Vancouver

Chris Wyness

LONELY PLANET PUBLICATIONS
Melbourne · Oakland · London · Paris

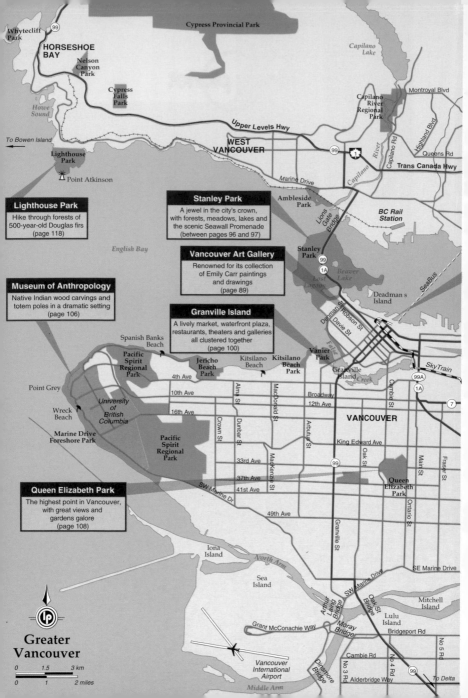

Whytecliff Park 99

HORSESHOE BAY

Nelson Canyon Park

Cypress Provincial Park

Capilano Lake

Cypress Falls Park

Montroyal Blvd

Capilano River Regional Park

Highland Blvd

Howe Sound

Upper Levels Hwy

Capilano River

Capilano Rd

Queens Rd

To Bowen Island

WEST VANCOUVER

99 1

Trans Canada Hwy

Lighthouse Park

Marine Drive

△ Point Atkinson

Ambleside Park

Lions Gate Bridge

BC Rail Station

Lighthouse Park
Hike through forests of 500-year-old Douglas firs
(page 118)

Stanley Park
A jewel in the city's crown, with forests, meadows, lakes and the scenic Seawall Promenade
(between pages 96 and 97)

Stanley Park

99

Beaver Lake

English Bay

Lost Lagoon

Deadman's Island

Vancouver Art Gallery
Renowned for its collection of Emily Carr paintings and drawings
(page 89)

SeaBus

Museum of Anthropology
Native Indian wood carvings and totem poles in a dramatic setting
(page 106)

Granville Island
A lively market, waterfront plaza, restaurants, theaters and galleries all clustered together
(page 100)

Denman St

Davie St

Robson St

Spanish Banks Beach

Pacific Spirit Regional Park

Jericho Beach Park

Kitsilano Beach

Kitsilano Beach Park

Vanier Park

Granville Island

SkyTrain

4th Ave

Creek

99A

Point Grey

University of British Columbia

10th Ave

16th Ave

Alma St

MacDonald St

Broadway

Cambie St

1A

7

Wreck Beach

VANCOUVER

12th Ave

Marine Drive Foreshore Park

Pacific Spirit Regional Park

Crown St

Dunbar St

Mackenzie St

Arbutus St

King Edward Ave

Oak St

Main St

Fraser St

33rd Ave

Queen Elizabeth Park
The highest point in Vancouver, with great views and gardens galore
(page 108)

37th Ave

41st Ave

SW Marine Dr

99

Queen Elizabeth Park

Ontario St

49th Ave

Granville St

SE Marine Drive

Iona Island

North Arm

Sea Island

SW Marine Drive

Mitchell Island

Arthur Laing Bridge

Oak St Bridge

Lulu Island

Bridgeport Rd

No 5 Rd

Grant McConachie Way

Moray Bridge

LP

Greater Vancouver

Dinsmore Bridge

Vancouver International Airport

Cambie Rd

No 3 Rd

No 4 Rd

99

Alderbridge Way

To Delta

Middle Arm

0   1.5   3 km

0   1   2 miles

2   Contents

PLACES TO STAY   127

PLACES TO EAT   138

ENTERTAINMENT   155

SHOPPING   166

EXCURSIONS   175

INDEX   211

VANCOUVER MAP SECTION   217

Contents

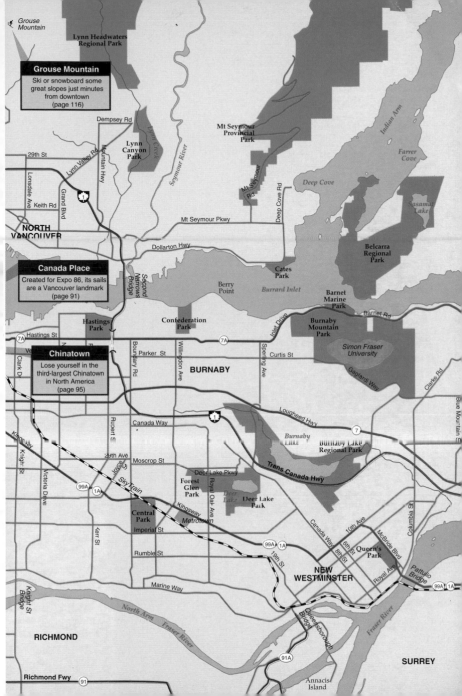

Grouse Mountain

Lynn Headwaters
Regional Park

Grouse Mountain
Ski or snowboard some
great slopes just minutes
from downtown
(page 116)

Dempsey Rd

Lynn
Canyon
Park

Mt Seymour
Provincial
Park

Farrer
Cove

29th St

Lonsdale Ave

Keith Rd

Grand Blvd

Lynn Valley Rd

Mountain Hwy

Seymour River

Mt Seymour Rd

Deep Cove

Sasamat
Lake

Indian Arm

**NORTH
VANCOUVER**

Mt Seymour Pkwy

Deep Cove Rd

Dollarton Hwy

Cates
Park

Belcarra
Regional
Park

Canada Place
Created for Expo 86, its sails
are a Vancouver landmark
(page 91)

Second
Narrows
Bridge

Berry
Point

Burrard Inlet

Barnet
Marine
Park

Barnet Rd

Hastings
Park

Confederation
Park

Inlet Drive

Burnaby
Mountain
Park

7A Hastings St

Ve

Chinatown
Lose yourself in the
third-largest Chinatown
in North America
(page 95)

Clark Dr

Boundary Rd

Parker St

Willingdon Ave

7A

Sperling Ave

Curtis St

*Simon Fraser
University*

Gaglardi Way

Clarke Rd

BURNABY

Rupert St

Canada Way

Trans Canada Hwy

Lougheed Hwy

7

Blue Mountain St

Knight Way

Knight St

Victoria Drive

29th Ave

Moscrop St

Joyce

SkyTrain

99A   1A

Deer Lake Pkwy

Forest
Glen
Park

Royal Oak Ave

*Deer
Lake*

Deer Lake
Park

*Burnaby
Lake*

Burnaby Lake
Regional Park

Canada Way

10th Ave

McBride Blvd

Columbia St

Central
Park

Kerr St

Kingsway

Metrotown

Imperial St

6th St

8th St

Queen's
Park

Pattullo
Bridge

Rumble St

99A   1A

6th Ave

**NEW
WESTMINSTER**

Royal Ave

99A   1A

Knight St
Bridge

Marine Way

Victoria Drive

Queensborough
Bridge

North Arm   Fraser River

Fraser River

RICHMOND

91A

SURREY

Annacis
Island

Richmond Fwy

91

Vancouver
1st edition – May 1999

Published by
Lonely Planet Publications Pty Ltd A.C.N. 005 607 983
192 Burwood Rd, Hawthorn, Victoria 3122, Australia

Lonely Planet Offices
Australia PO Box 617, Hawthorn, Victoria 3122
USA 150 Linden St, Oakland, CA 94607
UK 10a Spring Place, London NW5 3BH
France 1 rue du Dahomey, 75011 Paris

Photographs
BC Archives, Barrett & McKay, Scott Darsney/Mountainworld
Images, Diarama Stock Photos Inc (Wes Bergen, Fred Chapman,
Duncan McDougall, Yvonne McDougall), John Elk, Ric Ernst, Lee
Foster, David R Frazier, Rick Gerharter, Margaret Livingston (chapter
end), Gunter Marx, Chuck Pefley, Doug Plummer, Tim Thompson,
Vancouver Public Library, Nik Wheeler, Chris Wyness
Some of the images in this guide are available for licensing from
Lonely Planet Images.
email: lpi@lonelyplanet.com.au

Architectural Drawing
Robin Wood

Front cover photograph
Lions Gate Bridge, Vancouver (Stuart Dee)

ISBN 0 86442 659 3

text & maps © Lonely Planet 1999
photos © photographers as indicated 1999

Printed by Colorcraft Ltd, Hong Kong

The Author

Chris Wyness

Chris was born in Vancouver and, aside from a five-year stint in BC's East Kootenay region, grew up on the city's North Shore. Chris discovered a love for travel and the art of living on $10 a day when, at the age of 20, he hit the backpacker's trail around Europe for eight months. On returning to Canada, and after a number of jobs, he attended Toronto's Ryerson Polytechnical University where he earned a journalism degree. After two years on the Canadian prairies working for the Medicine Hat News, he traveled for a year and a half through Sri Lanka, India, Southeast Asia and Australia, making a 'living' as a freelance writer and photographer. He returned to Vancouver to edit The Examiner, a business publication, and then immigrated to Australia, where he was as an editor and a writer at New Idea, a weekly entertainment magazine in Melbourne. Another stint of travel took him and his wife, Amanda, to Asia, North America and Europe for two years, a year of which was spent in London where he worked as deputy editor at Diver magazine. He returned to Melbourne, where he is an editor at Lonely Planet, and lives with his wife and son Lachlan. This is the first book Chris has written for Lonely Planet.

FROM THE AUTHOR

My thanks in triplicate to Bruce Baird and his five boarders for putting up with me for nearly seven weeks while I kept the machinery oiled with the homebrew and made sure the keyboard got a good workout. A special thanks also for responding to my email queries, which went beyond the call of duty.

Thanks to Sean Collins for showing me the many highlights of Victoria; to John Kibblewhite for revealing the mysteries of Richmond, not to mention the delights of tapas and sangria; to Debi and Cliff Shannon for introducing me to the wonders of White Rock; and to Kent Spencer whose article on the Canadian Football League is a great addition to this book.

Thanks also to Joanne Morgan for her informative and entertaining article on Vancouver's film and TV industry; to Paul I Brooks at Zulu Records for providing me with information on the city's current music scene; to the staff at the Tourist InfoCentres and the Vancouver Public Library for all their help; and to Lonely Planet's Oakland office for bringing this book to life.

A special thanks to my mother, Constance Wyness, for her understanding, homecooked meals, conversation, tea and sympathy. But most of all, my thanks, appreciation and gratitude go to my wife, Amanda, and son, Lachlan, for their understanding, patience, support and love, not only for the time it took me to research and write this book, but for always.

This Book

FROM THE PUBLISHER

This first edition of *Vancouver* was edited and indexed in Lonely Planet's Oakland office by Susan Charles. Julie Connery and Paige R Penland assisted with editing, and Joslyn Leve, Paige and Julie proofed the text and maps. Design and production were executed by Margaret Livingston, who drew the maps and laid out the book, with oversight from Alex Guilbert and Scott Summers. Rini Keagy designed the cover. Illustrations were done by Hayden Foell, Rini, John Fadeff and Hugh D'Andrade. Special thanks to Raincoast Books for reviewing the manuscript, and to Vancouverites Deb Miller and Oliver Hamilton who helped in innumerable ways. Hearty thanks to senior editor Carolyn Hubbard for her editorial advice, guidance and support throughout the project.

Foreword

ABOUT LONELY PLANET GUIDEBOOKS

The story begins with a classic travel adventure: Tony and Maureen Wheeler's 1972 journey across Europe and Asia to Australia. Useful information about the overland trail did not exist at that time, so Tony and Maureen published the first Lonely Planet guidebook to meet a growing need.

From a kitchen table, then from a tiny office in Melbourne (Australia), Lonely Planet has become the largest independent travel publisher in the world, an international company with offices in Melbourne, Oakland (USA), London (UK) and Paris (France).

Today Lonely Planet guidebooks cover the globe. There is an ever-growing list of books and there's information in a variety of forms and media. Some things haven't changed. The main aim is still to help make it possible for adventurous travelers to get out there – to explore and better understand the world.

At Lonely Planet we believe travelers can make a positive contribution to the countries they visit – if they respect their host communities and spend their money wisely. Since 1986 a percentage of the income from each book has been donated to aid projects and human rights campaigns.

Updates Lonely Planet thoroughly updates each guidebook as often as possible. This usually means there are around two years between editions, although for more unusual or more stable destinations the gap can be longer. Check the imprint page (following the color map at the beginning of the book) for publication dates.

Between editions up-to-date information is available in two free newsletters – the paper *Planet Talk* and email *Comet* (to subscribe, contact any Lonely Planet office) – and on our website at www.lonelyplanet.com. The *Upgrades* section of the website covers a number of important and volatile destinations and is regularly updated by Lonely Planet authors. *Scoop* covers news and current affairs relevant to travelers. And, lastly, the *Thorn Tree* bulletin board and *Postcards* section of the site carry unverified, but fascinating, reports from travelers.

Correspondence The process of creating new editions begins with the letters, postcards and emails received from travelers. This correspondence often includes suggestions, criticisms and comments about the current editions. Interesting excerpts are immediately passed on via newsletters and the website, and everything goes to our authors to be verified when they're researching on the road. We're keen to get more feedback from organizations or individuals who represent communities visited by travelers.

Lonely Planet gathers information for everyone who's curious about the planet – and especially for those who explore it firsthand. Through guidebooks, phrasebooks, activity guides, maps, literature, newsletters, image library, TV series and website we act as an information exchange for a worldwide community of travelers.

Research Authors aim to gather sufficient practical information to enable travelers to make informed choices and to make the mechanics of a journey run smoothly. They also research historical and cultural background to help enrich the travel experience and allow travelers to understand and respond appropriately to cultural and environmental issues.

Authors don't stay in every hotel because that would mean spending a couple of months in each medium-sized city and, no, they don't eat at every restaurant because that would mean stretching belts beyond capacity. They do visit hotels and restaurants to check standards and prices, but feedback based on readers' direct experiences can be very helpful.

Many of our authors work undercover, others aren't so secretive. None of them accept freebies in exchange for positive write-ups. And none of our guidebooks contain any advertising.

Production Authors submit their raw manuscripts and maps to offices in Australia, USA, UK or France. Editors and cartographers – all experienced travelers themselves – then begin the process of assembling the pieces. When the book finally hits the shops, some things are already out of date, we start getting feedback from readers and the process begins again...

WARNING & REQUEST

Things change – prices go up, schedules change, good places go bad and bad places go bankrupt – nothing stays the same. So, if you find things better or worse, recently opened or long since closed, please tell us and help make the next edition even more accurate and useful. We genuinely value all the feedback we receive. Julie Young coordinates a well-traveled team that reads and acknowledges every letter, postcard and email and ensures that every morsel of information finds its way to the appropriate authors, editors and cartographers for verification.

Everyone who writes to us will find their name in the next edition of the appropriate guidebook. They will also receive the latest issue of *Planet Talk*, our quarterly printed newsletter, or *Comet*, our monthly email newsletter. Subscriptions to both newsletters are free. The very best contributions will be rewarded with a free guidebook.

Excerpts from your correspondence may appear in new editions of Lonely Planet guidebooks, the Lonely Planet website, *Planet Talk* or *Comet*, so please let us know if you *don't* want your letter published or your name acknowledged.

Send all correspondence to the Lonely Planet office closest to you:

Australia: PO Box 617, Hawthorn, Victoria 3122
USA: 150 Linden St, Oakland, CA 94607
UK: 10A Spring Place, London NW5 3BH
France: 1 rue du Dahomey, 75011 Paris

Or email us at: talk2us@lonelyplanet.com.au

For news, views and updates see our website: www.lonelyplanet.com

HOW TO USE A LONELY PLANET GUIDEBOOK

The best way to use a Lonely Planet guidebook is any way you choose. At Lonely Planet we believe the most memorable travel experiences are often those that are unexpected, and the finest discoveries are those you make yourself. Guidebooks are not intended to be used as if they provide a detailed set of infallible instructions!

Contents All Lonely Planet guidebooks follow the same format. The Facts about the Country chapters or sections give background information ranging from history to weather. Facts for the Visitor gives practical information on issues like visas and health. Getting There & Away gives a brief starting point for researching travel to and from the destination. Getting Around gives an overview of the transport options when you arrive.

The peculiar demands of each destination determine how subsequent chapters are broken up, but some things remain constant. We always start with background, then proceed to sights, places to stay, places to eat, entertainment, getting there and away, and getting around information – in that order.

Heading Hierarchy Lonely Planet headings are used in a strict hierarchical structure that can be visualized as a set of Russian dolls. Each heading (and its following text) is encompassed by any preceding heading that is higher on the hierarchical ladder.

Entry Points We do not assume guidebooks will be read from beginning to end, but that people will dip into them. The traditional entry points are the list of contents and the index. In addition, however, some books have a complete list of maps and an index map illustrating map coverage.

There may also be a color map that shows highlights. These highlights are dealt with in greater detail later in the book, along with planning questions. Each chapter covering a geographical region usually begins with a locator map and another list of highlights. Once you find something of interest in a list of highlights, turn to the index.

Maps Maps play a crucial role in Lonely Planet guidebooks and include a huge amount of information. A legend is printed on the back page. We seek to have complete consistency between maps and text, and to have every important place in the text captured on a map. Map key numbers usually start in the top left corner.

Although inclusion in a guidebook usually implies a recommendation we cannot list every good place. Exclusion does not necessarily imply criticism. In fact there are a number of reasons why we might exclude a place – sometimes it is simply inappropriate to encourage an influx of travelers.

Introduction

Travel brochures and guidebooks love to wax lyrical about the natural wonders that surround Vancouver, and with good reason: there aren't many cities in the world that offer such a wonderful combination of urban living and outdoor pursuits so close to each other. Vancouverites like to boast that you can go skiing in the morning, sailing in the afternoon and still be home in time for a night on the town.

This proximity to mountains, forests and ocean impresses most visitors when they first arrive in Vancouver. Indeed, it is these very elements that make Vancouver one of the most beautiful cities in the world, and they are the same ingredients that have encouraged people for more than 10,000 years to call this part of the world home.

It's easy to forget that where the city now stands was once thick, virgin rain forests of cedar, fir and hemlock. Without those forests, and the wealth derived from them, the city would never have come into existence. Vancouver was, after all, founded around a sawmill (and a saloon), and it's only been in recent times that its industrial core, which for years took center stage in the city's development, has been displaced by projects such as Granville Island, False Creek and much of the waterfront along Burrard Inlet.

Vancouver, however, did take a long time to find itself. For far too many years it denied that it had a rich and diverse ethnic mix of cultures that deserved to be celebrated; ignored the proposition that its architecture should

BY SEA LAND AND AIR WE PROSPER

embrace, and be enhanced by, the natural beauty of its surroundings; and despaired that artistically it was too far away from other cultural centers to make world-class contributions. Today, Vancouver isn't afraid to embrace all of these things and more.

Vancouver has reshaped and redefined itself as a young and vibrant city. No longer is it a frontier town on Canada's Pacific coast, but rather a modern cosmopolitan center that has much to offer the visitor. There is an almost embarrassing abundance of parks in Greater Vancouver, including two forest reserves within city boundaries,

Stanley Park and Pacific Spirit Regional Park. This abundance of green space, and easy access to the water, means that any outdoor activity you desire to try is only a bus ride away. There isn't a form of entertainment, whether it be the arts, theater, music or professional sports, that can't be sampled here. And when it comes to food, well, the selection of restaurants is simply staggering. But, perhaps more than anything else, the neighborhoods, with their mix of ethnic and countercultural communities, make Vancouver an exciting and interesting city to explore.

Facts about Vancouver

HISTORY
The First Inhabitants

People have been living along this part of the West Coast for more than 10,000 years, although the culture discovered by the first European explorers didn't start to take shape until around 500 AD. The Marpole people, as they are known, lived in villages consisting of large rough-hewn plank houses arranged in rows, often surrounded by a stockade, and with totem poles set up nearby. Inside the plank houses, areas were separated into rooms by hanging mats, allowing different family groups to share one house.

Their society was based on a relaxed class structure that was not nearly as rigid as that found in the Haida and Tsimshian cultures farther up the coast. The Marpole people used dugout canoes as well as tools, ornaments and carvings made from copper, stone, jade, bone and wood. They lived off the ocean and the land, which was abundant in salmon, shellfish, seal, porpoise, sturgeon, deer, elk, bear, goat and a variety of birds. They also gathered wild berries, fruit, edible roots and the wapato, a type of potato that grew along the Fraser River. Much of the food was dried and smoked in small smokehouses to preserve it for the cool, wet winters.

By the time the Europeans arrived in the late 1700s there were some distinct groups living in this area. Burrard Inlet, English Bay and the mouth of the Fraser River were home to the Musqueam, although they shared some of this area with the Squamish, who were largely based in villages at the head of Howe Sound but also had villages along the coast of North and West Vancouver, and at Kitsilano Point, Stanley Park and Jericho Beach. The area around New Westminster was controlled by the Kwantlen, while Delta and Richmond were home to the Tsawwassen. A group called the Tsleil'waututh occupied much of North Vancouver, while Coast Salish tribes such as the Cowichan, Nanaimo and Saanich set up seasonal camps along the Fraser River when the salmon were running.

European Exploration

Eager to discover the fabled Northwest Passage (the water route across North America from the Pacific Ocean to the Atlantic Ocean) and gain control of the region north of San Francisco, the Spanish sent three expeditions to the northern Pacific Coast between 1774 to 1779; however, none of the voyages ventured into Georgia Strait. British explorer Captain James Cook, arriving from the South Pacific in 1779 on his trip up the coast from Oregon to Alaska, also in search of that elusive northern shortcut to Europe, spent some time in Nootka Sound, but like those before him he believed that the west coast of Vancouver Island was actually the coast of the Mainland.

Captain George Vancouver

Although the Spanish, French and British continued to maintain a presence along the west coast of Vancouver Island, it wasn't until 1791 that Georgia Strait was discovered by the Spanish navigator José María Narváez who sailed into Burrard Inlet (he thought that Point Grey was actually a group of islands and named them Islas de Langara). In 1792, Captain George Vancouver, the British navigator who had sailed with Cook in 1791, returned to explore and chart the area, as did two Spanish ships, one under the command of Dionisio Alcalá Galiano. Both Vancouver and Galiano explored Burrard Inlet at the same time, sharing their information and charting the coastline.

As Spanish influence in the area declined in favor of the British, explorers such as Simon Fraser (who reached the mouth of the Fraser River in 1806, and returned in 1808, as an agent for the North West Company, to establish trading posts), Alexander Mackenzie and David Thompson mapped the interior of the province, opening it up for overland travelers and the arrival of the Hudson's Bay Company.

Permanent Settlement

In 1824, the Hudson's Bay Company, under the leadership of James McMillan, began setting up a network of fur-trading posts. In his initial exploration McMillan took note of an area along the Fraser River, about 50km from its mouth, that he thought would make an ideal location for a permanent settlement, and in 1827 returned to start building Fort Langley, the region's earliest European settlement. The original site, however, was abandoned in 1839 and a new fort was built 35km upriver where today, although it has been largely reconstructed, it's a National Historic Park. Fur trading was the fort's first commercial enterprise, but by the late 1840s salted salmon was its main source of income, followed by farming.

In 1858, 25,000 American prospectors flocked to the region to cash in on the Fraser River gold rush. Concerned that the influx of American prospectors might inspire the US to think about expanding north, the

Fort Langley (1862)

BC ARCHIVES #A-04313

Mainland followed the lead of Vancouver Island, a crown colony since 1849, and declared itself a British colony. James Douglas, who was already the governor of the colony of Vancouver Island, was sworn in as governor of the colony of British Columbia (BC).

Douglas asked the British government for support, so the Royal Engineers, under the command of Colonel Richard Moody, arrived at the end of 1858 to build roads and select a site for a military reserve. Alarmed by the poor strategic location of Fort Langley, Moody selected a new site on the Fraser River that became New Westminster, the capital of the colony (see the New Westminster section in the Things to See & Do chapter for details). In 1859, a trail (known today as North Road) was built from New Westminster to Burrard Inlet to provide an ice-free harbor in winter, and in 1860 the first trail, more or less where Kingsway is now, was built linking New Westminster with False Creek.

The first sawmills were set up along the Fraser River in 1860 and their logging operations provided cleared land for the new farms established in areas such as Surrey and south Vancouver. An interesting footnote is that in 1859, before the first sawmill began production, wood had to be imported from California to build the first permanent church in the new colony. However, it wasn't long before sawmills were established on both the north and south shores of Burrard Inlet (see the Gastown and North Shore sections in the Things to See & Do chapter for details).

In 1867, Edward Stamp's British-financed Hastings Mill, on the south shore of Burrard Inlet, established the starting point of a town that would become Vancouver. First called Gastown after John 'Gassy Jack' Deighton who opened the first saloon near the Hastings Mill, it was officially given the name Granville Townsite in 1870.

In 1866, the two colonies of Vancouver Island and British Columbia were united. With the creation of a new country called Canada on the eastern side of the continent in 1867, the colony of British Columbia started to become concerned about its future and feared that it could easily be swallowed up by the USA. So with the promise of access to a national railway, British Columbia joined the Canadian Confederation in 1871, although it would be another 15 years before the railway would actually reach the West Coast.

Port Moody, at the eastern end of Burrard Inlet, was slated to be the western terminus of the Canadian Pacific Railway (CPR). This was a thriving community that had developed around a sawmill and was where, in 1882, the first electric lights north of San Francisco were switched on. However, a CPR official, who was also an influential businessman and owner of land around Granville, discovered that the eastern end of Burrard Inlet wasn't a practical harbor for large ships and, much to the dismay and outrage of Port Moody citizens, Granville was selected instead.

Birth of the City

With the selection of Granville, the CPR negotiated with the provincial government for 2400 hectares, making it the townsite's largest private property holder. The story goes that in 1884, while the CPR's general manager William Van Horne was rowed around what would later become Stanley Park, he commented that the new city needed a name that would live up to its future stature as a great city. Since Granville was an unknown name, he said it should be called Vancouver after the man who everyone knew was responsible for literally putting the area on the map.

The new name was approved by the CPR directors and in April 1886 the town of Granville, with a population of 400 people, was incorporated as the City of Vancouver. The first piece of business by the new city council was to lease a 400-hectare military reserve from the federal government and establish it as the city's first park, which officially opened as Stanley Park in 1888.

However, on July 13, 1886, a fire, which came to be known as the 'Great Fire,' moved with incredible speed through the new City of Vancouver and in 45 minutes destroyed Vancouver's 1000 wooden structures and killed as many as 28 people and left 3000 people homeless. Within hours the rebuilding got underway, but this time with stone and brick. (Today, many of these buildings can be seen in Gastown.) In July of 1886 the first scheduled CPR transcontinental passenger train pulled into Port

The first CPR train, No 374 (1887)

VANCOUVER PUBLIC LIBRARY PHOTOGRAPH NUMBER 509

JW Horne's real estate office near Georgia & Granville Sts (1886)

Moody (the train stopped here until the track to Granville was completed) and the port of Vancouver saw its first cargo arrive – a shipment of tea from China. Another year passed before the first CPR passenger train, No 374, pulled into Vancouver. Within four years of the railway arriving in Vancouver, the city had grown to a population of 13,000, and between 1891 and 1901 the population skyrocketed to more than 29,000.

Growth of the City

As a major landowner in the city, and with a need to develop property for railway and shipping access, the CPR was responsible for shaping much of the city as it exists today. The CPR built Granville St from Burrard Inlet to False Creek, cleared and paved Pender and Hastings Sts, and developed the land around False Creek for railway yards and housing. Other areas developed by the

CPR for housing included the West End, originally designed to be an upper-income neighborhood, Kitsilano and Shaughnessy Heights (once known as 'CPR Heaven') in south Vancouver, which was created to be the home of Vancouver's new upper classes, just so long as they weren't Jewish or Asian (the deeds of sale contained a clause forbidding the re-sale of property to people from either of these groups).

Anti-Asian feelings weren't new to Vancouver: they had been expressed in 1887 when a white mob destroyed a Chinese camp in False Creek and again in 1907 when an anti-Asian riot ripped through Chinatown and Japantown. To make things worse, these racist sentiments were sanctioned by the government through legislation that, among other things, prohibited the Chinese from working on provincial government projects, did not allow Chinese women to immigrate unless they were married to a white man and denied all Asians the vote in federal elections.

The city benefited enormously with the opening of the Panama Canal in 1914, which allowed a quicker route to Europe for ships containing Canadian grain. (Today, more grain is shipped from Vancouver than from any other port in Canada.) That same year, BC Rail began life as Pacific Great Eastern Railway with passenger service between North Vancouver and Whytecliff near Horseshoe Bay, the beginning of its push into the center of the province. The following year saw the opening of the CPR station on Burrard Inlet, now Waterfront Station, and the creation of the University of British Columbia. In 1921, the completion of the Pacific Hwy to the Canadian-US border allowed for easier travel between Vancouver and Seattle.

During the first 30 years of the 20th century all the suburbs around the city grew substantially – by 1928 the population outside the city was about 150,000 people. When Point Grey and South Vancouver amalgamated with the city in 1929, bringing in a combined population of more than 80,000, Vancouver became the third-largest city in Canada.

Despite the Great Depression of the 1930s, which was as hard on the city as it was on the rest of the country and indeed the world, Vancouver saw some major developments, such as the construction of the Marine Building, Vancouver City Hall, the third and present Hotel Vancouver and the Lions Gate Bridge, and the inauguration of the first transcontinental passenger air service from Vancouver to Montreal in 1939.

WWII helped to pull Vancouver out of the depression by creating instant jobs at shipyards, aircraft-parts factories and canneries, and in construction building rental units for the increased workforce. Following the bombing of Pearl Harbor in 1942, however, Japanese Canadians were shipped to internment camps in the province's interior and all their land and property was seized. Chinese and East Indians (immigrants from the Indian subcontinent, which also includes Pakistan) were finally given the provincial vote in 1947, followed by the Japanese and Native Indians in 1949.

The City Comes of Age

By the start of the 1950s the city's population was 345,000 and Vancouver was thriving. One of the standout events during the '50s was the hosting of the 1954 British Empire Games where England's Roger Bannister defeated Australia's John Landy in the 'Miracle Mile,' the first race in which two runners ran the mile in under four minutes. This was also the first sports event to be broadcast live throughout North America. Also during this decade, the Second Narrows Bridge collapsed during its construction in 1958, killing 19 men.

Vancouver became environmentally aware in the '60s, particularly in 1969 when the Don't Make a Wave Committee formed, later to become Greenpeace, the world's largest environmental organization (see the Making Waves boxed text later in this chapter). This decade also saw Simon Fraser University open its doors in Burnaby, Whistler open as a ski resort, and also the government-operated BC Ferries begin its services, taking over ferry routes from private companies.

The '70s saw the creation of greater economic links with Asia, particularly with the opening of the coal port at Delta's Roberts Bank. This decade also witnessed the development of Granville Island into a successful public market and the entry into the National Hockey League with the Canucks. In the '80s nothing was more important to Vancouver than the 1986 international exposition, Expo 86, which welcomed more than 21 million visitors. It is generally agreed that Expo 86 helped Vancouver gain a more international profile and to come of age as a city. The '80s also saw the opening of Sky-Train, the creation of Pacific Spirit Park and the courage of Terry Fox as he attempted to run across Canada to raise money for cancer research (see the Terry Fox & the Marathon of Hope boxed text in the Things to See & Do chapter).

The suburbs that make up Greater Vancouver have grown at a phenomenal rate. By

Bridging the Gap Across First Narrows

The first proposal for a bridge across the First Narrows of Burrard Inlet came from the Burrard Wire Cable Bridge Company in 1909 that wanted to erect a bridge 'somewhat after the pattern of the Eiffel Tower' at Prospect Point. Park officials and city council refused to even consider the possibility of cutting a road through the center of Stanley Park, quickly turning the idea down.

A delegation representing British interests again approached the park board and city council in 1926 with the idea of building a bridge, but the following year the idea was overwhelmingly rejected by Vancouver voters in a plebiscite. When in 1933 British developers, led by the Guinness family, again proposed to build a bridge across the First Narrows, the scheme received greater public acceptance as the project was seen as a solution to the unemployment caused by the Great Depression.

Guinness' British Pacific Syndicate had paid $50 a hectare for 1600 hectares on Hollyburn Ridge in West Vancouver and was keen to get a return on its investment. A bridge would make the area more accessible and would hasten the sale of the lots on what had come to be known as British Properties. However, the plan to build a 2.4km causeway through the center of Stanley Park remained a highly contentious issue that received a lot of public attention and debate at the time.

Eventually the plan was approved and construction began in 1936. The project was completed in 1938 at a cost of $6 million. The British Empire's longest suspension bridge was officially opened by King George VI and Queen Elizabeth in 1939. Originally it had just two lanes but it wasn't long before three lanes were laid out with the center lane designated as a passing lane. The provincial government bought the bridge in 1963 for $6 million and soon removed the tolls. In due time, overhead lane controls were put in place to help control the flow of traffic as it changes throughout the day. Today, a total of about 63,600 vehicles cross over the bridge each day. The lights, a gift from the Guinness family, were added in 1986.

Over the years, Lions Gate Bridge has become more and more inadequate as a crossing. Various suggestions have been made and studies conducted on how the bridge might be remodeled to accommodate more traffic but a consensus has yet to be reached. Part of the

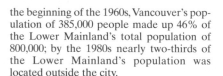

the beginning of the 1960s, Vancouver's population of 385,000 people made up 46% of the Lower Mainland's total population of 800,000; by the 1980s nearly two-thirds of the Lower Mainland's population was located outside the city.

Along with continued growth – much of it spurred on by an influx of Asian immigration – the '90s saw Vancouver become the third-largest film-production center in North America, the venue for the annual Molson Indy Race, the site of a two-day summit between Presidents Bill Clinton and Boris Yeltsin, and the home to the Grizzlies of the National Basketball Association. Although the suburbs continue to grow at a substantial rate, the city has regained a 26% share of the population with an increase of 107,000 people from 1981 to 1995; in 1997, the city's population was estimated at 544,000 people. The new high-rise developments being built in the city center are testament that this trend is expected to continue.

Vancouver has become a truly international city, with people from almost 100 different countries now living here, and it is in part this cultural diversity that will help Vancouver to reach its potential to be one the great cities of the 21st century.

For more detailed accounts of the history of some of Vancouver's neighborhoods, see those sections in the Things to See & Do chapter.

problem in making a decision is the number of parties involved - the bridge is owned by the provincial government, the City of Vancouver leases the park from the federal government, and the north end of the bridge crosses Capilano Indian Reserve No 5.

One suggestion is to build a two-lane tunnel under the inlet and turn the bridge back to two lanes, that way retaining the heritage value of the bridge. The cost of doing this would be about $350 million, about the same as the cost of building a new four-lane bridge, another one of the options under consideration. Another option is a four-lane tunnel from downtown Vancouver to the North Shore at a cost of $600 million.

Lions Gate Bridge (1939)

BC ARCH VES #B-00659

GEOGRAPHY

Greater Vancouver straddles the lowlands of the Fraser River and the Coast Mountains of southwest British Columbia. The Coast range, at only 20 million years of age, is one of North America's youngest mountain ranges. The North Shore Range of the Coast Mountains stretches from Black Mountain in the west to Mt Seymour in the east. Separated by Indian Arm of Burrard Inlet, the Golden Ears mountain group dominates the Fraser Valley. Cathedral Mountain at 1723m is the highest peak in the North Shore Range, while the highest peak of the Golden Ears group is 1706m. Four valleys separate the North Shore Range, including, from west to east, Cypress Creek, the Capilano River, Lynn Valley and the Seymour River.

Greater Vancouver is bordered to the west by Georgia Strait and to the north by Howe Sound. The City of Vancouver is bordered to the north by Burrard Inlet, which extends east as far as Port Moody, and to the south by the North Arm of the Fraser River.

The North Shore is on the north side of the inlet, and Richmond, which is built on islands formed from sedimentary deposits at the mouth of the Fraser River, is to the south of Vancouver. The South Arm of the Fraser River separates Richmond from Delta and Surrey, which in turn are bordered to the south and southwest by Boundary Bay.

Making Waves

It all started in 1969 in a Vancouver living room, where a group of concerned individuals gathered to discuss a one-megaton nuclear bomb dropped as easily and quietly as a raindrop on Amchitka, an ecologically diverse island near the tip of Alaska's Aleutians. It was the first bomb in a series of US atmospheric nuclear tests, scheduled intermittently over the next few years.

The visitors to that living room were mostly strangers of all ages and occupations, but they shared a common belief: no one had the right to drop nuclear weapons in the Earth's oceans or atmosphere. This was enough to prompt them to organize and do something to stop it.

The meeting marked the birth of the Don't Make a Wave Committee, whose plan was to sail north to disrupt US atomic activity before the next bomb fell on Amchitka. The trip to Amchitka was scheduled in 1971 during a stormy West Coast winter in an old fishing boat nicknamed *Greenpeace*. The weather, however, proved too much for the small boat, so a bigger boat was purchased. This one was also forced to turn back due to bad weather.

Meanwhile, the energy generated by the Don't Make a Wave Committee swelled beyond Amchitka. The wave had become a tsunami and rolled into the creation of an organization with a wider environmental scope, dedicated to creating a greener, more peaceful world, hence the new name Greenpeace.

Although Greenpeace's first two attempts to reach Amchitka failed, the group succeeded in sparking public interest. It showed the world that a group of determined and committed individuals with a specific environmental agenda could cast out a line of protest and, as a byproduct, net the public's attention. The strategy worked. By 1972, all atomic testing ceased on Amchitka.

Through demonstrative acts of civil disobedience, Greenpeace became the environmental leader in getting people's attention. Since Amchitka, Greenpeace has sailed many stormy waters, through language barriers and political agendas, infiltrating eco-vocabularies worldwide.

Throughout the 1980s and '90s, the protests, boycotts and public outcries brought Greenpeace to the forefront of radical environmentalism. From confronting Russian whalers to parachuting into an Ontario nuclear power plant, from convincing the *New York Times* to cancel all contracts with logging giant MacMillan Bloedel to ending clearcutting in BC's Clayoquot Sound, Greenpeace has combined creative protest with dedication to get high-profile media and public attention on environmental issues surrounding hydroelectric industries, forestry, commercial fishing, nuclear and chemical testing.

Greenpeace opponents have argued that the organization's renegade environmentalism and impromptu confrontations cause more harm than good. Like a pesky mosquito that just won't go away, Greenpeace has emitted an incessant, irritating buzz in the ear of many corporations, creating sleepless nights and public relations nightmares.

However annoying and aggressive, the buzz has made a difference: by forcing companies to wake up to global environmental problems and potential catastrophes, Greenpeace's eco-warfare has increased the standard for corporate accountability, or at least brought environmental concerns out of the cold and into the boardroom. Greenpeace's success has inspired a generation of activists.

In 1979, national Greenpeace organizations in Australia, Canada, France, Netherlands, New Zealand, the UK and US formed Greenpeace International, now headquartered in Amsterdam. There are organizations in more than 30 countries worldwide.

From Greenpeace's humble beginning in a Vancouver home, this organization has gone on to protect rain forests, whales and drinking water, among many other things. As for Amchitka, the island is now a flourishing bird sanctuary.

Debra Miller

The Fraser River, which essentially cuts through the center of the Lower Mainland, has its source in the Rocky Mountains and travels 1375km to its delta on Georgia Strait. It drains a basin the size of Britain. The Fraser's tributaries include the Coquitlam, Chilcotin, Nechako, Pitt and Thompson Rivers. Not only is this Canada's third-largest river, it is also the country's fifth-largest river system, and is the richest salmon river in North America.

CLIMATE

Compared to just about any other city in Canada, besides Victoria, Vancouver has the mildest climate in the country. The average January temperature is 2°C (35°F) while the July average is 17°C (62°F). It rarely snows in the city, and when it does, which might amount to a total of a week or two over the course of the winter, it tends to melt quickly or get washed away by the rain. Conversely, it seldom gets oppressively hot; for Vancouverites a stretch of 26°C (78°F) to 28°C (82°F) is considered to be a heat wave. The hottest day on record is 33.3°C (92°F), and the coldest day is -26°C (-15°F), which was accompanied by gale winds and 43cm of snow.

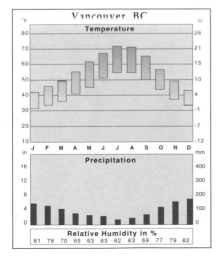

Vancouver, BC

What Vancouver is guaranteed to get, and to get by the bucket load, is rain. The surrounding mountains, which on a clear day look close enough to touch, disappear completely when the clouds settle in and the rain pours down, which can be for days on end. The record for Vancouver's longest rainy stretch is 29 days.

Vancouver's annual precipitation averages 1113mm. However, that is a deceptive figure because the rain isn't dispersed evenly throughout the Lower Mainland; annual rainfall declines in a north to south pattern. Areas such as Tsawwassen and White Rock in the southern end of the Lower Mainland get only about one-third of the rain that the North Shore receives (1100mm vs 3000mm), and it's estimated that in the mountain watershed below the Lions, annual rainfalls of up to 5000mm are common.

ECOLOGY & ENVIRONMENT

Greater Vancouver compares well against other cities in the world when it comes to air, water and soil qualities; in Canada there are 10 major centers with worse air pollution. However, this is not to say that Vancouver doesn't have its share of environmental problems.

At one time Vancouver's air quality suffered greatly from all the sawmills in the city center. (One of the reasons West Vancouver became a popular place to visit in the early 1900s was that the clean air was a nice relief from the smell and haze generated by the sawmills on Burrard Inlet and False Creek.) These days those problems have been replaced by pollution created by automobiles; on a warm, windless day this can often be seen as a brown haze over the city. Unfortunately, if the predictions hold true, this situation is unlikely to change until after the beginning of the 21st century.

It is estimated that about 900 million cubic meters of sludge – including agricultural and urban runoff, domestic sewage and industrial waste – flows into the Fraser River annually, from the town of Hope to Georgia Strait. Fortunately for the people who use the river for many recreational activities, and for the salmon that live in it, the water

Shake, Rattle & Roll

Most people would put San Francisco, Los Angeles, Mexico City, Kobe and Tokyo on their list of cities that sit in earthquake zones, but not many would think to include Vancouver. However, the threat of being hit with the 'big one' is as real in Vancouver as it is in those other 'capitals of shake.'

Vancouver sits on top of the most active earthquake zone in Canada, the Cascadia Subduction Zone, a 1400km-long fault line that runs south from Alaska along the west coast of the Queen Charlotte Islands and Vancouver Island all the way to Oregon. There are three different tectonic plates along this line – the North American Plate, the Pacific Plate and the Juan de Fuca Plate – that fit together while at the same time shift eastward. These plates are currently static but when they shift significantly, releasing all that built up tension, well, look out.

Every year there are about 300 minor quakes in the southwest region of BC. Most go unnoticed, with larger quakes happening every 20 to 50 years, such as the one that took place north of Courtenay on Vancouver Island in 1946 which measured 7.3 on the Richter scale. Every 300 to 600 years the region has been hit by a major quake measuring 8.5, and that's the one seismologists are concerned may be due since the last one of this magnitude occurred in 1700.

The worst-case scenario is that an 8.5+ quake would result in landslides and tsunamis along the coast; severe damage to up to 30% of the homes in Greater Vancouver and upwards of 60% of older unreinforced buildings such as those in Gastown; and to 15% of the city's high-rises. Bridges and schools would be severely damaged, flooding from the tsunamis and the broken dikes in the Fraser Valley would wreak havoc, and the death rate would be in the thousands. It is estimated that the financial cost would be up to $30 billion.

In recent years both the province and the City of Vancouver have taken the threat of earthquakes very seriously. About $300 million is being spent to reinforce bridges, tunnels, buildings and other structures such as the Cleveland Dam in North Vancouver. An Emergency Operations Centre for Greater Vancouver has been built at Rupert and Hastings Sts. Three saltwater pumping stations with earthquake-resistant piping have been built around Vancouver to act as a backup in case the main water supply fails or is shut down, although other waterlines are being gradually upgraded. The city also has an ongoing program to prepare and inform the public about what to do in the event of an emergency such as an earthquake, including a pamphlet that has been translated into five languages.

quality is rated at being fair to good. Even so, the Fraser River Action Plan was devised in 1991 to help protect the future of the river and its salmon runs.

Another problem facing Greater Vancouver is the clear-cut logging that is still allowed around some of Vancouver's mountain lakes and reservoirs. With a lack of forest cover to hold back the increased runoff, more silt has found its way into the drinking water. Rather than stop the logging, officials have chosen to deal with the problem by treating the dirty water with

increased chlorine – to such an extent that you can sometimes smell the chlorine when you turn on the tap.

In recent years recycling has pretty much become a way of life in Greater Vancouver. To combat the problem of disposing of garbage in landfill sites that can no longer cope with the quantity of waste, municipalities are encouraging households to separate their garbage. Newsprint, plastics, aluminum and tin cans, glass bottles and jars, motor oil, scrap tires, lead-acid batteries, gypsum wallboard and even old refrigerators are all recycled in some way. Paint is required to be disposed of at depots (a surtax on paint purchases covers the cost). Several municipalities even supply compost bins to residents at a subsidized rate so that organic waste can be turned into plant food rather than ending up on the garbage heap.

FLORA

Vancouver's mild climate and long growing season make it an ideal environment for many types of trees, shrubs, flowers and vegetables. Many Vancouverites maintain beautiful gardens, and the city's numerous parks and public gardens are ideal places to sample the delights available. One of the more distinctive trees you'll see is the indigenous arbutus, an evergreen with broad glossy green leaves and reddish-brown peeling bark.

Many properties are divided by holly, laurel and boxwood hedges, while many city streets are lined with ornamental flowering cherry and plum trees. In fact, there are more than 100,000 trees lining the streets of Vancouver, including maples, chestnuts, acacias and elms. If you are interested in finding out more about these trees, you can call the Vancouver Board of Parks & Recreation's 'Street Trees' at ☎ 604-257-8600.

In Stanley Park, and in many of the forests throughout the Lower Mainland, you'll find hemlock, Douglas fir, yellow cedar and red cedar. Also in Stanley Park, near the pitch-and-putt golf course, you'll find a collection of ornamental trees, including magnolias, camellias, azaleas, rhododendrons, beech and white pine.

It is said that in Queen Elizabeth Park you can find a specimen of every tree native to Canada, but one highlight here would have to be the giant dogwood with its distinctive white flowers, the province's floral emblem. For details on other parks to visit, see the Things to See & Do chapter. A good reference book is the *Trees of Vancouver* by Gerald Straley. For more information about Vancouver's flora and on the city's garden clubs and societies, call the VanDusen Botanical Library at ☎ 604-878-9274.

FAUNA

The many forests, lakes, rivers and bogs, as well as the Pacific Ocean, provide habitats for a large variety of wildlife in the Greater Vancouver region. You do not have to venture too far in some of the North Shore's forested parks to possibly meet a bear or a deer, or to see mountain goats in the upper regions of Golden Ears Provincial Park.

In the heart of the city, especially in and around Stanley Park, you can see coyotes, raccoons and skunks, and at Burnaby Lake there is a large population of beaver.

Another area where you'll find beaver, plus 23 other species of mammals including muskrat and deer, as well as 150 species of birds, is Burns Bog in Delta. This 4000-hectare site off Hwy 91 is the largest peat bog in North America and one of the largest in the world, although the only protected part is the 60-hectare Delta Nature Reserve.

Also in Delta is the Reifel Wildfowl Sanctuary, on Westham Island at the mouth of the South Arm of the Fraser River, where it's possible to see many of the 371 species of birds that either visit or live in this part of the West Coast. The most spectacular sight here is the 50,000 snow geese that stop off in the fall and again in early spring on their journey from and to Wrangel Island off the coast of eastern Siberia. The birds in the refuge can be viewed from 3.2km of designated paths that lead to an observation tower and some blinds. Keep in mind that there is very little activity here in summer. Call ☎ 604-946-6980 for information.

Other birds you'll see around Vancouver include the Crested Myna, pigeons, finches, crows, ducks, grebes, loons, geese, swans, sandpipers, herons, robins, wrens, sparrows, swallows, hummingbirds, larks, hawks, eagles, turkey vultures, grouse, doves, owls and of course gulls. For information about birds in Vancouver, and throughout the province, call the Federation of BC Naturalists at ☎ 604-737-3057.

Marine life is also abundant although not quite as easy to see unless you visit the Vancouver Aquarium, or if you are a diver. Compared to other temperate oceans, the

Orcas attain a length of 6.1m to 9.1m

North Pacific has the greatest number of species and many of these tend to be larger than closely related animals found in other oceans. Some examples of this are the giant octopus, starfish, halibut, mussels, shrimp, sea urchin and chinook salmon.

In the tidal pools along the rocky coastline you can find, among other creatures, crabs, sea anemones, sea cucumbers, whelks, pricklebacks and sculpins. Out at sea there are herring, perch, rockfish, sea perch, lingcod, flounders, skates, cabezons, sculpins, wolf eels and a variety of sharks.

In spring, the waters of the Fraser River will often push freshwater varieties such as sturgeon and carp into the harbor, and smelt can be found along the beaches. All five species of North American Pacific salmon – coho, chinook, sockeye, chum and pink – are found around Vancouver and spawn in late summer and autumn. Steelhead trout can also be spotted. Orcas (killer whales) can sometimes be spotted at the mouth of the Fraser River looking for salmon, or even straying into the harbor in search of seals. Besides the whales, other marine mammals interested in feasting on some of the spawning salmon are harbor seals and sea lions.

GOVERNMENT & POLITICS

The City of Vancouver has a mayor and 10 councilors who are elected to office for a period of three years. Provincial party politics do not have a direct bearing on city government, although there are affiliations. In Vancouver, when it comes time for an election, there are civic political parties, including the Committee of Progressive Electors (COPE) and the Non-Partisan Association (NPA), that put forward candidates, although many individuals run and have been elected as independents. However, these political parties don't seem to have much bearing on the actual policy implemented by the mayor or councilors during their tenure.

As a framework for its future, Vancouver adopted in 1995 what it calls CityPlan to help guide policy decisions, capital work projects, budgets and other priorities. This plan is an amalgamation of ideas collected over a three-year period from various community groups and interested individuals who suggested how they thought Vancouver should grow and develop (more than 20,000 people actively participated in its preparation). The issues included transportation, housing, pollution and community services, and it is a great example of participatory government at work.

Greater Vancouver consists of 20 municipalities – each with its own elected government consisting of a mayor and councilors – and two electoral areas: Electoral Area A (University Endowment Lands and Pacific Spirit Regional Park) and Electoral Area C (Bowen Island, Barnston Island, Howe Sound and Indian Arm).

The Greater Vancouver Regional District (GVRD), which was incorporated in 1967, oversees the joint interests of the municipalities in the Lower Mainland. This is a voluntary federation designed to deliver essential services more economically, efficiently and equitably. These services include water, sewerage and drainage, housing, hospital planning and development, solid waste management, air quality management and regional parks. The GVRD also initiated the Livable Region Strategic Plan, a strategy for growth management in the Greater Vancouver region.

The GVRD board, which meets once a month to set policy and vote on decisions, consists of a number of directors who are mayors and city councilors from participating municipalities. The directors, who are selected by their respective municipalities, serve one-year terms and can be re-appointed. The board elects a chairperson and vice-chairperson from among its members.

ECONOMY

Vancouver is the economic heart of BC, and is the principal manufacturing, trade and service center. It is one of North America's busiest ports and the leading dry-cargo port on the Pacific Coast. The city is also an important railway terminus. Plus, it has become an important financial center: most of the major industrial concerns in BC have their head offices in the city.

Because the economies of Vancouver and BC are so closely connected, its difficult to talk about one without mentioning the other. The resource industries of forestry, mining, agriculture and fishing remain the backbone of the economy and contribute to the high standard of living. The forest industry accounts for about half of BC's manufactured output and a quarter of the direct jobs, while mining contributes about $4 billion, with the most important minerals being coal, copper, zinc, gold and silver, as well as gas and oil. About one-third of BC's exports are to Asia, with the majority going to Japan, translating into about $9 billion worth of goods.

Service industries such as tourism, high technology and food processing are also fueling the economy. Tourism, which is Greater Vancouver's largest industry and second in the province only to forestry, alone brings $4.5 billion into BC, $3.52 billion of which stays in Vancouver. More than 5 million tourists visit BC every year, and in Vancouver that supports 63,000 jobs.

BC has a $352-million deficit, a growth rate of 1% and an unemployment rate of 8%.

POPULATION & PEOPLE

About 1.9 million of BC's 3.7 million people live in the Greater Vancouver area. Although Britain and Ireland are the ancestral homelands of many residents, successive migrations, especially since WWII, have produced a multicultural society with people coming from dozens of ethnic backgrounds, including Chinese, Indian, Ukrainian, Scandinavian, Dutch, Italian, Greek, Japanese, Iranian, Vietnamese, and many smaller groups, especially from the West Indies, Korea and Central and South America.

In terms of the province's original inhabitants, the United Native Nations Society estimates there are up to 60,000 people with aboriginal origins living in the Greater Vancouver area. Of these, just under 50% live on reservations, which is a drop of about 14% since 1976.

In terms of immigrant population, BC is the fastest-growing province in Canada, with a 25% growth rate in the past five years, making BC the most popular province to immigrate to. Between 1991 and 1996, BC received more than 250,000 immigrants; more than 70% live in Greater Vancouver.

Greater Vancouver is ranked second among cities in Canada (only Toronto is higher) for the highest percentage of minority residents, which make up 31% of the population. The largest groups are Chinese (from Hong Kong, Taiwan and China) who make up half of all newcomers, South Asian (mostly from the Punjab region of India), Filipino, Japanese, Southeast Asian, Arab/West Asian and Korean. Four out of five new arrivals in the Lower Mainland between 1991 and 1996 came from Asia or the Middle East, while just one in 10 came from Europe. This is a huge difference when compared to immigration statistics prior to 1961, when less than 10% of immigrants came from Asia and the Middle East, and 85% came from Europe.

ARTS
Literature

There is no shortage of writers in or from Vancouver. Some scratch out a living, or at least fulfill a need, by producing works that aren't read outside of Greater Vancouver, while others have moved on to fame and fortune elsewhere. Still others have come here from distant regions and have decided to call Vancouver home, believing it offers a good environment in which to create poetry and prose.

Some of the writers who have spent time in Vancouver, but are difficult to classify as being Vancouver writers, include Margaret Atwood, Simon Gray, Alice Munro, Margaret Laurence, Malcolm Lowry, Sinclair Ross, George Ryga and Ethel Wilson.

Vancouver – A Star is Born

The year was 1970. Director Robert Altman arrived in Vancouver with his stars Warren Beatty and Julie Christie to shoot the Warner Bros feature, *McCabe & Mrs Miller*. It was the city's first major Hollywood production. A ragtag crew had been strung together using local stagehands gathered from across Canada. Meanwhile, a convoy of trucks motored up the Pacific Coast Hwy from Hollywood with cameras, equipment and all the key production people in tow.

Vancouverites were beside themselves with excitement over the prospect of having 'real movie stars' in town. Today, dressing-room trailers are permanent fixtures around the city. Nearly 25,000 people work in the industry – at times servicing over 30 productions simultaneously – making Vancouver the third-largest production center in North America behind Los Angeles and New York.

Locals barely batted an eyelash when actor/comedian Robin Williams flexed his improv muscles at a local comedy club while in town filming the feature *Jumanji*, or when actress Sharon Stone strolled down Robson St to do a bit of shopping between takes on *Intersection*. In 1997 alone, 24 features, 20 TV series and 53 television movies were filmed in Vancouver, injecting more than $630 million into the local economy.

So what's the appeal of Vancouver for filmmakers from Bruce Beresford to Joel Schumacher? Unquestionably it's the variety of locations. Over the years Vancouver and environs, with its ocean, forest, mountain and urban settings all in such close proximity, have served as the backdrop for such locations as: Tibet in *K2* and in director Martin Scorsese's film *Kundun*; backstreet New York in Jackie Chan's *Rumble in the Bronx*; Washington State in the Jack Nicholson classic *Five East Pieces*; Argentina in director Jean Jacques Annaud's *Wings of Courage*; Scandinavia in *The 13th Warrior* starring Antonio Banderas; Seattle in *The Accused* starring Jodie Foster, and *Stakeout* starring Richard Dreyfuss; and almost everywhere else in the USA during *The X-Files'* five seasons of filming in Vancouver. Combine that variety with an extensive infrastructure of skilled crews, production services, facilities and weather suitable for year-round filming, then top it off with a cheap Canadian dollar, well, let's face it, you've got an unbeatable location.

Television has become a mainstay in Vancouver with the production and servicing of such major series as *Outer Limits*, *Highlander*, *Millennium*, *Poltergeist*, *The Sentinel* and *The X-Files* to mention just a few – and in fact the city attracts so many TV movies-of-the-week, it's been dubbed 'MOWtown.'

But the industry hasn't just been importing its talent, Vancouver has also produced and exported its own cadre of international TV and film stars over the years. Some of these include Raymond Burr, Michael J Fox, Margot Kidder of *Superman* fame, Jason Priestley (*Beverly Hills 90210*), Bruce Greenwood (*St Elsewhere*, *Nowhere Man* and, among other films, *Exotica* by director Atom Egoyan), Cynthia Stevenson (*The Player* and *Home for the Holidays*), Fairuza Balk (*Valmont* and *The Craft*) and the next tier, new teen heartthrob Joshua Jackson (*The Mighty Ducks*).

Film and TV production in Vancouver has come a long way since *McCabe & Mrs Miller* came to town – it's no longer just a business, it's an industry.

Joanne Morgan, a Vancouver Journalist

This section is by no means inclusive. If you would like to know more about the city's authors, read *Vancouver and its Writers* by Alan Twigg.

Both an established author and illustrator, Nick Bantock achieved international success with his 1991 novel *Griffin & Sabine*, followed by the award-winning *Sabine's*

Notebook and *The Golden Mean.* A novelist and a poet, Earle Birney, who died in 1995, is one of Vancouver's, indeed Canada's, better-known authors, producing experimental poetry and novels that include *Down the Long Table* and *Turvey.*

The recipient of the Governor General's Award for poetry and fiction, George Bowering has more than 40 titles to his name, including the novels *Burning Water*, about Captain George Vancouver, and *Caprice.* Denise Chong's *The Concubine's Children* is about a family reunion in China. Internationally, one of the better-known writers to have come from Vancouver is Douglas Coupland, best known for his novel *Generation X*, as well as *Shampoo Planet* and *Microserfs.*

William Deverell writes best-selling thrillers, including *Needles*, *High Crime*, *Mecca*, *Platinum Blues* and *Kill all the Lawyers.* Another Vancouver-based author of thrillers is Christopher Hyde, who has written *Hard Target*, *The Icarus Seal* and *Abuse of Trust.*

Science-fiction author William Gibson, who was born in North Carolina, has achieved international success with his novels *Neuromancer*, *Idoru*, *Mona Lisa Overdrive* and *Virtual Light.* Another well-known science-fiction writer who now calls Vancouver home is Spider Robinson, author of *Stardance* and *Callaghan's Crosstime Saloon.*

Multi-award-winning crime writer Laurence Gough was born in Vancouver and his novels include *The Goldfish Bowl*, *Hot Shots*, *Crimes* and *Killers.* The author of numerous children's books such as *Raven's Cry* and *Something Weird is Going On*, Christie Harris was a longtime Vancouver resident before moving to Victoria. Lynn Johnston, whose cartoon strip *For Better or For Worse* is published in 1400 newspapers worldwide, grew up and studied art in Vancouver.

Best known for his novel *Shoeless Joe*, which was made into the film *Field of Dreams*, WP Kinsella lives in White Rock and has also written a number of Native Indian-related stories that appear in collections such as *The Fencepost Chronicles*, *The Moccasin Telegraph* and *Brother Frank's Gospel Hour.* Joy Kogawa has written two novels about the internment of Japanese Canadians, *Obasan* and *Itsuka.*

SKY Lee received the City of Vancouver book award for *Disappearing Moon Café*, her novel about four generations of a Chinese family in Vancouver, and has also published *Bellydancer*, a collection of short stories.

Lee Maracle writes about the struggles of Native Indians, particularly from a woman's perspective, in *I am Woman*, *Bobbi Lee, Indian Rebel*, *Ravensong* and *Sundogs.* Humorist, playwright and journalist Eric Nicol is best known for his books *The Roving I*, *Shall We Join the Ladies?*, *Girdle Me a Globe* and *Dickens of the Mounted.* Jane Rule, originally from New Jersey, came to Vancouver in the late '50s and her novels include *Desert of the Heart*, *The Young in One Another's Arms* and *Contact with the World.* Ian Slater, originally from Australia, writes many of his novels about technological and ecological disasters including *Firespill*, *Deep Chill* and *Sea Gold.*

Audrey Thomas, who lives on Galiano Island, is best known for her short-story collections, including *Ladies and Escorts*, *Real Mothers* and *The Wild Blue Yonder*, but has also written novels including *Intertidal Life*, *Blown Figures* and *Latakia.* David Watmough, originally from England, writes about life as an immigrant and as a homosexual in novels such as *Thy Mother's Glass*, *Ashes for Easter* and *The Time of the Kingfishers.*

The author of about 150 books, and one of BC's most respected authors, George Woodcock (1912-1995) was, among other things, a poet (*Tolstoy at Yasnaya Polyana* and *The Cherry Tree on Cherry Street*), a historian, a literary scholar, a biographer and a travel writer. LR Wright is a well-known mystery writer whose books include *Neighbours*, *Mother Love* and *The Suspect.* Michael Yates is best known for his experimental writing, a combination of poetry and prose, in such works as *abstract beast* and *man in the glass octopus.*

Music

Vancouver's role in the international music scene is best represented by artists such as Bryan Adams, Sarah McLachlan, kd lang, 54-40, Spirit of the West, NoMeansNo and Bif Naked. The fact that these artists rarely perform in Vancouver is primarily because they are touring the world. Some of them call Vancouver home, but the majority of these musicians simply used the city as a springboard to get their careers started, which in itself says something about the vitality of the music industry here.

Groups that helped to put Vancouver on the map in the '70s include Chilliwack, Loverboy, Terry Jacks and the Poppy Family (most notably for *Seasons in the Sun*), Bachman-Turner Overdrive (BTO), Heart (although originally from Seattle) and punk rockers DOA. Twenty years later, DOA,

Bryan Adams – Local Boy

No other Vancouver musician has received more acclaim, had greater record sales or reached higher levels of international stardom than Bryan Adams. He fills concert halls and stadiums everywhere he goes with his brand of guitar-orientated rock, and he has sold more than 50 million albums worldwide.

Adams, who was born in Kingston, Ontario, in 1959, spent his first 14 years traveling the world with his family – his father was a captain in the British military. After his parents' marriage came to an end he settled in North Vancouver with his mother and brother in 1974. Always interested in music (the first album he owned was the Beatles' *Sgt Pepper's Lonely Hearts Club Band*), he quit school at the age of 16 to join the band Sweeney Todd, a rather forgettable group whose best-known song was *Roxy Roller*.

In 1978 Adams met his future writing partner Jim Vallance in a record store, and after producing songs for the likes of Kiss, Joe Cocker and Bachman-Turner Overdrive, they signed a deal to record the disco hit *Let Me Take You Dancing* in 1979. Adams' first couple of albums didn't sell well outside of the local market, but his 1982 album *Cuts Like a Knife* resulted in the title track and *Straight From the Heart*, becoming his first major hits. It was during this time that he established his reputation as a performer, especially in the USA where he toured as a support act with The Kinks, Loverboy and Foreigner.

However, *Reckless,* in 1984, was the album that really brought Adams an international audience, and with it he became the first Canadian to earn a diamond album for selling 1

million copies nationally. In 1986 and 1987 he had six top-20 songs in 12 months. His 1991 *Waking up the Neighbors* album, written and produced with new partner Robert 'Mutt' Lange, was his second album to earn a diamond award, and the song *(Everything I Do) I Do it for You* from the film *Robin Hood, Prince of Thieves* set a record in the UK by staying at No 1 in the charts for 16 weeks. In 1996 Adams released the album *18 'Til I Die* and in 1998 he became one of the many musicians to release an *Unplugged* album.

These days Adams spends most of his time in places other than Vancouver, such as London, England, although in 1998 he opened The Warehouse, a $2 million state-of-the-art recording studio in a Gastown heritage building.

though gray but not the least bit lethargic, still honors its punk-rock mandate by performing regularly. Bands such as Prism, Trooper and Jerry Doucette once filled concert halls across the country. Bands to come out of Vancouver in the '80s include the Payola$, Doug and the Slugs, Images in Vogue, Skinny Puppy and Grapes of Wrath, as well as guitar-sensation Colin James, who moved here from Regina.

Vancouver's music scene remains diverse. The punk spirit lives on in gob, d.b.s. and Brand New Unit. The nine-piece Superconductor was once infamous for having six guitarists. Zumpano shares one thing in common with Superconductor and that's the same vocalist, but its sound is more in keeping with the kind of music you're likely to hear on AM 'pop' stations. Also look out for Moist, Rose Chronicles, Pure and Salvador Dream.

The Molestics is a tongue-in-cheek jazz ensemble that plays the tunes of Louis Armstrong and the Hot Five and the Hot Seven. The Molestics will make you want to dance and take you back to a different era. For the serious jazz fan there is Tony Wilson, who pieces together quintets, sextets and septets and more from the reservoir of Vancouver's hottest jazz musicians. Wilson, a guitarist, tends to lean towards the post-bop and avant garde stylings of musicians such as John Coltrane or Ornette Coleman. Some of his associates to look out for include Talking Pictures, and John Korsrud and the Hard Rubber Orchestra. From Nanaimo, acclaimed jazz pianist and vocalist Diana Krall can almost be considered a local. Veda Hille and Kinnie Starr represent the city's folk-jazz scene; Hille creates fierce and literate jazz with angular pop, while Starr embraces rich sounds with elements of hip-hop.

Country music fans should look out for Neko Case, a former member of Cub. Rockabilly is represented by the Saddlesores and Bughouse 5, and bluegrass is performed by Great Northern. Long-time Vancouver blues guitarist and vocalist (and sometime actor) Jim Byrnes is always worth catching in one of the clubs around the city.

For more information about music, particularly classical and opera, and venues, see the Music section in the Entertainment chapter.

Painting & Sculpture

The natural beauty of Vancouver, with its many landscapes, colors, textures and ever-changing light, is surely an inspiration to artists, no matter what they've chosen as their theme or medium. Vancouver has long had an active art scene and the following are just some of the city's more important artists.

Emily Carr (1875-1945), who was born in Victoria, is one of the better-known artists to have lived and worked in Vancouver. Her vision of the coastal forests and the Native Indians who called them home is truly remarkable (see The Life & Work of Emily Carr boxed text in the Things to See & Do chapter). Two former Group of Seven painters, Frederick Horsman Varley (1881-1969) and Lawren Harris (1885-1970), are known for both their landscapes and their influence on the Vancouver art community.

WP Weston (1879-1967) did for the mountains in his paintings what Carr had done for the West Coast forests in hers. A commercial artist and landscape painter, Paul Rand (1896-1970) was interested in making painting accessible to everyone, while Charles H Scott (1886-1964) was more interested in finding new ways of depicting the landscape. Charles Marega (1879-1939) is best known for his public sculptures, including the lions on the south side of Lions Gate Bridge.

Two Native Indian carvers who preserved the past while contributing to a new generation of Native artists were Charles Edenshaw (1839-1920), the first professional Haida artist, who worked in argillite, gold and silver, and Mungo Martin (1881-1962), a Kwakiutl master carver of totem poles. Martin passed on his skills to Bill Reid (1920-1998), the outstanding Haida artist of his generation and the first Haida artist to have a retrospective exhibition at the Vancouver Art Gallery.

Charles Edenshaw's great-grandson Robert Davidson (1946-) explores innovative ways to transform Haida art, while his great-great-grandson Jim Hart (1952-) is best known for his large carvings. Both artists apprenticed under Bill Reid. Another family connection comes by way of Henry Hunt (1923-) and his son Tony Hunt (1942-), the son-in-law and the grandson of Mungo Martin, who have continued the carving tradition and the totem preservation work at the Royal British Columbia Museum in Victoria. Roy Henry Vickers (1946-) of Tofino is another Native artist who has found new ways to express traditional themes, often through wildlife paintings, while Susan Point (1952-), a Coast Salish artist, has combined a distinctive personal style with traditional themes in a variety of mediums.

Jack Shadbolt (1909-) is one of the better-known artists in Vancouver whose experimental work is very often of an abstract composition, as are the paintings of Gordon Smith (1919-). Toni Onley (1928-) has a very distinctive style that imparts the feeling of the West Coast landscape through abstract elements, while EJ Hughes (1913-) paints more realistic landscapes. Julie Duschenes (1953-) paints still lifes and landscapes using abstract forms, while the landscapes, cityscapes and still lifes of Vicki Marshall (1952-) are more traditional.

Richard Prince (1949-) is a sculptor who specializes in machines that often move with the wind, while Alan Storey (1960-) also likes to create moving machines, such as *Pendulum* in the Hongkong Bank building on West Georgia St. Video art is best represented by the works of Paul Wong (1955-).

Theater & Dance

Vancouver has long had an active and innovative dance scene, winning many of the country's top awards. As well, the city hosts the annual modern dance festival, Dancing on the Edge, at the Firehall Theatre (see Special Events in the Facts for the Visitor chapter for details). For information on Vancouver's dance companies and theaters, see the Entertainment chapter.

Architecture

No one has done more to shape the look of Vancouver than architect Arthur Erickson, both through his own designs and those that have been created through his influence. Starting in the early '60s, Erickson and his protégés have been designing buildings that are specific to Vancouver by taking into account the city's climate and geography and incorporating those into a unique style.

Some of Erickson's most important structures include Simon Fraser University, Robson Square and the courthouse, the redevelopment of the building that is now the Vancouver Art Gallery, the MacMillan Bloedel building on West Georgia St and the Museum of Anthropology at UBC.

When Vancouver rose phoenix-like from the ashes of the Great Fire of 1886, Gastown was where the city's first architects built stone and brick buildings, keeping with the styles of the time. Nathaniel Stonestreet Hoffar, who emerged as the most important architect of this period, is responsible for the buildings along the 300 block of East Cordova in Gastown, plus the Yale Hotel near the Granville Bridge.

The six-year period between 1907 to 1913 became known as 'Vancouver's Golden Years of Growth,' when much of the financial district along West Hastings St was first developed, and when two buildings – the 13-story Dominion Trust Building at Hastings and Cambie Sts, and the 17-story Sun Tower at Beatty and Pender Sts – both claimed the record for being the tallest building in the British Empire in their time. WT Whiteway, who designed the Sun Tower, also designed The Landing in Gastown.

Also during this golden period, JE Parr and Thomas Fee designed the Hotel Europe in Gastown, many of the buildings along Granville St and the fabulous Manhattan Apartments on Thurlow and Robson Sts. The Winch Building, now part of the Sinclair Centre on Hastings and Granville Sts, was designed by Thomas Hooper, who also designed the south facade of what is now the Vancouver Art Gallery, the rest of that building was designed by Francis Rattenbury and renovated by Arthur Erickson.

Many of the period's more elegant buildings, such as the Toronto-Dominion Bank at Hastings and Seymour Sts, were designed by Woodruff Marbury Somervell, an American who came to Vancouver by way of New York and Seattle. A firm to emerge during this period, and stay in business for 80 years, was Sharp & Thompson. It was responsible for the pre-WWI buildings at UBC, the Vancouver Club and, in the early 1930s, the galleries of the Burrard Bridge.

Post-WWI buildings of note include the moderne City Hall on Cambie St, designed by Townley and Matheson, while McCarter Nairne and Partners designed the exquisite art deco Marine Building at the north end of Burrard St.

Despite these few impressive structures, and the high-rise development in the West End in the '50s, the overall skyline of Vancouver didn't change much between WWI and the late '60s. The False Creek area was an industrial enclave surrounded by mills, warehouses and railway yards. From City Hall, most of the North Shore was visible from the shoreline up to the mountains, and the downtown peninsula's tallest structure was the BC Hydro building on Burrard St, completed in 1957 and now a condominium residence called The Electra.

Since then, in just over 30 years, Vancouver has been transformed into a 'new' city with some outstanding modern developments such as Canada Place, Library Square, Cathedral Place, the BC Gas building, Robson Square and Granville Island. False Creek is being developed into a multi-purpose area that, if all goes according to plan, should be an example for other cities to follow, as will the continued development of the waterfront along Burrard Inlet.

When it comes to preserving its heritage, the city has done a good job protecting some of its more notable buildings, such as the Sinclair Centre and those in Gastown, but it hasn't been quick enough to save others from the onslaught of developers. This attitude is changing for the better, however, and the city is now taking pride in its past while it looks ahead to the future.

RELIGION
Protestant denominations make up the largest religious group in Vancouver at 39%, followed by those with no religious affiliation at 25.2%, Catholics at 14%, Sikhs at 7%, Buddhists at 5.6%, Muslims at 4%, Jews at 2.7% and Hindus at 2.5%.

LANGUAGE
Vancouver is primarily an English-speaking city and English is the mother tongue for almost 60% of the population. Canada's other official language is French, and federal government offices in Vancouver, as well as across the country, work in English and French. Only 1.5% of Vancouverites consider themselves to be French speakers.

Chinese is the second-most-common language, with 18.5% of the population speaking it, followed by Punjabi, German, Italian, Tagalog (Filipino), Vietnamese and Spanish.

Facts for the Visitor

WHEN TO GO

In many respects, Vancouver is a year-round destination. The best weather is likely to be found from mid-spring (May) through mid-autumn (October), with the best of the summer weather coming in July, August and September. But it's not uncommon for Vancouver to get its best summer weather in June, then rain more or less throughout July and August, with another shot of summer coming in September.

Those interested in the ski slopes will enjoy the winter months (December through April), even though at times the city itself feels like it's trapped inside one huge rain cloud (or at worst gets hit with a snowstorm, which is guaranteed to shut down the city). Be that as it may, Vancouver can still get some lovely days in winter when the temperatures are in the low teens, the sky is clear and the mountains are in their full glory.

Many of the hotels divide their prices up into four seasons with December to February being the lowest and June to August being the highest. The costs in this book reflect the high-season prices. During the winter months you can get some great package deals which include room, breakfast and at least one dinner plus discounted tickets to a show or sports event. Tourist attractions are open throughout the year although some have restricted hours during the winter months. And if all else fails you can always explore one of Vancouver's many indoor shopping centers where the weather, no matter what the season, isn't a factor.

ORIENTATION

Vancouver (population 543,871) is built on a series of peninsulas bounded on the north by Burrard Inlet and on the south by the Fraser River. Directly behind the city to the north rise the Coast Mountains, while to the west Georgia Strait is cluttered with islands. The many bays, inlets and river branches, as well as the Pacific coastline, are a major feature of the city. Much of the city's recent growth has pushed suburbs far up the Fraser River to the east.

Surrounding the City of Vancouver, the region referred to as Greater Vancouver (population 1.9 million), or the Lower Mainland as it's also called, consists of a number of communities: Lions Bay, West Vancouver and North Vancouver to the north; Burnaby, New Westminster, Belcarra, Anmore, Port Moody, Coquitlam, Port Coquitlam, Pitt Meadows and Maple Ridge to the east; Richmond, Delta, Surrey, White Rock and Langley to the south and southeast; and the University Endowment Lands to the west.

To the south, Hwy 99 begins at the Canadian-US border where I-5 comes to an end. It's about an hour's drive from the border to the city center. Hwy 99 enters the south end of the city by way of the Oak St Bridge and then cuts over to Granville St and continues into the center. Hwy 99 continues through Downtown Vancouver, over Lions Gate

JOHN ELK

Bridge and north by way of the Upper Levels Hwy (Hwys 1 and 99) to Horseshoe Bay, Squamish, Whistler and beyond.

To the east, the Trans Canada Hwy (Hwy 1) skirts the edge of the city (Hastings St leads to Downtown Vancouver) and continues across the Second Narrows Bridge to North Vancouver and into West Vancouver, where it becomes the Upper Levels Hwy (Hwys 1 and 99), eventually ending at Horseshoe Bay. Other highway routes around the city are described in more detail in the relevant sections of the Things to See & Do chapter.

BARRETT & MCKAY

Downtown Vancouver

Vancouver's downtown center is itself on a peninsula, cut off from the southern portion of the city by False Creek and from the northern mainland by Burrard Inlet. The tip of this peninsula is preserved as Stanley Park, one of Vancouver's greatest treasures. Three bridges link the southern part of the city, known confusingly as the West Side, with downtown. Only one bridge, the high-flying Lions Gate, links Downtown Vancouver to the northern suburbs, resulting in traffic nightmares.

Because Downtown Vancouver is on a small peninsula tilted slightly askew, the streets running parallel to Granville St actually run northeast-southwest, while the streets parallel to West Georgia St run northwest-southeast. For the purposes of this book, streets parallel to Granville St will be referred to as north-south routes, and streets parallel to West Georgia St will be referred to as east-west routes.

The corner of Granville and West Georgia Sts is the city's center point and includes the Pacific Centre, a 2½-block complex of shops, restaurants and services. West Georgia St and, two blocks south, Robson St are the two principal east-west streets. Robson St is lined with boutiques and restaurants. Only West Georgia St continues through Stanley Park to Lions Gate Bridge, although once it reaches the park it is known as the Stanley Park Causeway. Davie St, between Robson St and English

Bay-False Creek, is a secondary commercial and shopping street.

The main north-south streets are, from west to east: Burrard, Howe, Granville and Seymour. North of West Georgia St, bordered by Howe and Burrard Sts, is the main office, banking and financial district. At the water's edge at the foot of Howe St is the impressive Canada Place, the convention center and cruise-ship terminal, with its five jagged white 'sails.' Much of Granville St, from Nelson St north to West Hastings St, is closed to cars. It's not a true mall as buses, and service and emergency vehicles are still permitted; it has never worked very well as a central showcase.

The high-density area to the west of the downtown shopping area is known as the West End – *not* to be confused with the West Side across False Creek and English Bay, or with West Vancouver on the North Shore.

Three downtown districts are worth noting. Yaletown, on Hamilton and Mainland Sts between Davie and Nelson Sts, is currently the 'hot' part of town with old warehouses being converted into hip bars, restaurants and loft apartments. Gastown is along Water St, north of West Hastings St between Richards and Columbia Sts. This is the historic center of old Vancouver, with many restored Victorian buildings. Bustling Chinatown is just to the southeast, in the area more or less bordered by Carrall and Gore Sts and Hastings and Keefer Sts.

Neighborhoods

To the south of Downtown Vancouver, over False Creek, lies most of the City of Vancouver – a vast area that's primarily residential. Heading west after crossing either Burrard Bridge or Granville Bridge is Kitsilano, filled with students and young professionals. Farther west is Point Grey, another affluent neighborhood, which borders Pacific Spirit Regional Park and the University Endowment Lands where the University of British Columbia (UBC) is found. Between Kitsilano and south to the North Arm of the Fraser River are some of the city's most exclusive areas, such as Shaughnessy Heights.

East of Downtown Vancouver, running south from East Hastings St, Commercial Drive was once the center of Vancouver's Italian community but is now the focal point for a developing alternative and student-oriented neighborhood. To the southeast of downtown, on Main St between 48th and 51st Aves, is the Punjabi Market where Vancouver's Indian community has created a lively and vibrant neighborhood.

The City of Burnaby, east of Vancouver proper, is another residential area and contains Simon Fraser University. Southeast of Burnaby is the City of New Westminster, once the capital of BC and now an industrial area along the Fraser River. Across the river on the south side from New Westminster is Surrey, and farther south again, near the Canadian-US border, is the beachside community of White Rock.

Directly south of the City of Vancouver, across the Fraser River, is the rapidly growing City of Richmond, which is built on several islands at the mouth of the river, including Sea Island where the Vancouver international airport is located. Still farther south is Delta, which includes the port of Tsawwassen and the BC Ferries Terminal from where you can catch ferries to Vancouver Island and the Gulf Islands.

Over Lions Gate Bridge and Second Narrows Bridge lie North Vancouver and West Vancouver, collectively known as the North Shore. These are essentially middle-class residential areas, although there are some very exclusive neighborhoods, such as the British Properties, above the Upper Levels Hwy in West Vancouver. The shore of Burrard Inlet in North Vancouver is lined with commercial docks. To the east are two provincial parks, Lynn Canyon Park and Mt Seymour Provincial Park. To the north, off Capilano Rd, are Capilano River Regional Park, Grouse Mountain and the North Shore Range of the Coast Mountains.

In West Vancouver, to the north is Cypress Provincial Park and to the south, on Marine Drive, is Lighthouse Park. Horseshoe Bay marks the northwest boundary of the North Shore and it is from the BC Ferries Terminal here that you can take ferries to Bowen Island, the Sunshine Coast and Vancouver Island. Just north of Horseshoe Bay is the tiny residential community of Lions Bay.

Street Savvy

Generally, the avenues in Greater Vancouver run east to west and the streets go north to south. Some of the streets in the downtown area, as well as many of the avenues in the Greater Vancouver area, are given east or west designations. So Hastings St, for example, is divided into West Hastings St and East Hastings St. As a general rule the dividing cross street is Main St. However, for numbering purposes, the downtown east-west streets begin numbering at Carrall St, near Chinatown; on the West Side they start with Ontario St. North-south streets begin numbering at Waterfront Rd, along Burrard Inlet. As a reference in downtown addresses, Robson St begins the 800 block. Don't be confused on the West Side, in Kitsilano, when numbered avenues don't predict the street addresses. For instance, West 1st Ave is, for numbering purposes, the 1600 block.

Vancouver doesn't really have a freeway system to carry trunk traffic through the city, and congestion on the surface streets can be extreme. Especially to be avoided during rush hour (roughly 4.30 to 6.30 pm) is Lions Gate Bridge between downtown and West Vancouver. Only three lanes wide, the center

Aerial view of Downtown Vancouver, Stanley Park & the West Vancouver mountains

Lions Gate Bridge & the North Shore mountains

Queen Elizabeth Park in full bloom

RICK GERHARTER

CHUCK PEFLEY

TIM THOMPSON

DAVID R FRAZIER

Embracing Vancouver's cultural diversity

View of Vancouver skyline at sunset from North Vancouver

CHUCK PEFLEY

Dominion Building & Harbour Centre Tower

GUNTER MARX

Haida artist Bill Reid's *Jade Canoe*

JOHN ELK

Exterior detail on Marine Building

DOUG PLUMMER

Diners seen against mural in waterfront restaurant

CHUCK PEFLEY

The SkyTrain traveling through the city to Burnaby, New Westminster and Surrey

BC ferry near Horseshoe Bay, West Vancouver

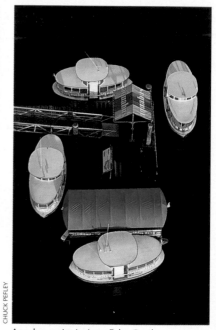

Aquabus water taxis on False Creek

lane changes direction during the day to accommodate traffic flow.

MAPS

The maps in this book are likely all you'll need to navigate around the city; however, consider purchasing a detailed city map if you need to find your way to the surrounding suburbs.

Free city maps are available from the Travel InfoCentres at the airport and in the city center. Several of the free visitors' guides to the city, which are found at the tourist offices or at many hotels, come complete with a map.

If you need a more detailed street map, it's worthwhile to purchase the *Greater Vancouver Street Wise Map Book*. It is available in convenience stores and bookstores at a cost of $4 for the standard 88-page book or $9 for the deluxe edition, which includes the Fraser Valley. Large foldout-type maps are also available at convenience stores, bookstores and many service stations for around $4.

A rather unique map that could double up as a nice souvenir of the city is *MapEasy's Guidemap to Vancouver*, which calls itself 'a location map and guidebook' in one. This foldout map has illustrations of the main attractions and shows by way of a color-coded system where some of the city's hotels, restaurants and retail shops are located. There are also detailed sections on Granville Island, Stanley Park and Robson St. It costs about $6.

TOURIST OFFICES

The Travel InfoCentre (Map 2; ☎ 604-683-2000, 800-663-6000 outside the Lower Mainland, fax 602-6901 for information, 683-2772 for bookings), Plaza Level, Waterfront Centre, 200 Burrard St, is open in the summer daily from 8 am to 6 pm, and the rest of the year weekdays from 8.30 am to 5 pm, Saturday from 9 am to 5 pm. Though usually busy, the staff is friendly and helpful, but don't forget to take a number!

The staff will help you with booking accommodations, tours, transportation and activities. You can also obtain transit tickets,

schedules and passes here. At the InfoCentre get a free copy of *The Vancouver Book*, the official visitors' guide, which has information on shopping, accommodations, entertainment, local transportation, convention and business services and more. Also useful are the free booklets *Where Vancouver*, *Visitor's Choice* and *Discover Greater Vancouver Visitors Guide,* available around town, often at hotels.

On the corner of West Georgia and Granville Sts (at Eaton's) is an information kiosk open in summer Tuesday to Friday from 10 am to 6 pm. There are also InfoCentres at the Vancouver airport (arrivals, level 2), at the Tsawwassen ferry terminal and at the Canadian-US border on Hwy 99. Other Travel InfoCentres where you can get information on various areas of the Lower Mainland, as well as on the rest of the province, are as follows:

Burnaby Travel InfoCentre
   (☎ 604-431-8046) Metrotown on Kingsway, in the pedestrian concourse to the Eaton Centre, open daily May to September
New Westminster Travel InfoCentre
   (☎ 604-526-1905) Westminster Quay Public Market, 810 Front St, open daily
North Vancouver Travel InfoCentre
   (☎ 604-980-5332) Capilano Rd at Marine Dr, open daily from May to September
Richmond Travel InfoCentre
   (☎ 604-271-8280) Hwy 99, 100m north of the Massey Tunnel, open daily
White Rock Travel InfoCentre
   (☎ 604-536-6844) Ground floor of the Town Centre Hall, 15150 Russell Ave, open daily

Other Information Offices

For general information about British Columbia, and to make reservations anywhere in the province, call Discover British Columbia at ☎ 604-663-6000 or 800-663-6000 from outside the city, including the USA. This is just a phone service. If you want information by mail, the address is Parliament Buildings, Victoria, BC V8V 1X4.

The British Columbia Automobile Association (BCAA; ☎ 604-268-5555) 4567 Canada Way, Burnaby, provides its members, and the members of other auto clubs, with travel information, maps, travel insurance and accommodations reservations. For 24-hour emergency road service call ☎ 604-293-2222.

DOCUMENTS
Visas
Visitors from nearly all western countries, including Mexico, need only a valid passport and do not require a visa, the exceptions being Portugal and South Africa. Tourists from Korea and Taiwan need a visa as do visitors from developing or third world countries. Residents of most Eastern European countries need visas as do those from Central and South American countries and also those from Communist nations. Visitor visas cost $75, or the equivalent in the currency of the country where the visa is obtained, and are granted for a period of six months. Visa requirements change frequently, and since visas must be obtained before arrival in Canada, check before you leave – Europeans included. A separate visa is required for visitors intending to work or to go to school in Canada.

Visitors from the USA, Greenland (Denmark) and Saint Pierre and Miquelon (France) do not need passports if they are entering from their areas of residence, but they do need to be in possession of valid identification such as a driver's license, birth certificate or a certificate of citizenship or naturalization. US citizens arriving in Canada from somewhere other than the USA should be in possession of a passport.

A passport and/or visa does not guarantee entry. Admission and duration of permitted stay is at the discretion of the immigration officer at the point of entry. The decision is based on a number of factors, including being of good health, being law abiding, having sufficient funds to support your stay in Canada and possibly being in possession of a ticket out of the country. This latter requirement will not often be asked of any legitimate traveler, especially from a western country.

If you are refused entry but have a visa, you have the right of appeal at the Immigra-tion Appeal Board at the point of entry. Those under 18 years of age traveling on their own should have a letter from a parent or guardian.

Visa Extensions An application for a visa extension must be submitted one month before the current visa expires. The fee for an extension is $75. The length of the extension is at the discretion of the particular immigration officer who is handling your application. Requirements for receiving an extension include having a valid passport, an onward ticket and adequate funds. In Vancouver, extensions must be applied for at the Canada Immigration Centre. Because the office does not provide a walk-in service, you must first call ☎ 604-666-2171 with your inquiry and then you will be given the appropriate information and/or instructions on how to proceed with your application.

Travel Insurance
Residents of BC are covered by the provincial health-care system which provides them with good, inexpensive medical care. Visitors to the province, however, are not covered under this system so you are well advised to take out travel insurance before you leave home. Not only does it cover you for medical expenses (see the Health section later in this chapter) and luggage theft or loss, but also for cancellations or delays in your travel arrangements under certain circumstances, such as becoming seriously ill the day before your scheduled departure. Check what's already covered by your local insurance policies or credit card as you might find that you won't need to take out a separate policy. However, in most cases this secondary type of coverage is very limited with lots of tricky small print. For peace of mind and guaranteed security, take out a separate insurance policy at the highest affordable level. It's also advisable to purchase travel insurance as early as possible so that you are covered if, for example, your plans are delayed due to strikes or industrial action.

Driver's License & Permits

You will need to show a valid driver's license when renting a car. You may want to obtain an International Driving Permit (IDP) at your local automobile association before leaving home; however, your local license is valid documentation for up to six months. The IDP is valid for one year but must be shown in conjunction with your original license.

US citizens planning a trip to Canada may want to investigate the Canadian Non-Resident Interprovince Motor Vehicle Liability Insurance Card which is only available in the USA. Visitors with US or British passports are allowed to bring their vehicles into Canada for up to six months. If you have rented a car, trailer or any other vehicle in the USA and intend on driving it into Canada, be sure to have a copy of the rental agreement with you to avoid any possible problems at the border. The rental agreement should stipulate that taking the vehicle to Canada is permitted. This also applies to those who have rented a vehicle in Canada and intend on taking it into the USA.

Useful Cards

A Hostelling International (HI) card is useful at the official youth hostels – non-members are welcome but pay between $4 to $7 more per night. If you don't get a HI card before leaving home you can buy one at youth hostels in BC.

An International Student Identity Card (ISIC) will get you admission discounts at museums, galleries and other attractions. If you don't have an ISIC card, be sure to have a valid student card from your school so you can prove you are eligible for the student admission fee.

Photocopies

All important documents (passport data page and visa page, credit cards, travel insurance policy, travel tickets, driver's license, etc) should be photocopied before you leave home. Leave one copy with someone at home and keep another one with you, separate from the originals.

EMBASSIES & CONSULATES
Canadian Embassies

Unless otherwise noted, details are for embassies. Diplomatic representation abroad includes:

Australia
  High Commission:
    (☎ 06-273-3844)
    Commonwealth Ave, Canberra, ACT 2600
  Consulate General:
    (☎ 02-9364-3000, Visa Immigration Office ☎ 02-9364-3050)
    111 Harrington St, Level 5, Quay West, Sydney, New South Wales 2000

Denmark
  (☎ 33-12-22-99)
  Kr Bernikowsgade 1, 1105 Copenhagen K

France
  (☎ 01-44-43-29-00)
  35 Avenue Montaigne, 75008 Paris

Germany
  (☎ 228-8123410)
  Godesberger Allee 119, 53175 Bonn

Ireland
  (☎ 1-478-1988)
  65-68 St Stephen's Green, Dublin 2

Italy
  (☎ 6-44-59-81)
  Via GB de Rossi 27, Rome 00161

Japan
  (☎ 3 408-2101)
  3-38 Akasaka 7-chrome, Minato-ku, Tokyo 107

Netherlands
  (☎ 070-361-4111)
  Sophialaan 7, 2500 GV The Hague

New Zealand
  High Commission:
    (☎ 4-473-9577)
    61 Molesworth St, Thorndon, Wellington
    (Note: visa and immigration inquiries are handled by the Consulate General of Canada in Sydney, Australia.)

Spain
  (☎ 1-431-4300)
  Edificio Goya, Calle Nunez de Balboa 35, Madrid

Sweden
  (☎ 8-613-9900)
  Tegelbacken 4 (7th floor), Stockholm

Switzerland
  (☎ 31-352-63-81)
  Kirchenfeldstrasse 88, CH-3005 Berne

UK
>   High Commission:
>   (☎ 0171-258-6600;
>   from 22 April 2000 ☎ 020-7258-6600)
>   Macdonald House, 1 Grosvenor Square,
>   London W1X 0AB

USA
>   (☎ 202-682-1740)
>   501 Pennsylvania Ave NW,
>   Washington, DC 20001
>   There are also many cities with Consulate
>   Generals. For information, check the Blue Pages
>   under 'Consulates.'

Consulates in Vancouver

In Vancouver there are 47 consulates but no embassies, which are located in Ottawa, Ontario, the country's capital. For those consulates not listed here check the Yellow Pages under 'Consulates & Other Foreign Government Representatives.' Consulates include:

Australia
>   (☎ 604-684-1177) 602 - 999 Canada Place

Denmark
>   (☎ 604-684-5171) 755 - 777 Hornby St

France
>   (☎ 604-681-2301) 1201 - 736 Granville St

Germany
>   (☎ 604-684-8377) 704 - 999 Canada Place

Ireland
>   (☎ 604-683-8440) 1400 - 100 West Pender St

Italy
>   (☎ 604-684-7288) 705 - 1200 Burrard St

Japan
>   (☎ 604-684-5868) 900 - 1177 West Hastings St

Netherlands
>   (☎ 604-684-6448) 475 Howe St

New Zealand
>   (☎ 604-684-7388) 1200 - 888 Dunsmuir St

UK
>   (☎ 604-683-4421) 800 - 1111 Melville St

USA
>   (☎ 604-685-4311, fax 685-7175)
>   1095 West Pender St

CUSTOMS

Along with your personal possessions, you are allowed to bring into Canada a duty-free allowance of 1.1L (40oz) of liquor or wine, or 24 375ml (12oz) bottles of beer, as well as 200 cigarettes, 50 cigars or 400g of tobacco. Alcohol and tobacco products can be brought in only by someone who is at least 19 years old, the age of an adult in BC. You are allowed to bring in gifts up to a total value of $60.

Sporting goods, including 200 rounds of ammunition, cameras and film, and two days' worth of food can be brought into the country. It's probably worthwhile to register excessive or expensive sporting goods and cameras with customs as this will save you time and trouble when leaving, especially if you plan on crossing the Canadian-US border a number of times.

If you are bringing a dog or cat into the country you will need proof that it has had a rabies shot in the past 36 months. For US citizens this is usually easy enough, but for residents of other countries there may well be more involved procedures. To avoid problems check with the Canadian government or a representative before leaving home.

For boaters, pleasure craft may enter Canada either on the trailer or in the water and stay for up to one year. An entry permit is required and is obtainable from the customs office at or near the point of entry. All boats powered by motors over 10hp must be licensed.

Pistols, fully automatic weapons and any firearms less than 66cm (26 inches) in length are not permitted into the country. Most rifles and shotguns will be admitted without a permit.

MONEY
Currency

The Canadian dollar ($) is divided into 100 cents (¢). Coins come in denominations of 1¢ (penny), 5¢ (nickel), 10¢ (dime), 25¢ (quarter), $1 (loonie) and $2 (twoonie) pieces. There is also a 50¢ coin but this is seldom seen. Notes come in $5, $10, $20, $50 and $100 denominations. Bills in larger denominations are produced but rarely used in general circulation, and even the $50 and $100 bills can prove difficult to cash, especially at smaller businesses or at night. Service stations, for example, are sometimes reluctant to deal with larger bills. Canadian bills are all the same size but vary in their colors and images. Some denominations have two styles as older versions in good condition continue to circulate.

All prices in this book are in Canadian dollars unless otherwise noted.

Exchange Rates

At press time exchange rates were:

country	unit		dollar
Australia	A$1	–	C$0.95
France	1FF	=	C$0.28
euro	€1	=	C$1.76
Germany	DM1	=	C$0.92
Hong Kong	HK$10	=	C$1.99
India	R10	=	C$0.36
Japan	¥100	=	C$1.34
New Zealand	NZ$1	=	C$0.81
UK	£1	=	C$2.53
USA	US$1	=	C$1.55

Exchanging Money

Changing foreign currency or traveler's checks is not a problem during normal banking hours, and most banks can deal with most currencies, especially those branches located in the city center. Thomas Cook has a number of offices in Vancouver, including one (Map 2; ☎ 604-687-6111) at 1016 West Georgia St, open Monday to Saturday from 9.30 am to 6 pm, and another one at 130 - 999 Canada Place, open Monday to Saturday from 9 am to 5 pm. American Express (Map 2; ☎ 604-669-2813) is at 666 Burrard St (the entrance is actually on the corner of Hornby and Dunsmuir Sts) and is open weekdays from 8 am to 5.50 pm and Saturday from 10 am to 4 pm.

There are several 24-hour currency exchange machines placed throughout the airport which dispense 15 foreign currencies – each machine has a different selection. Royal Bank also has several outlets at the airport. There are also a number of currency exchange offices in the city, usually in the heavily touristed areas such as Gastown or Robson St, and most are open daily. However, they charge a commission fee and give poor exchange rates. Still, if it's late or it's Sunday and you need money these outlets are convenient and include:

Custom House Currency Exchange
(Map 3; ☎ 604-482-6000) 375 Water St (Gastown). Open weekdays from 9 am to 5 pm, and weekends from 10 am to 5 pm.

International Securities Exchange
(☎ 604-683-9666) 1169 Robson St. Open Monday to Thursday from 9 am to 7 pm, Friday and Saturday from 9 am to 9 pm, and Sunday from 10 am to 7 pm.

Maple Leaf GST Refund Service Ltd
(☎ 604-893-8478) 900 West Georgia (Hotel Vancouver), open Monday to Saturday from 8 am to 8 pm, and until 6 pm on Sunday.

Money Mart
(☎ 604-606-9555) 1195 Davie St. As well as cashing checks, you can send and receive telegraphic transfers here; open 24 hours.

Traveler's Checks

Traveler's checks offer protection from theft or loss. American Express, Thomas Cook and Visa are widely accepted and have efficient replacement policies.

Keeping a record of the check numbers and the checks you have used is vital when it comes to replacing lost checks. Keep this record in a separate place from the checks.

You will save yourself trouble and expense if you buy traveler's checks in Canadian dollars. The savings you might make on exchange rates by carrying traveler's checks in a foreign currency don't make up for the hassle of exchanging them at banks and other facilities. Restaurants, hotels and most stores accept Canadian-dollar traveler's checks as if they were cash, so if you are carrying traveler's checks in Canadian dollars the odds are you will rarely have to use a bank or pay an exchange fee. Fast-food restaurants, smaller businesses and out-of-the-way establishments not use to seeing tourists may refuse checks, so ask at the outset of a meal or a purchase if they will be accepted. Traveler's checks in US dollars will also be readily accepted by most businesses but the exchange rate offered will be much lower than what you'll get at a bank or other exchange facility.

Take most of the checks in large denominations ($50s and $100s) as it won't be until the end of a stay that you may want to change a small check to make sure you aren't left with too much local currency.

Banks & ATMs

The major national banks such as the Bank of Nova Scotia, CIBC, Canada Trust, Royal Bank and Toronto Dominion have branches throughout the city and most have automatic teller machines (ATMs), usually referred to as 'banking machines' in Canada. The main downtown branches have foreign exchange departments. There are also about 25 foreign banks in the city. Banks are generally open weekdays from 9.30 am to 4 pm. Quite a few banks around town are open Saturday, including Bank of Nova Scotia, West 41st Ave and Cambie St (Oakridge Shopping Centre), open 9.30 am to 3.30 pm; CIBC, on the corner of Denman and Robson Sts (West End), open 9.30 am to 3.30 pm; Canada Trust, on the corner of East Pender and Main Sts (Chinatown), open from 9 am to 3 pm; Toronto Dominion, on the corner of 10th Ave and Alma St (Kitsilano), open 9 am to 3 pm.

At the airport, Royal Bank has four outlets open daily from 5.30 am to 9.45 pm.

Credit & Debit Cards

North America is a credit-card orientated market: major credit and charge cards are widely accepted everywhere. Indeed, car rental agencies, travel agents and most hotels prefer them to cash. The most commonly accepted cards are Visa, MasterCard (which are both affiliated with European Access Cards) and American Express. Diners Club-enRoute cards are also accepted by many businesses. Banks that issue Visa and MasterCard also offer debit cards that deduct payment directly from your savings or checking account.

If you lose your credit cards or they get stolen, contact the company immediately by calling the following 24-hour numbers:

American Express	☎ 800-268-9824
Diners Club-enRoute	☎ 800-363-3333
MasterCard	☎ 800-826-2181
Visa	☎ 800-336-8472

International Transfers

If you need money, you can instruct your bank at home to send you a draft. Specify the city, bank and branch to which you want your money directed, or ask your home bank to tell you where a suitable one is, and make sure you get the details right. The procedure is easier if you've authorized someone at home to access your account.

Money sent by telegraphic transfer should reach you within a week; by mail allow two weeks. When it arrives it will most likely be converted into local currency – you can either take it as is or buy traveler's checks.

You can also transfer money by American Express, Thomas Cook or Western Union, though the latter has fewer international offices.

Costs

Vancouver is not a bargain-travel destination: it ranks as one of the most expensive cities in North America both to visit and to live in. However, if you are on a strict budget and are prepared to stay in a hostel, cook many of your own meals and be selective about how you entertain yourself then you could get by on $45 to $50 a day. Staying in a very cheap hotel, eating in inexpensive restaurants and allowing yourself a bit more latitude with your entertainment dollar will cost you about $100 a day. At $150 a day you can live quite comfortably and after that, well, you are only limited by your imagination and expense account.

Tipping

Tipping is expected in restaurants, bars and better hotels, as well as by taxi drivers, hairdressers, barbers and baggage carriers. In restaurants, bars and clubs, the waitstaff is paid minimum wage and rely on tips to make a reasonable living. Tip at least 10%, but if you think the service was exceptional then tip up to 15%. Keep in mind that the tip is calculated on food and drink amounts and should not include the taxes, which are itemized separately at the bottom of the bill before being added to the grand total. A few restaurants have the gall to include a service charge on the bill in which case no tip should be given. Never tip in fast-food, take-out or buffet-style restaurants where you serve yourself. In a bar, if a big tip is given on the first order you probably won't have to worry about going thirsty for the rest of the night.

Taxi drivers expect 10% and hairdressers and barbers get 15% if their service is satisfactory. Baggage carriers (in airports or hotels) receive $1 for the first bag and 50¢ for each additional bag. In 1st-class and luxury hotels, tipping can reach ludicrous proportions as door attendants, bellhops and parking attendants all expect to be tipped at least $1 for each service performed, including simply opening a taxi door for you. However, saying 'thank you' to an attendant who does something that you could have just as easily done yourself is OK.

Taxes & Refunds

The Goods & Services Tax (GST), also known as the Gouge & Screw Tax, adds 7% to just about every product, service and transaction, with groceries being one of the few exceptions. The provincial sales tax adds another 7% to the bill and is applied to most items with the exception being groceries, books and magazines. The provincial sales tax is nonrefundable; however, items shipped out of BC directly by the seller are exempt. Keep in mind that when you are looking at the price of a product in a store, or the price of a hotel room, be sure to add on another 14% so that you aren't surprised when you are handed the bill.

Some guesthouses and B&Bs don't charge GST for rooms, and foreign visitors should try asking for an exemption from the GST on their hotel bill when making payment. If paid, however, the GST added to all accommodations (except campsites) is refundable.

Besides a refund on accommodations, foreign visitors also get a GST refund on nonconsumable goods bought for use outside Canada, provided the goods are removed from the country within 60 days. Tax paid on services or transportation is not refundable nor is the tax paid on consumable items such as restaurant meals, gas and tobacco. The value of the goods taxed must be over $100 and you must have original receipts; credit-card slips and photocopies are not accepted as proof of purchase. Most 'tourist' or duty-free shops, hotels and tourist offices have GST rebate booklets and mailing forms, or you can contact Revenue Canada, Custom, Excise & Taxation, Visitors' Rebate Program, Ottawa, Ontario K1A 1J5. Expect to wait four to six weeks for your refund check, which is paid in Canadian dollars. The receipts are not returned.

For those driving to the USA, you can claim an immediate cash rebate at the Heritage Duty-Free Shop (☎ 604-541-1244) at the main border crossing on Hwy 99. Be sure to have the original receipts and proof of residence (picture identification such as a passport or driver's license). The shop is open daily from 5 am to midnight.

POST & COMMUNICATIONS
Post

The main post office (Map 2; ☎ 604-662-5722, 800-267-1177), 349 West Georgia St between Homer and Hamilton Sts, is open weekdays from 8 am to 5.30 pm. There is no separate poste-restante counter so you must join the queue, show some identification and the person behind the counter will look for your mail. The post office will keep poste-restante mail marked 'c/o General Delivery' for two weeks and then return it to sender. The American Express office, 666 Burrard St, will also hold mail for their customers – being in possession of one of their traveler's checks is enough to qualify.

Some other postal outlets in the city offering full service include:

Bentall Centre (☎ 604-482-4296) 595 Burrard St

Chinatown (☎ 604-688-7225) 523 Main St

East Vancouver
  Tomson's Copy & Stationery (Map 4; ☎ 604-254-3003) 2458 East Hastings St
  Commercial Drug Mart (Map 4; ☎ 604-253-3266) 1850 Commercial Drive

West End
  Shoppers Drug Mart (☎ 604-685-0246) 1125 Davie St

Yaletown (☎ 604-899-6201) 1165 Pacific Blvd

Aside from the post offices themselves, stamps and postal services are often available at other outlets such as pharmacies, gift shops and convenience stores (look for the Canada Post sign in the front window). These outlets often have the advantage of being able to provide you with basic postal services seven days a week. Hotel concessions will often stock stamps.

Mail is delivered locally on weekdays. All mail, whether it's going to a local or an international destination, can be placed into the red mailboxes that are found on the streets throughout the city, often on street corners.

Both the main post office on West Georgia St and the outlet in the Bentall Centre have good philatelic counters, as well as photocopiers.

Postal Rates A standard 1st-class airmail letter is limited to a maximum of 50g to North American destinations but as much as 500g to other international destinations. First-class letters or postcards within Canada are 45¢ for up to 30g, while 1st-class letters or postcards to the USA are 52¢ for up to 30g. To all other destinations, 1st-class letters or postcards are 90¢ for up to 20g. Aerogrammes, which are not common, cost the same. To the USA, heavier mail can go either by surface or, more expensively, by air in small packet mail. Anything over 1kg goes by surface parcel post.

To other international destinations, letter packages up to a maximum of 2kg can be sent by air. Small packet mail up to the same weight can go by either surface or air. Packages over 2kg are sent by parcel post and different rates apply. For full details go to a post office and pick up a pamphlet which explains all the options, categories, requirements and prices. Suffice it to say there are numerous methods for posting something, depending on the sender's time and money limitations. Rates vary according to destination. Mail over 10kg goes surface mail only. For added security, speed or other requirements, there's registered mail and special delivery. Canada Post also offers an international courier service.

Some countries require a customs declaration on incoming parcels; check at the post office.

Telephone

Canada has an excellent telephone system. Rates tend to be low for local use and rather costly for long distance. BC Tel operates the phone system in BC, although recently they have had to open the market to other long-distance providers which has resulted in cheaper rates. The following information is based on using BC Tel as the provider. However, other companies may be able to offer cheaper long-distance rates.

Phone numbers within Canada consist of a three-digit area code followed by a seven-digit local number. If you're calling locally just dial the seven-digit number. If you're calling long distance, dial ☎ 1 + the three-digit area code + the seven-digit number. If you're calling Vancouver from overseas, the international country code for Canada is 1.

Area Codes Vancouver phone numbers are in the 604 area code, which also applies to the Lower Mainland, Fraser Valley, Sunshine Coast, Bowen Island and Whistler/Howe Sound regions. The rest of the province, including Vancouver Island, has the 250 area code. Generally within the 604 area the rule is that if the location of a call is across two stretches of water from where it originates then a toll charge applies. Note: you don't need to use the area code if you're calling from within the city.

All toll-free numbers are given with a 800 or 888 area code. Note that some toll-free numbers are good for anywhere in North America, others may be within Canada only, while still others may cover just the province. Sometimes you won't know until you try the number.

Rates Calls made from a private phone within the metropolitan area are free of charge. Local calls made from a coin or pay phone cost 25¢. Cellular phones from outside BC can be connected to the existing network for a fee for the service and a user fee – a major credit card is required for reference and charges. Call ☎ 800-661-2355 for information.

Hotels, motels and guesthouses often add a service charge of up to $1 for every call made from a room phone; they also have hefty surcharges for long-distance calls. If cost is a factor then use a public phone, which can be found in most hotel lobbies, public buildings, shopping malls, and on the streets. You can pump in quarters, use a phone or credit card, or make collect calls from pay phones. An alternative is a phone debit card that allows purchasers to pay in advance. These are available at BC Tel PhoneMarts, pharmacies and convenience stores.

Long-distance calls to anywhere in the world can be made from any phone but the rate varies depending on how it's done and when. If you wish to speak to an operator (☎ 0) to get information about rates or services you will be connected free of charge. However, don't ask the operator to put your call through because operator assisted calls are much more expensive than direct-dial calls. A call made without the assistance of an operator (which can be done if you know the area code as well as the number) is not only cheaper but faster. With operator assistance, calls in increasing order of cost are, station to station (you'll talk to whomever answers the phone), collect (reverse charge) and person to person.

If you use BC Tel as your provider, long-distance rates for calls made to destinations in BC, Canada and the USA are cheapest from 11 pm to 8 am daily. The second most economical time to call is from 6 to 11 pm daily except Sunday when this rate runs from 8 am to 11 pm. The most expensive time to call is from 8 am to 6 pm weekdays. Reductions can also apply to calls to the USA or overseas. All international codes are listed at the front of the White Pages. For international rates call the operator (☎ 0).

If you don't want to fumble with change at a pay phone then make your national or international calls at Payless Communications (☎ 604-687-2040), 470 West Cordova St, near Richards and Water Sts. It offers direct-dial service from private booths, and promises that international calls will cost 25% less than you will pay at a hotel or by using the assistance of an operator. The rate for calls throughout North America is 49¢ per minute. It also offers fax and money-transfer services.

International Calls To make an international call direct, dial ☎ 011 + the country code + the area code + the phone number. To find a country code look in the front of the White Pages or call the operator (☎ 0). International rates vary depending on the time of day, the destination and the telephone provider used. If going through BC Tel, for example, the cheapest time to call London from Vancouver is between 6 pm and 9 am, while it's cheapest to call Sydney and Tokyo between midnight and 8 am.

Directory Assistance There is no charge from a public phone for dialing local directory assistance at tel 411. To obtain telephone numbers for other locations in BC, Canada, or the USA dial ☎ 1 + the area code + 555-1212. To find out if a business has a toll-free number call ☎ 800-555-1212.

Fax, Telegraph & Internet Access
Faxes can be sent and received through the front desk of most hotels. Business centers such as Kinko's (☎ 604-734-2679), 1900 West Broadway, offer reasonably priced fax service on a 24-hour basis as well as computer and photocopying services. Another company to try is Mail Boxes Etc with nine

locations in the Lower Mainland. Two of its downtown locations are (☎ 604-689-1243) 125A - 1030 Denman St in Denman Place

Internet Resources

There are many useful websites on the Internet for gathering information for your visit to Vancouver. Listed below are a few that will give you somewhere to start.

Bob's British Columbia Links

www.arc.ab.ca/individuals/erkamp/bc.htm
This site will let you link up with some other interesting sites about not only the city, but the province as well, such as ferry schedules, the Yellow Pages, Victoria, Whistler and a site called Hidden Vancouver.

City of Vancouver

www.city.vancouver.bc.ca
The city's official website has just about anything you'd want to know about Vancouver, including tourist attractions, bicycle routes and the address of the mayor's office so you can tell him how much you enjoyed your visit (or not).

Enjoy Vancouver Electronically (EVE)

www.webzines-vancouver.bc.ca
This 'webzine' includes reviews and listings of restaurants, pubs, clubs and general up-to-date information on the city.

In Vancouver

www.vancouver-bc.com
Another site with complete listings of attractions, pubs, clubs and restaurants.

Lonely Planet

www.lonelyplanet.com
Access this site for the Thorn Tree bulletin board, travel news, updates and links.

The *Vancouver Sun* and the *Province*

www.vancouversun.com
www.vancouverprovince.com
The two daily newspapers are online and are worth a read to find out what's going on in the city.

and (☎ 604-688-8848) 141R - 757 West Hastings St in the Sinclair Centre.

Telegrams can be sent anywhere in Canada or overseas through AT&T Canada (☎ 888-353-4726).

Email access is available at most large, corporate hotels. In addition, Internet cafes offer online computer use at hourly rates, although they tend to go out of business rather quickly. One place to try is BC Internet Coffee (Map 2; ☎ 604-682-6668), 1104 Davie St, which has 11 computer stations offering email access and Internet browsing. Wild Web Cafe (☎ 604-879-0770), 2325 Cambie St, also provides Internet access as does Digital U Cyber Cafe (Map 5; ☎ 604-731-1011) 101 - 1595 West Broadway. The cost at any of these places is about $8 an hour for Internet access. Magpie Magazine Gallery (Map 4; ☎ 604-253-6666, fax 255-6913, magpie@lynx.bc.ca), 1319 Commercial Drive, offers an email sending and receiving service for $1 an email. It is open daily from 10 am to 7 pm, and until 9 pm on Thursday and Friday.

You can also find out the locations of 'cyber cafes' in Vancouver and around the world by connecting to www.cyberiacafe.net before your departure.

BOOKS

Most books are published in different editions by different publishers in different countries. As a result, a book might be a hardcover rarity in one country while it's readily available in paperback in another. Fortunately, bookstores and libraries are able to search by title or author, so your local bookstore or library is the best place to find out about the availability of the following recommendations.

Lonely Planet

Lonely Planet's *Canada* and *Pacific Northwest* are good supplemental guidebooks for travelers heading to Vancouver.

Guidebooks

There are quite a few special-interest guidebooks to Vancouver and the surrounding area, covering activities such as walking,

hiking, cycling and things to do with the kids. Jack Christie is a Vancouver journalist, author and outdoor enthusiast who has written several informative and entertaining guides to Vancouver including *One-Day Getaways from Vancouver*, *Day Trips with Kids* and *Whistler Outdoors Guide*, all published by Greystone Books.

Nature Walks Around Vancouver (Greystone Books) by Jean Cousins details 35 walks in and around Vancouver with descriptions of the flora and fauna found along the way. Also by the same author is *Easy Hiking Around Vancouver* with 35 hikes, including maps and seasonal tips. *109 Walks in British Columbia's Lower Mainland* and *103 Hikes in Southwestern British Columbia* (Douglas & McIntyre) by Mary and David Macaree offer detailed information on walks and hikes in and around Vancouver, although *109 Walks* might be of more interest to the short-term traveler to Vancouver; it has walks around False Creek, Point Grey and Stanley Park, among others.

Heritage Walks Around Vancouver (Whitecap Books) by Michael Kluckner and John Atkin calls itself the 'sidewalk historian's handbook' and takes walkers through eight of the city's more interesting neighborhoods and commercial districts. *Bicycling Vancouver* (Lone Pine Publishing) by Volker Bodegom has 32 entertaining and well-planned routes around the Lower Mainland. One of the routes takes in some of the best bakeries in Vancouver.

The Complete Guide to Fun with Kids in Greater Vancouver (Redpath Publishing) by Sandra Ferguson and Mary Jane Oberhofer offers a staggering 450 suggestions from toddler playgrounds to concerts in the park. *52 Weekend Activities Around Vancouver* (Greystone Books) by Sue Lebrecht and Judi Lees is divided into seasons and outlines such eclectic pursuits as underwater hockey, summer skiing and nudism. *BC for Free and Almost Free* (Whitecap Books) by Pat Kramer devotes nearly a third of its contents to Vancouver and Victoria; it could be a worthwhile purchase for those who are visiting one or both of these cities.

A Traveller's Guide to Aboriginal BC (Whitecap Books) by Cheryl Coull is a complete guide to Native Indian sites, history and culture with a full range of touring options. Even though this book covers the entire province, it's a good resource book for those interested in the Native Indian peoples located in and around the Lower Mainland.

If you are heading over to Victoria then you might be interested in purchasing *Victoria – The Insider's Guide* (Orca Book Publishers) by Robert Moyes. This pocket-size guide not only details the standard sites but also outlines some of the more unusual attractions and restaurants. *Victoria & Vancouver Island – The Almost Perfect Eden* (Hilltop Publishing) by Kathleen and Gerald Hill covers all you need to know about the provincial capital and beyond (although the maps in the book are conspicuous by their absence). *Hiking Trails I, Victoria & Vicinity* (Vancouver Island Trails Information Society) by Susan Lawrence is a no-nonsense and informative guide on hikes in the Victoria area.

History
Making Vancouver 1863-1913 (UBC Press) by Robert AJ McDonald looks at the years from when Vancouver began to when it became a full-fledged city, and how the different groups of people who came to Vancouver during those years helped to mold and shape it into the city it has become. Through pictures and text, *Vancouver at the Dawn* (Harbour Publishing) by John A Cherrington details the city's early history as chronicled by Sara McLagan, a newspaper woman and social activist at the turn of the 20th century. *Vancouver – A City Album* (Douglas & McIntyre) is, for the most part, a pictorial history of Vancouver from its beginnings in 1860, when Captain Edward Stamp built his first sawmill on First Narrows, to the early 1990s.

General
In *Vancouver's Many Faces* (Whitecap Books), Vancouver journalist Kevin Griffin explores more than 30 cultural groups in the

Lower Mainland, detailing their backgrounds. The book is part social history, part neighborhood guide and part reference. A different aspect of Vancouver's cultural background is looked at by Kay J Anderson in *Vancouver's Chinatown* (McGill-Queen's University Press). This book is a study of race and racism and is based on the premise that Chinatown, as a creation of the white community over a 100-year period, is the result of cultural domination.

Legends of Vancouver (Douglas & McIntyre) by Pauline Johnson is a city classic. Written in 1911 by this writer and performer, the book has been in print ever since and tells the legends and stories behind many prominent natural features in and around Vancouver. What city is worth its weight if it doesn't have its own coffee-table book? Perfect for display or reading, *Greater Vancouver* (Altitude Publishing) by Douglas Leighton has lots of glorious photos and would make a great gift or souvenir; it also comes in French and Japanese.

Vancouver's Famous Stanley Park – The Year-Round Playground (Heritage House Publishing) by Mike Steele details everything you'd want to know about the park, including its history, attractions and sites, complete with maps, suggested walks and photographs. *The Greater Vancouver Book – An Urban Encyclopaedia* (Linkman Press) edited by Chuck Davis is the definitive resource book on anything and everything to do with the city. When it comes to Vancouver, if it isn't in this book then it probably isn't worth knowing about.

NEWSPAPERS & MAGAZINES

The city's two daily newspapers are the *Vancouver Sun* and the *Province*. Both are published by Pacific Press so there really isn't much competition between the two. The *Vancouver Sun*, published every morning except Sunday, tries to be the more serious newspaper of the two while the *Province*, published every morning except Saturday, works hard at living up to its 'tabloid' image, although it has somehow always missed the mark. The major Chinese newspaper is the *Sing Tao Daily*.

The *Georgia Straight* is a free news and entertainment weekly published on Thursday and found in coffee shops, music stores, convenience stores and many other locations throughout the city. It's the best source of information on what's going on in the city. The weekly *West Ender/Kitsilano News*, generally found in the West End and Kitsilano, and the *North Shore News*, found in North and West Vancouver and published three times a week, are free publications full of local news and entertainment information. In fact, it's worth checking these out for restaurant ads offering two-for-one meal deals. The local gay newspapers are *Xtra West*, *Angles* and *The Loop*, all distributed free at many locations around the city.

There are a lot of local publications that cover a wide variety of interests, so if you want something in particular, go to a good newsstand and tell them what you want (see the Books & Magazines section in the Shopping chapter for information).

Some local magazines include *Vancouver Magazine*, a general-interest city magazine published eight times a year and found at newsstands. It also produces a yearly *City Guide*. Another lifestyle magazine focusing on travel and recreation, food, fashion and home design is *Western Living*, published 10 times a year. *Coast: The Outdoor Recreation Magazine*, is a free publication which is produced eight times a year and covers such outdoor sports as bicycling, hiking and skiing. For those interested in fishing, hunting and other types of outdoor recreation, check out *BC Outdoors*, published eight times a year. If boating news and information is what you're after then you'll want to look at the monthly *Pacific Yachting*. *Business in Vancouver* is a weekly tabloid covering business news in the Greater Vancouver area, while *BC Business* is a monthly magazine covering the province and has information on business opportunities and trends.

Although based in Toronto, the *Globe & Mail* is Canada's national newspaper and is easily found throughout the city. Also based in Toronto, *Maclean's Magazine* is Canada's weekly news journal, which also produces a

Chinese (Cantonese) edition. Canada's newest national daily newspaper, *National Post*, is also available in Vancouver.

RADIO & TV
Radio
If your radio is hooked up to cable, there are about 40 radio stations you can listen to in Vancouver, but if you are listening to a car radio, you will have to make do with about 20 stations (most of the additional stations are piped in from Seattle). The local stations listed here are identified by both their standard call number and the number where you'll find them if you are listening to a radio hooked into the cable network. All of the stations on cable are found on the FM frequency.

On AM frequencies, CKBD (600, 90.9) has talk, while CISL (650, 91.3) plays those old hits from the '50s through to the '70s. The commercial-free national broadcaster CBU-CBC (690, 93.1) has news, talk and music. For current top-40 hits there is CKLG (730, 94.7), or for news, sports, talk and middle-of-the-road music try CKNW (980, 96.3). CKST (1040, 88.5) has a variety of music and talk, and CKWX (1130, 97.1) plays country. CHMB (1320, 97.5) plays easy-listening music and CFUN (1410, 100.1) plays those easy-listening soft-rock favorites. CJVB (1470, 103.3) is a multicultural station.

On FM, CJJR (93.7, 92.5) plays country, KISS (96.6, 103.9) plays soft rock, CBUF-CBC (97.7, 102.3) is the French station, CFOX (99.3, 99.7) plays adult album-oriented rock and CFMI (101.1, 105.3) plays light rock. CITR (101.9), which is broadcast from UBC, plays alternative music of all kinds, and CFRO (102.7, 102.9) is a community station offering a mixed bag of information and entertainment. CHQM (103.5, 106.1) plays easy-listening music and CBU-CBC (105.7, 107.1) is for the classical music lovers.

TV
Why is it that no matter how many stations one has to choose from, it can still be difficult to find something worth watching? The selection of TV stations in Vancouver is

Art for City's Sake

In 1990 the Vancouver City Council became, in a manner of speaking, a patron of the arts when it decided to institute the Public Art Program in an attempt to bring art to the people by decorating public space.

The program is carried out in three different ways: through the art the city adds to civic projects, through neighborhood art programs, and through the commitment imposed on the developers of large construction projects. With the latter, developers must spend 95¢ per construction foot on public art.

Some of the results of the program can be seen in places such as Homer St where three time capsules make up the work called *Refuse Collection*; Pacific Blvd where *Footnotes* can be found inset in the sidewalk; and at the foot of Davie St on False Creek where *Street Light* consists of 14m-high bronze girders from which hang images either stamped in metal or etched in glass.

Other Lower Mainland cities, such as Richmond and Surrey, have either instituted similar programs to help beautify their public spaces or are considering doing so.

large, especially if all the cable and additional pay-TV channels are included. Not every TV will have access to every station: it can be a bit of a search-and look operation to find out what's on where. Also, finding any particular station will be determined by where you are in the Lower Mainland and who the cable provider is for that area. Check the local TV listings printed daily in the newspapers, or tune in to channel 2 for the regularly updated TV guide.

The government-funded Canadian Broadcasting Corporation's (CBC) station in Vancouver is CBUT (3) and the French version is CBUFT (7). The Canadian Television Network (CTV), the country's commercial station, is BCTV (11) in Vancouver and CHEK (6) in Victoria. Besides the two Canadian networks, the US networks such as ABC (10), CBS (15), FOX (28), NBC (16) and PBS (9) are broadcast from Seattle. Other stations that might be of interest are the Weather Network (23), CBC Newsworld (26), the Women's Television Network (27) and the multicultural station (20).

On the cable channels there are a variety of stations offering sports (TSN, 30), music (MuchMusic, 29; Nashville Network, 32; MusiquePlus, 35), news (CNN, 33; Headline News, 37) and general interest (The Learning Channel, 34; Arts & Entertainment, 31; The Discovery Channel, 42), just to name a few. Besides these channels there are additional pay-TV stations offering movies, more sports and business news.

PHOTOGRAPHY & VIDEO
Film & Equipment
Print film is widely available at supermarkets and discount drugstores (both of which offer the best prices). Slide film might prove a bit more difficult to find and you might have to go to a camera store to get what you want.

Drugstores are a good place to get your film cheaply processed, especially at one of the London Drugs stores. If you drop it off by noon you can usually pick it up the next day. However, if you want your pictures right away you can find one-hour processing outlets throughout the city, but be prepared to pay double the overnight cost. The cost of developing a roll of 35mm color film with 24 exposures is about $12, including tax.

Carrying an extra battery for your built-in light meter or compact camera is a good idea because you know it will die at the most inopportune time.

Video Systems
Canada uses NTSC color TV standard, which is not compatible with other standards (PAL or SECAM) used in Africa, Asia, Australia and Europe unless it is converted. If you are visiting from anywhere outside the Americas or Japan, keep in mind that if you buy a pre-recorded video tape

here it might not be playable at home – check your unit's requirement before leaving home. Shops might stock PAL versions but very few have tapes in SECAM.

TIME
Vancouver, and indeed most of BC, is on Pacific Standard Time (PST), which is eight hours behind Greenwich Mean Time (GMT); four hours behind Atlantic Standard Time (encompassing the Maritime Provinces apart from Newfoundland which is 4½ hours behind); three hours behind Eastern Standard Time (including Montreal, Ottawa and Toronto); two hours behind Central Standard Time (including Winnipeg and Regina); and one hour behind Mountain Standard Time (including Edmonton and Calgary).

CHUCK PEFLEY

Almost all of Canada (Saskatchewan is the exception) observes daylight saving time; clocks go forward one hour from the last Sunday in April to the last Sunday in October, when the clocks are turned back one hour.

ELECTRICITY
Canada uses 110 volts and 60 cycles, and plugs have two or three pins (two flat pins often with a round 'grounding pin'). Plugs with three pins don't fit into a two-hole socket, but adapters are available at Radio Shack, other electronic stores and hardware stores.

WEIGHTS & MEASURES
Canada officially changed from imperial measurement to the metric system in the 1970s. Most citizens accepted this change only begrudgingly and even today you'll find that both systems remain for many day-to-day uses.

All speed-limit signs are in metric – so don't go 100mph! Gasoline is sold in liters but items such as ground beef and potatoes are still often sold by the pound. Radio stations will often give temperatures in both Celsius and Fahrenheit degrees.

The expensive changeover has really resulted in a bit of a mess. The old system can never be eliminated completely as long as the USA, Canada's largest trading partner, still uses its version of imperial measure.

For help in converting between the two systems, see the chart on the inside back cover of this book. Note that the US system, basically the same as the imperial, differs in liquid measurement, most significantly (for drivers) in the size of the gallons.

LAUNDRY

Whether it's a coin-operated laundry you're after or a dry cleaners, there is no shortage of laundry facilities in Vancouver. Many hotels, especially the more upscale ones, offer laundry services but charge very high prices. Some coin laundries offer a drop-off service where you leave your clothes for the day and they will wash, dry and fold your laundry for about $1 a pound. Self-service washing machines generally cost $1.25 for a 25-minute cycle, while it will take about another $1.25 to get your clothes dry. Check the Yellow Pages under 'Laundries' to find one close to you. Some laundries around town include:

Davie Laundromat
(Map 2; ☎ 604-682-2717)
1061 Davie St, West End

Great West Coin Laundromat
(Map 6; ☎ 604-734-7993)
2955 West 4th Ave, Kitsilano

Vicious Cycle Laundro & Leisurama
(Map 4; ☎ 604-255-7629)
2017 Commercial Drive, East Vancouver

TOILETS

Public toilets, which are more commonly referred to as washrooms or restrooms, are free to use, easy to find and are located in shopping malls, department stores, most restaurants, bars and service stations. You may have to ask for a key, but as long as you look reasonably well presented, or especially desperate, you shouldn't have a problem. You will also find toilets in some public parks but these aren't cleaned as often as they should be and, depending on the location, can be a hangout for drug users, which means that you'll have to keep an eye out for discarded needles. For this reason it's a good idea to accompany a child into these particular facilities.

HEALTH

You don't need any special vaccinations to visit Canada and, aside from protecting yourself from those inevitable wet days for which Vancouver is famous, you are unlikely to encounter any serious threat to your health. Up-to-date tetanus, polio and diphtheria immunizations are always recommended no matter where you are traveling.

You are well advised to take out travel insurance before leaving home. A visit to a hospital or a dentist could put a serious dent in your budget. The standard rate for a bed in a city hospital is at least $500 a day and up to $2000 a day for nonresidents. The largest seller of hospital and medical insurance to visitors to Canada is John Ingle Insurance. They offer hospital medical care (HMC) policies for a minimum of seven days to a maximum of one year, with a possible renewal of one additional year. The 30-day basic coverage costs $90 for an adult under the age of 55, $110 for ages 55 to 64 and $126 above that. Family rates are available. Coverage includes the hospital rate, doctor's fees, extended health care and other features. Visitors to Canada are not covered for conditions they had prior to arrival. If you are planning a side trip to the USA be sure to inquire about coverage details. Ingle also offers insurance policies (at reduced rates) for foreign students and to those visiting Canada on working visas. For more information call ☎ 604-684-0668, or visit one of their agents.

In the city try Customplan Financial Services (☎ 604-687-7773) 1440 - 1055 West

Hastings St. Their pamphlets are available in about 15 languages and can be found at post offices, pharmacies, doctor's offices and some shopping centers. Read the information carefully as there are exclusions and conditions which should be clearly understood. Also check the maximum amounts payable as different policies allow for greater payments.

For minor health concerns visit a pharmacy and consult the pharmacist. For 24-hour service go to the Shoppers Drug Mart in Kitsilano (☎ 604-738-3138), at 2302 West 4th Ave, or in the West End (☎ 604-685-6445) at 1125 Davie St.

If you would like information regarding AIDS and other sexually transmitted diseases call ☎ 604-872-6652, or ☎ 660-6161 for testing. AIDS Vancouver (☎ 604-687-2437), 1107 Seymour St, can also be of assistance if you need help or information.

For a walk-in clinic downtown go to the Care Point Medical Centre (Map 2; ☎ 604-681-5338), 1175 Denman St; in Kitsilano go to the Khatsahlano Medical Clinic (Map 6; ☎ 604-731-9187), 2689 West Broadway; or in East Vancouver go to the Care Point Medical Centre (Map 4; ☎ 604-254-5554), 1623 Commercial Drive.

If you have a dental emergency call the College of Dental Surgeons (☎ 604-736-3621) to get a referral.

Hospitals include the following:

BC Children's Hospital
(☎ 604-875-2345) 4480 Oak St at 29th Ave
BC Women's Hospital
(☎ 604-875-2424) 4490 Oak St at 29th Ave
Burnaby Hospital
(☎ 604-434-4211) 3935 Kincaid St, Burnaby
Lions Gate Hospital
(☎ 604-988-3131) 231 East 15th St, near Lonsdale Ave, North Vancouver
St Paul's Hospital
(☎ 604-682-2344) 1081 Burrard St, near Davie St
UBC Pavilions
(☎ 604-822-7121) 2211 Westbrook Mall, off University Blvd
Vancouver General Hospital
(☎ 604-875-4111) 855 West 12th, near Oak St

WOMEN TRAVELERS

Vancouver is generally a safe city for women traveling on their own, although the usual precautions apply. The Main and Hastings Sts area is best avoided and it's probably not a good idea to go for a walk in Stanley Park on your own after dark.

There are a number of women's organizations in the city that can be found under that heading in the Yellow Pages. A good place to start is the UBC Women's Resources Centre (☎ 604-482-8585), 1144 Robson St, where you can find information and literature directed specifically to women. Also worth investigating is the Women's Research Centre (☎ 604-734-0485), 101 - 2245 West Broadway. The South Asian Women's Center (☎ 604-325-6637), 8163 Main St, is another one to try. Those interested in making business contacts and getting information about doing business in Vancouver can contact the Western Businesswomen's Association (☎ 604-688-0951), 302 - 1107 Homer St. For free legal advice, general information and counseling, with referrals available to feminist lawyers, contact the Vancouver Status of Women (☎ 604-255-5511), 301 - 1720 Grant St. To get information about health issues contact the Vancouver Women's Health Collective (☎ 604-736-5262), 219 - 1675 West 8th Ave.

In a time of crisis contact:

Battered Women Support Services
(☎ 604-687-1867)
Rape Crisis Centre (☎ 604-255-6344, 24 hours)
Rape Relief & Women's Shelter (☎ 604-872-8212)

GAY & LESBIAN TRAVELERS

When it comes to gay-friendly cities, Vancouver is up there with the best of them. It may not have the reputation that San Francisco enjoys, or host a yearly show like the Mardi Gras in Sydney, but the gay and lesbian scene is alive and well in Vancouver. This of course has not always been the case. Homosexuality was only decriminalized in Canada in 1969, and even in 1980 the Vancouver City Council voted down a proposal to establish a Gay Unity Week.

The gay rights movement in Canada began in Vancouver when, in 1964, a group of feminists and academics started the Association for Social Knowledge, the first gay and lesbian discussion group in the country. In 1971, a 'kiss-in' was held by the Gay Liberation Front in the Castle pub on Granville St which, even though the pub recognized it had a primarily gay clientele, enforced a no-touching policy. That, and a march at the courthouse steps, were two of the first organized gay protests in the country. The first AIDS organization in the country, AIDS Vancouver, was started in 1983.

In 1990, Vancouver played host to the week-long Celebration 90: Gay Games III and Cultural Festival, which many local gays and lesbians believe marked the turning point in the community's development. It brought in nearly $15 million, and attracted 8500 participants in 29 sports and 14 cultural events. Today, the city's gay and lesbian communities continue to be active, but in a comfortable, self-confident and open way much like any other special-interest group. Traditionally the West End was the area where gay men tended to live and play while the lesbian community was found around Commercial Drive. However, in recent years there has been more of a mix between the two communities.

The Stonewall Festival (☎ 604-660-6143) in Grandview Park, on Commercial Drive between Charles and Williams Sts, is a one-day event held in June featuring live music, entertainment, food and craft booths. The Gay Pride Society (☎ 604-737-7433, www.vanpride.org) parade at English Bay is held in August. There is also the annual Whistler Gay Ski Week (☎ 604-258-4883, www.outontheslopes.com) in February which has been going since 1991 and now attracts up to 2000 participants in an eight-day frenzy of skiing, dining, dancing, drinking and all-round good times.

The Gay & Lesbian Centre (☎ 604-684-6869 for the helpline, or 684-4901 for programs and services) is at 1170 Bute St, or you can call the Gay & Lesbian Counselling & Consulting Services at ☎ 604-222-7807. If you would like information about gay-and-lesbian-friendly businesses in Vancouver, call the Gay & Lesbian Business Association at ☎ 604-253-4307.

For more information on what's going on in the city, check the gay and lesbian publications distributed for free at music stores, bookstores, convenience stores, theaters and newsstands including *Xtra West, Angles* and *The Loop.*

For information about where to get tested for HIV or other sexually transmitted diseases see the Health section.

DISABLED TRAVELERS

When it comes to making it easy for disabled people to get around, no city in Canada does it better. Vancouver became the first city in Canada to provide scheduled bus service for people with disabilities. BC Transit runs lift-equipped buses on more than half of its 161 routes in the Greater Vancouver area and plans to have all the routes covered by 2007. All the SkyTrain stations, except Granville Station, are wheelchair accessible, as is the West Coast Express which travels between the city and Mission.

HandyDART is a custom door-to-door service that can be booked up to four days in advance. For information about Handy-DART, to apply for a HandyPass or to purchase Taxi Saver coupons, call BC Transit's Accessible Transit Department at ☎ 604-540-3400. For information on accessible bus schedules and stops call ☎ 604-521-0400.

There are more wheelchair-accessible taxis in Vancouver than in any other Canadian city. Vancouver Taxi (☎ 604-255-5111) runs 30 accessible cabs in Vancouver alone, and in the Lower Mainland another 18 taxi companies have accessible cabs.

About 90% of the sidewalks in the city center have sloping ramps for easy wheelchair access, and audible crosswalk signals have been installed at about 70 intersections. Public and private parking lots have specially identified spaces for disabled drivers. For information on a disabled parking permit, call ☎ 604-736-4367.

The Coalition of People with Disabilities (☎ 604-875-0188, fax 875-0188) distributes a free guidebook called *Accessible Vancouver* which details how to get around the city. The Handicapped Resource Line (☎ 604-875-6381) can help travelers looking for information about services in Vancouver. Also take a look at the website www.access able.com; it has a Web page for travelers with disabilities. Other helpful sources of information include:

Airlines Attendant Fare Discount
    Air Canada (☎ 604-688-5515)
    Canadian Airlines (☎ 604-279-6611)
BC Parks Disabled Access Pass in Victoria
    (☎ 604-387-5002)
Disabled Sailing Association (☎ 604-222-3004)
Disabled Skiers Association (☎ 604-738-7175)
Greyhound Lines of Canada (☎ 604-662-3222);
    has lift-equipped bus information
Sport and Fitness Council for the Disabled
    (☎ 604-737-3039)
We're Accessible Newsletter for Wheelchair
    Travellers (☎ 604-731-2197)

In the USA, the Society for the Advancement of Travel for the Handicapped (SATH; tel 212-447-7284), 347 Fifth Ave No 610, New York, NY 10016, has information sheets on a wide range of destinations around the world, or they can research your specific requirements. Membership is $45 a year ($25 for seniors and students); the information charge for nonmembers is $5, which covers costs. Mobility International (☎ 541-343-1284), PO Box 10767, Eugene, OR 97440, offers international educational exchanges but will also answer questions and help travelers with special needs.

SENIOR TRAVELERS
Because of the West Coast's relatively mild winters and warm summers, many people come to live in Vancouver or Victoria after they have retired. This has resulted in a large network of services and centers for residents, although not necessarily much in the way for travelers. Seniors are generally considered to be people who are over the age of 60, although in some cases you must be 65 to qualify for a discount. You might be asked to show proof of age so carry your passport or driver's license with you.

Discounts are available for seniors at restaurants, pharmacies, banks, movies, attractions and other entertainment venues. There are special discounts for seniors on BC Transit, and the HandyDART system is also available to seniors who have difficulty walking (see Disabled Travelers for details). Travel on BC Ferries is free for seniors who are BC residents Monday to Thursday, except on public holidays. There are also seniors' discounts on BC Rail, Via Rail and the various bus companies.

The country's main seniors' organization is the Canadian Association of Retired Persons (CARP; ☎ 416-363-8748), 1304 - 27 Queen St East, Toronto, Ontario M5C 2M6. It's a good resource for travel bargains and information. A one-year membership for Canadian residents costs $10.

Elderhostel, with branches in many countries, is also found in Canada. It specializes in inexpensive, educational packages for those over 60 years of age. The standard type of program consists of talks and lectures in the mornings, followed by afternoon field trips and visits to related sights. Participants stay in university dorms or similar type of accommodations. There is generally a full-package price that includes meals, lodging and some transportation. The courses are of varying lengths but may be several weeks long. Subject matter is drawn from a variety of interests including history, nature, geography and art. For more information contact Elderhostel Canada (☎ 613-530-2222) 308 Wellington St, Kingston, Ontario K7K 7A7.

VANCOUVER FOR CHILDREN
Lonely Planet's *Travel with Children* by Maureen Wheeler is a good place to start if you want some tips on the fundamentals of traveling with youngsters. Much of her advice is valid in Vancouver, where there's much to attract the attention of children. In fact, according to the *Kids' Guide to Vancouver*, a free brochure published by Creative Options (☎ 604-266-8986, fax 266-3643),

6 - 5729 West Blvd, and available at the Vancouver Travel InfoCentre, there are more than 100 places to take your youngsters for a fun time.

Vancouver is a very child-friendly city and unless you want to dine at an upscale restaurant, you shouldn't have a problem finding places that have high chairs and even children's menus. Facilities for feeding infants or changing diapers are reasonably easy to find, especially in shopping centers and department stores, and are free.

Kid Friendly! British Columbia (☎ 604-925-6063, fax 925-6064) is a nonprofit organization which annually reviews and accredits businesses and services offering programs for children and families including hotels, restaurants, attractions, stores and public facilities. Contact them for their free directory or pick up a copy at the Travel Info-Centre.

Special events and activities aimed at children take place throughout the year. The biggest of these is the Vancouver International Children's Festival (☎ 604-687-7697), which is held annually in Vanier Park in Kitsilano, during the last week in May. The festival is a world of fun and entertainment for children of all ages and attracts about 200 Canadian and international acts, including musicians, actors, mimes, clowns, puppeteers, jugglers and storytellers.

For more information check with the Travel InfoCentre, or try the following options, most of which are described in more detail elsewhere in the book:

Stanley Park – the Children's Farmyard and Miniature Railway, the Variety Kids Water Park, the Vancouver Aquarium with its orcas and beluga whales, the beach pool at Second Beach, or renting bikes and cycling around the Seawall Promenade

Science World & the OMNIMAX Theatre – hands-on exhibits, demonstrations and 3-D laser shows, plus the theater with its huge dome screen at the end of False Creek

Kids Only Market – a store just for the young, and young at heart, at the entrance to Granville Island

Playland – more than 35 rides and attractions at Hastings Park

Variety Kids Water Park in Stanley Park

Pacific Space Centre & Vancouver Museum – experience some of the city's history in the museum in Kitsilano and then go next door to take a trip through space in the planetarium

SplashDown Park – a waterpark with 13 slides and 10 acres of activities about three minutes from the Tsawwassen Ferry Terminal

Capilano Salmon Hatchery – learn about the life cycle of the salmon at the hatchery in North Vancouver

Nat Bailey Stadium – watch the Vancouver Canadians play baseball in this picturesque location next to Queen Elizabeth Park

Bloedel Conservatory – a tropical paradise of floral displays and exotic birds under a 'triodetic' dome in Queen Elizabeth Park

Lighthouse Park – a great dense forest with old-growth Douglas fir trees, rock formations, trails, tidal pools and a 1914 lighthouse in West Vancouver

There's also a children's library at the Vancouver Public Library; see the Libraries section for information.

If you want a break from the kids for an evening out or for an afternoon of shopping, you might consider leaving them with a qualified baby-sitting service. Some hotels offer such a service, or they can advise you on whom to contact. Generally, the better agencies use people over 18 years of age who have been trained in first aid and CPR, have had a security clearance through the police and are insured. There is usually a three-hour minimum, and the cost is approximately $11 an hour. Two such agencies to check out are Just Like Mum! (☎ 604-325-4225), 120 - 8415 Granville St, and KidScenes

(☎ 800-665-9296, www.canadianrockies.net /kidscenes), which provides service through-out western Canada.

LIBRARIES

Completed in 1995, the Roman Coliseum-style building occupying a city block, bounded by West Georgia, Homer, Robson and Hamilton Sts, is the main branch of the Vancouver Public Library (Map 2; ☎ 604-331-4000). A six-story atrium leading in from the West Georgia St entrance acts as a promenade between the circular library and the adjoining 22-story office tower and houses a bookstore, coffee shops and retail outlets. On the lower level you'll find a chil-dren's library, complete with child-size fur-nishings, in addition to a reading and play area.

Other features include a computerized lab with a variety of software (☎ 604-331-3685 to reserve a time); specialized data-bases; Internet and Freenet access; the Online Public Access Catalogue (OPAC); a language center which has self-tutoring in up to 90 languages; a glass-enclosed area for rare, historic books; and three meeting rooms available for public use (☎ 604-331-4045 for information). If you are interested in obtaining a temporary library card call ☎ 604-331-3600 for information. The library is open Monday to Wednesday from 10 am to 9 pm, and Thursday to Saturday from 10 am to 6 pm; it's open September to April on Sunday from 1 to 5 pm.

In addition to the main library there is the Carnegie Reading Room on the corner of Hastings and Main Sts. Completed in 1903 with a $50,000 grant from US steel magnate and philanthropist Andrew Carnegie, this was Vancouver's first purpose-built library and still serves as a small branch library and reading room today. Although it's not in the greatest part of town, it is worth taking a look inside this building if only to see the stained glass windows around the inside stairwell.

There are also another 20 branch libraries located throughout the city where visitors are welcome to browse.

CAMPUSES

Vancouver is home to two universities, the University of British Columbia (UBC; ☎ 604-822-2211) with a student population of about 35,000, and Simon Fraser Univer-sity (SFU; ☎ 604-291-3111) with a student population of about 20,000. The British Columbia Institute of Technology (BCIT; ☎ 604-434-5734), in Burnaby, with a full-time student population of about 15,000, is the major technical institute in the province, offering certificate and diploma programs. Aside from these learning institutes there are numerous community colleges and spe-ciality schools located throughout the Lower Mainland.

The large UBC campus is in an area called the University Endowment Lands; part of this area also makes up the forested 763-hectare Pacific Spirit Regional Park and University Hill. Locals often simply refer to the UBC area as Point Grey. Not only is UBC respected worldwide with such well-known people as scientist David Suzuki on staff, it is also home to the Nitobe and Botanical Gardens, the Museum of Anthro-pology, Wreck Beach and the aforemen-tioned Pacific Spirit Regional Park (all are discussed in the Things to See & Do chapter).

Situated on Burnaby Mountain in Burnaby, SFU's main campus was designed in part by Arthur Erickson, who is responsi-ble for designing some of the more notable buildings in Vancouver. There is also a satel-lite campus in Harbour Centre near Water-front Station. In existence since 1965, SFU was at one time considered to be Vancou-ver's 'alternative' university. It was the site of student protests in the '60s and '70s, and the school pioneered such things as the year-round trimester system as well as a more relaxed approach to admission require-ments, where life experience counts as much as grades do. Today SFU is setting up the TeleLearning Research Network (TL-RN) that puts researchers, other universities and organizations onto the Internet in a com-bined Virtual University, the first networked multimedia system in the world.

CULTURAL CENTERS

A full list of cultural centers and associations can be found in *Exploring Ethnic Vancouver* by Anne Garber, John TD Keyes and Lorraine Gannon.

Vancouver's major cultural centers include:

Alliance Française
(☎ 604-327-0201) 6161 Cambie St

Australia-New Zealand Association
(☎ 604-876-7128) 3 West 8th Ave

Chinese Cultural Centre
(☎ 604-687-0729) 50 East Pender St

Croatian Cultural Centre
(☎ 604-879-0154) 3250 Commercial Drive

Goethe Institute
(☎ 604-732-3966) 944 West 8th Ave

Hispanic Community Centre
(☎ 604-872-4431) 125 East 12th Ave

Hungarian Cultural Society
(☎ 604-876-4720) 728 Kingsway

India Cultural Centre
(☎ 604-274-0026) 8600 No 5 Road, Richmond

Italian Cultural Institute
(☎ 604-688-0809) 708 - 1200 Burrard St

Jewish Community Centre
(☎ 604-257-5111) 950 West 41st Ave

Polish Community Centre
(☎ 604-874-8620) 4015 Fraser St

Portuguese Club
(☎ 604-251-2042) 1144 Commercial Drive

Russian Community Centre
(☎ 604-732-9223) 2114 West 4th Ave

Scottish Cultural Centre
(☎ 604-263-9911) 8886 Hudson St

Spanish Association
(☎ 604-524-2506)
759 Carnarvon St, New Westminster

DANGERS & ANNOYANCES

The emergency number for police, fire department and ambulance is ☎ 911; the Vancouver police can also be contacted at ☎ 604-665-3535.

All federal, provincial and city government offices appear in the blue pages at the back of the White Pages directory; the front of every phone book also contains a complete list of community organizations that might be useful.

By world standards Vancouver is a small city and certainly doesn't have many of the problems you might encounter in places like Los Angeles or Johannesburg. Violent crime is unusual but theft is common, especially in regards to car break-ins, car theft and bicycle theft. Always lock your car and take anything of value with you or secure it in the trunk, and always lock your bicycle. As in any city, you should always be aware of your surroundings and never leave personal belongings such as shoulder bags or backpacks in a location where you can't watch them at all times.

Perhaps the panhandlers, of which there seems to be a very large number, are the greatest annoyance in Vancouver. Because of Vancouver's relatively mild winter climate (at least compared to the rest of the country) a lot of people end up here without a job and no place to live so they resort to begging in order to scratch out an existence. There is also a large drug problem here so many of the panhandlers are only after enough money to pay for their next fix. Generally these people are harmless enough, if not irritating, and many of them will bring out all the tired old lines like 'I only need another 70¢ to make up my bus fare,' 'My wallet was stolen, can you help me?' or 'I've just lost my job and my baby son needs food.' Some beggars simply sit under a blanket in a doorway with their hand extended out or, in a couple of places around the city, they work a street corner with a squeegee washing windshields. Unfortunately, it's impossible to differentiate between those truly in need and someone on the hustle.

The areas where you'll be hassled the most by beggars is on Granville St, especially between Pender and Davie Sts, around the Gastown area, and along Commercial Drive. Hastings St, running east from about Homer St, is a pretty downtrodden part of the city and you'll see lots of people down on their luck here, especially close to the corner of Main St where there are numerous old hotels (which act as long-term accommodations), dingy taverns and pawnshops.

This is not an area to dawdle at night, especially for a woman on her own.

Prostitution has always been a problem on Vancouver's streets and all the authorities have ever been able to do is to shift it out of one neighborhood and into another. These days the majority of the streetwalkers tend to be located in East Vancouver in areas that tourists aren't likely to find themselves in unless, of course, they are looking for this particular service.

LEGAL MATTERS

If you are arrested you are allowed to remain silent. There is no legal reason to speak to a police officer; however, never walk away from an officer until given permission. If arrested you must be formally told of the charges and are allowed to make one phone call. You also have the right to an interpreter if English is not your first language. If you don't have a lawyer or someone who can help you, call your consulate. The police will give you the number upon request.

If you want legal advice or referral to a lawyer, contact the Legal Aid-Legal Services Society at ☎ 604-601-6100; this is a taped message but if you listen long enough you will eventually find the information you need, hopefully before you're due to appear in court. You can also visit the Legal Resource Centre, 200 - 1140 West Pender St.

BUSINESS HOURS

There aren't many things you can't get in Vancouver seven days a week, with a few exceptions. Stores open around 9 or 10 am and close around 5 or 6 pm. On Thursday and Friday many stores, especially the shopping malls and large department stores, stay open until 9 pm. Bookstores and specialty shops often maintain regular night hours staying open until 9 or 10 pm daily.

Sunday has more limited hours with department stores and some shopping centers not opening until noon and closing at 5 pm. In areas like Gastown or Robson St you'll find many of the shops are open seven days a week until early evening. Throughout the city there are restaurants, convenience stores and service stations that stay open 24 hours. A few drugstores and grocery stores stay open 24 hours as well, although many more are open daily from 8 am to midnight. There is even a gym, Fitness Unlimited Athletic Club (☎ 604-279-9220), 150 - 2251 No 5 Rd, Richmond, which is open 24 hours Monday to Thursday and from 6 am to 10 pm Friday to Sunday.

Bars, pubs and lounges are open seven days a week and generally last call is just before 1 am, although this may be earlier in smaller neighborhood-type pubs. Clubs stay open until 2 am. Liquor stores, which are operated by the provincial government, keep regular business hours (Monday to Saturday from 9.30 am to 6 pm) although a few stay open to 9 pm, and the stores at 2020 West Broadway (near Maple St) and 1716 Robson St (near Denman St) are open to 11 pm. Liquor stores are closed on Sunday and public holidays, but beer and wine stores, which are attached to pubs and hotel bars, are open daily until 11 pm.

PUBLIC HOLIDAYS

National public holidays are celebrated throughout Canada. Banks, schools and government offices (including post offices) are closed and transportation, museums and other services are on a Sunday schedule. Holidays falling on a weekend are usually observed the following Monday. The following is a list of the main public holidays:

January
  New Year's Day (January 1)
March-April
  Easter (Good Friday, Easter Monday)
May
  Victoria Day (Monday preceding May 24)
July
  Canada Day (July 1)
August
  BC Day (first Monday)
September
  Labour Day (first Monday)
October
  Thanksgiving (second Monday)

November
>   Remembrance Day (November 11 – banks and government closed)

December
>   Christmas Day (December 25)
>   Boxing Day (December 26 – many retailers open, other businesses closed)

SPECIAL EVENTS

Just about any month you visit Vancouver there will be a festival of some sort taking place, whether it's to do with the arts, food, drink, cultural celebrations or just an excuse to have a good time. In fact, Vancouver puts on about 33 annual festivals throughout the year.

Following is a list of the major events. For up-to-date information get a copy of *The Vancouver Book* from the Travel InfoCentre, or pick up a copy of *Visitor's Choice,* available for free at many tourist attractions and hotels.

January

Polar Bear Swim
>   This popular, chilly affair has been taking place on English Bay Beach annually on New Year's Day since 1819, and might just be the ultimate cure for a hangover. Anywhere from up to 2000 people charge into the ocean at 2.30 pm. Not many dally for long but some do swim the 90m to a buoy and back to the beach. If you can't handle the water, watching is allowed. Call ☎ 604-732-2304 for information.

Chinese New Year
>   The date of the lunar new year varies from late January to early February each year but the fireworks crackle in Chinatown for days before and days after. The festivities take place over 15 days and besides lots of good food it features the Dragon Parade, music, dancing, art exhibits and storytelling. Call ☎ 604-662-3207 for information.

February

Women in View Festival
>   Showcasing the work of women in the performing arts, this four-day festival of music, dance, theater, comedy and literary events takes place at the end of the month in various venues around Commercial Drive. Call ☎ 604-257-1650 for information.

April

Story Telling Festival
>   No matter what your age, if you like a good yarn then you'll enjoy this three-day event that takes place early in the month at a variety of venues in the West End. Call ☎ 604-876-2272 for information.

Vancouver Playhouse International Wine Festival
>   With more than 500 wines to sample from more than 125 wineries from around the world, not to mention some good food to taste as well, this is one of the largest annual wine shows in North America. This festival takes place at the Vancouver Trade and Convention Centre over a week during the month of April, although it is sometimes held in March. Call ☎ 604-873-3311 for information.

May

Vancouver International Marathon
>   Strap on your running shoes and race through the city streets with runners from around the world. The run starts at BC Place and takes you into Stanley Park and over to Kitsilano. Almost as good as a city tour, really. It takes place on the first Sunday of the month. Call ☎ 604-872-2928 for information.

Music West
>   A celebration of pop and rock music, this takes place in the second weekend of the month. As well as being an international music festival, there is also a conference and a skateboarding competition. The Vancouver Trade and Convention Centre is the hub for the activities, although many of the clubs in the city act as venues for the participating bands. Call ☎ 604-684-9338 for information or check it out on www.musicwest.com.

Hyack Festival
>   New Westminster comes to life during this annual event that takes place over nine days in the middle of the month and coincides with the Victoria Day holiday weekend. There are more than 60 events, including a fireworks display, an impressive parade, a '21-gun' salute to the sovereign using anvils instead of canons and lots of dancing around maypoles. Call ☎ 604-522-6894 for information.

Vancouver International Children's Festival
>   The red-and-white tents go up in Vanier Park on the last Monday of the month and stay up for seven days while 70,000 people enjoy Canadian and international acts dedicated to keeping the young, and young of heart, totally entertained. Call ☎ 604-687-7697 for information.

June

Bard on the Beach Shakespeare Festival

Starting around the second Tuesday of the month and going through to the end of September, this summerlong celebration of all things 'Bill' takes place in a 500-seat tent at Vanier Park, with English Bay acting as a backdrop. Usually two plays are performed throughout the summer and other special events include Champagne and Shakespeare, Symphony and Shakespeare and Peak Performances. Call ☎ 604-737-0625 for information.

Canadian International Dragon Boat Festival

Held during the third weekend of the month, about 2000 competitors from around the world take part in the Dragon Boat races on False Creek, plus there is music, theater and food pavilions at the Plaza of Nations. Call ☎ 604-688-2382 for information.

DuMaurier International Jazz Festival

Some of the biggest names in jazz take the stage at 25 venues in the Vancouver area including Dr Sun Yat-Sen Classical Chinese Garden and Grouse Mountain. In addition, a two-day New Orleans-style street festival takes place in Gastown. The festival starts on the third Friday of the month and runs for 10 days. Call ☎ 604-682-0706 for information.

July

Canada Day Celebrations

Canada Place is the main location for the celebrations marking the country's birthday on July 1, which includes music, food and fireworks. Festivities begin at 10 am and the fireworks are at 10 pm. On the same day you can travel over to Richmond to take in the **Steveston Salmon Festival** (☎ 604-277-6812).

Dancing on the Edge

Leading dance companies from across Canada gather at the Firehall Arts Centre, 280 East Cordova St, for 10 days at the start of the month to perform the latest in dance. Call ☎ 604-689-0691 for information.

Harrison Festival of the Arts

Held during the second week of the month, this 10-day celebration of theater, world music, dance and visual arts takes place on the shores of Harrison Lake, about a 1½-hour drive east of the city. Call ☎ 604-681-2771 for information.

Vancouver Sea Festival

During this festival in mid-July there are concerts, parades, fireworks and salmon barbecues, all of which take place on the shores of English Bay. There is also the famous Nanaimo-to-Vancouver Bathtub Race. Call ☎ 604-684-3378 for information.

Vancouver Folk Music Festival

Jericho Beach Park is the venue for this festival which has musicians performing on seven stages throughout the third weekend of the month and attracts about 30,000 people. The Little Folks Festival is for the kids, with one of the stages set aside especially for family entertainment, and there are children's activity areas as well. Call ☎ 604-876-6777 for information.

Caribbean Days Festival

Great music, dancing, performances and food highlight these two days of fun held during the last weekend of the month at Waterfront Park, Lonsdale Quay, North Vancouver. Call ☎ 604-303-1455 for information.

Benson & Hedges Symphony of Fire

This, the world's largest musical fireworks competition, starts at the end of July and goes to the beginning of August. Three competing countries (which change each year) put on their most spectacular display of fireworks over three nights, with all of them coming together to put on a dazzling display on the final night. The displays are held at English Bay and start at 10.15 pm. Car traffic to the West End is cut off at 7.30 pm, an hour earlier at Kits Point, so get to the beach early to claim your spot. If you aren't close enough to hear the music then tune your Walkman into CKNW (980 AM) or CFMI (101.1 FM). Call ☎ 604-738-4304 for information.

Vancouver International Comedy Festival

Granville Island is the location for this celebration of comedy and laughter which takes place over 10 days in the end of July. Call ☎ 604-683-0883 for information.

Vancouver Chamber Music Festival

Considered to be one of the finest music festivals of its kind in the country, the two-week event, which starts at the end of July, brings together the finest Canadian and international chamber musicians, as well as outstanding young talents. Call ☎ 604-602-0363 for information.

Early Music Festival

This celebration of Medieval to Baroque music takes place from late July to early August at the UBC School of Music. Call ☎ 604-732-1610 for information.

August

Abbotsford International Air Show

Held on the second weekend of the month, this is known as 'Canada's national air show' and has been voted the world's best. If it flies, you'll probably find it here. It takes place in Abbotsford, 56km southeast of the city near the Canadian-US border. Call ☎ 604-852-8511 for information.

Gay Pride Day

Also in the early part of the month, watch for the outrageous feature parade drawing 15,000 people along Denman St. Call ☎ 604-737-7433 for information, or check www.vanpride.org.

Harmony Arts Festival

A showcase for the best visual, musical and performing arts on the North Shore, this festival is held in the middle of the month at various venues throughout West Vancouver. Call ☎ 604-925-7268 for information.

StreetFare

Also known as the Vancouver International Street Performers Festival, this event attracts about 25 buskers who entertain with music, magic, clowning, mime and comedy. There's even a special Kids Only Stage. It takes place on the last weekend of the month and most of the action happens around the Vancouver Art Gallery from noon until 10 pm. Call ☎ 604-685-7811 for information.

September

Molson Indy Vancouver

The roar of the engines can be heard far and wide during Labour Day weekend when these Indy cars race around False Creek to find out who really is the fastest and the best. Call ☎ 604-684-4639 for information.

Vancouver International Fringe Festival

This popular theater event presents drama, musical theater, comedy and dance from around the world. It takes place over 10 days starting at the beginning of the month and is held in various venues in East Vancouver, with Commercial Drive being the center point. Call ☎ 604-257-0350 for information.

Vancouver International Film Festival

Although it doesn't have the star-studded glamour of some other film festivals, this is the third-largest one in North America with 400 screenings of 300 films from 50 countries. The festival takes place over 17 days from the end of September to mid-October in seven city theaters. Call ☎ 604-685-0260 for information.

October

Vancouver International Writers Festival

Held during the third week of the month at venues on Granville Island, this event attracts more than 50 authors, poets and playwrights

from across Canada and around the world. Some of the events include the Great Canadian Spelling Bee, the Literary Cabaret, the Poetry Bash and the Bill Duthie Memorial Lecture. Call ☎ 604-681-6330 for information.

December

Christmas Carolship Parade

This is a uniquely Vancouver tradition which takes place from around the 5th to the 23rd. About 100 boats of all sizes, which are lit up and decorated like Christmas trees, take part in a flotilla that on different nights sails past False Creek, English Bay, Point Grey, West Vancouver, or up Burrard Inlet to Port Moody. On many of the boats carolers sing through sound systems, while other boats play taped music. Whether you're lucky enough to be on one of the boats or simply hear the carols from the shore, this is a great way to help bring on the Christmas spirit. Call ☎ 604-878-9988 for information.

DOING BUSINESS

As Canada's gateway to Asia and the third-largest city in the country, Vancouver has become a focal point for doing business. Both the federal and provincial governments are doing their utmost to encourage businesses to set up shop here. They offer a wide range of support networks and information packages to make it easy for foreign investors, or newly arrived immigrants who want to start their own business, to understand everything from tax laws to how to identify business opportunities.

If you are coming to Vancouver to set up a business, or simply to do business, the trade office at the Canadian embassy in your home country can probably provide initial information and help establish the necessary contacts, as can your embassy's trade office in Ottawa. In Vancouver, two good places to start are the British Columbia Trade & Investment Office (☎ 604-844-1900, 660-2457), 730 - 999 Canada Place, and the Canada/British Columbia Business Service Centre (☎ 604-775-5525, fax 775-5520, www.sb.gov.bc.ca/), 601 West Cordova St in Waterfront Station. The latter is a joint venture between the federal and provincial governments where you can get information about starting a new business, entering new markets, accessing government programs and services, and taxation and regulations. Another organization that can help you get started is the British Columbia Chamber of Commerce (☎ 604-683-0416, fax 683-0416), 1607 - 700 West Pender St.

Business Services

If you need an office and secretarial services while you are in Vancouver, whether it be for an hour or a month, try Executive Office Centre (☎ 604-669-8727), 404 - 999 Canada Place. Office space with a basic reception service for an hour/day is $15/80, plus more for any extras you may need such as photocopying and faxing services or the use of a stenographer or access to the Internet. The cost of long-term office rental is negotiable depending on the length of stay and the services required. There are also boardrooms available, complete with reception service, ranging in cost from $15/80 an hour/day for a four- to six-seat room to $30/150 for a 20-seat room. Because this service is part of the Pan Pacific Hotel, any catering you might require for your board meeting can easily be handled.

Another service to try if you need an office and plan to be in Vancouver for at least two months is Shelley Morris Business Services Ltd (☎ 604-687-5500), 600 - 890 West Pender St. The cost for the minimum two-month rental with full secretarial service is $875. Boardrooms are available and cost $75/150 for a half/full day.

If you only need the services of a secretary, the companies listed above, along with many others in the city, can provide that as well. For a full list of services in and around the city check under 'Secretarial Services' in the Yellow Pages. If you need any translating or interpreting done, try Berlitz Translation Services (☎ 604-685-9331), 808 West Hastings St, or Sino Translation Services Ltd (☎ 604-682-8932), 501 - 535 Thurlow St.

If you want to rent a cellular phone, call Rent Express (☎ 604-713-7368), or go to

their kiosk at the Vancouver airport's mid-point business center in the international arrivals area; or try Nedco (☎ 604-736-3326), 1820 Burrard St.

Exhibitions & Conferences

Vancouver has become the most popular city in North and South America in which to hold a convention, beating out such rival cities as San Francisco, Washington, DC, and Montreal. And this is despite the fact that the city ranks only 54th in North America in terms of the size of convention space available. Vancouver plays host to around 40 conventions and 180 major meetings each year.

The major luxury hotels, such as The Coast Plaza Hotel at Stanley Park (see Places to Stay), are often used for modest meetings and shows and have the facilities to handle gatherings from 10 to 1000 people.

The city's largest facility by far is BC Place Stadium (☎ 604-669-2300, fax 661-3412), 777 Pacific Blvd South, which seats 60,000 people and is often used for major trade shows. The Vancouver Trade & Convention Centre (☎ 604-641-1987, fax 641-1436), 200 - 999 Canada Place, holds up to 10,000 people and is used for major trade shows and conventions.

The Robson Square Conference Centre (☎ 604-482-1800, fax 685-9407), 800 Robson St, holds smaller conferences and seminars. Left over from Expo 86, the Plaza of Nations (☎ 604-682-0777, fax 682-7724), B100 - 750 Pacific Blvd South, is a large, covered outdoor area which is used for cultural fairs and festivals. As if this isn't enough, there is a new $250-million convention facility, including a 1000-room hotel, planned to be built on the waterfront next to Canada Place, and when completed it will double Vancouver's existing capacity.

WORK

Work permits must be obtained outside Canada and may take six months; however, these are difficult to get as opportunities go first to Canadians. Without a Social Insurance (SI) number it can be very difficult to obtain employment anywhere in Canada. If you are caught working without a bona-fide

SI number you will be told to leave the country. That said, however, employers hiring casual, temporary service workers (hotel, bar, restaurant) or construction, farm or forestry workers won't necessarily ask for a work permit and may turn a blind eye to the fact that you don't have a SI number, especially if they can pay you cash.

Many young European women come to Canada as nannies. Japan has a program called Contact Canada that includes one-year work permits with pre-arranged work generally on farms. Many countries have agencies where you can obtain details on these types of programs.

Opportunities for Australians

Of particular interest to Australian students may be the Student Work Abroad Program (SWAP). Organized by the National Union of Students (NUS) and the Canadian Feder-ation of Students (CFS), the program allows Australians between the ages of 18 and 25 to spend a year in Canada on a working holiday. This program only has space for 200 people a year and applicants must be enrolled in a post-secondary educational institution. For full details contact the NSU (☎ 03-9348-1777), PO Box 1130, Carlton, Victoria 3053.

The Working Holiday Program is another program which is open to all Australians between the ages of 18 and 25, and they need not be enrolled in a post-secondary educational institution. This program has an annual quota of 3000 people. Application forms can be obtained by contacting the Canadian Consulate General in Sydney, Australia. See the Embassies & Consulates section earlier in this chapter for the address. Applications for this program take up to two months to process.

Getting There & Away

Vancouver is Canada's Pacific gateway to Asia and the Pacific Northwest. There is an international airport, three seaplane terminals (on the Fraser River at the south airport, on the harbor near Canada Place and in New Westminster), a helicopter terminal on the harbor near Waterfront Station, and a large train and bus station close to the city center. This is the most important transportation hub in Western Canada.

AIR

Vancouver international airport (YVR; www.yvr.ca) is 13km south of the city center, located in Richmond, on a small island called Sea Island, at the mouth of the Fraser River. The airport, which is Canada's second busiest, handles 13 million passengers a year.

An Array of Airport Art

The airport recently underwent a $500 million refurbishment which turned it into a showcase of floor-to-ceiling glass walls stretching upwards to skylights, large open spaces and some fabulous art such as Bill Reid's large bronze sculpture titled *The Spirit of Haida Gwaii, The Jade Canoe*. Also look out for the *Spindle Whorl*, a 4m-high Musqueam cedar carving, located at the top of the escalator as you make your way to Canada Customs and the arrivals hall. You'll be greeted at the bottom of the escalator by *Welcome Figures*, a 5.2m-high red cedar carving of a Native Indian man and woman displaying a traditional Coast Salish welcome. Overall, the new terminal's architecture and collection of art is designed to evoke BC's natural and artistic splendor.

The main airport has two terminals: international and domestic. The international terminal handles all flights to the USA as well as other international destinations. Arrivals are on level 2 along with Canada Customs and Immigration, a business center, tour and cruise-ship operators and the reception area.

Departures are on level 3 and here you'll find the check-in counters (US check-ins are in concourse E and other international check-ins are in concourse D), US Customs and Immigration pre-clearance, a children's play area and parent's facilities, *The Spirit of Haida Gwaii, The Jade Canoe*, a chapel and a host of shops and restaurants. In fact, there are about 60 retail outlets scattered throughout the airport. There is a tourist information counter on each level where you can be assisted in 10 languages, as well as foreign exchange kiosks, ATMs and six branches of the Royal Bank.

The domestic terminal, which is the original airport, handles arrivals on level 2 and departures on level 3, where you'll find the airline check-in counters. On level 3, in the passageway that connects the domestic and international terminals, you'll find a children's nursery and a large play area.

The smaller south airport terminal, off Inglis Drive, handles regional airlines and floatplanes. There is no regular transportation service between this terminal and the main ones so contact your airline to have it arranged or take a taxi, as it's definitely too far to walk.

For information about getting to/from the airport, see the Getting Around chapter.

Departure Taxes

There is an airport departure tax of $55 levied on all international flights out of Canada, except those to US destinations. To US destinations the tax is 7% of the ticket value plus $6 to a maximum of $55.

Most tickets purchased in Canada for international flights out of Canada include

this tax; tickets purchased outside of Canada may not include it. If your ticket doesn't include the departure tax you will be asked to pay it after you pass through customs and immigration. When you're changing money, consider saving enough to cover it.

In Vancouver you have to pay an additional tax known as the airport improvement tax. If you are on a flight leaving Canada for a US destination you will be taxed $10, if you are on any other international flight you will be taxed $15. This tax is not included with the ticket price and must be paid at the airport; the desk is by the doors before you pass through the security check.

Remember, too, that if you intend to apply for a GST rebate this is your last chance to get a form (see the Taxes section in the Facts for the Visitor chapter for more details).

Airlines

Both major Canadian airlines, Air Canada and Canadian Airlines International, fly to Vancouver, as do many US and Asian airlines – check the Yellow Pages under 'Airlines.' Air BC is a local airline run by Air Canada, serving Vancouver Island, some points in the interior of the province, Seattle and Portland. Some Canadian and foreign airlines with offices in Vancouver are:

Air Canada (and Air BC)
    (☎ 604-688-5515) 1070 West Georgia St
Air China
    (☎ 604-685-0921) 1040 West Georgia St
Air India
    (☎ 604-879-0271) U6 - 601 West Broadway
Air New Zealand
    (☎ 604-606-0150, 800-663-5494)
    1250 - 888 Dunsmuir St
Air Pacific
    (☎ 604-214-3831, 800-227-4446)
    109 - 10651 Shellbridge Way, Richmond
Air Zimbabwe
    (☎ 604-681-8955) 320 - 1040 West Georgia St
Alaska Airlines
    (☎ 800-426-0333)
    Vancouver international airport
British Airways
    (☎ 800-247-9297) 1188 West Georgia St

Canada 3000 Airlines International
    (☎ 604-273-0930)
    5455 Airport Rd South, Richmond
Canadian Airlines International
    (☎ 604-279-6611) 1030 West Georgia St
Cathay Pacific Airways
    (☎ 604-606-8888, 800-607-3388)
    500 - 550 West 6th Ave
Japan Airlines
    (☎ 604-606-7715, 800-525-3663)
    710 - 777 Hornby St
Korean Air
    (☎ 604-689-2006, 800-438-5000)
    103 - 1185 West Georgia St
Lufthansa Airlines
    (☎ 800-563-5954) 1401 - 1030 West Georgia St
Malaysia Airlines
    (☎ 604-681-7741, 800-552-9264)
    919 - 885 West Georgia St
Pacific Coastal Airlines
    (☎ 604-273-8666, 800-663-2872)
    4440 Cowley Crescent, Richmond
Qantas Airways
    (☎ 800-227-4500) 1111 West Georgia St
Reno Air
    (☎ 800-736-6247)
    Vancouver international airport
Singapore Airlines
    (☎ 604-689-1223) 1111 - 1030 West Georgia St
West Coast Air
    (☎ 604-688-9115)
    Foot of Burrard St, west of Canada Place

Buying Tickets

The plane ticket will probably be the single most expensive item in your budget, and buying it can be intimidating. Rather than just walking into the nearest travel agency or airline office, it pays to do some research on the current market. Start looking early – some of the cheapest tickets and best deals must be bought months in advance, some popular flights sell out early and special offers may only be advertised in newspapers and magazines.

Look at the travel sections of magazines like *Time Out* and *TNT* in the UK, or the Sunday editions of newspapers such as the *New York Times* and *Los Angeles Times* in the USA or the *Sydney Morning Herald* and *The Age* in Australia. Ads in these publications offer cheap fares, but don't be surprised if they are sold out when you contact

Air Travel Glossary

Bucket Shops These are unbonded travel agencies specializing in discounted airline tickets.

Bumped Just because you have a confirmed seat doesn't mean you're going to get on the plane (see Overbooking).

Cancellation Penalties If you have to cancel or change a discounted ticket, there are often heavy penalties involved; insurance can sometimes be taken out against these penalties. Some airlines impose penalties on regular tickets as well, particularly against 'no-show' passengers.

Check-In Airlines ask you to check in a certain time ahead of the flight departure (usually one to two hours on international flights). If you fail to check in on time and the flight is over-booked, the airline can cancel your booking and give your seat to somebody else.

Confirmation Having a ticket written out with the flight and date you want doesn't mean you have a seat until the agent has checked with the airline that your status is 'OK' or confirmed. Meanwhile you could just be 'on request.'

Courier Fares Businesses often need to send urgent documents or freight securely and quickly. Courier companies hire people to accompany the package through customs and, in return, offer a discount ticket that is sometimes a phenomenal bargain. In effect, what the companies do is ship their freight as your luggage on regular commercial flights. This is a legit-imate operation, but there are two shortcomings – the short turnaround time of the ticket (usually not longer than a month) and the limitation on your luggage allowance. You may have to surrender all your allowance and take only carry-on luggage.

Full Fares Airlines traditionally offer 1st class (coded F), business class (coded J) and economy class (coded Y) tickets. These days there are so many promotional and discounted fares avail-able that few passengers pay full economy fare.

ITX An ITX, or 'independent inclusive tour excursion,' is often available on tickets to popular holiday destinations. Officially it's a package deal combined with hotel accommodations, but many agents will sell you one of these for the flight only and give you phony hotel vouchers in the unlikely event that you're challenged at the airport.

Lost Tickets If you lose your airline ticket, an airline will usually treat it like a traveler's check and, after inquiries, issue you another one. Legally, however, an airline is entitled to treat it like cash; and if you lose it, then it's gone forever. Take good care of your tickets.

MCO An MCO, or 'miscellaneous charge order,' is a voucher that looks like an airline ticket but carries no destination or date. It can be exchanged through any International Association of Travel Agents (IATA) airline for a ticket on a specific flight. It's a useful alternative to an onward ticket in those countries that demand one, and is more flexible than an ordinary ticket if you're unsure of your route.

No-Shows No-shows are passengers who fail to show up for their flight. Full-fare passengers who fail to turn up are sometimes entitled to travel on a later flight. The rest are penalized (see Cancellation Penalties).

On Request This is an unconfirmed booking for a flight.

Onward Tickets An entry requirement for many countries is that you have a ticket out of the country. If you're unsure of your next move, the easiest solution is to buy the cheapest onward ticket to a neighboring country or a ticket from a reliable airline that can later be refunded if you do not use it.

Open Jaw Tickets These are return tickets on which you fly out to one place but return from another. If available, these can save you backtracking to your arrival point.

Overbooking Airlines hate to fly with empty seats and since every flight has some passengers who fail to show up, airlines often book more passengers than they have seats. Usually excess passengers make up for the no-shows, but occasionally somebody gets bumped. Guess who it is most likely to be? The passengers who check in late.

Point-to-Point Tickets These are discount tickets that you can buy on some routes in exchange for waiving your right to a stopover.

Promotional Fares These are officially discounted fares, available from travel agencies or direct from the airline.

Reconfirmation At least 72 hours prior to departure time of an onward or return flight, you must contact the airline and 'reconfirm' that you intend to be on the flight. If you don't do this, the airline can delete your name from the passenger list and you could lose your seat.

Restrictions Discounted tickets often have various restrictions on them – such as advance payment, minimum and maximum periods you must be away (eg, a minimum of two weeks or a maximum of one year) and penalties for changing the tickets.

Round-the-World Tickets RTW tickets give you a limited period (usually a year) in which to circumnavigate the globe. You can go anywhere the carrying airlines go, as long as you don't backtrack. The number of stopovers or total number of separate flights is decided before you set off, and they usually cost a bit more than a basic return flight.

Stand-By This is a discounted ticket on which you fly only if there is a seat free at the last moment. Stand-by fares are usually available only on domestic routes.

Travel Agencies Travel agencies vary widely and you should choose one that suits your needs. Some simply handle tours, while full-service agencies handle everything from tours and tickets to car rental and hotel bookings. If all you want is a ticket at the lowest possible price, then go to any agency specializing in discounted tickets.

Transferred Tickets Airline tickets cannot be transferred from one person to another. Travelers sometimes try to sell the return half of their ticket, but officials can ask you to prove that you are the person named on the ticket.

Travel Periods Ticket prices vary with the time of year. There is a low (off-peak) season and a high (peak) season, and often a low-shoulder season and a high-shoulder season as well. Usually the fare depends on your outward flight – if you depart in the high season and return in the low season, you pay the high-season fare.

the agents: they are usually low-season fares on obscure airlines with conditions attached. Talk to other recent travelers if possible – they may be able to stop you from making some of the same old mistakes.

Note that high season in Canada is mid-June to mid-September (summer) and the week before and after Christmas. The best rates for travel to and in Canada are found November through March.

Call travel agencies for bargains (airlines can supply information on routes and timetables; however, except at times of fare wars, they don't supply the cheapest tickets). Airlines often have competitive low-season, student and senior citizens' fares. Find out the fare, route, duration of the journey and any restrictions on the ticket. Fares change constantly, and sometimes fares that include accommodations may be as cheap as roundtrip (return) fares.

Outside Canada, cheap tickets are available in two distinct categories: official and unofficial. Official tickets have a variety of names, including budget, advance purchase, Apex and super-Apex. Unofficial tickets are simply discounted tickets that the airlines release through selected travel agencies (not through airline offices).

Wherever you buy your tickets, the cheapest ones are often nonrefundable and require an extra fee for changing your flight, if you are allowed to change your flight at all. Many insurance policies cover this loss if you have to change your flight for emergency reasons. Look into buying roundtrip tickets as they are often much cheaper than two one-way fares.

You may decide to pay more than the rock-bottom fare by opting for the safety of a better known travel agent. Established firms like Council Travel or STA Travel, which have offices internationally, or Travel CUTS in Canada, offer competitive prices to most destinations.

Many people going across the continent find it cheaper to go, say, from Buffalo to Seattle rather than from Toronto to Vancouver. If you're flying to Vancouver from Asia, it also may be cheaper to fly into US West Coast cities rather than into Vancouver.

Once you have your ticket, write down its number, together with the flight number and other details, and keep the information somewhere separate. If the ticket is lost or stolen, this will help you get a replacement.

The fares quoted in this book should be used as a guide only and don't necessarily constitute a recommendation for the carrier.

Round-the-World Tickets Round-the-world (RTW) tickets that include travel within Canada are popular and can be real bargains. Prices start at about UK£900, A$2200 or US$1300. The cost, however, largely depends on the carriers you use, the seasons you are traveling in any given part of the world and the number of stops included in the ticket.

Official RTW tickets are usually put together by a combination of two airlines and permit you to fly anywhere you want on their route systems as long as you do not backtrack. Other restrictions are that you must usually book the first sector in advance and that you are liable for normal cancellation penalties. There may be restrictions on the number of stops permitted, and tickets are usually valid up to a year. You can also see if your travel agent can create a de facto RTW pass using a combination of discounted tickets.

Although most airlines restrict the number of sectors that can be flown within Canada and the USA to four, and some airlines black out a few popular routes (like Honolulu to Tokyo), stopovers are otherwise generally unlimited. In most cases a 14-day advance purchase is required. After the ticket is purchased, dates can be changed without penalty and tickets can be rewritten to add or delete stops for about $50 each.

Many airlines offer RTW tickets including British Airways, Canadian Airlines, Qantas Airways and TWA.

Circle Pacific Tickets For Circle Pacific tickets, two airlines link up to allow stopovers along their combined Pacific Rim routes. Rather than simply fly from point A to point B, these tickets allow you to swing through much of the Pacific and eastern

Asia taking in a variety of destinations, as long as you keep traveling in the same circular direction.

Circle Pacific routes essentially have the same fares: $3128 when purchased in Canada; US$2579 when purchased in the USA; A$3299 when purchased in Australia; and NZ$4049 when purchased in New Zealand.

Circle Pacific fares include four stopovers with the option of additional stops for $65 each. There's a seven- to 14-day advance-purchase requirement, a 25% cancellation penalty and a maximum stay of six months.

Canadian Airlines has Circle Pacific fares from Vancouver in partnership with Qantas Airways, Air New Zealand, Singapore Airlines, Garuda Indonesia, Cathay Pacific Airways or Malaysia Airlines.

Qantas Airways offers Circle Pacific routes in partnership with, among others, United Airlines, Delta Air Lines, Japan Airlines, Northwest Airlines and Continental Airlines.

Air New Zealand offers the ticket in conjunction with, among others, Japan Airlines, Thai Airways International, Cathay Pacific and Singapore Airlines. United Airlines offers the ticket in combination with more than a dozen Pacific Rim carriers.

Itineraries can be selected from scores of potential destinations. For example, a Canadian-United ticket could take you from Vancouver to Honolulu, on to Tokyo, south to Manila, followed by Sydney and back to Vancouver.

Keep in mind that Circle Pacific fares are high and you may find better deals elsewhere. Air New Zealand, for instance, has a 'Backpacker' fare from Vancouver for $2035 roundtrip that allows stopovers at two destinations, including New Zealand, Australia, Tahiti, Hawaii, Fiji, the Cook Islands, Western Samoa and Tonga, within a one-year period. Each additional stop is $165.

Travelers with Special Needs

If you have any special needs – dietary restrictions, dependence on a wheelchair, responsibility for a baby, fear of flying – let the airline know as soon as possible so that they can make arrangements accordingly. Remind them when you reconfirm your booking (at least 72 hours before departure) and again when you check in at the airport. It may also be worth phoning several airlines before you make a booking to find out how they can handle your particular needs.

Airports and airlines can be surprisingly accommodating to passengers in wheelchairs, but they do need advance warning. Most international airports provide escorts from the check-in desk to the airplane if necessary, and there should be ramps, lifts, accessible toilets and reachable phones. Aircraft toilets, on the other hand, are likely to present a problem; travelers should discuss this with the airline at an early stage and, if necessary, with their doctor.

Guide dogs for the blind often have to travel in a specially pressurized baggage compartment with other animals, away from their owners, though smaller guide dogs may be admitted to the cabin. Guide dogs are not subject to quarantine as long as they have proof of being vaccinated against rabies.

Deaf travelers can ask for airport and in-flight announcements to be written down for them.

Children under two travel for 10% of the standard fare (or free on some airlines) as long as they don't occupy a seat (they don't get a baggage allowance either). 'Skycots' should be provided by the airline if you request them in advance; these take a child weighing up to approximately 10kg. Children between the ages of two and 12 usually occupy a seat for half to two-thirds of the full fare and they do get a baggage allowance. Strollers can often be taken on as hand luggage.

Baggage

On most domestic and international flights you are limited to two checked bags, or three if you don't have carry-on luggage. There could be a charge if you bring more or if the size of the bags exceeds the airlines limits. It's best to check with the individual airline if you're worried about this. On some international flights the luggage allowance is based on weight.

If your luggage is delayed upon arrival (which is rare), some airlines give a cash advance to purchase necessities. If sporting equipment is misplaced, the airline may pay for rentals. Should the luggage be lost, it's important to submit a claim. The airline doesn't have to pay the full amount of the claim, but they can estimate the value of your lost items. It may take them anywhere from six weeks to three months to process the claim and pay you.

Illegal Items Items that are illegal to take on a plane, either checked or as carry-on luggage, include aerosols of polishes, waxes etc; tear gas and pepper spray; camp stoves with fuel; and divers' tanks that are full. Matches shouldn't be checked in with your baggage.

Arriving in Canada

Aboard the plane, on the international leg of the flight, passengers are given standard immigration and customs forms to fill out. The cabin crew will help you if you have any questions. After the plane lands, you first go through immigration. There are two lines: one for Canadian citizens and residents, the other for nonresidents. Immigration formalities are usually straightforward if you have the necessary documents (passport and visa). Occasionally, you may be asked to show your ticket out of Canada, but this doesn't happen often.

You then collect your baggage and pass through customs. If you have nothing to declare, you'll probably clear customs quickly and without a luggage search, but you can't rely on it. (See also Customs in the Facts for the Visitor chapter.) Once through customs you are officially in the country.

Leaving Canada

You should check in for international flights two hours before the scheduled departure. During check-in procedures, you may be asked questions about whether you packed your own bags, whether anyone else has had access to them since you packed them and whether you've received any parcels to carry. These are simply security measures.

Within Canada

The *Vancouver Sun*, *Vancouver Province*, *Globe & Mail* and other major newspapers all produce weekly travel sections with numerous travel agencies' ads. Travel CUTS has offices in all major cities; see the Travel Agencies section later in this chapter.

Air travel within Canada is not cheap, certainly when compared to airfares in the USA, but there are ways to save money. There are often seat sales that you might be able to take advantage of, especially if you have a friend in Canada who can book the ticket for you before you arrive. Also, if you book a ticket well in advance of your desired departure date you will always pay less than if you need to leave the following day. Late-night flights, often referred to as 'red-eye' specials, can save you anywhere from $50 to $100.

Some one-way fares with either Canadian Airlines or Air Canada from Vancouver include Calgary $150, Winnipeg $543, Toronto $553, Montreal $594, Halifax $814, Whitehorse $550 and Yellowknife $768. Canada 3000 Airlines is a discount charter airline with flights from Vancouver to other major cities in Canada and if you choose to fly standby, you can get to Calgary one way for $65, or all the way to Toronto for $155.

For courier flights contact FB On Board Courier Services at ☎ 604-278-1266.

To/From Victoria Both Air Canada and Canadian Airlines connect the airport of Vancouver with Victoria. The normal pre-tax economy fare is about $220 roundtrip, but weekend roundtrip specials can often lower this to around $120.

Aside from the regular airline service between Vancouver and Victoria, harbor-to-harbor seaplane service is offered by Harbour Air (☎ 604-688-1277 in Vancouver, 250-384-2215 in Victoria, 800-665-0212). It operates 20 flights a day during the week and eight flights a day on the weekend for $75 one-way. The trip takes about 30 minutes. It also has service to the southern Gulf Islands and to Maple Bay (near Duncan) on Vancouver Island for $65 one-way. West Coast Air (☎ 604-688-9115) also offers a harbor-to-harbor seaplane service for $116/130 one-way/roundtrip. Both these services operate from the terminal off Waterfront Rd West, about three blocks west of Canada Place. There are also services from the south airport terminal.

If helicopters are your preferred mode of travel, then you can fly harbor to harbor in a Helijet Airways (☎ 604-273-1414) 12-passenger S-76 Sikorsky. The daily flights start at $139 roundtrip and leave from the downtown terminal at 455 Waterfront Rd East, next to Waterfront Station.

The USA

The *San Francisco Examiner*, *Los Angeles Times*, *New York Times* and other major newspapers all produce weekly travel sections with numerous travel agencies' ads. Council Travel (☎ 800-226-8624) and STA Travel (☎ 800-777-0112) have offices in major cities across the USA.

The magazine *Travel Unlimited*, PO Box 1058, Allston, MA 02134, publishes details of the cheapest airfares and courier possibilities. A US discounter, Reno Air, flies into Vancouver, linking it with California and the US Southwest.

Flights to Vancouver, with any carrier, from Seattle cost $156 (US$100) and from San Francisco cost $248 (US$164). To Vancouver from Los Angeles with Reno Air is $240 (US$160), and from New York with Cathay Pacific is $388 (US$260).

Australia & New Zealand

In Australia and New Zealand, STA Travel (☎ 800-637-444) and Flight Centres International are major dealers in cheap airfares; check the travel agencies' ads in the Yellow Pages. Qantas Airways/Canadian Airlines flies to Vancouver from Sydney, Melbourne (via Sydney or Auckland) and Cairns. Air New Zealand also offers similar flights. United Airlines flies to San Francisco and Los Angeles from Sydney.

The cheapest tickets have a 14-day advance-purchase requirement, a minimum stay of seven days and a maximum stay of 60 days. Qantas Airways/Canadian Airlines flies from Melbourne or Sydney to Vancouver for a top price of A$2273 in the high season, but the usual standard, advance-purchase fare runs A$1873. Flying with Air New Zealand can sometimes run cheaper, and both Qantas Airways and Air New Zealand offer tickets with longer stays or stopovers, but you pay more.

Roundtrip flights from Auckland to Vancouver on Qantas Airways cost NZ$2015 in the low season. Canada 3000 Airlines flies between Vancouver and Sydney from November to April only for the remarkably low roundtrip fare of C$1100.

Asia

Hong Kong was once the discount plane ticket capital of the region, but now Bangkok and Singapore, which have a number of bucket shops, are better places for getting the cheapest fares. STA Travel has branches in Hong Kong, Tokyo, Singapore, Bangkok and Kuala Lumpur. Many flights to Canada and the USA go via Honolulu.

Japan Japan Airlines and Northwest Airlines have direct flights from Tokyo to Vancouver with connections to other US West Coast cities such as Seattle, San Francisco and Los Angeles. Japan Airlines also flies to Honolulu from Osaka, Nagoya, Fukuoka and Sapporo. United Airlines has flights to Honolulu from Tokyo with connections to US West Coast cities.

If you are flying to Vancouver from Tokyo, expect to pay around $1500.

Southeast Asia Numerous airlines fly to Canada and the USA from Southeast Asia; bucket shops in places like Bangkok and Singapore should be able to come up with the best deals. Tickets to Vancouver or US West Coast cities often allow a free stopover in Honolulu.

Malaysia Airlines flies to Honolulu from Hong Kong, Bangkok, Manila, Seoul and Singapore, with connections to Vancouver and other US West Coast cities. Korean Air and Philippine Airlines also have flights from a number of Southeast Asian cities to Honolulu, with onward connections.

Some fares from Vancouver are Hong Kong $1550, Bangkok $1700, Singapore $1750 and Delhi $2200.

UK & Ireland

If you are traveling from the UK, you will probably find that the cheapest flights are advertised by obscure bucket shops. Many are honest and solvent, but there are a few rogues who'll take your money and disappear, only to reopen elsewhere a month or two later under a new name. If you feel suspicious, don't pay for the ticket all at once – leave a deposit of 20% or so and pay the balance on receiving the ticket. If they insist on cash in advance, go elsewhere. Once you have the ticket, phone the airline to confirm that you are booked on the flight.

Check the ads in magazines such as *Time Out* and *City Limits*, plus the Sunday papers and *Exchange & Mart*. Also check the free magazines widely available in London – start by looking outside the main railway stations.

Most British travel agents are registered with the Association of British Travel Agents (ABTA). If you've paid for your flight at an ABTA-registered agent who then goes out of business, ABTA will guarantee a refund or an alternative. Unregistered bucket shops are riskier but sometimes cheaper.

London is arguably the world's headquarters for bucket shops, which frequently place ads and can usually beat published airline fares. Two good, reliable agents for cheap tickets in the UK are Trailfinders (☎ 0171-937-5400; from 22 April 2000 ☎ 020-7937-5400), 194 Kensington High St, London W8 7RG, and STA Travel (☎ 0171-937-9971; from 22 April 2000 ☎ 020-7937-9971), 86 Old Brompton Rd, London SW7 3LQ. Trailfinders produces a lavishly illustrated brochure including airfare details.

The Globetrotters Club publishes a newsletter called *Globe* that covers obscure destinations and can help you find traveling companions. You can write to them at BCM Roving, London WC1N 3XX.

The fare to Vancouver from London is £536 (although with Canada 3000 Airlines a roundtrip fare is as low as £355), from Edinburgh is £575 and from Dublin is IR£461.

Continental Europe

Though London is the travel-discount capital of Europe, several other cities offer a range of good deals, especially Amsterdam and Athens. Many travel agencies in Europe have ties with STA Travel, where cheap tickets can be bought and STA Travel tickets can be altered free of charge (first change only).

In the Netherlands, NBBS Reizen is a popular travel agency; it has offices in Amsterdam at Roken 38 (☎ 624 09 89) and Leidestraat 53 (☎ 638 17 26). In Paris, Council Travel (☎ 01 44 55 55 65) has its main offices at 22 rue des Pyramides (1er). In Athens try International Student & Youth Travel Service (☎ (01) 323-3767), Nikis 11.

Some fares to Vancouver include Paris FF4978, Amsterdam f1778, Frankfurt D1662, Rome L1,577,580 and Athens 315,747dr.

Mexico & South America

Most flights from Mexico and Central and South America to Vancouver go via Miami, Houston, Los Angeles and/or San Francisco. Often the ticket has to be combined between a carrier leaving one of these countries and a carrier flying into Vancouver. Japan Airlines is one of the few carriers that has direct flights between Mexico City and Vancouver.

In the USA, airlines such as United and American serve these destinations as do the various countries' international carriers such as Aerolíneas Argentinas and LanChile Airlines. Continental has flights from about 20 cities in Mexico, Central and South America, including Lima, San Jose, Guatemala City, Cancún and Mérida, most of which arrive at Dallas-Fort Worth airport with connections to the rest of the USA and Canada.

Some fares to Vancouver include Mexico City $520, Costa Rica $730, Caracas $819, Buenos Aires $1570 and Rio de Janeiro $1650.

BUS

The bus station is part of Pacific Central Station, 1150 Station St. Greyhound (☎ 604-662-3222), Maverick Coach Lines (☎ 604-662-8051, 255-1171) and Pacific Coach Lines (☎ 604-662-8074) stop here.

Greyhound buses link Vancouver with Seattle and other cities in the USA, as well as to points east in Canada. Greyhound does not have service to Victoria. Some examples of one-way fares with Greyhound (including tax) from Vancouver are: Kelowna $50 (eight buses daily); Banff $100 (five buses daily); and Calgary $105 (five buses daily). Children under 11 travel for half-price.

Pacific Coach Lines has eight buses daily to Victoria, leaving the bus station every hour at 10 minutes to the hour from 5.50 am to 8.45 pm. The one-way fare is $25 including ferry; the journey takes about three hours.

Maverick Coach Lines operates eight buses daily to Nanaimo for $18 one-way (including ferry); the trip takes 3½ hours. It also has buses to the Sunshine Coast and Powell River, Squamish, Whistler ($17 one-way, seven buses daily) and Pemberton. Perimeter (☎ 604-266-5386) operates a service during the ski season between the Vancouver international airport (including drop-off and pickup at various Vancouver hotels) and Whistler for a one-way fare of $45/24 adults/children (five to 11).

If you're heading for the USA, Quick Coach Lines (☎ 604-940-4428, 800-665-2122 in Canada) operates a daily bus shuttle to downtown Seattle for $39 one-way; the bus also makes stops at Seattle's Sea-Tac airport and the Bellingham airport. Buses leave downtown Vancouver from most major hotels.

You can also catch a BC Transit city bus to White Rock, close to the US border. Take bus No 351, 352 or 354 south on Granville St.

An alternative bus service is Bigfoot's Backpacker Adventure Tours (☎ 604-278-5220, or book through an HI hostel) which does a two-day trip to Banff via Kamloops with interesting stops along the way. The price is $95/190 one-way/roundtrip, which does not include accommodations en route.

See the Train section for details on bus service offered by VIA Rail and Amtrak.

Canada Pass

Greyhound's Canada Pass is potentially useful if you plan on doing a lot of bus travel out of Vancouver. A pass costs $223 for seven days of unlimited travel, $295 for 15 days, $402 for 30 days and $509 for 60 days (these rates apply in any season). You can get on and off at any Greyhound terminal and it is also good for travel in the USA. The pass must be purchased at least seven days prior to your first journey. International travelers can purchase an International Canada Pass for a bit less at overseas travel agencies.

TRAIN

Trains operating out of Vancouver travel across the country, to the Rockies, through the province or into the USA.

VIA Rail

Vancouver is the western terminus for VIA Rail. The magnificent Pacific Central Station is off Main St at 1150 Station St between National and Terminal Aves. For 24-hour information on fares and reservations call ☎ 800-561-8630. The ticket office is open restricted hours: Monday and Thursday from 8 am to 8 pm; Tuesday, Wednesday and Friday from 8 am to 3.30 pm; Saturday from 12.30 to 8 pm; and Sunday from 8 am to 1.30 pm. Left luggage is open from 8 am to 10 pm (closed between 3.30 and 4 pm).

The route east goes through Kamloops, Jasper and Edmonton. Trains leave Monday, Thursday and Saturday at 8 pm. Stopovers are permitted but you must re-reserve.

VIA Rail also provides a bus service between the towns of Kamloops and Penticton, Edmonton and Calgary and Saskatoon and Regina. This provides a connection to major towns no longer part of the rail system.

Amtrak

Amtrak's (☎ 604-585-4848 for reservations, 800-872-7245 for information) *Mt Baker* line connects Vancouver to Bellingham and

Seattle with one train daily. In addition, Amtrak runs three buses a day from Vancouver to connect with other main-line departures in Seattle, and connections to other US destinations can be made in Seattle. The bus fare to/from Vancouver/ Seattle is US$19 one-way.

Rocky Mountaineer

The privately owned *Rocky Mountaineer* train travels through some of the country's most scenic landscapes from BC to Banff and Calgary (VIA Rail no longer provides service along this route). This isn't really a service for people just trying to get from place to place, unless you have a lot of money to spend. Tickets come with accommodations (there's an obligatory overnight stay in Kamloops) and meals, with more extensive packages available on both the Vancouver and Alberta ends. The cheapest off-season fare from Vancouver to Banff or Jasper is $475; a basic four-day package runs $975.

The service runs between the middle of May and early October. There are seven trips a month in summer. For information contact a travel agent or Rocky Mountaineer Railtours (☎ 604-606-7200, 800-665-7245 reservations), 130 - 1150 Station St, in Pacific Central Station.

BC Rail

British Columbia has its own railway system (☎ 604-984-5246, 800-663-8238) which operates the *Cariboo Prospector* with service from North Vancouver to Squamish, Whistler, Lillooet, 100 Mile House, Williams Lake, Quesnel and Prince George, where it connects with VIA Rail. One train leaves daily at 7 am with service as far as Whistler and Lillooet; the one-way fare to Whistler is $30/27/18/6 adults/seniors/children/infants, and the trip takes about 2½ hours (the train departs Whistler for North Vancouver at 6.10 pm). Three days a week – Sunday, Wednesday and Friday – the train continues on to Prince George; one-way fare to Prince George is $190/171/114/38 and the trip takes about 13 hours. Reservations are advised.

Trains leave from North Vancouver, at BC Rail Station, 1311 West 1st St at the southern end of Pemberton Ave. To get to the station take bus No 239 west from the SeaBus terminal at Lonsdale Quay.

Train Passes

If you are planning to do a fair amount of train travel outside Vancouver, consider getting VIA Rail's CANRAILPASS. The pass gives you 12 days of economy-class travel across Canada within a 30-day period. The cost for an adult is $569 in the peak season (June 1 to October 15) and $49 for each additional day of travel up to a maximum of three days, or $369 in the low season (October 16 to May 31) and $31 for each additional day. For a youth under 25 or a student with an International Student Identification Card (ISIC), or a senior over 60, the cost is $499 in peak season ($44 for each additional day) and $339 during low season ($28 for each additional day).

The North America Rail Pass, a partnership between VIA Rail and Amtrak, allows you to travel throughout Canada and the USA on over 45,000km of track, with unlimited stops to more than 900 destinations, and is valid for 30 days. An economy-class ticket is $895 in the peak season and $625 in the low season.

CAR & MOTORCYCLE

If you are coming from the USA (Washington State) you'll be on I-5 until the border town of Blaine. At the border is the Peace Arch Provincial and State Park. The first town in BC is White Rock. Hwy 99 veers west, then north to Vancouver. Close to the city, the highway passes over two arms of the Fraser River and eventually turns into Granville St, one of the main thoroughfares of downtown Vancouver. In the center of town Granville St becomes a pedestrian mall and traffic – other than buses, taxis and emergency vehicles – is forbidden. Remember, there is a network of one-way streets around here too.

If you're coming from the east, you'll almost certainly be on the Trans Canada Hwy (Hwy 1), which takes the Port Mann Bridge over the Fraser River and snakes through the eastern end of the city, eventu-

The Great Dividing Line

Just a 30-minute drive from Vancouver, south of Tsawwassen on Georgia Strait, and across Boundary Bay from White Rock, there is a little knob of land called Point Roberts. This 12.5-sq-km peninsula is detached from Washington State by water and land, but because it is on the south side of the 49th parallel, the dividing line between Canada and the USA, it is a US possession.

Even though an exception was made for Vancouver Island when, in 1846, it was decided the border would follow the 49th parallel west to the Pacific Ocean, no such exception was made for Point Roberts. The area comes under Washington State's jurisdiction and there is an official border crossing open 24 hours. However, the area has been utilized far more by Canadians than it has been by Americans, and over the years Canada has provided most of the services (water, gas, electricity, police etc).

Canadians have owned summer homes here for a long time, mainly to make use of the long stretches of sandy beach and the shallow bay's warm water – in fact, the beach at Point Roberts has been ranked one of the top 15 beaches in the USA – and because property prices have remained relatively low. You'll find a marina, a small airport, shops, restaurants, two taverns and the 7-hectare Lighthouse Park with campsites and picnic areas.

At one time this was little more than a farming community settled by Icelandic immigrants. In time, the fishing and canning industries became the main sources of employment, along with the taverns, which for many years were a reason for Canadians to make the trip from Vancouver.

Starting in the late 1940s, Point Roberts became a popular place to come for cheap beer and music at two of the largest taverns in the USA, The Reef and Breakers, especially on a Sunday when bars and clubs in BC were closed. In recent years there has no longer been that attraction and the area is now mostly enjoyed for the beaches, the boating and the fishing, and of course the novelty of being in the USA while still being in Canada.

To get to Point Roberts from Vancouver, follow Hwy 99 south, turn south onto Hwy 17 (the road to the BC Ferries Terminal at Tsawwassen) and at 56th St (Point Roberts Rd) turn south again.

ally meeting with Hastings St. It continues over the Second Narrows Bridge to North Vancouver and eventually on to West Vancouver and Horseshoe Bay. If you want to go downtown, turn left onto Hastings St and follow it into the city center.

If you are coming from Horseshoe Bay in the north, the Trans Canada Hwy (Hwy 1) heads through West Vancouver and North Vancouver before going over the Second Narrows Bridge into Burnaby. If you're heading downtown, leave the highway at the Taylor Way exit in West Vancouver (it's also a part of Hwy 99) and follow it over the Lions Gate Bridge into Stanley Park and into the city center.

Speed limits, which are posted in kilometers, are generally 50km/h in built-up areas and 100km/h on highways. The use of seat belts is compulsory, as is the wearing of helmets for motorcyclists, and children under the age of five must be secured in infant restraint systems. At a red light a right turn is permitted after you have come to a complete stop, as is a left turn from one one-way street onto another one-way street. The blood-alcohol limit when driving is 0.08%. Gasoline, which is sold in liters, is reasonably priced (about 55¢ a liter) although compared to gas prices in the USA it will seem expensive. You may notice that the vast majority of drivers keep their headlights on throughout the day; this is not mandatory but is recommended and newer cars have driving lights that turn on and off automatically with the ignition.

The British Columbia Automobile Association (BCAA; ☎ 604-268-5555) 4567 Canada Way, Burnaby, provides its members, and the members of other auto clubs, with travel information, maps, travel insurance and accommodations reservations.

For 24-hour emergency road service call ☎ 604-293-2222.

For more information about driving, see Car & Motorcycle in the Getting Around chapter.

Driveaways

If you are ready to leave town and know where you want to go, or conversely don't care where you end up, you may want to check out the uniquely North American Driveaway system. The basic concept is that you drive someone else's car to a specific destination. Usually the car belongs to someone who has been transferred for work and has had to fly, or doesn't have the time, patience or ability to drive a long distance. Arrangements are made through a Driveaway agency.

After the agency matches you up with a suitable car, you put down a deposit of $300 to $500 and are given a certain number of days to deliver the car. If you don't show up the police are notified. You are usually given a route to take and a rough kilometer guideline which translates into the most direct route from A to B.

You are not paid to deliver the car and generally you pay for gasoline. With two or more people, this can be an especially great deal. The company will want to know who will be driving.

In summer, when demand is highest, cars may be more difficult to obtain and you could be asked for a nonrefundable administrative payment of, perhaps, $100.

One thing to ask about is what happens if the car breaks down. Get this information in writing if possible. Generally, minor car repairs of around $100 or less are paid by you. Keep the receipt and you will be reimbursed upon delivery. If bad luck strikes and a major repair is required there may be hassles. The agency might get in touch with the owner and ask how to proceed. This might take time and could involve some inconvenience. Usually the cars offered are fairly new and in good working order or the owners probably wouldn't bother having them transported.

You'll require good identification, a valid driver's license, the deposit and a couple of photos. Look for Driveaway companies in the Yellow Pages under 'Automobile & Truck Transporting,' or contact Vancouver Driveaway (☎ 604-985-8016), 1080A Marine Drive, North Vancouver.

HITCHHIKING

Hitching is never entirely safe in any country in the world and we don't recommend it. Travelers who decide to hitch should understand that they are taking a small but potentially serious risk.

Hitching on the Trans Canada Hwy is illegal until 40km past the city limits. One possibility is to take bus No 9 along East Broadway to Boundary Rd, then walk south to Grandview Hwy (which connects with the Trans Canada Hwy) and stick your thumb out. Alternatively, take the SkyTrain to Scott Rd Station then bus No 502 to Langley along the Fraser Hwy before getting onto the main route.

If you want to get up to Squamish or Whistler, first take the West Vancouver Blue Bus to Horseshoe Bay. You can catch the bus from outside The Bay department store on West Georgia St, near Granville St. Ask the driver to let you off at the point where Marine Drive almost connects with the Upper Levels Hwy, and before the bus turns to go down into Horseshoe Bay. From there walk up to the highway and along to a point where drivers can see you are heading north on Hwy 99.

FERRY

BC Ferries Corporation (☎ 888-223-3779 for schedules and information, or 888-724-5223 for reservations) operates the ferry routes in BC's coastal waters with a fleet of 40 ferries. The two main ferry routes are from Tsawwassen (about an hour's drive south of the city center) to Swartz Bay (30-minute drive north of Victoria), and from Horseshoe

NIK WHEELER

Bay (30-minute drive north of the city center) to Nanaimo. From Tsawwassen, ferries also go to Nanaimo and the Gulf Islands. From Horseshoe Bay, ferries also go to Bowen Island and the Sunshine Coast (see those sections elsewhere in the book for details).

During the summer months, from 7 am to 10 pm there are hourly sailings between the Mainland and Vancouver Island. During the rest of the year this is generally dropped back to a sailing every two hours, except during holidays. The crossing takes 90 minutes to two hours. Friday evening, Sunday afternoon and evening, and holiday Monday are the busiest times, and if you have a car there is often a one- or two-ferry wait. To avoid long delays it's worth planning your crossing for less busy times.

The one-way fare on all Mainland to Vancouver Island routes in the summer, or peak season (end of June to the middle of September), is $9/4.50 adults/children (five to 11), $32 for a car (driver not included), $52 for a vehicle over 7ft high and up to 20ft long, $16 for a motorcycle (or $24 if it has a sidecar and/or trailer), $2.50 for a bicycle and $4 for a kayak or canoe. These rates are slightly lower if you travel midweek (Monday to noon Friday, unless one of these days is a public holiday) and are substantially lower in the winter, or low season.

To get to Tsawwassen by city bus, catch the southbound bus No 601 (South Delta), from either Howe St or from the corner of Granville St and West 4th Ave, to the Ladner Exchange. From the exchange take bus No 640 (Tsawwassen Ferry) to the ferry termi-

nal. A quicker way is to catch the SkyTrain to Scott Road Station and there catch bus No 640. The fare either way is $1.50, or $3 if you travel in peak traffic time. From Swartz Bay you can take bus No 70 into Victoria. To get to the Horseshoe Bay ferry terminal from Vancouver take the West Vancouver Blue Bus No 250 or 257 (Horseshoe Bay) north-bound on West Georgia St. The bus stops in front of The Bay department store between Granville and Seymour Sts.

TRAVEL AGENCIES

Vancouver isn't exactly a discount-fare paradise, but there are deals to be had if you are willing to shop around. Package deals are always your best bet, but those are usually only good if you are going to a holiday destination as opposed to looking for an onward flight out of Vancouver. The following agencies will at least give you a place to start when looking for a ticket:

American Express Travel
 (☎ 604-669-2813) 666 Burrard St
ANZA
 (☎ 604-734-7725) 210 - 1847 West Broadway.
 Specializes in travel to Australia and New Zealand.
BCAA Travel
 (☎ 604-268-5622) 999 West Broadway. The provincial auto club has 11 offices in Vancouver.
Budget Cruise & Travel
 (☎ 604-685-7399) 1402 - 1166 Alberni St
 (☎ 604-732-8801) 102 - 1500 West 2nd Ave
Flight Centre
 (☎ 604-682-3104) 655 West Pender St. It has eight offices around Vancouver and offers very competitive prices.
Travel CUTS
 (☎ 604-681-9136) 567 Seymour St
 (☎ 604-874-7498) 555 West 8th Ave. The official student agency with six offices in Vancouver.

ORGANIZED TOURS

If you have seen the sights in Vancouver and want to explore farther afield, there are any number of options available. Most of the tours take in Victoria or Whistler (see the following section for details) but if you really want to get out of town then there are tours available into the interior of the province and beyond to the Rockies.

Gray Line and Brewster bus lines (☎ 604-879-3363) have put together a number of packages that, for example, take in areas such as the Fraser River, the Thompson River or the Rockies, and range in duration from two to nine days. The seven-day Rockies Circle Tour, from mid-May to mid-October, starts at around $1640.

BC Rail (☎ 604-984-5246) has a number of vacation packages that are anywhere from two to nine days in duration. For example, the three-day Pacific Coastal Circle tour goes from North Vancouver to Prince George, then after a night in Prince George you take VIA Rail to Prince Rupert where, after an overnight stay, you fly back to Vancouver. The cost is $665 based on double occupancy and includes all meals served on board the train.

To/From Victoria

A number of companies offer a variety of tours to Victoria from Vancouver. The standard tour is a one-day trip from/to Vancouver that takes in Butchart Gardens along the way. Some involve overnight stays in Victoria returning to Vancouver the following day, while others give you the option of going one-way on the bus and returning by helicopter. Still others offer a marine wildlife tour as part of the trip to Victoria. There are many companies offering escorted tours to Victoria and the following is a list of just a few available.

Gray Line (☎ 604-879-3363) offers a one-day (about 13 hours) fully escorted trip to and around Victoria taking in Butchart Gardens along the way. During the summer (mid-June to mid-September) there are three daily departure times, 7.30, 8.30 and 9.15 am, and you can be picked up at your hotel a half-hour before your scheduled departure. During the rest of the year the daily departure times are reduced. The cost is $96/89/59 adults/seniors/children. If you want to return to Vancouver in just 35 minutes by helicopter the cost on weekdays is $225/188/144, and on weekends and holidays it's $176/169/139. If you want to stay overnight in Victoria the tour/hotel packages start at $301/228/207 for single/double/

triple occupancy. There is also a two-night, three-day package available.

Pacific Coach Lines (☎ 604-662-7575) has a standard daily escorted tour which includes Butchart Gardens for $66/33 adults/children (five to 11). The Marine Wildlife Adventure Tour takes in a two-hour trip around Victoria's inner harbor and the southern part of Vancouver Island in a small boat with a naturalist, and costs $109/69. You can be picked up at your hotel half an hour before departure times or you can catch the bus at Pacific Central Station.

Town Tours (☎ 604-451-1777) offers the standard Victoria-and-Butchart Gardens tour but in smaller 24-seat mini-buses. The daily escorted tours run from June to October and cost $84/80/43 for adults/seniors/children (four to 12). Pickup is at your hotel at 9.15 am.

To/From Whistler

The scenery on the way up to Whistler, not to mention at Whistler itself, is spectacular and there are several types of tours that let you see the natural splendor to its best advantage. The following is a list of some of the tours available.

Alpine Adventure Tours (☎ 604-683-0209) will take you to Whistler and back by train or you can do a bus/train combination. The train departs daily from the BC Rail Station in North Vancouver at 7 am and breakfast is served en route to Whistler, where the train arrives at about 9.30 am. The train departs Whistler at 6 pm and dinner is served on the return trip to Vancouver, where the train arrives at 8.40 pm. If you choose the bus/train option, the bus leaves Vancouver at 10 am arriving in Whistler at noon. The train option is $62/59/42 for adults/seniors/children, while the bus/train option is $79/76/45.

Gray Line (☎ 604-879-3363) offers a daily 9½-hour tour to Whistler from mid-April to mid-October which takes in the 330m Shannon Falls and the Railway Heritage Park in Squamish on the way. The cost is $56/52/34 for adults/seniors/children. For an additional cost the *Royal Hudson* steam train from North Vancouver to Squamish can be added in as part of the package. If you want to stay overnight in Whistler the packages start at $275/188/149 for single/double/triple occupancy. There are also two-night, three-day packages available.

West Coast Sightseeing (☎ 604-451-1600) has year-round daily trips to Whistler taking in Shannon Falls and the Bald Eagle Watch in Squamish, where more than 3000 bald eagles gather along the river to feed during the winter. The cost is $55/52/32 for adults/seniors & students/children (four to 12).

Alaska Cruises

Although you will have likely booked your cruise long before you get to Vancouver, this section wouldn't be complete without at least a passing mention of what has become one of the world's most popular, and profitable, cruise destinations. Most of the 25 ships that make the Alaska cruise, which run from May through to October, either start or finish in Vancouver. More than 600,000 passengers from more than 270 separate sailings a year are processed by the Port of Vancouver, although it is expected that by the 21st century this number will reach more than 1 million passengers a year.

Even though Canada Place was designed to handle as many as five ships at a time, due to the increased size of the new ships it can now only accommodate two ships. The other ships dock at the Ballantyne Cruise Terminal at Ballantyne Pier, a cargo terminal in East Vancouver which has been upgraded to accommodate the cruise ships and their passengers. Ballantyne Pier is at the foot of Heatley Ave about five blocks east of Main St.

For more information about the cruises, or to make reservations, contact a travel agent or Cruise Holidays (☎ 604-737-8100, 888-702-7245). As well, *Porthole* magazine (☎ 800-776-7678, www.porthole.com) is a good source of information.

WARNING

The information in this chapter is particularly vulnerable to change: prices for international travel are volatile, routes are introduced and canceled, schedules change, special deals come and go, and rules and visa requirements are amended. Airlines and governments seem to take a perverse pleasure in making price structures and regulations as complicated as possible. You should check directly with the airline or a travel agent to make sure you understand how a fare (and ticket you may buy) works. In addition, the travel industry is highly competitive and there are many packages and bonuses.

The upshot of this is that you should get opinions, quotes and advice from as many airlines and travel agents as possible before you part with your hard-earned cash. The details given in this chapter should be regarded as pointers and are not a substitute for your own careful, up-to-date research.

Getting Around

TO/FROM THE AIRPORT

There are two ways to get between the airport and downtown by bus. The quickest option is to take a Vancouver Airporter bus (☎ 604-946-8866) which runs to/from the Pacific Central Station and all major central hotels for $10/8/5 adults/seniors/children (five to 12); roundtrip prices are $17/16/10 with no time limit. Tickets can be purchased from the ticket office on level 2 of the airport (outside the main terminal adjacent to the bus departure zone), or from the driver; they can also be purchased from the hotels. Buses depart from level 2 at the airport every 30 minutes starting at 6.30 am, take about 30 minutes to get downtown and the last one departs about 12.10 am. At Pacific Central Station, buses leave from bay 9 on level 1 starting at 6.10 am. You can also flag the buses down at bus stops on Granville St and Broadway, or at Granville St and 41st Ave.

To get to the airport by city bus, take No 20 south on Granville St to 70th Ave. From there transfer to bus No 100 which will take you to the airport terminal. From the airport, do the reverse. The total travel time is one hour and the fare is $1.50 ($3 during peak traffic time). You need to have exact change.

A taxi from the airport to the city center takes about 25 minutes and costs around $30.

A four-story parking garage with 2400 parking spaces (don't forget to take note of where you have parked) is connected to the international and domestic terminals by covered walkways. Parking costs about $4 an hour. Baggage carts, which cost nothing to use, can be found in the garage, outside by the main doors and inside the terminal near the baggage carousels.

Rental car outlets are located on level 1 of the garage.

PUBLIC TRANSPORT

For BC Transit information call ☎ 604-521-0400 or obtain one of the two publications they produce on getting around the city, or check out their website at www.bctransit .com. The *Transit Route Map & Guide* is a map of Greater Vancouver showing the bus, SkyTrain, SeaBus and West Coast Express routes, plus information on fares and schedules. It costs $1.50 and can be bought at convenience stores and bookstores. *Discover Vancouver on Transit* (includes Victoria, too) lists many of the city's attractions and how to get there. It's available for free at Travel InfoCentres. For information about traveling on BC Transit with a disability, see the Disabled Travelers section in the Facts for the Visitor chapter.

BC Transit offers several modes of public transportation: electric trolley buses that are connected to overhead cables and standard diesel-powered buses; SeaBus passenger ferries that operate between Waterfront Station near Canada Place and Lonsdale Quay in North Vancouver; the SkyTrain elevated light-rail system that runs from Waterfront Station to King George Station in Surrey; and the West Coast Express trains that run only during the morning and afternoon peak traffic hours from Waterfront Station to Mission.

The transport system is divided into three zones: the inner zone covers central Vancouver; the next zone includes the suburbs of Richmond, Burnaby, New Westminster, North Vancouver, West Vancouver and Sea Island; and the outer zone covers Ladner, Tsawwassen, Delta, Surrey, White Rock, Langley, Port Moody, Pitt Meadows, Maple Ridge, Belcarra, Coquitlam, Port Coquitlam and Lions Bay.

On weekdays before 6.30 pm the fare depends on how many zones you travel across: $1.50 for one zone, $2.25 for two and $3 for three. After 6.30 pm, and on weekends and public holidays, the fare is a flat $1.50. Concession (or discount) fares, which are given to seniors (65 and over), students (14 to 19 with a valid GoCard), children (five to

13) and HandyPass holders, are $1 for one zone, $1.50 for two, $2 for three and a flat $1 during non-peak times.

The fare is good for travel on buses, the SkyTrain and the SeaBus, and is valid for 90 minutes for travel in either direction from the time of purchase. Service on most of the routes ends at about 1 am daily, except on major streets when a limited service comes into effect until about 3 am (although you might feel like you've been waiting an eternity by the time a bus comes along, especially if it's raining).

If you start your journey on a bus be sure to get a transfer from the driver as proof of payment. Exact payment must be made on buses as drivers do not carry change. Before boarding the SkyTrain or SeaBus purchase a ticket from the red ticket machines in the station or terminal. These machines accept coins, $5 and $10 bills; they return change; and they will issue a fare receipt automatically (which also serves as a transfer).

All-day transit passes called DayPasses are good for one day's unlimited travel any day of the week and cost $6 for adults and $4 for those who qualify for a discounted fare. They can be purchased at SeaBus terminals, SkyTrain stations or from shops displaying the 'FareDealer' sign. You can also save money by purchasing a book of 10 tickets called FareSaver Tickets. These are available for travel in one zone for $13.75, two zones $20.50 and three zones $28. A booklet of 10 discount tickets is available for one-zone travel only and costs $10.

If you are going to be in Vancouver for an extended period and plan on doing a lot of traveling on BC Transit then you might want to look into the monthly passes called Fare-Cards which cost $54 for one zone, $78 for two zones and $103 for three zones. The concession FareCard costs $35 for unlimited travel.

SkyTrain

The wheelchair-accessible SkyTrain connects Downtown Vancouver with Burnaby, New Westminster and Surrey. The trains are fully computerized (meaning there's no driver!) and travel mostly above ground along a specially designed track that stretches for a total distance of 29km. From downtown the four-car trains depart from Waterfront Station about every three to five minutes, and a trip to King George Station at the other end takes about 40 minutes. The trains are scheduled to connect with buses.

There are a total of 20 stations. The downtown stops, heading eastbound after Waterfront Station, include Burrard Station (near Dunsmuir St), Granville Station (near West Georgia St), Stadium Station (near Dunsmuir and Beatty Sts, and close to GM Place and BC Place Stadium), Science World-Main Street Station (near Terminal Ave and Pacific Central Station), and Broadway Station (at Commercial Drive).

SeaBus

These super-modern catamarans zip back and forth across Burrard Inlet between Waterfront Station near Canada Place and Lonsdale Quay in North Vancouver. The two 400-passenger ferries, the *Burrard Beaver* and the *Burrard Otter*, take about 13 minutes to make the trip; it's worth taking the journey if only to see the fabulous views.

They leave every 15 minutes on weekdays between about 6 am and 6.30 pm, on Saturday between about 10 am and 6 pm, and on Sunday and holidays during the summer between about 11 am and 6 pm; the rest of the time they leave every 30 minutes. Try to

CHUCK PEFLEY

SeaBus in action

avoid rush hour when many commuters crowd aboard. The ferries are wheelchair accessible and bicycles can also be taken on board at no extra charge.

West Coast Express

This is essentially a commuter train service for people who live in the eastern suburbs and the stations are Mission ($13.65 roundtrip), Port Haney, Maple Meadows, Pitt Meadows ($9.75 roundtrip), Port Coquitlam, Coquitlam and Port Moody ($7.80 roundtrip). During weekdays the trains travel westbound in the morning from Mission to Waterfront Station, leaving every half-hour from 5.27 to 7.27 am, and in the afternoon they make the return trip eastbound leaving about every half-hour from 3.50 to 6.20 pm. The trip from Mission to Waterfront Station takes about 85 minutes. The trains are wheelchair accessible and bicycles can also be taken on board free of charge. There are some special weekend services as well; call ☎ 604-689-3641 to find out when these services are in effect. The West Coast Express tickets and passes provide free transfers to all other BC Transit services. Call ☎ 604-683-7245 or 488-8906 for information.

CAR & MOTORCYCLE

See the Car & Motorcycle section in the Getting There & Away chapter for general information about road rules, documents etc.

If you are driving, you will notice the city doesn't have any expressways; everyone must travel through the city or around it. Congestion is a big problem, especially along the Lions Gate Bridge (probably best avoided at rush hour) and the Second Narrows Bridge. Very few downtown streets have left-hand turn signals, and traffic can backup for blocks during peak traffic hours, particularly with traffic trying to get onto West Georgia St from the south. Keep in mind that most of the north-south streets in the city center are alternate one-way streets, Burrard St being the exception. The city map at the back of this book has arrows on the streets indicating in which one-way direction they run.

Parking

As in most cities, meter parking on downtown streets is difficult to find, and at best is limited to short durations, costing around $2 an hour. Your best bet is to park in a city lot or multi-story parking garage where the hourly rate is about $2.50 an hour or around $10 a day. Most of the main parking garages, both attended and metered, accept credit cards as well as cash. The main parkades are at Pacific Centre (entrance on Howe and Dunsmuir Sts), Robson Square (entrance on Smithe and Howe Sts), The Bay department store (entrance on Richards St near Dunsmuir St), Seymour St (just across Pender St) and in the West End on Denman St (near Barclay St). Many of the larger downtown hotels provide parking to guests but some don't, so ask about it when you make a reservation.

In some areas of the city, such as the West End, street parking is reserved for residents with parking permits; without one, your car will be ticketed and even towed away. Keep in mind that on most major streets parking is not permitted at all during peak traffic times, generally 7 to 9.30 am and 3.30 to 6.30 pm, but check the parking meters and street signs for exact times. You will definitely be ticketed and towed if your car is parked on one of these streets during these times. Parking in commercial alleys is illegal. Throughout Stanley Park pay parking (in the lots and on the streets) is in effect, and ticket machines are easy to find.

If your car has been towed there is one of two companies responsible for the dirty deed. If you have been towed from the street, Unitow (☎ 604-688-5484) will have your car at 1410 Granville St, beneath the bridge on Pacific St, and the charge will be around $25. If you have been towed from a private lot, Busters (☎ 604-685-8181) will have your car at 104 East 1st St, near Quebec St, and the charge will be around $70. Both lots are open 24 hours and they accept credit cards as well as cash.

When all is said and done, it's probably best to take public transport if you are going into the city for the day. Not only will you save some money but you'll be doing your nervous system a favor as well.

Car Rental

There are many car rental companies in Vancouver; the larger ones have several offices around town and some also have offices at the international airport. Some have discount coupons which are available at various stores, hotels and Travel Info-Centres.

Generally the daily rate starts at around $32 a day for a small car like a Toyota Tercel, but if you rent by the weekend, week or the month, it'll cost less. Weekend rates are often the cheapest and can include three or even four days, so building a schedule around this can save money. For example, if you pick up a car Friday morning and return it Monday evening, it may be billed as just three days.

Beware that prices can be deceptive. The daily rate may be an enticing $29 but by the time you finish with insurance, gasoline (you should fill it up before taking it back or you'll pay their prices plus a fee for doing it), the number of kilometers, provincial sales tax and GST, and any other bits and pieces, you can be handed a pretty surprising bill.

Rental agencies will also try to sell you options on personal insurance coverage at about $15 a day. You don't need this if your travel insurance, or vehicle insurance at home, includes coverage for this type of liability. Ask about this when you take out your travel insurance, or call up your vehicle insurer before leaving home: the rental company will need to see proof that you are in fact covered. Also, some credit cards, such as Visa Gold, MasterCard Gold or American Express, cover collision insurance if you rent for 15 days or less and charge the full cost of rental to your card.

To rent a car you must be at least 21 years of age and in some cases 25. Depending on your age you might be asked to buy additional insurance. You must have a valid driver's license and present a major credit card.

Check the Yellow Pages for a complete listing of car rental companies. Following is a

small selection with their downtown addresses and an example of their starting daily rates:

Budget
  (☎ 604-668-7000) 450 West Georgia St ($33)
Enterprise
  (☎ 604-872-1600) 415 East 5th Ave ($30, but say they will beat any other price in town by at least 10%)
Hertz
  (☎ 604-688-2411) 1128 Seymour St ($36)
Lo-Cost
  (☎ 604-689-9664, 800-886-1266) 1105 Granville St ($30)
National Tilden
  (☎ 604-685-6111, 800-387-4747) 1130 West Georgia St ($33)
Rent-A-Wreck
  (☎ 604-688-0001, 800-327-0116) Sheraton Wall Center, 1083 Hornby St ($23)
Thrifty
  (☎ 604-688-2207) Landmark Hotel, 1400 Robson St ($28)

Recreational Vehicle Rental

Renting recreational vehicles (RVs) or camper vans, or various trailers (caravans) is another option. These should be booked early in the year as they are very popular, especially with European visitors. The summer season is the most expensive with mid- to large-size vehicles costing around $200 a day. These are good for five to seven people and include six appliances. Make sure to ask for a diesel engine as this will save considerably on running costs. Cheaper camper vans are also available but these should be booked even earlier. Two companies to try are: Canada Camper RV Rentals (☎ 604-327-3003), 1080 Millcarch St, Richmond; and Go West Campers International (☎ 604-987-5288), 1577 Lloyd St, North Vancouver. Some of the car rental companies, such as Lo-Cost, also rent RVs.

Motorcycle Rental

A number of companies in Vancouver rent motorcycles. Although not a cheap form of rental transportation (a Honda Gold Wing will set you back about $145 a day or $725 a week), if you do get the urge to test out the highway to Squamish on two wheels, then at least you have that option. Look in the Yellow Pages under 'Motorcycle Renting' or contact Alley Cat Rentals (☎ 604-684-5117), 1779 Robson St, and Cruise Canada Motorcycle Rentals (☎ 604-946-5775), at 7731 Vantage Way, Delta.

TAXI

Taxi drivers in Vancouver are generally reliable and will get you to where you want to go without taking you for a ride. Taxis can be hailed on the streets, and they are available if the sign on the roof is illuminated. There are also taxi stands around the city. The meter starts at $2.10 and runs at $1.20 for each km. Four of the companies are Black Top & Checker Cabs (☎ 604-731-1111), MacLure's (☎ 604-731-9211, 683-6666), Vancouver Taxi (☎ 604-871-1111) and Yellow Cab (☎ 604-681-1111). They all offer much the same service, although Vancouver Taxi has about 30 wheelchair-accessible taxis that can also be used by travelers who have a lot of luggage. Taxi companies also offer special rates for city tours (see the Organized Tours section at the end of this chapter for details).

BOAT
Mini Passenger Ferries at False Creek

Two companies operate mini-ferry shuttles around False Creek. False Creek Ferries (☎ 604-684-7781) runs from the Aquatic Centre on Sunset Beach Bay at the foot of Thurlow St, to Granville Island (every five minutes) and to Vanier Park on Kitsilano Point (every 15 minutes). From Granville Island it makes the trip to Stamps Landing near the Cambie St Bridge (every 30 minutes), to Science World (every hour) and to the Plaza of Nations (every hour). In summer the daily service between the Aquatic Centre and Granville Island is from 7 am to 10 pm, and until 8 pm in winter. The other routes have varying times and schedules depending on the season. The basic fare from the Aquatic Centre to Granville Island, or to Vanier Park, is $1.75/$1 adults/seniors & children, while the trip from Granville Island to Science World is $4/3/2 adults/seniors/children.

The privately run Aquabus (☎ 604-689-5858) travels between the foot of Hornby St to the Arts Club Theatre on Granville Island. From Granville Island it goes to Stamps Landing, to the Concord Pacific Presentation Centre/Yaletown dock and to Science World. Fares and times are similar to the False Creek Ferries.

BICYCLE

Cycling is a good way to get around town, though be aware that riding on the sidewalk is illegal and bicycle helmets are mandatory. There are several designated bicycle routes throughout the city which make up the Vancouver Bicycle Network, plus a few bike paths downtown. One of the city's most popular bicycle routes is the 9km Seawall around Stanley Park.

The *Cycling in Vancouver* map is available at libraries, community centers and bicycle stores, or by contacting the Bicycle Hotline at ☎ 604-871-6070. For more information about cycling in the city, visit the city's website (www.city.vancouver.bc.ca).

Bicycles can be taken on the SeaBus and the West Coast Express, but not on the SkyTrain. Three buses are equipped with bicycle racks but can only carry two adult bicycles: these are bus No 404 (airport/Ladner exchange), No 351 (Crescent Beach/Vancouver) and No 601 (South Delta/Vancouver).

You are not allowed to ride a bicycle through the George Massey Tunnel under the Fraser River on Hwy 99 south of the city. However, from May to September a shuttle

DOUG PLUMMER

service is available at designated times. Call ☎ 604-271-0337 for information.

Aquabus (☎ 604-689-5858) will transport bicycles from one of its five docks along False Creek. It even has a 'cyquabus' ferry specifically designed to carry 12 bicycles and cyclists. See the Ferry section earlier in this chapter for details. Also see the Activities section in the Things to See & Do chapter for information regarding suggested bicycle routes.

Rental

There are a number of places to rent bicycles around the city, with many rental shops around Robson and Denman Sts (and there is no prize for guessing that the reason is the proximity to Stanley Park). Some shops also rent in-line skates.

Generally the cost, which includes a helmet (or other assorted protective gear if you are renting in-line skates), is around $4.50 an hour, $13 for a half day (four hours), and $16 for a full day. During the summer the shops are open daily from 9 am to 9 pm, with more restricted hours the rest of the year. Following is a list of outlets near Stanley Park; however, there are others so check the Yellow Pages under 'Bicycle Rental':

Action Rentals
  (Map 2; ☎ 604-683-7044) 1793 Robson St
Alley Cat Bike Rentals
  (Map 2; ☎ 604-684-5117) 1779 Robson St
Spokes Bicycle Rental & Espresso Bar
  (Map 2; ☎ 604-688-5141) 1798 West Georgia St
Stanley Park Cycle
  (Map 2; ☎ 604-608-1908) 1741 Robson St

WALKING

Vancouver is a very walkable city, and on a sunny day there aren't many places in the world that compare with the views around the harbor area. The city center is compact enough that walking around it is very easy and, in fact, there really isn't any other way you'd want to experience it. If it does start raining, buses are never too far away or you can duck into one of the indoor shopping malls, such as the Pacific Centre, the Royal Centre or the Sinclair Centre.

Away from the center of the city there are plenty of walking possibilities. Granville Island is made for walking around, as is False Creek which, if the mood strikes, you can follow all the way around to the Science Centre at the far end. If you still have energy to burn, continue around False Creek to the Plaza of Nations and then on to the foot of Hornby St, across from Granville Island, where you can walk back to the center of the city. If you get tired along the way, you can always catch one of the False Creek mini-ferries.

Vancouver is blessed with an abundance of parks and the sparkling jewel in this crown is Stanley Park. The 9km Seawall around Stanley Park may just be the best walk, run, or bicycle ride in not only Vancouver, but in just about any city you'd care to mention. But don't think the Seawall is the only place in the park to stretch the legs because inside the 408-hectare reserve there are numerous safe walking trails that wind their way through thick forests. See the special Stanley Park color section later in this book.

In Kitsilano, below Cornwall Ave, Kitsilano Beach Park continues east to Hadden Park and then on to Vanier Park to make a great seaside walk with some fabulous views of English Bay and the city skyline, with the North Shore mountains acting as a backdrop. Going west from Kitsilano, starting a couple of blocks past Alma St off 4th Ave, you'll find Jericho Beach Park which becomes Locarno Beach, then Spanish Banks Beach, Point Grey Beach, Tower Beach and finally around Point Grey to Wreck Beach, where you have the option of taking your clothes off if you want to soak up a few rays (you might as well because no one else around you will be wearing anything).

Some other parks close to the city that are worth keeping in mind for a leisurely stroll, or an all-out power walk, are Pacific Spirit Regional Park beside UBC, Queen Elizabeth Park off Cambie St, Capilano River Regional Park off Capilano Rd in North Vancouver, and Ambleside Park and Lighthouse Park which are both off Marine

Drive in West Vancouver. Are you feeling tired yet?

See the Organized Tours section later in this chapter for information about walking tours. Also, see the Things to See & Do chapter for suggested walking tours of Downtown Vancouver.

ORGANIZED TOURS

If your time in Vancouver is limited, or you simply like to sit back and let someone else do the driving, or you are after an experience that is a bit out of the ordinary, you'll find the wide variety of organized tours appealing. You can do city tours by bus, trolley, taxi, boat, helicopter, seaplane, bicycle or on foot. You can take a dinner cruise in the harbor, take a horse-drawn carriage through Stanley Park or learn about BC's Native Indian culture. If you want to leave the city for the day, you can take a steam train to Squamish, or have dinner on a train that goes as far as Porteau Cove, about halfway between Horseshoe Bay and Squamish. Following is a list of just some of the tours available.

Bus Tours

Gray Line (☎ 604-879-3363) offers a few different city tours on big buses. The tours begin at the Hotel Vancouver, but a pick-up and drop-off service from/to the place you're staying or the cruise-ship terminals is included in the ticket price, and all major hotels sell tickets. The Deluxe Grand City Tour is a 3½-hour tour of the best the city has to offer for about $40/38/29 for adults/seniors/children. There are daily departures at 9.15 am and 2 pm, and the tour is offered in five languages – Cantonese, French, German, Japanese and Spanish. Another tour is Vancouver by Night which lasts two hours and departs daily at 7.15 pm from the beginning of May to the end of October; it costs $25/23/13. The double-decker bus tour allows you to see the city in your own time as you can hop on and off at any of 20 stops from 8.30 am to 6.30 pm over two days. The cost is $22/21/11.

Town Tours (☎ 604-451-1777) offers tours in smaller minibuses. The 3½-hour City

Highlights tour departs twice daily at 9 am and 2 pm from June to October, and costs $25/23/16 for adults/seniors & students/children. Pickup and drop-off anywhere in Vancouver is included. Private tours in a foreign language are also available.

Vancouver Trolley Company (☎ 604-451-5581) operates red replicas (on wheels) of the famous San Francisco trolleys. You can get on or off the trolley at 15 different attractions throughout the day from 9 am to 6 pm. The entire circuit takes two hours and the trolleys depart every half-hour. The cost of this tour is very reasonable at $18/10 for adults/children (four to 12 years); children under four ride for free. You can simply pay the driver.

West Coast City & Nature Sightseeing (☎ 604-451-1600) has among its tours a couple of interesting options. One is the daily five-hour City & North Shore Combination tour which spends two hours in the city and three hours in North Vancouver. This can be done separately or as a combined package. The combination tour, which departs at 10 am, costs $44/42/27 for adults/seniors & students/children. The other option is the Native Culture Tour which is a good introduction to the culture, lifestyle and philosophy of the West Coast Native Indians. The four-hour tour takes in the totem poles at Stanley Park, and the Museum of Anthropology and the replica of a Haida village at UBC. The daily tours leave at 8.30 am and cost $41/39/25. As well, city tours are available in English, German and Mandarin.

Boat & Train Tours

Harbour Cruises (☎ 604-688-7246), at the north foot of Denman St in Coal Harbour by Stanley Park, offers a variety of boat tours, some in conjunction with other tour operators. The MPV *Constitution*, Vancouver's only authentic paddlewheeler, operates 70-minute tours around the harbor daily at 11.30 am, 1 and 2.30 pm for $16. The paddlewheeler is also used for the three-hour Sunset Dinner Cruise which leaves daily at 7 pm and costs $50 (or $55 if you book it through Gray Line which includes hotel pickup). Both these tours run from the beginning of May to the end of October.

For sports fans the Canuck Grizzly Dinner Cruise, which operates during the hockey and basketball seasons (November to mid-April), is an interesting option that includes a two-hour cruise from Coal Harbour to the Plaza of Nations at False Creek (during which time you have either an appetizer or a buffet-style dinner), a ticket to the game and post-game transfer back to Coal Harbour. The price depends on which sport you are going to see and whether you have appetizers or the full meal. The Grizzlies/appetizer option is $56, while dinner is $79; the Canucks/appetizer option is $79, while dinner is $99. GM Place seat upgrades are available at additional cost, and hotel packages are also available. Call ☎ 604-899-4263 or 800-663-1500 for information.

The *Royal Hudson* steam train, one of the last operating steam trains in Canada, runs between the BC Rail Station in North Vancouver and Squamish, at the head of Howe Sound. The train operates Wednesday to Sunday (and public holidays) from the end of May to mid-September, leaving North Vancouver at 10 am and returning at 4 pm, with a two-hour stop in Squamish. Another option is to take the MV *Britannia*, operated by Harbour Cruises, one way to Squamish and the *Royal Hudson* the other way. The MV *Britannia* departs from Harbour Cruises at 9.30 am and returns at 4.30 pm. A shuttle service between the BC Rail Station and Coal Harbour is provided. The train costs roundtrip $47/41/13 adults/seniors (60) & youth (12 to 18)/children (five to 11; children under five free); the train/boat combination costs $78/66/22. Another option is to travel Parlour Class both ways on the train for a flat rate of $85, regardless of age. You will be served lunch on the way up and afternoon tea on the return trip. Call ☎ 604-984-5246 for information. Gray Line also offers the train/boat combination as one of its tour packages.

The *Pacific Starlight* Dinner Train is another tour offered by BC Rail from the beginning of May to the end of October, plus

Royal Hudson **Steam Train**

on special occasions such as New Year's Eve and Valentine's Day. The train has nine vintage cars, including three dome cars and six salon cars, which have been refurbished in art deco style. Each car is named after a famous big-band tune or jazz locale. The train leaves the BC Rail Station in North Vancouver at 6.15 pm and travels along the scenic route to Porteau Cove, on Howe Sound not far from Squamish, with dinner served on the way. After a 45-minute stop at Porteau Cove the train returns to North Vancouver, arriving at 10 pm. The rates are $71 for salon seating and $86 for dome seating. Call ☎ 604-984-5246 for information.

False Creek Ferries (☎ 604-684-7781) offer scenic harbor tours during the summer in one of its small passenger ferries. The tours depart from the Granville Island dock next to Bridges restaurant from 10 am to 5.30 pm. The half-hour tour is $6/4/3 for adults/seniors/children and the one-hour tour is $8/6/4.

Starline Tours (☎ 604-272-9187) offers a unique boat tour from Steveston but you'll have to be in Vancouver at the right time of year to enjoy. From late March to mid-May as many as 700 sea lions from Alaska and California take up residence on the 8km Steveston jetty to gorge themselves on Fraser River fish. The trip to see them takes 1½ hours and costs $20/17/10 adults/seniors & students/children. Call for departure times. It also offers other interesting tours such as a trip to Harrison (east of the city) via the Fraser River with lunch at the Harrison Hotel, and a six-hour trip to Pitt Lake (northeast of the city), the world's largest freshwater tidal lake, to see pictographs.

Air Tours

Harbour Air (☎ 604-688-1277) offers seaplane tours such as the 20-minute Panorama Tour of the city, for $72 a person, or 2½-hour wilderness excursions to secluded mountain lakes and quiet fjords which start at around $210 a person. It also has a Fly 'n' Dine tour to Bowen Island that involves a seaplane ride one-way and a ferry and limousine ride the other (your choice), with dinner at Snug Cove, all for $130 a person. Full-day tours to the Sunshine Coast, Whistler and Victoria are also available. The terminal is about three blocks west of Canada Place off Waterfront Road West.

Vancouver Helicopters (☎ 604-270-1484, 800-987-4354) has a number of tours that, although not cheap, are guaranteed to be spectacular. The Burrard Explorer, essentially a city tour from above, lasts about 10 minutes and costs $55 a person, minimum three people, while the North Shore Discoverer flies over Vancouver and the North Shore mountains for $195 a person. It also offers tours from the heliport on top of Grouse Mountain. The harbor heliport is just east of Waterfront Station.

Walking Tours

Walkabout Historic Vancouver Tours (☎ 604-808-1650) is a great way to get some exercise while learning something about the city's past. The 1½-hour tours leave from the northwest corner of Howe and West Georgia Sts daily throughout the summer at 9 am, noon, 3 and 6 pm. The cost is $10/$8 for adults/seniors & students.

World in a City Tours (☎ 604-738-9223) specializes in cultural and historical walking tours of Vancouver's ethnic communities, plus it offers a general Vancouver tour. The China in Vancouver tour takes about five hours and costs $75; the India in Vancouver tour takes about four hours and costs $70; and the Vancouverite for a Day tour takes eight hours and costs $115. All the tours include lunch and must be booked at least 48 hours in advance. The tours meet at the Tourist InfoCentre, 200 Burrard St.

Other Tours

Stanley Park Horse-Drawn Tours (☎ 604-681-5115) is a leisurely and informative way to see the park. The daily one-hour narrated tours in a 20-passenger carriage depart about every 20 to 30 minutes from beside the information booth on Park Drive, east of the rowing club. The cost is $12/9.50/7.25 adults/seniors & students/children (three to 12 years), and children younger than three ride for free as long as they are not occupying a needed seat.

Taxi tours of the city are offered by Black Top & Checker Cabs (☎ 604-731-1111) and Yellow Cab (☎ 604-681-1111). These tours do not have fixed prices and are simply an approximation of what the meter will clock up over a set route. The tours they offer are similar, with the basic 1½-hour city tour, including Stanley Park, costing around $60. Taxis take up to five passengers, so this could be an economical way to get a taste of the city.

Lotus Land Tours (☎ 604-684-4922) will take you on a wilderness experience not that far from the city. The four-hour tour to North Vancouver, which is described as being for the 'inexperienced and the unfit,' includes a guided kayaking trip in Indian Arm off Deep Cove, a barbecued salmon lunch on Twin Island, and a chance to explore the forest and beach for $120. You will be picked up and dropped off at your hotel or residence. It also offers guided cycling and hiking trips.

Things to See & Do

You would have to be here a long time (some would argue a lifetime) before you tire of what Greater Vancouver has to offer. Whether it be galleries, museums, historic sites, parks or the many sports and outdoor activities that are found here, there is something of interest for everyone. Also keep in mind that some of the areas that are a part of the region of Greater Vancouver, but are not included in this book, are also worth searching out and exploring (see the Orientation section in the Facts for the Visitor chapter for a description of the areas that make up Greater Vancouver).

Included here are just some of the neighborhoods that make up the City of Vancouver which, for the purposes of this book, is divided into Downtown Vancouver (City Center & Yaletown, Gastown, Chinatown

and the West End) and the West Side (Granville Island, Kitsilano and the University of British Columbia). Other neighborhoods that make up Vancouver, plus some of the bordering cities, include East Vancouver (Commercial Drive and the Punjabi Market, Burnaby and New Westminster), the North Shore (North and West Vancouver) and Richmond (including Steveston).

Each of these areas has its own character and history and, for the visitor, offers something of interest. But if what is here does fail to impress, what you definitely won't tire of in a hurry (at least on the clear days) are the stunning views that present themselves from one side of the city to the other.

Downtown Vancouver

Downtown Vancouver – bordered on two sides by water and on a third by enormous Stanley Park – consists of the City Center, including Yaletown, the waterfront along Burrard Inlet as far as about Main St, Gastown, Chinatown, the north side of False Creek, the West End and Stanley Park. This constriction of water and parkland has forced the city upward and, while none of the business towers are startlingly high, the cumulative effect of so many high-rise buildings gives Vancouver its modern appearance.

Another anomaly of Downtown Vancouver is that the vast majority of the high-rises in the West End, the area bordered by Stanley Park and English Bay, are residential towers erected in the 1950s. A *lot* of people live right downtown, and this has kept small markets and other neighborhood facilities in operation. Day or night, Downtown Vancouver has a real lived-in quality unusual in a North American city of this size.

CITY CENTER & YALETOWN (Map 2)

Generally, the City Center (or Central Business District as it's sometimes called) is the area that is bordered to the west by Burrard St, to the north by Burrard Inlet, to the south by False Creek, and to the east by Gastown and Chinatown. The City Center radiates from West Georgia and Granville Sts where the business, financial and shopping areas meld into one.

Vancouver is a very walkable city and, in fact, walking is really the only way to discover its hidden treasures and scenic delights. This section begins with a suggested walking tour followed by detailed descriptions of some of the main sites. The corner of West Georgia and Granville Sts is an ideal location to begin this walking tour.

Walking Tour

This tour takes in most of the interesting sites in the City Center and will require anywhere from four hours to an entire day, depending on how fast you feel like walking and how many stops you want to make along the way. However, this tour can be done in stages, or joined or left at any point; public transit is always close at hand, whether it's a bus or the SkyTrain. To get to the starting point at West Georgia and Granville Sts take either the SkyTrain to the Granville Station or one of the many buses that travel from various parts of the city to and along Granville St (bus Nos 4, 5, 6, 7, 8, 10, 16, 50).

At the corner of West Georgia and Granville Sts you'll find Canada's two major department stores sitting kitty-corner from each other. Eaton's and The Bay, which was built in 1913 (although it has had a store on this site since 1888) and is a designated heritage building, are above the Pacific and Vancouver Centres, two underground shopping malls.

Start the tour on the south side of West Georgia St and walk one block west to the **Vancouver Art Gallery**, originally the Vancouver Provincial Courthouse. It was designed in the early 1900s by Francis Rattenbury, who also designed Victoria's Parlia-

ment Buildings and Empress Hotel. The 1910 granite lions were modeled after those in London's Trafalgar Square, and the Centennial Fountain, which pumps around 1.3 million liters of water an hour, was built in 1966 to commemorate the union of the crown colonies of Vancouver Island and British Columbia in 1866.

Continuing west on West Georgia St, the **Hotel Vancouver** (completed in 1939) is a fine example of the chateau-style hotels built across the country by Canada's two railways. Although it was built by Canadian National Railway, it was jointly managed by it and Canadian Pacific Railway, and is now operated by CP Hotels & Resorts. Check out the fine relief work, Renaissance detail and the gargoyles, supposedly reproductions of 11th-century cathedral carvings.

Across West Georgia St on the northwest corner of Hornby St, **Cathedral Place** (completed in 1991) is worth taking a look at for its art deco-inspired features in the lobby, the sculpted nurses that were once a feature of the site's previous occupant, the Georgia Medical Dental Building, and the roof and gargoyles which complement Hotel Vancouver's. The **Canadian Craft Museum**, in the tranquil Cathedral Place Courtyard, is directly behind it on Hornby St.

Next to Cathedral Place on West Georgia St, in the lobby of the **Hongkong Bank**, is a wonderful piece of kinetic art called *Pendulum*. The 27m-long buffed aluminum sculpture, designed by Alan Storey, is hollow from top to bottom, weighs 1600kg and moves about 6m (the swing is assisted by a hydraulic mechanical system at its top). Also in the lobby is a granite sculpture, *Wings of Prey*, by George Schmerholz, plus an ever-changing art exhibit.

On the northeast corner of West Georgia and Burrard Sts, **Christ Church Cathedral** (completed in 1895) is the city's oldest surviving church and was declared a heritage building in 1974. The Gothic-inspired sandstone structure was originally an Anglican parish church (for what was then a residential neighborhood) and became a cathedral in 1929. If open, it's worth going inside to

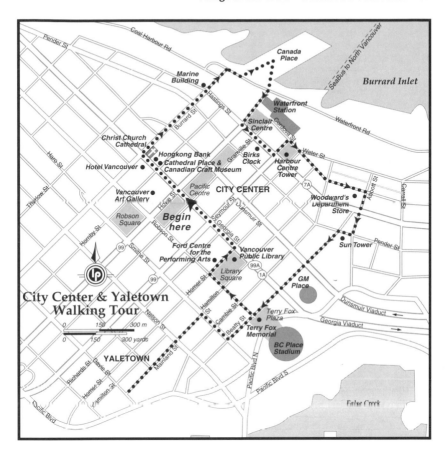

City Center & Yaletown Walking Tour

take a look at the timber framework and stained-glass windows.

Cross Burrard St, turn right passing the entrance to the Royal Centre, another underground shopping mall, and continue north on Burrard St for three blocks, past the Hyatt Regency and the Bentall Centre, to the **Marine Building**, 355 Burrard St, at Hastings St. This spectacular example of art deco architecture was completed in 1930 and is a 22-story tribute to transportation and Vancouver's maritime history, which is depicted on relief panels near the base. Sea horses, waves and marine fauna are depicted on a frieze that wraps around the front of

the building, while a ship's prow sails forth over the Burrard St entrance. Step inside the ornate lobby to see the maritime theme continued with blue and green tiles, and an array of sea creatures on both the walls and the brass doors. For more than 10 years this was the tallest building in the British Empire.

Continue down Burrard St, going past the Waterfront Centre and the Travel InfoCentre at 200 Burrard St, and around the corner into **Canada Place** with its five white fabric sails. From here there are some great views of the harbor, Stanley Park to the west and across Burrard Inlet to North Vancouver.

The art deco-inspired Marine Building

Leaving Canada Place, walk south along Howe St and straight ahead on Cordova St is the rear entrance to the **Sinclair Centre** (which can also be accessed by way of a pedestrian overpass from Granville Square); the main entrance is at 757 West Hastings St. This upscale shopping center is actually a melding of four heritage buildings, the cornerstone being the city's previous main post office on the northwest corner of Granville and Hastings Sts (completed in 1910). The large clock in the tower underwent a renovation in 1985 when the mechanical works were replaced by an electronic mechanism. However, the restored winding mechanism and old bell can be seen in the center's atrium.

Vancouver's most famous timepiece, however, is the **Birks clock** across the street at the southeast corner of Hastings and Granville Sts. Built in 1905, Vancouver's first public clock has been at three locations along with its owner, jeweler Henry Birks & Sons. For more than 80 years this city icon was in front of the Birks store, across from The Bay, at the corner of West Georgia and Granville Sts, where generations of Vancouverites arranged to meet 'under the Birks clock.' Ironically, with the store's move in 1994, the clock has ended up across the street from its original location. The clock,

which has its original wooden movement, is hand-wound every Tuesday morning.

A block east at 555 West Hastings St, is the rather unattractive **Harbour Centre Tower** which, at 174m, is the tallest building in BC. The 360° views are everything you'd expect and just about worth the $8/7/5 adults/seniors/students it costs to be whisked up in the glass 'Skylift' elevators to 'The Lookout' at the top. Open daily in summer from 8.30 am to 10.30 pm, and in winter from 9 am to 9 pm. The tickets are valid all day.

There's also the Top of Vancouver Revolving Restaurant (☎ 604-669-2220) above 'The Lookout,' but there are better and cheaper places in the city to dine. However, if you do have lunch or dinner here, the ride up is free.

If you leave Harbour Centre Tower by way of the Cordova St doors, to your left you'll be looking across at **Waterfront Station**, the old Canadian Pacific Railway Station. Opened in 1915, this was the CPR's western terminus from where transcontinental passenger trains either ended or began their journeys. These days it acts as a transportation hub for SkyTrain, SeaBus and West Coast Express services. Inside this designated heritage building there are offices, cafes and retail shops.

At the front of the station, the bronze statue of the angel carrying a dead soldier upward, *Angel of Victory* by Couer de Lion MacCarthy, was commissioned by the CPR in 1922 to commemorate employees who had died in WWI, and later the dates of WWII were added. Exact copies of this statue are also in front of the CPR stations in Montreal and Winnipeg.

Follow Cordova St east, bypassing Gastown (see the Gastown section later in this chapter), and continue for three blocks to Abbott St. As you approach the corner of Cordova and Abbott Sts, the old **Woodward's Department Store** (first built in 1908 but with various additions over the years) is on your right. The company is now out of business but this heritage building is in the process of being developed. On the roof a large red 'W' rotates on top of a miniature

Eiffel Tower, and this one-time 'advertising gimmick,' which could be seen from just about anywhere in the city, is now a designated heritage sign.

Turn south (right) onto Abbott St and go up two blocks to Pender St. Cross Pender St and turn west (right) and you are in front of the **Sun Tower** at the corner of Beatty St. When it was built in 1912, this 17-story highrise was, for two years at least, the tallest building in the British Empire. It was built to house the *Vancouver World* newspaper and, in fact, was originally called the World Tower until it was bought out by the *Vancouver Sun* in 1937, which continued to publish from here until 1965. Take a look up toward the beaux arts copper dome and about half way up the building you'll see nine risqué maidens acting as caryatids, or columns.

As you continue south down Beatty St you'll bypass **GM Place**, a sports arena built in 1995 which is home to the Vancouver Canucks of the National Hockey League (NHL) and the Vancouver Grizzlies of the National Basketball Association (NBA); see Spectator Sports in the Entertainment chapter for details. Continue on to Terry Fox Plaza in front of **BC Place Stadium** (where inside you'll also find the **BC Sports Hall of Fame & Museum**). At the east end of Robson St, the **Terry Fox Memorial** – a postmodern-style arch made of steel, tile and brick, and topped by four fiberglass lions – is a tribute to Terry Fox whose run across Canada to raise money for cancer research was cut short by his own fight with the disease (see the boxed text later in this chapter).

At this point, if you feel up to it, you can take in Yaletown; if you want to shorten the tour then just skip down to the next paragraph. Continue south on Beatty St for about one block and at Smithe St turn west (right) and follow it for two blocks. This brings you to the top of Mainland St which runs three blocks south to Davie St. Mainland St, and the next two parallel streets going west – Hamilton and Homer Sts – make up the area known as **Yaletown** where you'll find lots of restaurants, bars and retail stores. From here head north up Homer St to the Vancouver Public Library.

If you choose not to take in Yaletown then head west up Robson St about three blocks to Homer St and turn north (right) at the Roman-Colosseum-like **Vancouver Public Library**. Designed by Moshe Safdie and completed in 1995, this striking building has become a new landmark in the city. The main square is actually one block up at 350 West Georgia St. Inside the complex, which includes a 21-story office building as well as the seven-level library, you'll find cafes, shops and three levels of underground parking. For more information on the library see the Facts for the Visitor chapter.

Across Homer St, and also designed by Safdie, the **Ford Centre for the Performing Arts** is an 1800-seat venue designed to stage large-scale productions, mostly of the lavish Broadway-musical variety. The theater, which opened in 1995 with *Show Boat*, has a magnificent foyer complete with a glass cone and mirrored staircase, while the stage is surrounded on three sides by three levels of seating.

At West Georgia St turn west (left) and walk three blocks to Granville St – you'll find yourself back where you started.

Vancouver Art Gallery

The Vancouver Art Gallery (☎ 604-662-4719), 750 Hornby St, is right at the center of things between Robson Square and West Georgia St. In the 1970s, noted architect Arthur Erickson designed Robson Square and at the same time turned what had been a courthouse into a world-class art gallery. The gallery presents both contemporary and historical exhibitions of painting, sculpture, graphic arts, photography and video by distinguished regional, national and international artists.

The gallery's collection includes works by Canadian artists, paintings by 17th- and 18th-century Dutch artists and works by British artists from the mid-20th century. The centerpiece, however, is the paintings and drawings of renowned BC artist Emily Carr. This is the largest permanent collection

The Life and Work of Emily Carr

Emily Carr was born in Victoria in 1871 to prosperous parents. Her parents died when she was young and by the age of 16 she was waging war with the family to be permitted to attend art school in San Francisco, California. However, her dedication to painting was deemed 'unladylike,' and she was forced to make a living from teaching.

It wasn't until 1899, when she accompanied a churchman to his mission at Ucluelet on the west coast of Vancouver Island, that her career as an artist took a pivotal turn. The life and arts of the Native Indian village had a profound effect on Carr and, inspired by what she saw, she began using both the landscape and Native Indians as her subject matter. She soon realized, however, that she needed to learn technique, so she went to London to study landscape painting.

In 1906, after traveling to Europe, Toronto and the Cariboo region of BC, Carr moved to Vancouver where she taught art classes and rented a studio at 570 Granville St. However, she felt that the power of nature she so desperately wanted to capture on canvas was still missing from her work. Therefore, in 1910, at the age of 39, she went to Paris to absorb some of the more modern painting techniques and styles. It was during this time that Carr developed her unique style that combined the use of dark colors, strong brush strokes and the subject matter of the province's West Coast forests and Native culture.

Returning to Vancouver in 1912, Carr rented a studio at 1465 West Broadway to exhibit her French paintings; she had another exhibit of 200 paintings at a hall she rented in 1913. Her work, however, wasn't taken seriously. Some of her paintings were even found to be offensive, resulting in the removal of students from her art classes. A social outcast at 42, and with no means of support, she returned to Victoria to live on family property and to work as a landlady to make ends meet.

It wasn't until the late 1920s that her scorned 1912 paintings were shown in eastern Canada and in a sense discovered. She then met the members of the increasingly well-known and influential school of painters called the Group of Seven, and with renewed energy and confidence Carr continued her development as an artist. Over the next 10 years she revisited many of her cherished Indian locales and painted some of her best-known works.

As her health failed and she became bedridden, she took to writing. Her book *Klee Wyck*, meaning 'laughing one,' the name given to her by the Kwakiutl people, is a collection of stories recalling her life among the Native Indians. *The Book of Small* chronicles her childhood in Victoria and *The House of All Sorts* describes her years as a landlady.

Her house in Victoria, the Carr House, is open to the public, and her paintings can be viewed at the Vancouver Art Gallery and the Art Gallery of Greater Victoria, as well as at all of the major galleries across the country.

Carr produced a rich body of work unlike that of any other Canadian artist and is regarded as Canada's first major female artist.

of her work in Canada (see the boxed text). In recent years the gallery has concentrated its acquisitions on the works of BC artists and on contemporary international art.

The gallery has four floors with the changing exhibits on the 1st, 2nd and 4th floors, while the 3rd floor is reserved for Emily Carr and other BC artists. The gallery hosts various traveling shows which usually include one major international exhibit. For those interested in doing research, the gallery also maintains a 25,000-volume reference library and a slide library (☎ 604-662-4709), which is open Sunday to Friday, except Tuesday, from 1 to 5 pm.

The Gallery Shop has especially good gifts and local crafts. The Gallery Cafe, which overlooks the Sculpture Garden, is a great place for coffee and a snack.

During summer the gallery is open Monday to Friday from 10 am to 6 pm, and Thursday to 9 pm; Saturday from 10 am to 5 pm, and Sunday from noon to 5 pm. From mid-October to Easter weekend the gallery is closed Monday and Tuesday. Admission is $7.50/5/3.50 adults/seniors/students, and free for children under 12. Admission is by donation on Thursday from 5 to 9 pm.

To get to the gallery, either take the Sky-Train to Granville Station and walk two blocks west along West Georgia St to Hornby St or take bus No 5 west on Robson St.

Canadian Craft Museum

This pleasant museum (☎ 604-687-8266), 639 Hornby St, in the Cathedral Place Courtyard, is dedicated to the role of craft, both historical and contemporary, in human culture. Dominating the permanent collection are works from Canada; touring shows and special collections frequently have a more international focus. Once you have seen an exhibit here you'll probably be left wondering what the defining line is between 'craft' and 'art.'

The museum, founded in 1980, was originally on Granville Island. In 1988 the City of Vancouver, recognizing its importance, granted it a 99-year lease on its current location. The museum presents crafts in glass, wood, clay, metal and fiber, and each year

shows about six major exhibits in the Main Gallery and six smaller ones in the Mezzanine Gallery.

As you might expect, the gift shop here is wonderful, and a great place to find a truly unique handmade gift. The museum is open Monday to Saturday from 10 am to 5 pm (Thursday till 9 pm), and Sunday and holidays from noon to 5 pm. Admission is $4/2 adults/seniors & students, and free for children under 12. Closed Tuesday from September to May.

To get to the museum, take the SkyTrain to Burrard Station and walk one block east on Dunsmuir St, then about half a block south up Hornby St.

Canada Place

Canada Place, built to coincide with Expo 86 when it was used to house the government of Canada's pavilion, juts into the harbor at the foot of Howe St. The building's stridently modern design invites comparisons. Does it resemble an ocean liner with tent-like sails, the white exoskeleton of a very large and spiny insect, or just the Sydney Opera House? In any case, Canada Place has become a major city landmark. It's home to the World Trade Centre, the Vancouver Trade & Convention Centre, a cruise-ship terminal, The Prow Restaurant, the Pan Pacific Hotel, retail shops, a food court and the CN IMAX Theatre. To get here take either the SkyTrain or the SeaBus to Waterfront Station, which is just east of Canada Place.

CN IMAX Theatre This theater (☎ 604-682-4629, 800-582-4629), at the north end of Canada Place, has a five-story-high screen and wraparound IMAX Digital Sound – all in all it's a pretty exhilarating experience. The 35- to 45-minute films are on themes such as wildlife, natural wonders, space travel or popular destinations, all of which usually involve on-the-edge-of-your-seat action. Films, some of which are 3-D, are specially made for these theaters.

Show times change depending on what is being shown and on what day, but generally there are shows throughout the day starting at noon and going to about 9 pm. Admission for a single show in the afternoon is $8/7/6 for adults/seniors/children (four to 12), and for a double show in the evening is $11.50/10.50/9.50.

BC Place Stadium

Opened in 1983, BC Place Stadium (☎ 604-669-2300 for general information, 661-7373 for events), 777 Pacific Blvd South, is covered by a translucent dome-shaped roof. The roof is 'air-supported,' which means it is inflated by huge fans (no, not sports fans) and kept in place by crisscrossed steel wires, hence its quilted appearance. Concerts, trade shows, sports events and other large-scale gatherings are held during the year in this stadium, which can hold up to 60,000 people. It is also the home field of the BC Lions football team, part of the Canadian Football League (CFL); see the Spectator Sports section in the Entertainment chapter for details.

To get to the stadium, either take the Sky-Train to Stadium Station, or take bus Nos 2, 5 and 17, which all travel along Beatty St.

BC Sports Hall of Fame & Museum This

small museum (☎ 604-687-5520), Gate A at BC Place Stadium, is a showcase for BC athletes who have achieved success in their chosen fields of endeavor, both amateur and professional. It's a fun place for children to learn about sports through interactive displays, and equally enjoyable for sports fans of all ages to relive some of those great moments in sports.

There are a number of rooms, or galleries, showing different aspects of sports in BC. The History Gallery takes you through sports in BC from the time before Europeans arrived to the present. The Discovery Gallery shows what it takes to make a champion athlete, while the Hall of Champions tells the stories of BC's top athletes. In the Participation Gallery you can try your hand at a few athletic endeavors such as seeing how fast you can get a baseball to travel, how fast you can run along a 14m track or what it's like to climb a rock wall. You can even have a game of

ice hockey, even if it is just the miniature version.

The galleries dedicated to BC athletes Terry Fox, who ran his 'Marathon of Hope' across Canada to collect money for cancer research (see boxed text), and Rick Hanson are the center points of the museum. Hanson, who became a paraplegic at the age of 15 due to a motor vehicle accident, embarked in 1985 on what he called his 'Man-in-Motion' wheelchair journey around the world to create awareness of the potential of people with disabilities. Along the way he raised millions of dollars for research into spinal-cord injury. Hanson, who was a friend of Fox's and was inspired by his show of courage and determination, was a top wheelchair athlete winning 19 international wheelchair marathons, including three world championships.

If you are interested in purchasing sports memorabilia, you'll like the shop, but keep in mind that this stuff doesn't come cheap.

Open daily from 10 am to 5 pm. Admission is $6 for adults and $4 for everyone else, and children under five are free. A family ticket (up to four people) is $15; each additional member is $3.50.

Yaletown

This converted warehouse-and-loft district, between Mainland and Homer Sts and Davie and Smithe Sts, is still trying to define itself. Despite all the retail stores that have moved into the area it's still zoned as a commercial district. Large industrial garbage containers sit on the streets, there is little in the way of proper street lighting (making it rather unappealing at night, especially when it's wet and gloomy) and parking is next to nonexistent.

However, this is currently the trendy part of town so there are plenty of restaurants, bars, clubs and shops, including more designer-furniture stores than you have probably ever seen gathered together in one area. A lot of offices have moved into the converted warehouses, so a few professionals like lawyers and chartered accountants wander around as well. If you have lots of money to dispose of, or simply enjoy

Terry Fox & the Marathon of Hope

People like Terry Fox don't come along all that often, and when they do their efforts often go unrecognized. However, Canadians were quick to applaud the contribution this Port Coquitlam resident made to raise money for cancer research. A young man who possessed the wonderful combination of having a dream, extraordinary courage and the desire to help others, Terry became a national hero in 1980.

At the age of 18, while studying kinesiology at Simon Fraser University in 1977, Fox lost his right leg to cancer. Inspired by a magazine article he read while in the hospital about a one-legged runner named Dick Traum who competed in the New York Marathon, Fox decided that he would start training as soon as he was able. After his operation he began to run every day, building up strength and developing his own technique. In January 1979 he ran his first half kilometer, and by August he was running 19km a day.

After two years he was ready to run what he called the 'Marathon of Hope' across Canada. His goal was to raise $1 from every Canadian to go toward cancer research. With limited sponsorship, and little media coverage, Fox began his run on April 12, 1980, from St John's, Newfoundland. By the time he reached Ontario, he was a household name and donations were pouring in from around the country.

Fox averaged a remarkable 37km a day (he aimed to run 42km a day), most of it in pain, until after 144 days and 5376km a recurrence of cancer forced him to end his run 29km outside Thunder Bay, Ontario. The cancer had spread to Fox's lungs and he died on June 28, 1981, just one month before his 23rd birthday. His Marathon of Hope raised more than $24 million, surpassing his goal.

Fox's legacy lives on in the Terry Fox Run, an annual event held in September in towns and cities across the country, which continues to raise money for cancer research. Also, a park and mountain in BC carry his name (near Hwys 16 and 5 in the central eastern part of the province near the Alberta border), as does an icebreaker (the MV *Terry Fox*); an 83km stretch of highway in Ontario between Nipigon and Thunder Bay (the Terry Fox Courage Hwy); and a $5 million scholarship fund established by the Canadian government (The Terry Fox Humanitarian Award). Monuments have been erected in his honor in Vancouver, Port Coquitlam, Ottawa and Thunder Bay.

---

window-shopping, then Yaletown is a good place to spend an hour or two during the day, ideally around lunchtime or dinnertime so that you can finish off by having a meal.

In case you were wondering, the area took its name from the CPR workers who settled in the area at the turn of the century to be close to the railway yards that dominated False Creek. Many of them had worked at the CPR yards in Yale, about 180km northeast of Vancouver.

If you are interested in the history of the CPR you can do a quick detour from here down to the **Roundhouse Community Centre** at the eastern end of Davie St on Pacific Blvd. The 'roundhouse' was once used to service the railway's locomotives, and now houses engine No 374, which brought the first passenger train into the city in 1887.

To get close to Yaletown, take bus Nos 1, 2, 15, 17 or 20, all of which can be caught at various points around the city.

GASTOWN (Map 3)

This is the city's birthplace and Victorian-era business district that takes its name from John 'Gassy Jack' Deighton. Deighton was an English sailor who forsook the sea to become a publican, first in New Westminster to cash in on the miners traveling up to the Caribou gold rush in 1862, and then on the south shore of Burrard Inlet in 1867 to service the area's developing timber mills. The story goes that Deighton rowed into Burrard Inlet with his Native Indian wife, a yellow dog and a barrel of whiskey and told the workers at the Hastings Mill that if they helped him build a tavern drinks were on him. Within 24 hours the Globe Saloon was in business, and when a village sprang up around his establishment it was called Gastown.

After the center of Vancouver moved elsewhere, Gastown became a warehouse district and slowly declined in importance. The decline continued until the 1960s when people interested in Vancouver's heritage became alarmed by government plans to demolish the area in favor of a new development. Gastown property owners began to renovate their buildings, street vendors set up stalls, historic walking tours began, and in 1970, The Old Spaghetti Factory

opened, attracting people who were looking for somewhere different to dine. In 1971 the provincial government designated Gastown an historic site (it's one of two in the city, Chinatown being the other one) and the real restoration began, simply pushing Vancouver's seedier characters a little farther south to Hastings St.

The old Victorian buildings now house restaurants, bars, boutiques and galleries (most of which sell expensive Native Indian art) and some of the city's best nightlife happens here. The brick streets have been lined with old lamps and trees, and street vendors and buskers add to the holiday feel of the area. The historic flavor is only a little marred by the multi-level parking lot on Water St.

Water St is the main thoroughfare and is where most of the attractions are found; however, Gastown does branch off to a couple of side streets – Cambie and Abbott Sts – and continues a block or so off the streets that intersect at Maple Tree Square – Alexander, Powell and Carrall Sts. Start your tour of Gastown at the top of Water St where it intersects with Cordova and Richards St, just east of Waterfront Station where you can arrive by SkyTrain or SeaBus. Bus Nos 1 and 50 also travel up Water St.

The Landing, at 375 Water St, is a beautifully restored heritage building which houses 25 very upscale clothing and specialty shops, restaurants and the Steamworks Brewing Co; the harbor views are pretty good, too. Walking east to the corner of Water and Cambie Sts you'll come to the **steam clock**, perhaps Vancouver's most photographed attraction. This is the world's first steam-powered clock and, despite its antique appearance, was built in 1977. The clock stands on a steam tap that vents the steam lines that were formerly used to heat local businesses. You can see the steam works through the side glass panels. It blows off steam and whistles every 15 minutes, and chimes every hour, so you might want to wait around to see the clock do its thing before continuing along Water St.

LEE FOSTER

Statue of Gassy Jack

The **Byrnes Block**, at 2 Water St, was built shortly after the Great Fire of 1886 and is Vancouver's oldest heritage building still on its original site (the 1865 Hastings Mill Store is now on Alma St in Kitsilano). It was one of the city's first brick buildings and stands on the site of Gassy Jack's second saloon, a two-story hotel and billiard parlor called Deighton House. In the 1960s it was also the first building in Gastown to be renovated, breathing some new life into the then downtrodden area.

Behind the Byrnes Block you'll find **Gaolers Mews**, the location of the city's first jail, customs house and home to Gastown's first constable, Jonathan Miller, who also held the posts of custom collector and postmaster. Today it houses an information and police office.

At the end of Water St at Maple Tree Square is the narrow Hotel Europe which, when it was completed in 1909, was the best hotel in town and, for architecture buffs, is the first reinforced-concrete building in Vancouver. It is no longer a hotel and what was once an interesting bar on the ground floor is now, unfortunately, a poster and greeting-card shop. Around the corner in the square you'll come to the **statue of Gassy Jack** in about the same place where the Globe Saloon was located.

If you want to learn more about this colorful area, there are free guided walking tours from June to September. The 1½-hour tour meets at the statue in Maple Tree Square daily at 2 pm. Call ☎ 604-683-5650 for information.

Vancouver Police Centennial Museum

Close to but not in Gastown, this funny little museum (☎ 604-665-3346), at 240 East Cordova St next to the Firehall Arts Centre on the corner of Gore Ave, is on the way to Chinatown. The unusual museum, housed in the old Coroner's Court Building, was created in 1986 to commemorate the centennial of the Vancouver Police Force.

The displays include an autopsy room in the old morgue complete with bits and pieces of damaged body parts on the wall (a bit gruesome), a forensic laboratory display, a jail cell and a radio dispatch room. There are also old uniforms, police cars and motorcycles, a huge weapons display, counterfeit money and re-creations of famous crime scenes. The museum is open weekdays from 9 am to 3 pm, and in the summer on Saturday from 10 am to 3 pm. Admission is $5/3 for adults/seniors & youths (seven to 13).

From Carrall St (Gastown) the museum is about three blocks east on Cordova St. To get there by public transit take any one of the buses that travel along Hastings St as part of their route (such as bus Nos 10, 16 or 20) and get off at, or near, Gore Ave and walk north one block.

CHINATOWN (Map 3)

In the late 1800s Victoria was the port of call for ships arriving from Asia, but Vancouver was the town of choice for the new arrivals from China who called it 'Salt Water City.' By 1886, when the City of Vancouver was incorporated, Shanghai Alley was the location of a small Chinese settlement close to what is now Carrall and Pender Sts. It wasn't long before the settlement grew and developed along the shores of False Creek.

Ironically, it was the Great Fire in 1886 that helped Chinatown develop. In an attempt to rebuild the city, 60 hectares of forested land was leased to some of the Chinese immigrants who were given a 10-year rent-free lease on the condition they clear and farm their own land. By the end of that year almost 90 Chinese lived on Dupont St (now Pender St) west of Westminster Ave (now Main St) on farms producing either produce or pigs.

It wasn't long before two-story wooden buildings sprang up along Pender and Carrall Sts, which became a gathering place for banking (to wire money home) and socializing, as well as providing shelter for new arrivals. The Chinese were enticed by the opportunity to make money working in sawmills, lumber camps, fish canneries, mines and on railroad construction gangs. In 1883 alone, of the nearly 2000 gold miners in BC, 1500 were Chinese, and between 1881 and 1885 more than 11,000 Chinese arrived by ship to work on the construction of the CPR – which paid $1 a day, half of what white workers were paid but 95¢ a day more than they were paid at home.

Today, roughly 35,000 people of Chinese descent live in the area around Pender St, roughly bordered by Abbott St and Gore Ave, while thousands of others come here to shop, making this one of the largest China-towns in North America.

Chinatown is a designated heritage area. For the most part, this is a real Chinese market and business district where nearly all the signs are in Chinese, including the street signs, and English is rarely spoken. The colors, smells, signs and occasional old Chinese-style balcony can make you believe for a second that you're in Hong Kong. Throughout the day the streets are full of people going in and out of stores selling hanging ducks, bales of strange dried fish, exotic fruit, or Eastern remedies. The numerous restaurants and bakeries make this a good place to come for dim sum.

For years the area has contended with the run-down blights of Hastings and Main Sts, which is finally taking a toll. Now that newer arrivals from Hong Kong have colonized Richmond, the center of Chinese Canadian business and culture has at least in part relo-cated to the suburbs, but there's still plenty of vitality in Chinatown.

During the summer there is a great **night market** which captures all the fun, food, noise and excitement of its counterpart in Asia and has done a lot to bring life back to the streets of Chinatown at night. The night market is held on Pender and Keefer Sts, east of Main St, from May to the end of September, every Friday to Sunday from 6.30 to 11.30 pm. And don't forget the Chinese New Year celebrations if you are here during the Lunar New Year (see Special Events in the Facts for the Visitor chapter).

Around the block bordered by Pender, Carrall, Keefer and Columbia Sts, you'll find the world's narrowest commercial building; **China Gate** (originally used for the China pavilion at Expo 86); a sculpture depicting the Chinese railworkers and a bust of Dr Sun Yat-Sen; the **Chinese Cultural Centre**,

JOHN ELK

Storefronts in Chinatown

which has its own garden; the new **Museum & Library Complex** which contains archives and exhibits of early Chinese pioneers in BC, plus a Chinese-English library; and the Dr Sun Yat-Sen Classical Chinese Garden.

To get to Chinatown, take bus Nos 19 or 22 which travel along Pender St (No 19 continues up Main St), or you can take one of the buses that travel along Hastings St and get off at Main St. Another option is to take the SkyTrain to the Science World-Main St Station and walk north, or catch a bus, down Main St about four blocks to Chinatown.

World's Narrowest Office Building

Called the Sam Kee, this building at 8 West Pender St, near the corner of Carrall St (where Shanghai Alley used to be), has made it into Ripley's *Believe It or Not* and *The Guinness Book of Records*. It's easy to miss not only due to its narrowness but because it looks like the front of the larger building behind, to which it is attached. The reason for such a narrow building is that businessman Chang Toy, the owner of the Sam Kee Co, bought land at this sight in 1906, but in 1926 all but a 1.8m-wide strip was expropriated by the city. His way of thumbing his nose at city hall was building the world's narrowest office building.

Just for trivia's sake, you might be interested to know that, accessed by way of a winding staircase beneath the building, there

Stanley Park
The Jewel in the City's Crown

Of all of the parks in Greater Vancouver none is loved more by Vancouverites than Stanley Park. In many ways this 405-hectare reserve, with its forests of cedar and fir, meadows, lakes, attractions, restaurants and numerous hiking, biking and jogging trails, including the 10.5km Seawall Promenade, is the heart, if not the soul, of the city: you only have to visit on a sunny Sunday afternoon to see how much the citizens of Vancouver enjoy spending time here.

As you enter Stanley Park from West Georgia St, you are on Stanley Park Drive, the one-way road that goes around the park's perimeter. Or you can enter via the scenic Seawall Promenade, an ideal biking, walking, jogging and in-line skating trail that hugs the park's shoreline. Pass the Vancouver Rowing Club on the right and you'll come to a parking area, an **information booth** and the starting point for the horse-drawn tram tours. North of here you'll find Painters Corner, where artists work and sell their paintings; the outdoor theater Malkin Bowl; the Rose Garden; the Stanley Park Pavilion; what remains of the Zoo; the Vancouver Aquarium (the bronze sculpture in front of the aquarium, *Killer Whale,* is by Haida artist Bill Reid) and the Children's Farmyard and Miniature Railway.

The **Vancouver Aquarium** (☎ 604-659-3474), Canada's largest, with nearly 9000 sea creatures representing 250 species, is one of the city's premier destinations. The most popular attraction is the dolphins and the killer whale. There is also a special (albeit controversial) tank for the five beluga whales. Other exhibits include octopuses, eels and a wide variety of local sea life and freshwater fish. The Indonesian Reef Exhibit is also a standout, as is the Amazon Rainforest, a re-creation of a tropical rain forest, complete with crocodiles, toucans, piranhas, tree frogs and hourly rainstorms. The Vancouver Aquarium is also Canada's largest marine mammal rescue-and-rehabilitation center. Open year-round; call for hours and admission. Inquire about the 40-minute behind-the-scene tour with a naturalist guide that takes place daily at 1 pm.

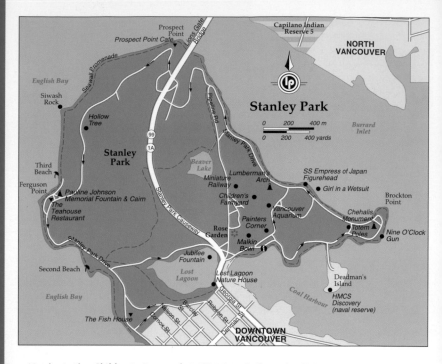

Nearby is the **Children's Farmyard & Miniature Railway** (☎ 604-257-8351), where children can interact with the llamas, sheep, goats, cows, hens and other small animals, and everyone, no matter what their age, will enjoy the 10-minute ride on the train. The engines are replicas of actual locomotives, one being CPR engine No 374 that pulled the first train into Vancouver. Open daily in summer, and in winter on weekends (weather permitting). Call for hours and admission.

Head back down to Stanley Park Drive, continue east and you'll pass **Deadman's Island**. This small island, which is used today as a naval reserve, has quite an illustrious history: it has been a Native Indian battleground, a Native Indian burial site, a quarantine station during the smallpox epidemic of 1888-90, a logging camp, a squatters village, the site of numerous jurisdictional battles and a military installation (HMCS *Discovery*) since 1943.

At **Brockton Point**, which refers to the eastern end of the park as well as the eastern tip of the peninsula, you'll find the Brockton Oval playing field and cricket ground, a good collection of **totem poles** from several different Native Indian groups, and the **Nine O'Clock Gun** on Hallelujah Point – an electrically fired cannon which sounds at 9 pm every day and was originally used to allow ships' captains to set their chronometers. This area was originally cleared by Edward Stamp in 1865 for the location of his sawmill. However, when he discovered it was impossible to keep log booms in the swift waters of Burrard Inlet, he abandoned the site and moved his operations farther along the shores of the protected harbor. The **Brockton Point Lighthouse** was completed in 1915. Around the point the *Chehalis* **Monument** commemorates the loss of a tugboat that was struck by the CPR ship *Princess of Victoria* in 1906, killing nine of the 15 people aboard.

Continuing west you'll see *Girl in a Wetsuit*, a bronze figure by Elek Imredy, and the **SS *Empress of Japan* Figurehead** that commemorates Vancouver's early trade with Asia. Just west, the area known as **Lumberman's Arch** was once the location of a Coast Salish village. Here you'll find the structure which gives the area its modern-day name, an arch donated by the Lumberman's and Shingleman's Society. You'll also find the Variety Kids Water Park beside the Seawall Promenade.

Follow the road along the shoreline and it will cut into the park and over the causeway. You'll be at **Prospect Point**. Up until 1939 there was

a beacon on the bluffs, but this was removed leaving only the terraces and steps, which provide great views of the Lions Gate Bridge, Burrard Inlet and the North Shore. The cairn here commemorates the 1888 wreck of the *SS Beaver*, a Hudson's Bay Company steamship that was the first to travel the entire west coast of North America. Also here you'll find the Prospect Point Cafe, a gift shop and a large colony of cormorants nesting in the bluffs.

Continue along Stanley Park Drive and park the car at the **Hollow Tree**, the remains of a tree that once measured 18.3m in diameter. Walk back up Stanley Park Drive about 150m and follow the trail to the left to the **Siwash Rock** lookout. This 15.2m monolith is, as Native Indian legend has it, a Squamish warrior named Skalsh who the god Q'uas the Transformer turned into a rock as a reward for being unselfish.

JOHN ELK

Back on Stanley Park Drive continue south to **Third Beach**, a popular place to swim or to enjoy the views from the beach, with perhaps the chance of seeing a seal or a bald eagle. At Ferguson Point there is The Teahouse Restaurant and the **Pauline Johnson memorial fountain and cairn** that actually marks the Native Indian poet's grave (1861-1913). Farther along at Second Beach you'll come to the outdoor swimming pool, Ceperley Meadow and Playground, the pitch-and-putt golf course, putting green, lawn-bowling green, tennis courts and The Fish House restaurant.

Near Second Beach, if you follow the road left, you will come to **Lost Lagoon**. At one time this was an extension of Coal Harbour, but by 1916 the bridge was replaced with a causeway, and in 1922 it was given its name from a poem, *The Lost Lagoon*, written by Pauline Johnson. By 1929 it was a true freshwater lake. Today it's a wild-bird sanctuary and the path around it makes for a wonderful walk. The **Jubilee Fountain**, originally a feature at the Chicago World's Fair, was installed in 1936 to commemorate Vancouver's 50th anniversary. On the city side of the lagoon, beneath the concession stand, is the **Lost Lagoon Nature House** with exhibits on the park's history and attractions, and information on the shoreline, forest, wildlife and birds.

GUNTER MARX

is a tunnel extending under Carrall St which once held baths, toilets and barber chairs.

Dr Sun Yat-Sen Classical Chinese Garden

Close to the Sam Kee building you'll find a tranquil oasis that, as the brochure states, really is 'refreshment for the heart.' This is the only full-scale classical Chinese garden (☎ 604-689-7133), at 578 Carrall St behind the Chinese Cultural Centre, found outside China and its design is subtle but exquisite in execution and effect. Modeled after the private classical gardens of the Ming Dynasty (1368-1644) in the city of Suzhou, it makes a real sanctuary in the center of the city.

The Taoist principles of yin and yang are incorporated in numerous ways throughout the garden – rugged and hard is balanced by soft and flowing, dark is balanced by light, large is balanced by small – with balance and harmony being the main themes. The four main elements of the garden, as tradition dictates, are buildings, rocks, plants and water. Everything in the garden, which is meant to be a microcosm of nature, has a specific purpose and this is reflected even in the placement of plants.

Completed in 1986 after a year of construction, the garden was designed and built by a 52-member team from Suzhou with the help of Vancouver architects. The architectural components such as carved woodwork, limestone rocks, roof tiles and the courtyard pebbles were shipped from China in 950 crates. As well, the garden was constructed using traditional tools.

The 45-minute guided tours, which are included with admission, are very worthwhile and are every hour in the summer (reduced times in winter). The garden is open daily throughout the year, June 15 to September 15 from 9.30 am to 7 pm, and September 16 to June 14 from 10 am to 6 pm. Admission is $6.50/5/4 for adults/seniors/students.

SCIENCE WORLD & ALCAN OMNIMAX THEATRE (Map 3)

Just south of Chinatown, Science World (☎ 604-268-6363), 1455 Quebec St, at Termi-

nal Rd, is another vestige of Expo 86. Inside the gleaming geodesic dome (or 'golf ball' as it's sometimes called), you'll find four galleries on two levels showing science, technology and natural-history exhibits with lots of interactive displays, plus a 170-seat 3D Laser Theatre. The 400-seat OMNIMAX Theatre is on the 3rd level. There is also a gift shop and cafeteria.

Even though people of all ages can have fun here, as well as learn a thing or two, the exhibits are aimed primarily at children. Hands-on experiments help explain scientific and physical phenomena and two of the galleries host traveling international exhibits. Kids especially love the films put on in the laser theater.

The OMNIMAX Theatre – with one of the world's largest domed screens at five stories high and 27m in diameter, and a 28-speaker wraparound sound system – shows films specially made for these venues.

Science World is open weekdays from 10 am to 5 pm, and weekends and holidays from 10 am to 6 pm. Admission to the museum is $10.50 for adults; $7 for seniors, students and children (four to 18); and children under four are free. Admission to the OMNIMAX Theatre is $9 and free for children under 4. Combination tickets to the museum and theater are $13.50 for adults and $9.50 for everyone else.

To get to Science World, take the Sky-Train to the Science World-Main St Station, or take a mini-ferry from False Creek or Granville Island.

WEST END (Map 2)

The West End is generally defined as the area bordered to the east by Burrard St, to the north by Burrard Inlet, to the west by Stanley Park and to the south by English Bay. Probably the first thing you'll notice about this section of the city are the large number of high-rise apartment buildings and condominiums. This is one of the most densely populated neighborhoods in Canada with nearly 40,000 people living here.

But in 1862 the only people who lived in this area were a small group of Musqueam and Squamish Indians, who had lived here for about 3000 years, and three settlers from England. 'The three greenhorns,' as they came to be known, paid $550 for a parcel of land that was pretty much the same area as today's West End. They had a vision of a 'New Liverpool' being built from Coal Harbour to English Bay – a dream they never saw realized.

When the CPR came to town in 1885, it purchased much of this property and slowly developed it for high-priced homes. By the turn of the century, summer revelers were coming to English Bay by way of the newly opened Robson and Denman streetcar line. Although English Bay was the preferred area for the wealthy to build their mansions, a housing boom from 1901 to about 1910 resulted in rows of two-story frame houses going up west of Burrard St.

During the next 50 years, houses and three-story apartment blocks defined the look of the West End, and until the 1950s the eight-story Sylvia Hotel, built in 1912, remained the area's tallest building. In the mid-1950s the city wanted to attract more people to the downtown shopping and business district so it decided on a plan to develop high-rise apartment buildings in the West End. During a 13-year period, 220 apartment buildings went up, and in so doing took away many of the fine old buildings that had made the West End a gracious place in which to live. Fortunately a few of these properties survived and have since been designated as heritage homes.

For the visitor, the West End is a lively place to spend time, especially along Robson, Denman and Davie Sts, or around English Bay. There are lots and lots of restaurants, bars, cafes and retail outlets to keep you entertained and, especially during the summer, everything goes from morning to late at night. Aside from a few heritage buildings there really aren't any major attractions in this area, so kick back and indulge yourself.

Walking Tour

This walking tour will take anywhere from four hours to an entire day, depending on

how fast you walk and how many shops you venture into. To get to the starting point either take the SkyTrain to Granville Station and walk south one block on Granville St, then west one block on Robson St, or take bus Nos 3 or 5.

Start the walk at **Robson Square**, between Howe and Hornby Sts, where you'll be looking across at the south side of the Vancouver Art Gallery. Robson Square was designed by noted architect Arthur Erickson and completed in 1970. At this low-rise multi-level development you'll find a skating rink (look down), restaurants and lots of places to sit. In fact, one of its attractions is that it's very 'people friendly.' To the south is a waterfall that forms one wall of the glass-roofed provincial courthouse.

If you like shopping you'll love **Robson St**. A collage of tourist shops, fashion boutiques, coffee shops and restaurants, Robson St is the best place in the city for people watching. Locals, international tourists and recent immigrants all throng here, giving the street the feeling of a mini United Nations. Part of the fun of browsing here is that the shops are really eclectic – you can find everything from Giorgio Armani suits, to hologram portraits of Elvis, to a shop dedicated to fancy condoms. At the northeast corner of Robson and Burrard Sts, the huge **Virgin Megastore** (the largest music store in Canada), which also houses a Planet Hollywood (☎ 604-688-7827) restaurant and bar, is a 1957 heritage building that was the previous home of the Vancouver Public Library.

If you are interested in getting a sense of what this area was like before the high-rises took over, continue west on Robson St for four blocks, turn south onto Broughton St and in one block you'll come to **Barclay Heritage Square**, a one-block site containing nine historic West End houses dating from 1890 to 1908. The showpiece is the 1893 Queen Anne-style Roedde House (☎ 604-684-7040), 1415 Barclay St, designed by Francis Rattenbury. The main floor of the house has been restored and authentically furnished, and the surrounding gardens are planted in period style. Admission is by guided tour

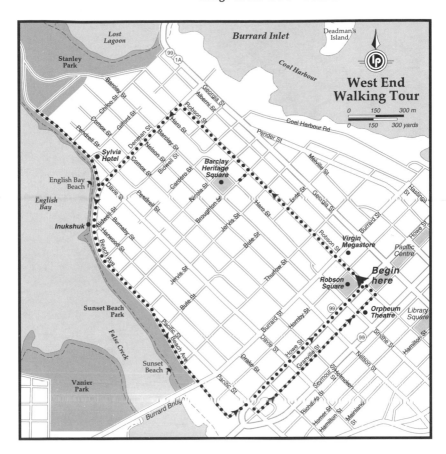

only, so phone to arrange a time if you want to see inside the house.

Walk back to Robson St and continue west to **Denman St**, where you can choose to continue on to Stanley Park or turn south and follow Denman St past numerous neighborhood-oriented cafes, shops and restaurants to English Bay. At **English Bay**, which can get packed with people on a nice day, you have a couple of options: you can follow either Beach Ave or the Seawall Promenade west around English Bay Beach, which will take you past the historic **Sylvia Hotel**, and into Stanley Park; you can head east up **Davie St**, another strip loaded with

restaurants (one of which, Romano's Macaroni Grill, is in a beautiful 1902 heritage mansion) and shops, back into the city and, if you choose, all the way down to Yaletown; or you can follow either Beach Ave or the Seawall Promenade east around English Bay to **Sunset Beach** and False Creek.

If you choose the latter option, you will pass **Inukshuk** facing out to the bay. This 6m figure at 31,500kg is a large version of an ancient Inuit symbol traditionally used as a navigational aid and landmark, and a symbol of northern hospitality. This was moved here in 1987 after being a part of the Northwest Territories' pavilion at Expo 86.

As you make your way toward Sunset Beach, you'll have good views over English Bay to Kitsilano and the West Side as far as UBC. If you like, beside the Vancouver Aquatic Centre at the foot of Burrard St, you can catch a mini-ferry to Vanier Park or Granville Island, or walk up to Beach Ave (if you're not already on it) and along to the foot of Hornby St where mini-ferries also travel to Granville Island. Otherwise, return to Robson St along either Howe or Granville Sts, the latter partly a pedestrian mall with colorful, if rather seedy street life, where there are shops, fast-food outlets, a couple of worthwhile restaurants and many of the city's cinemas.

If you do choose to return via Granville St, once referred to as the 'Great White Way' because of its variety of neon lights, you'll pass the **Orpheum Theatre**, 884 Granville St, near the northeast corner of Smithe St. Completed in 1927, the 2800-seat theater was originally built to accommodate vaudeville acts which traveled the North American circuit, and was the largest in Canada and the Pacific Northwest. Although not much to look at from the outside, the ornate interior is exquisitely decorated in a Spanish baroque motif, complete with 1000-bulb crystal chandeliers and the original Wurlitzer organ. It was eventually turned into a movie theater, but in the '70s it was restored as a concert venue and is now home to the Vancouver Symphony Orchestra.

West Side

Don't let the name confuse you: the West Side is in fact the long-established residential neighborhoods and bustling commercial centers south of Downtown Vancouver across False Creek and English Bay. The Cambie, Granville and Burrard Bridges lead to the West Side, and the main east-west arterial roads are 4th Ave and Broadway, both of which lead to the University of British Columbia (UBC) at the tip of the peninsula. Of interest to visitors are Granville Island, Kitsilano, UBC, Queen Elizabeth Park and the VanDusen Botanical Garden.

GRANVILLE ISLAND (Map 5)

On the south side of False Creek, under the Granville Bridge, this small one-time industrial 'island' has been redeveloped into a busy blend of businesses, restaurants, galleries, theaters and the Granville Island Hotel (see the Places to Stay chapter for details). Although now it's actually a tiny peninsula, at one time it was nothing more than two sandbars favored by the Squamish Indians as a winter fishing ground.

With the arrival of Europeans and industrialization, the sandbars were transformed into an island in 1916. Factories began to set up business to service the sawmills and rail yards that surrounded False Creek, and to be close to the channel with its access to shipping lanes. Industrial Island, as it was officially called, was administered by the government of Canada and underwent a number of ups and downs, including a couple of spectacular fires, before it was turned into a peninsula when dredging fill was dumped between the island and False Creek's south shore. This was actually part of an overall plan to completely fill in False Creek, but due to the expense the plan was fortunately abandoned. Interest in redeveloping the island as a people-friendly area took hold, and after a large financial commitment from the federal government, the Public Market opened for business in 1979.

The Granville Island **Information Centre** (☎ 604-666-5784), 1592 Johnston St, across from the Arts Club Theatre, is open daily from 9 am to 6 pm. There are lots of pamphlets here and great free maps of the island, plus a currency exchange, ATMs, a change machine for parking and a direct taxi line.

The center of activity, and a food lover's dream come true, is the **Granville Island Public Market** (open daily from 9 am to 6 pm, except Thanksgiving to Victoria Day when it's closed on Monday). Dozens of greengrocers, fishmongers, butchers, bakers, cheese shops, delicatessens and other food merchants squeeze into the bustling market, making this a great place to experience the natural bounty of the Lower Mainland. There are also coffee shops and take-out counters, although finding an empty table

Rehydrate at the Granville Island Brewery Co

can be tricky. The market fronts onto False Creek, and unless it's pouring with rain, the waterfront plaza behind the market is filled with shoppers, children, tourists, buskers and swarms of pigeons and gulls. It's estimated that about 250,000 people visit the market every month.

Granville Island is also an artisans' mecca with working studios and shops and several commercial art galleries. A number of the galleries and craft shops are in the **Net Loft** building (open daily from 10 pm to 6 am) across from the Public Market, but others are found throughout the island. The **Emily Carr Institute of Art & Design** (☎ 604-844-3800), at 1299 Johnston St, has frequent exhibits in its two galleries.

Children and adults alike will love the large two story **Kids Only Market**, right at the southern entrance to the island, open daily from 10 am to 6 pm, which has an astounding number of things to do, see and buy, including a giant beanstalk and a 'cafe' geared for youngsters. Not far away are the **Water Park** and adventure playground that the kids will love, plus a picnic area.

The combined **Model Ships & Sport Fishing Museums** (☎ 604-683-1939), 1502 Duranleau St, are probably only of interest to those who have a love for such things. The model ships are of a more general interest and children will probably enjoy them, but unless fishing is your passion, well, how many reels, rods, flies, outboard motors and stuffed fish do you want to see? The museums are open Tuesday to Sunday from

10 am to 5.30 pm. Separate admission to each is $3.50/2.50/2 for adults/seniors & students/children (under 12) and free for kids under six.

If you like beer, visit the **Granville Island Brewery Co** (☎ 604-688-9927), 1441 Cartwright St, and go on one of the half-hour tours, which are offered seven days a week year-round; call ☎ 604-687-2739 for tour times as they change seasonably. There is a tasting room and a retail/gift shop as well.

There are also a number of ship chandlers and recreational-equipment shops, including kayak and boat rentals, on the island. At night, the focus shifts from shopping to the performing arts when three theaters (Waterfront, Arts Club and the Arts Club Revue) open their doors; see the Entertainment chapter for details. Bridges Pub and the Arts Club Theatre Backstage Lounge, which has live music most nights and a very impressive selection of 55 blended and single-malt whiskies, are good places to have a drink or two, no matter the time of day. And with a choice of nine restaurants on the island, there is no shortage of places to eat.

To get to the island, take bus Nos 50 or 51, or take a mini-ferry.

KITSILANO (Map 6)

The south shore of English Bay, extending west roughly from Burrard to Alma Sts, and south as far as about West 16th Ave, is the neighborhood of Kitsilano. The area west from Alma St to UBC is Point Grey, a mostly affluent residential neighborhood. For the purposes of this book it is easier to refer to a portion of Point Grey as being part of Kitsilano. These divisions can get murkier still as the areas that border the south coast of Burrard Inlet's outer harbor, as you go west toward UBC, are also referred to locally as Jericho and Spanish Banks.

During the 1960s and '70s, Kitsilano was considered a hippie enclave and a center of countercultural sympathies and lifestyles. As times changed, the hippies turned into professionals and the neighborhood has become genteel. The old single-family homes are now unaffordable to the students who once gave the area its élan, and many old homes are now broken up into flats while some have been replaced with condominiums. Some apartment buildings rise upwards, hoping for glimpses of downtown across the bay.

Kitsilano, usually referred to as 'Kits,' is still a fun area to explore, particularly along West 4th Ave and Broadway, the primary commercial streets, which are lined with unusual shops, bookstores and ethnic restaurants. The old countercultural atmosphere can still be found here, mostly in the form of organic-food stores and vegetarian restaurants, but chances are they will be sitting beside a European clothing boutique or an upscale Italian restaurant. Plus, three of the city's main museums are located in Vanier Park.

To get to Kitsilano, take bus Nos 2 or 22, which run south on Burrard St and along Cornwall Ave.

To get to West 4th Ave, take bus Nos 4 or 7 which run south on Granville St. And to get to Broadway, take bus No 10, which also runs south on Granville St. Also, bus No 9 runs the entire length of Broadway from Boundary Rd to UBC. You can also take a mini-ferry to Vanier Park.

Vanier Park

Vanier Park, on English Bay below the Burrard Bridge, is home to the Pacific Space Centre, Vancouver Museum, Gordon MacMillan Southam Observatory and Vancouver Maritime Museum. Also here are the City of Vancouver Archives, Academy of Music, Burrard Civic Marina and the Canadian Coast Guard station.

During mid-May the 15 hectares of lawn, ponds and pathways are home to the Vancouver International Children's Festival, and during summer they're home to Bard on the Beach (see Special Events in the Facts for the Visitor chapter).

The park, which winds around the point and connects up with Kitsilano Beach Park (usually referred to as 'Kits Beach') to the southwest, is a popular area; when the weather's fine you'll see people strolling, jogging, cycling, walking their dogs or simply sitting and watching the ships anchored in English Bay. On a windy day Vanier Park is also an ideal and popular place to fly kites.

The history of Vanier Park is in many ways the history of Kitsilano. The point where the park now sits was originally the site of a Native Indian village called Sun'ahk, which the provincial government turned into a reservation in the late 1800s. However, in 1901 the government displaced this community – with some families going to the Capilano Indian Reserve on the North Shore while others moved to Squamish – with the idea of turning the area into an industrial site. Meanwhile, the CPR, which controlled the bulk of the property in this area, began to sell blocks of land for residential development. It was, in fact, the CPR that gave the area its name after Chief Khahtsahlanough, whose grandson August Jack was a resident of Sun'ahk.

Along with the first streetcar service to the area in 1905, and another line along 4th Ave to Alma St in 1909, came a mixture of housing, from the 'Vancouver Box' (two or 2½-story homes) to small apartment buildings to the development of some estates. During the 1950s and '60s many of these properties were converted into rooming houses which became popular with university students, thus creating the perfect mix for the countercultural community that Kitsilano became known for in the '60s and '70s.

Meanwhile, the area that is now Vanier Park remained in limbo with industrial concerns eagerly awaiting the opportunity to develop it as an extension of False Creek. During WWII the Royal Canadian Air Force used it as an equipment depot and, in 1956 when a high-rise apartment building went up nearby, the idea of industrializing it was dropped and it became home to its current occupants.

Because of the park's beginnings it's only fitting that *The Crab*, a stainless steel sculpture-fountain by George Norris, sits in front of the Pacific Space Centre and Vancouver Museum. This humble creature was considered by Native Indians to be the guardian of the harbor, and it's also the astrological sign for July 1– Canada's birthday.

Pacific Space Centre This space-science center (☎ 604-738-7827), which shares the same building as the Vancouver Museum at 1100 Chestnut St, has displays on the planet's geology, the chemical make-up of space and the mechanics of space exploration in the main gallery called the Cosmic Courtyard. It's all very hands-on with lots of interactive displays, computer games and even a moon rock you can touch – kids will love it.

But what the entire family will get a kick out of is the Virtual Voyages Simulator, a full-motion flight simulator that takes you on a 'ride': you could be on a mission to Mars, experiencing a collision with a comet, or going on a roller coaster. The flight simulator, which holds 30 people, lasts about five minutes. The ride time is included with ticket price.

In the GroundStation Canada Theatre, to your left as you enter the Space Centre, live and audio-visual presentations about the universe, lasting 20 minutes, are presented hourly throughout the afternoon starting at about 11.30 am, and are included with the ticket price. The HR MacMillan Star Theatre presents shows, some of which are geared to children, about various aspects of space on a 19m-diameter dome. The 40-minute shows, which are included with the ticket price, are put on hourly from 1 to 4 pm. In the evening this theater is used for laser-music shows – such as Pink Floyd Meets the Doors, or Laser U2 – for which there is a separate admission charge of $8; they are presented Wednesday to Sunday at 9 pm, and an additional show Friday and Saturday at 10.30 pm. These shows are popular so get here early or make reservations.

The Space Centre is to the left of the ticket booth, while access to the Star Theatre is by way of the elevator behind the booth. Open daily from 10 am to 5 pm, except from the beginning of September to the end of May when it's closed Monday. Admission is $12/9.50/8 for adults/seniors & youths/children (five to 10) and free for children under

five. A family ticket is $38 for five individuals, with a maximum of two adults, and $7.50 for each additional person.

Vancouver Museum This museum (☎ 604-736-4431), 1100 Chestnut St, specializes in the history of Vancouver and southwest BC. On display are historic photos and artifacts, including an exhibit on the archaeology and ethnology of the area, concentrating on the Salish Indians. There are examples of most Native Indian crafts.

At the time this book was being researched the museum was in the process of planning a two-year, $7 million refurbishment. A decision still hadn't been made on what the displays will feature, although they will continue with similar themes but with a greater emphasis on the history of Asian immigration. The museum will be a hands-on interactive-display kind of place. There might be a limited exhibit while the renovations are being done; however, it won't effect the operation of the Pacific Space Centre.

The museum is open daily July and August from 10 am to 5 pm, and closed Monday the rest of the year. Admission is $5 for adults and $2.50 for seniors, students, youths (11 to 18) and children (five to 10), and free for children under four. A family ticket costs $10.

Combined tickets for the Vancouver Museum and Pacific Space Centre are $15 for adults; $10 for seniors, students and youths; $9 for children; and free for children under four. A family ticket is $48 for five individuals, with a maximum of two adults.

Observatory The Gordon MacMillan Southam Observatory (☎ 604-738-2855), just next to the Pacific Space Centre and Vancouver Museum building, features a 500cm telescope available for free public viewing. Viewing takes place on Friday and Saturday from 7 to 11 pm, provided the weather is clear and volunteers are available.

Vancouver Maritime Museum This museum (☎ 604-257-8300), 1905 Ogden Ave at the foot of Cypress St, is a five-minute walk west from the Vancouver Museum. There are two parts to the museum – the museum itself and the *St Roch*.

The museum is probably of most interest to boat buffs and children, although it will seem very tame if you have come here from the Pacific Science Centre. There are lots of wooden models and some old rowboats on display, plus exhibits on shipwrecks and pirates. The reconstruction of the bridge of an actual tugboat working in Burrard Inlet is interesting, and the Children's Maritime Discovery Centre has lots of hands-on displays.

The *St Roch* is the 1928 RCMP Arctic patrol sailing ship that was the first vessel to navigate the legendary Northwest Passage in both directions. There are interesting guided tours on the ship every half-hour or so. Open daily in summer from 10 am to 5 pm, closed Monday from Labour Day to Victoria Day. Admission is $6/3 adults/ seniors & youths (six to 19), and free for children under five. A family ticket is $14.

Kitsilano Beach Park & West to UBC

The one thing that hasn't changed over the years in Kitsilano are the beaches. Kits, specifically Kitsilano Beach Park, bordered by Cornwall Ave west from Arbutus to Trafalgar Sts, faces onto English Bay and the sandy strand that flanks the water is a very popular gathering spot in summer. For a serious swim, however, go to the heated 137m **Kitsilano Outdoor Pool** (see the Activities section later in this chapter for details). While at Kits Beach you might want to check out some of the cafes and restaurants along Cornwall Ave or south up **Yew St**, which has some good places to get a meal or to have a drink.

From Forests to Urbanization – a Short History of Point Grey

It wasn't long after the Europeans first arrived at what is now Point Grey (named by Captain George Vancouver after a friend) that the enormous western red cedar, western hemlock and Douglas fir were being logged and floated through First Narrows to the Hastings Mill in the inner harbor near Gastown.

Although much of this area was leased to the Hastings Mill in 1865, the colonial government recognized the point's strategic importance and created reserves, one of which became UBC and the other Jericho Beach Park. The area's logging heritage is preserved in the name Jericho, which comes from either 'Jerry's Cove' or 'Jerry & Co,' named after a contract logger, Jeremiah Rogers, who had a logging camp near the old Native village.

In 1892 a nine-hole golf course was established at Jericho, the first west of the Mississippi, although this course was reverted to military use during WWII and the clubhouse burned down in 1948. There was minimal development until 1904 when the Jericho Boys' Industrial School for delinquent youth was established, and 1905 when a general store opened to service the dairy farmers who pastured their cows in the area.

By 1909 the first streetcar line came as far as Alma St, and the area's first large house, called Aberthau and now a heritage house and community center at 4397 West 2nd Ave, was built. With another streetcar line along West 10th Ave in 1912, the district was firmly established as a residential area and large houses became more and more common, such as the Brock House, at 3875 Point Grey Rd, a 1913 heritage house which is now used as a seniors' center and restaurant.

Despite the development, families continued to camp on the beach in the summertime up until the 1920s. In the early 1920s a flying boat air station was established at Jericho which remained in place until the 1970s. One of the barracks is now the HI Vancouver Jericho Beach hostel.

Jericho Beach Park Farther along West 4th Ave, just west of Alma St, Jericho Beach Park is another popular place to strut your stuff and sun worship. If you are out this way you might want to take a look at the **Hastings Mill Store Museum** (☎ 604-734-1212), 1575 Alma St, the city's oldest building and its first store (post office, church and meetinghouse). Built in 1865 and originally located at the foot of what is now Dunlevy Ave near Gastown, it was one of the few buildings to survive the Great Fire of 1886. It was floated to this site in 1930. Open June 1 to September 15 daily from 11 am to 4 pm, and the rest of the year weekends only from 1 to 4 pm. Admission is by donation.

If you are looking for more beaches, especially ones that don't get quite as crowded, then closer to the UBC Endowment Lands, which includes Pacific Spirit Regional Park, Jericho Beach eventually gives way to **Locarno Beach** (Map 7) which in turn becomes **Spanish Banks Beach** (Map 7). There are some stunning views from these beaches looking back at the city and across to West Vancouver, and the ships in Burrard Inlet look almost close enough to touch.

The British Columbia Golf House Museum

This museum (☎ 604-222-4653), 2545 Blanca St at the University Golf Course, just south of Spanish Banks Beach, is definitely intended for those who can't get enough of the game on the fairways. The small museum in the original 1931 UBC golf clubhouse details the history of golf in BC, with an international slant. There are lots of clubs, trophies, photos, paintings, more clubs and a reference library. Open Tuesday through Sunday from noon to 4 pm. Admission is by donation.

UNIVERSITY OF BRITISH COLUMBIA (Map 7)

The University of British Columbia (☎ 604-822-2211), often just called UBC, is at the most westerly point of Vancouver, on the peninsula jutting out into Georgia Strait. The huge 402-hectare campus, serving 35,000 students, is part of an area called the University Endowment Lands, much of which is still forest. Making up the rest of the area is the 763-hectare Pacific Spirit Regional Park, which is administered by the Greater Vancouver Regional District (GVRD).

The main roads going into UBC include West 4th Ave, becoming Chancellor Blvd at Blanca St; West 10th Ave, becoming University Blvd at Blanca St; and West 16th Ave. North-West and South-West Marine Drive is the main route that loops around the peninsula.

Besides the pleasant campus with its bustle of students, UBC offers some excellent gardens and a world-class museum of anthropology. The **UBC Aquatic Centre** is open to the public (see the Activities section later in this chapter for details). Free 1½-hour **walking tours** of the campus are offered May to September, weekdays at 10 am and 2 pm, and start at the Student Union Building just north of the bus loop. Call ☎ 604-822-8687 or 604-822-3131 for information.

Although UBC is often referred to locally as being in Point Grey, officially it is not a part of Vancouver. It is administered by the provincial government's ministry of municipal affairs. In 1908 the University Loan Act was established to set up a site for the province's first university and Point Grey was selected. However, the first classes didn't start here until 1925, and that was only after 1200 students marched in the 'Great Trek' from the makeshift campus, near Oak St and West 10th Ave, to the Endowment Lands to show their disgust with the lack of a permanent facility.

Building has continued steadily since then and the developed portion of the campus resembles a small town, if not a city. A portion of the revenue needed to build and maintain the university is supposed to come from housing developments cut out of the surrounding forests on the Endowment Lands, but due to wars and economic depressions this fortunately has not moved ahead as quickly as some planners would have liked.

Even though this area was heavily logged from 1861 to 1891 it wasn't clear-cut, mainly because many of the trees were too difficult to reach. This allowed the remaining trees to generate substantial re-growth. Because of these reasons, or perhaps in spite of them, there are still remarkable forests here today, which are now a part of Vancouver's legacy. With the creation of Pacific Spirit Regional Park in 1988, an area almost twice the size of Stanley Park has been preserved for future generations. For more information about UBC, see the Campuses section in the Facts for the Visitor chapter.

To get to UBC, take bus Nos 4 or 10 from downtown, or No 9 along Broadway; it takes about 30 minutes from downtown. The UBC bus loop is at the center of the campus.

Museum of Anthropology

This excellent museum (☎ 604-822-5087), 6393 North-West Marine Drive, another creation by architect Arthur Erickson, focuses on exhibits of art and artifacts from cultures around the world. Asia, Africa and the Pacific are all well represented but the emphasis is on the work of BC's Coastal Native Indians. The museum houses the best collection of totem poles and wood carvings in the world.

The design of the building is almost as exhilarating as the exhibits it houses. It was inspired by the post-and-beam longhouses favored by many coastal groups, and the Great Hall with its fabulous use of glass allows the huge totem poles and other artifacts inside to be set off against a backdrop of mountains and sea.

The museum has the world's largest collection of works by Haida artist Bill Reid, including the famous sculpture *The Raven and the First Men,* carved from a four-ton block of yellow cedar formed from 106 beams. Of the museum's 30,000 cultural objects and 200,000 archaeological specimens, almost half originated with Native Indians.

The other interesting aspect of the museum is how user-friendly it is. The open storage galleries, pioneered by the museum, allow more than 50% of its collection to be displayed. A database provides detailed information on the exhibits and a free guide will take you through the various galleries if you'd like. However, it's kind of fun poking around and seeing what you discover on your own.

Built in 1976, the museum was a gift to the province from the federal government to celebrate the 100th anniversary of BC entering the Canadian Confederation in 1871, and is the largest teaching museum in Canada. Also be sure to step outside to see the **Haida village**, a re-creation of a traditional village with a longhouse, a smaller mortuary house and 10 totem poles.

There is a fabulous, albeit pricey, gift shop featuring Native Indian jewelry, carvings, prints and an extensive collection of books on Native Indian history and culture.

Open daily in summer (Victoria Day to Labour Day) from 10 am to 5 pm, and to 9 pm Tuesday; the rest of the year it opens at 11 am and is closed Monday. Admission is $6/3.50 adults/seniors & students, and free on Tuesday between 5 and 9 pm.

If you drive, there is metered parking in front of the museum. If you take the bus (see the UBC introduction for bus numbers), from the bus loop walk west on University Blvd, turn right (north) on West Mall and follow it to the end; it's about a 10-minute walk.

Nitobe Memorial Garden

This beautiful Japanese-style garden (☎ 604-822-3825), near Gate 4 at the foot of Memorial Rd off West Mall, isn't far from the museum and, aside from the sound of the traffic on Marine Drive behind it, is a tranquil retreat perfect for quiet meditation. Designed by a leading Japanese landscape architect, it is considered to be the most authentic Japanese garden outside Japan. The garden has two parts: the Tea Garden, with its ceremonial Tea House, is designed for peaceful contemplation; and the Stroll Garden, the layout of which conforms to the map of the Milky Way, is a symbolic journey through life following the principals of yin and yang. It's enclosed within high walls that help to create the feeling that you are in another world.

During summer, guides are available at the gate when you buy a ticket. Open daily in summer from 10 am to 6 pm, and the rest of the year weekdays from 11 am to 3 pm. Admission during summer is $2.50/1.50 adults/seniors & students, and free the rest of the year.

See the Museum of Anthropology, above, for details on getting to the garden. However, if you are walking from the bus loop, instead of going to the end of West Mall, turn left (west) on Memorial Rd and follow it to the end.

UBC Botanical Garden

A real gem, this 44.5-hectare garden (☎ 604-822-9666), 6804 South-West Marine Drive, near the corner of West 16th Ave, is actually made up of about eight separate gardens containing 10,000 different trees, shrubs and flowers.

There are several thematic plantings, including gardens with plants specific to regions of the world and to particular environments such as the Alpine Garden and the Asian Garden, which has Canada's largest collection of rhododendrons; the BC Native Garden, with plants from many areas of the province; the Food Garden, containing seasonal vegetables, berries and fruit; and the Physick Garden, an enclosed 16th-century apothecary garden. Even 'out of season,' the Winter Garden features plants that bloom during the cooler months.

Even if you don't go into the garden itself, the Botanical Garden Centre, with a walkway leading to a scenic lookout, is worth visiting. There is a gift shop and plant yard (nursery) where you can buy books, seeds, gardening tools and unusual plants. The garden is open daily 10 am to 6 pm, and to 2.30 pm in winter. Admission in summer is $4.50/2.25 adults/seniors & students; in winter admission is free.

If you drive, there is free parking beside the center. If you take the bus (see the UBC introduction for bus numbers), from the bus loop walk west on University Blvd, turn left (south) on West Mall and follow it to the end.

Pacific Spirit Regional Park

This 763-hectare park is essentially a long, wide strip stretching northwest from Burrard Inlet on one side of the peninsula to the North Arm of the Fraser River on the other, and acts as a green zone between the campus and the city. From the north side of the peninsula, and going around the point to the other side, it connects with Point Grey Beach, Acadia Beach, Tower Beach and Wreck Beach, which is part of the Marine Drive Foreshore Park.

This is a fantastic area to explore with 35km of walking, jogging, cycling and even equestrian trails making their way through forests of giant cedar and fir that aren't much different from the forests the first Europeans found when they arrived.

In this park you'll find the 12,000-year-old **Camosun Bog**, a unique wetland which is the home of many native bird and plant species. The bog can be reached by a boardwalk starting at Camosun St and West 19th Ave. The Park Centre (☎ 604-224-5739), at West 16th Ave, near Blanca St, is where you'll find information and maps on the park and the bog. To get to the center from downtown either take bus Nos 4 or 10 to Blanca St and 10th Ave then walk south six blocks, or (and this is a longer route) take the SkyTrain to Nanaimo Station and from there take bus No 25 to UBC which will drop you off right next to the center.

Wreck Beach Although difficult to reach, the log-strewn beaches at the base of the embankment around Point Grey offer good views of Georgia Strait, and even on a hot day can be relatively quiet. The exception to this is the popular Wreck Beach, notorious for being the only nude beach in the city. It gets very busy in summer, but for the bashful there are lots of logs to lie between. At low tide the sandy beach gives way to mudflats that extend out to Georgia Strait and the mouth of the North Arm of the Fraser River. People do swim here but the thought of all that industrial waste emptying into Georgia Strait from the river can be a bit off-putting.

Once you have made your way down the steep path to the bottom, the thought of the hike back up will be enough to inspire you to take off your clothes and stay a while. If you need something to drink, eat or smoke, there are many enterprising individuals selling refreshments. Access to Wreck Beach is on South-West Marine Drive not far from Gate 6 at the foot of University Blvd; follow one of the trails marked No 4, 5 or 6 down the steep steps. On a warm day parking along Marine Drive is next to impossible unless you get here early. From the bus loop, walk west along University Blvd to Marine Drive where, on the west side of the road to the right (north), you'll find signs to Wreck Beach.

QUEEN ELIZABETH PARK (Map 1)

This park, the city's third largest at 53 hectares, is between Cambie and Ontario Sts, and West 29th and West 37th Aves. This is also the highest point in Vancouver and at 153m above sea level there are great views of the city from almost every direction. The park features a mix of sports fields, manicured lawns, formal botanical gardens, tennis courts, a pitch-and-putt golf course, lawn bowling greens, the city's only Frisbee golf course, one of Vancouver's top restaurants, Seasons in the Park (see the Places to Eat chapter for details), and the Bloedel Conservatory. The main route going into the park is West 33rd Ave.

The park began life as an area called Little Mountain, where in the 1870s there was a logging camp, then a small dairy farm, and by 1910 a Chinese vegetable farm. It was about this time that quarries were opened up on Little Mountain to provide slate for the city's newly created network of roads, and in the 1920s one of the mines was turned into Vancouver's main water reservoir. In 1939, with the visit of King George VI and Queen Elizabeth, Little Mountain was turned into a park and given its new name.

Over the years the two old quarries have been landscaped, creating the beautiful and impressive Quarry Gardens with their stunning seasonal floral displays, fountains and pools. This is a very popular spot to have wedding photos taken, and on a nice day wedding parties are virtually lining up to take their turn. The park's eastern slopes contain examples of just about every native shrub and tree in BC.

On the east side of the park is the wonderful (well, for baseball fans at least) Nat Bailey Stadium, home to the Triple A league Vancouver Canadians. On a warm summer night, or afternoon for that matter, there aren't many places in the city where you can have a more enjoyable beer and hot dog while being entertained at the same time (see Spectator Sports in the Entertainment chapter for details).

Also, while you're at the top of the park, check out the two sculptures near the conservatory: Henry Moore's bronze *Knife Edge (Two Pieces)*, behind the conservatory, sitting on the deck area covering the reservoir (copies of this sculpture can be found on Nelson Rockefeller's New York estate and outside the House of Lords in London); and the clever bronze piece called *Photo Session*, by J Seward Johnson Jr, beside Seasons in the Park restaurant.

To get to the park, take bus No 15, which runs the entire length of Cambie St, heading east on Robson St.

Bloedel Conservatory

Crowning the hill at Queen Elizabeth Park is this Buckminster Fuller-inspired, 'triodetic' domed floral-and-bird conservatory (☎ 604-257-8570). This 'garden under Plexiglas' has three climate zones, including desert, subtropical and rain forest. Living inside the conservatory are 400 species of plants – from Africa, the Americas, the Caribbean and Asia – and 150 free-flying tropical birds, or about 36 species. Plant and bird guides are provided with the admission. Almost as popular as the gardens for wedding photos, the conservatory hosts up to 30 wedding-photo sessions a day. It sort of puts a whole new slant on the expression 'watch the birdie,' doesn't it?

Open April to September, weekdays from 9 am to 8 pm, and weekends from 10 am to 9 pm; November to January daily from

10 am to 5 pm; and October, February and March daily from 10 am to 5.30 pm. Admission is $3.30/2/1.65 adults/seniors/children.

VANDUSEN BOTANICAL GARDEN (Map 1)

This 22-hectare park (☎ 604-299-9000 ext 7194), 5251 Oak St, between West 33rd and West 37th Aves, is only about four blocks west of Queen Elizabeth Park. The garden, which used to be a golf course, contains a small lake and a large collection of ornamental plants from around the world, plus Sprinklers Restaurant (☎ 604-261-0011).

There are various theme gardens, including a children's garden, a rose garden and a lakeside garden. Be sure to find your way through the Elizabethan Hedge Maze. There is also an interesting collection of sculptures. In the first week of June, the Flower & Garden Show takes place, and in December a section of the garden is illuminated with 19,000 Christmas lights for the popular Festival of Lights.

There are guided tours every Sunday at 2 pm, and every afternoon from April to October. Guide-driven electric carts are available from April to October for visitors with limited walking ability. Open daily from 10 am to 9 pm in summer; the time it closes the rest of the year depends on daylight hours. Admission is $5/2.50 for adults/students.

To get to the park, take bus No 17, which runs the entire length of Oak St, south on Burrard St from downtown.

East Vancouver

In Vancouver, the area east of Main Street has traditionally been the working class and, in some areas, the non-British section of the city. In 1865 Edward Stamp's new Hastings sawmill, just east of where Main St is now, set the foundation for what became an industrial and commercial area. The East End, as it was once called, developed from the houses and businesses that were built to support the people who worked in the mills and factories, or along the waterfront.

Even though some communities had a more defined neighborhood than others – in the early 1900s, for example, Powell St was the center of the Japanese community, while Union and Prior Sts were home to the Italian community – there really weren't any strict boundaries and Russians, Ukrainians, Scandinavians, Jews and blacks all added to the mix.

Over the years these communities grew, or moved to other parts of the city, although in many cases they have simply continued to shift east. For instance, with a large flux of Italian immigration from the 1950s to the '70s, the Italian community moved east to Commercial Drive, which until just recently was dubbed 'Little Italy.' Other groups – such as the Sikh community which before WWI was centered in Kitsilano near the Burrard Bridge and now has a neighborhood around Main and Fraser Sts below about East 49th Ave – have moved into East Vancouver continuing the tradition which has become the area's distinguishing characteristic.

Continuing east past Vancouver's borders are Burnaby and New Westminster, both of which are covered in this section. For visitors, these two cities, which are essentially suburbs of Vancouver, offer a number of attractions worth taking the time to see. Other areas east of Vancouver, which are not covered in this book but may also be of interest to the visitor, include Port Moody, Coquitlam, Port Coquitlam, Pitt Meadows, Maple Ridge and even farther east along the Fraser Valley, all of which are mostly residential and, in some cases, farming communities.

COMMERCIAL DRIVE (Map 4)

The first inter-urban rail line from New Westminster to Vancouver was constructed in 1891, and the first road built along the line was eventually called Commercial Drive. Development was slow to take off but by 1912 the surrounding area was covered in houses and Commercial Drive was the main shopping street.

It wasn't long before the city developed east along Hastings St and south from the waterfront, swallowing up what had been a distinct village.

In some ways Commercial Drive, or simply 'the Drive' as it's referred to locally, still has the feel of, if not quite a village, an area that is separate from the city. This has become the city's 'alternative-lifestyle, counterculture' neighborhood where a cross-section of nationalities, gays, artists, students and the politically aware meld into one.

Once the center of the city's Italian community and home to some of Vancouver's best Italian restaurants, it is no longer thought of as being just 'Little Italy,' although there are still many good Italian restaurants and cafes to be found here. The cultural diversity has broadened to include Portuguese, Latin American, Caribbean and Southeast Asian restaurants and markets stretching from around Venables St to East Broadway. The only off-putting aspect of the Drive is the number of panhandlers who have congregated along here, and sometimes the persistent begging can be annoying.

The Drive's political mix is in evidence with rainbow flags hanging in shop windows, and earnest political conversations taking place in vegetarian cafes and third-world solidarity coffee shops. The **Vancouver East Cultural Centre** (☎ 604-254-9578), 1895 Venables St, just off Commercial Drive, is a church converted into an avant-garde performance space which captures perfectly the area's left-of-center politics and artistic tastes.

To get to the Drive, take the SkyTrain to Broadway Station, or bus No 20 north on Granville St, or bus No 9 along Broadway.

PUNJABI MARKET (Map 1)

Often referred to as 'Little India,' this small strip of shops and restaurants is worth searching out if you want to experience a small taste of the Indian subcontinent in Vancouver. Granted, you won't find cows wandering the streets, or bicycle-rickshaws weaving between the traffic, but many of the sounds, smells and colors of India are condensed into an area in southeast Vancouver that stretches along Main St from about East 48th to 51st Aves.

The early history of Indians (or East Indians as these groups of people are collectively referred to) in Vancouver is not an altogether happy one. After hearing stories about this fabulous land from soldiers returning from London, a group of 45 Indians immigrated to Vancouver in 1904. In 1907 the provincial government not only denied Indians the vote, which was maintained until 1947, it also barred Indians from entering the medical and legal professions and from logging on crown land. Today, there are more than 130,000 Indo-Canadians living throughout Greater Vancouver, of which about 75,000 are Sikhs and 18,000 are Hindus.

This small commercial strip, complete with street signs in Punjabi, is one of several Indian shopping districts in the Lower Mainland. The focus here is on food markets, sari and fabric shops, music stores, jewelers and, of course, restaurants (see the Places to Eat chapter for details). Indian music spills out onto the street, as do the aromas from the restaurants and spice shops; close your eyes for a minute and you can almost believe you have been transported to India. If you really want to get a good hit of Indian aromas, walk into **Bombay Sweets** at 6556 Main St, which specializes in spices, dals and bulk food.

Although not in the market, but close enough to be worth the extra trip, the **Sikh Temple**, 8000 Ross St, just off South-East Marine Drive near Knight St is worth a look. Designed by Arthur Erickson, this building has the hallmark of traditional Indian architecture. Visitors are welcome to look inside as long as they follow the prescribed customs.

To get to the market, take bus No 3, which travels the length of Main St, north on Granville St.

BURNABY (Map 1)

The City of Burnaby, with a population of around 188,000, is the province's third-largest city. However, most Vancouverites tend to think of Burnaby (which was only incorporated as a city in 1992) not as a city in its own right, but as the eastern extension of Vancouver. Burnaby is bordered to the north by Burrard Inlet, to the south by the North Arm of the Fraser River and New Westminster, to the east by Coquitlam (North Rd) and to the west by Vancouver (Boundary Rd).

Perhaps the reason for this lack of identity, at least in the minds of Vancouverites, is that there is no clear dividing line between the two cities, nor does Burnaby have an easily defined center. Rather, Burnaby has evolved from its beginnings as a logging and agricultural center to an industrial and residential district made up of a number of small shopping areas and, more recently, large malls such as the **Metrotown Centre** (☎ 604-438-2444), at 4800 Kingsway.

Deer Lake Park
Just off Canada Way and the Trans Canada Hwy (Hwy 1), and close to Burnaby Lake Regional Park, this was once a Native Indian encampment. Now it serves as a cultural center and park. Just to confuse matters, the cultural facilities are actually in an area called Century Park. Here you'll find the Burnaby Heritage Village, the Burnaby Art Gallery (inside a heritage house), the Shadbolt Centre for the Arts (☎ 604-291-6864) the heritage Hart House and the Century Gardens.

And, if all that weren't enough, wooded parklands extend around the other side of the lake in an area called Oakalla Parksite. The lake, which is surrounded by a 5km shoreline covered in forest, is a good place to go for a paddle (see the Activities section later in this chapter for details). To get to the park, take bus No 123 east on Hastings St.

Burnaby Heritage Village This museum (☎ 604-293-6501), 6501 Deer Lake Ave, is a replica village that attempts to preserve both the artifacts and atmosphere of a southwestern BC town between the years 1890 and 1925. There's an old schoolhouse, printing shop, drugstore and other establishments. A large, working steam-train model is

next to the village. The real highlight is the restored carousel with 36 wooden horses. Friendly, informed workers are in period dress. Open April to September, daily from 10 am to 4.30 pm, and shorter hours the rest of the year. Admission is $7/5 adults/seniors & students.

Burnaby Art Gallery Ceperley Mansion, a heritage house, serves as the home of this gallery (☎ 604-291-9441), 6344 Deer Lake Ave, which specializes in contemporary art. The gallery shows work by local, regional, national and international artists. There are guided tours available, plus there is a gift shop and art reading room. Open Tuesday to Friday from 9.30 am to 4.30 pm, and weekends and holidays from 12.30 to 4.30 pm. Admission is $2 and free for children under 12.

Other Parks
Besides Deer Lake Park, there are some other wonderful parks in Burnaby that are well worth searching out. Contact Burnaby Parks and Recreation (☎ 604-294-7450) for information.

The **Barnet Marine Park**, 8383 Barnet Hwy, on the shores of Burrard Inlet, is a marine park with forest trails, swimming and boating; take bus No 160 from Burrard Station. **Burnaby Lake Regional Park** (☎ 604-432-6350), on Kensington Ave off the Lougheed Hwy, is teeming with wildlife, including beavers. The 160-hectare lake/marsh is surrounded by 9km of trails, a nature house and a viewing tower; take bus No 123 from Burrard Station.

Surrounding Simon Fraser University, **Burnaby Mountain Park**, Centennial Way off Gaglardi Way, has stunning views of Burrard Inlet and across to North Vancouver. There is a fabulous collection of totem poles as well as Ainu (aboriginal Japanese) sculptures. Take bus Nos 35 or 135 from Pender and Granville Sts. **Central Park**, Boundary Rd and Kingsway, combines quiet forest trails around small lakes. There's an outdoor swimming pool, a pitch-and-putt golf course and an award-winning playground. Take the

SkyTrain to Patterson Station, or bus No 19 east on Pender St.

Simon Fraser University

Opened in 1965, Simon Fraser University (SFU) is the province's second largest with a population of 20,000 students. SFU sits on top of Burnaby Mountain about 20km directly east of the city center (there is also a downtown campus in the Harbour Centre). A showcase of modern architecture, the university was designed by (you guessed it) architect Arthur Erickson whose unusual use of space and perspective was, and remains, controversial. There are huge courtyard-like quadrants all interconnected by a common courtyard with many fountains, including one on a roof. Some areas of the complex are reminiscent of Mayan ruin sites in Mexico.

The university's **Museum of Archaeology & Ethnology** (☎ 604-291-3325), Academic Quadrangle 8602, features a collection of Pacific Native Indian artifacts, and has a budget cafeteria. The museum is open Monday to Friday from 10 am to 4 pm; admission is by donation.

The **Art Gallery** (☎ 604-291-4266), Academic Quadrangle 3004, has collections from Pacific countries with an emphasis on BC and Canadian artists. Open Monday from noon to 6 pm, and Tuesday to Friday from 10 am to 4 pm; admission is free. Free 1½-hour walking tours of the campus are offered throughout the year between 9 am and 3.30 pm; however, tours must be arranged in advance as there is no set schedule. Call ☎ 604-291-3397 for information on walking tours.

See the Campuses section in the Facts for the Visitor chapter for more details on SFU. To get to the campus, take bus Nos 35 or 135 from Pender and Granville Sts.

NEW WESTMINSTER (Map 1)

New Westminster has a rich and colorful history and, for a brief time, was even the capital of the colony of British Columbia. However, what remains today is a city that is down on its luck and somewhat tattered around the edges, especially along Colum-bia St, just north of the market. There are some interesting things to see, to be sure, and the developed riverfront esplanade running in front of the Westminster Quay Public Market is pleasant enough to spend a couple of hours. However, this is a destination you could easily forgo if time is a factor.

New Westminster (or simply New West) is a small city with a population of about 528,000 in an area of only 9.6 sq km. It is bordered by Burnaby to the northwest, Coquitlam to the northeast, and across the Fraser River, Richmond, Delta and Surrey. The main route traveling through New West from Vancouver is the combined Hwys 1A and 99A (in Vancouver and Burnaby this is Kingsway, but becomes 10th Ave and McBride Blvd in New West, and then after crossing Pattullo Bridge into Surrey becomes the King George Hwy). South-East Marine Drive, which turns into Marine Way in Burnaby, follows the Fraser River through Vancouver and Burnaby into New West where it crosses the Queensborough Bridge and joins Hwy 91A.

With the discovery of gold on the Thompson and Fraser Rivers in the mid-1800s it was decided that a new town was to be built that would be both a commercial center as well as the colony's new capital. Colonel RC Moody, the commander of the Columbia Detachment of Royal Engineers, chose this site in 1859 for its accessibility to rail and river transportation, and in 1860 New West became the first city to be incorporated in Canada west of the Great Lakes.

The city's first name, however, was Queensborough in tribute to Queen Victoria, but at the suggestion of the Queen the name was changed thus giving it its nickname 'The Royal City.' It was named the colony's new capital, ousting Fort Langley, and in 1866, when the two colonies of British Columbia and Vancouver Island were united, New West became the capital of both. This honor was only to last two years before Victoria, which had been the capital of the Colony of Vancouver Island, was instead named the new capital of British Columbia.

Centennial Fountain

Vancouver Art Gallery

Library Square

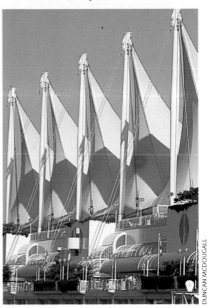
Canada Place

Gastown's piping steam clock – among the most photographed objects in Vancouver

Vancouver's ornamental Chinatown

Interior of a chic retail store in Yaletown

Dining on Granville Island

Hastings Mill Store Museum

Vancouver Maritime Museum, Vanier Park

Granville Island and the False Creek marina – year-round destinations for locals and tourists

NIK WHEELER

Totems at Museum of Anthropology, UBC

DOUG PLUMMER

Beach Closed
Sunset to 8 am

Clothing
is optional
at beach
ahead.

At the Wreck Beach trailhead

WES BERGEN

Science World and the 'golf ball'

JOHN ELK

Street signs marking Punjabi Market

JOHN ELK

The world-class VanDusen Botanical Garden

During those early years a fleet of stern-wheelers worked up and down the Fraser River, while along the banks sawmills, canneries and shipyards were established, making this the most important city on the mainland. In 1886 the CPR arrived and by the end of the 1800s New West was the commercial center for the Fraser Valley, although by this time it had lost out to Vancouver as the Mainland's premier city. There was also a large Chinatown here at the foot of 10th St, but nothing of it remains today.

In 1898 the commercial core along Columbia St was destroyed by fire, and although it was rebuilt and the industries along the river still thrive to this day, New West never really regained the importance it once held in the region.

The **Travel InfoCentre** (☎ 604-526-1905), on the esplanade in front of the market is open daily April to September from 9.30 am to 6.30 pm, and October to March from 10 am to 4 pm.

To get to New West, take the SkyTrain to New Westminster Station beside the market, or to Columbia Station on Columbia St.

Westminster Quay Public Market & Esplanade

This is another market modeled after the successful Granville Island Public Market. The Westminster Quay Public Market (☎ 604-520-3881), at the foot of 8th St, is home to 80 stores and services, offices and a hotel.

The 1st floor of the market is devoted to fresh food and shops plus the Paddlewheeler Pub (☎ 604-524-1894), while the 2nd floor is mainly take-out food and restaurants with good views. Beside the market is the Inn at Westminster Quay (see the Places to Stay chapter for details). The market is open daily from 9.30 am to 6.30 pm.

The riverside esplanade in front of the market is a pleasant place to stroll on a sunny day. To the right of the market you'll see the *Samson V*, a paddlewheeler that once worked on the river and is now a small maritime museum, only open during the summer. There is also a bust of Simon Fraser (1776-1867), the first European to come down the river that now bears his name.

To the left of the market past the tourist office is a rather odd tourist attraction, a Russian submarine. The *Foxtrot U-521* (☎ 604-520-1073) was part of the Soviet Union/Russian Navy's fleet for 20 years before it was decommissioned in 1993 and ended up here as the only one on display in North America. Open daily from 9.30 am to 6.30 pm. Admission is $7/5 for adults/seniors & children (under 13), or $20 for a family (two adults and two children).

Next to the tourist office, Paddlewheeler River Adventures (☎ 604-525-4465) offers a variety of river tours on an authentic sternwheeler (built in 1985) including the Fraser River Exploration Cruise, the Fort Langley Adventure Cruise, the Sunset Dinner Cruise and various special-event cruises. Call for times and costs.

Irving House Historic Centre

Built in 1865, this 14-room home (☎ 604-527-4640), 302 Royal Ave, about six blocks north of Columbia Station, is one of the oldest structures in BC and now functions as a museum of frontier life and early furnishings. The original owner, William Irving, was a riverboat captain on the Fraser River. Adjacent is the **New Westminster Museum & Archives**, which tells the story of this township. Open May 1 to mid-September, daily except Monday (although it is open holiday Mondays) from 11 am to 5 pm, and the rest of the year weekends only from 1 am to 5 pm. Admission is by donation.

North Shore

North and West Vancouver together make up the North Shore. There are three ways to get to this side of Burrard Inlet: Lions Gate Bridge, accessed by way of the causeway (Hwy 99) through Stanley Park; Second Narrows Bridge, a continuation of Trans Canada Hwy (Hwy 1) which goes through East Vancouver; and the SeaBus from Waterfront Station.

Like so much of the Lower Mainland, this area had its industrial beginnings as a logging and sawmilling center. In fact, before Edward Stamp built his Hastings Mill on the south shore of Burrard Inlet in 1865, Pioneer Mills had begun operation on the north shore in 1862 at a site about 6km east of First Narrows.

Stretching from Horseshoe Bay to Deep Cove, the District of North Vancouver, with a population of only a few hundred people, was incorporated in 1891. However, in 1907 and 1912 it had been subdivided into the City of North Vancouver and the Municipality of West Vancouver, respectively. Vancouverites often made the journey across the inlet, first by canoe and then by ferry, to hike or ski on Grouse Mountain, or to terrify themselves on the Capilano Suspension Bridge. The beaches of West Vancouver were popular picnic destinations; in the summer, tents lined the shore from what is now Ambleside Park to about 23rd St.

Transportation across the inlet started in 1866 by way of a rowboat operated by Navvy Jack Thomas, a gravel merchant, who charged a small fee to get mill workers over to Gassy Jack's Globe Saloon and home again. In 1873 Thomas eventually moved to what is now West Vancouver with his wife Row'i'a (the granddaughter of Chief Ki'ep'i'lan'o after whom the Capilano River is named), becoming the area's first white resident.

The first substantial ferry service to North Vancouver began in 1900. It proved to be such a success that in 1903 the Wallace Shipyards (later to become Burrard Dry Dock where the *St Roch* and numerous BC Ferries' vessels were built) started building many of the ferries that traveled back and forth across the inlet until the new Second Narrows Bridge opened in 1958. The last of these ferries is permanently docked beside Lonsdale Quay and functions as the Seven Seas Seafood Restaurant (see the Places to Eat chapter for details).

The new bridge, which replaced the first one built in 1925, was designed to take both trains and automobiles, cutting traveling time from Vancouver to a speedy 20 minutes. With it came the development of the Grouse Mountain Hwy and Scenic Resort.

Meanwhile, in West Vancouver, John Lawson began a regular ferry service in 1909. This service allowed more people to travel across Burrard Inlet to an area that for the most part, with the exception of day-trippers and summer campers, had been used as a base for logging and fish canning (Environment Canada's Pacific Research Laboratories on Marine Drive was a cannery from 1891 to 1967). The **wooden pier** where the ferries docked, until the service ended in 1947, is at the foot of 17th St in John Lawson Park, and the original **ferry building**, built in 1913 and now a heritage community gallery, is at 14th St in Ambleside Park.

Summer cottages and some permanent homes soon sprang up along the shore and a few housing developments were established. However, it wasn't until the opening of the Lions Gate Bridge in 1938 that the area really came into its own as a residential neighborhood.

For the visitor, the North Shore is still as appealing today as it was to those who came here on day trips in the early 1900s. From shops to restaurants, and from outdoor pursuits to some of the Lower Mainland's best parks, there is every reason to make the journey across the water.

NORTH VANCOUVER (Map 8)

North Vancouver extends west from Indian Arm to West Vancouver, with the Capilano River more or less acting as its western boundary. The District and the City, collectively known as North Vancouver (or simply North Van), have a combined population of over 127,000.

You can take in the shops and restaurants at Lonsdale Quay and the lower section of Lonsdale Ave, hike or ski on Grouse Mountain, visit a fish hatchery, walk across a suspension bridge or explore some of North Van's fabulous parks. Plus, the various train services offered by BC Rail leave from its station at the foot of Pemberton Ave running south off Marine Drive.

To get to North Van, take the SeaBus from Waterfront Station to Lonsdale Quay, a trip worth taking for the views of the harbor. At the quay, buses leave for various routes throughout North Van. Buses also travel to North Van west along West Georgia St to Lonsdale Quay, and east on Pender St to Phibbs Exchange, near the north end of the Second Narrows Bridge, where you can connect with other buses.

Lonsdale Quay Market

Aside from being a transportation hub, Lonsdale Quay Market (☎ 604-985-6261) is home to 80 stores and services, offices, apartments, a hotel and Waterfront Park. Following the success of both the SeaBus service, which was inaugurated in 1977, and of Granville Island Public Market, the quay was developed in the mid-1980s to breath life into the lower section of Lonsdale Ave, and to that end it has been very successful.

The 1st floor of the market is devoted to fresh and cooked food, while the 2nd floor has mainly specialty shops, as well as restaurants with good views. The Lonsdale Quay Hotel takes up the top floor (see the Places to Stay chapter for details). As you leave the ferry, there's a Travel InfoCentre, open May to September, daily from 9 am to 6 pm. The market is open daily from 9.30 am to 6.30 pm, and to 9 pm on Friday.

If you continue north up **Lonsdale Ave**, the commercial center of North Vancouver, you'll find shops, cafes, restaurants and businesses, as well as the large Lions Gate Hospital a block east on 15th St. Once you cross the Trans Canada Hwy (Hwy 1) this commercial strip becomes a residential thoroughfare.

North Vancouver Museum & Archives

This museum (☎ 604-987-5618), 209 West 4th St at Chesterfield Ave, just west of Lonsdale Ave, has rather good changing exhibits on the history of North Vancouver, covering a wide range of subjects such as transport and industry, with displays on antiques and Native Indian crafts, plus a fabulous collection of photographs. The museum is open Wednesday to Sunday from noon to 5 pm, and the archives are open Wednesday to Friday from 9.30 am to 4.30 pm. Admission is free.

To get to the museum, take the SeaBus to Lonsdale Quay or bus Nos 239 or 246.

Capilano Suspension Bridge

You might ask yourself, why do people want to spend money to walk on a bridge that essentially goes nowhere? Apparently this isn't a question on a lot of people's minds – they arrive here by the busload to do just that. This bridge (☎ 604-985-7474), 3735 Capilano Rd, adjoining Capilano River Regional Park, spans the Capilano River for almost 135m at a height of 69m.

The first bridge was built in 1888 by George Mackay to gain access to some of his 2400 hectares of property. Made of cedar planks and hemp rope, the bridge became a popular destination for people seeking a thrill. The suspension bridge, although no longer made of rope and wooden planks, is still *very* popular, and the crowds can be oppressive. As someone once said, 'Build it and they will come'! There are also history and forestry exhibits, a totem-pole and nature park, the Native Indian Carving Centre, a gift shop and restaurants. Open daily May to September from 8.30 am to 9 pm, October to April from 9 am to 5 pm.

Capilano Suspension Bridge

Admission is $8.95/7.50/6/3 adults/seniors/students/children (six to 12), and free for children under six.

To get to the bridge, take bus No 236 from Lonsdale Quay.

Capilano Salmon Hatchery

The hatchery is a fish farm (☎ 604-666-1790), 4500 Capilano Park Rd, run by the Federal Department of Fisheries and Oceans to help stop the depletion of valuable salmon stocks. It's in Capilano River Regional Park, off Capilano Rd about 2km north of the suspension bridge.

Although you can't see the holding pools, there are exhibits with good explanations of the whole process. Salmon in various stages of growth are on display in eye-level tanks, and you can see how they are channeled from the river into the hatchery when they head upstream to spawn. Open daily from 8 am to 4 pm. Admission is free.

To get to the hatchery, take bus No 236 from Lonsdale Quay.

Cleveland Dam

The dam (☎ 604-224-5739), built in 1954, blocks the 5.6km Capilano Lake, which supplies about 40% of the Lower Mainland's drinking water. To the north there are great views of the Lions: the West Lion at 1646m and the East Lion at 1599m are the two highest peaks of the North Shore Range of the Coast Mountains – and it's from them the Lions Gate Bridge takes its name. The dam is at the top of Capilano River Regional Park and there are picnic areas and trails. The dam is about half a kilometre north of the salmon hatchery off Capilano Rd, which becomes Nancy Greene Way.

The **Capilano River Regional Park** extends south from the dam along the Capilano River to the Upper Levels Hwy (Hwy 1). One of the trails in the park, the Capilano Pacific, extends south from the dam more or less following the Capilano River to its mouth at Ambleside Park in West Vancouver.

To get to the dam, take bus No 236 from Lonsdale Quay.

Grouse Mountain

With the Lower Mainland sprawling below it, Grouse Mountain (☎ 604-984-0661), 6400 Nancy Greene Way (the northern extension of Capilano Rd), is a must-see for visitors. Not only is this the city's most convenient ski and boarding area, with several runs even lit for night skiing, but in summer it's also great for walking and hiking, plus the Grouse Nest offers *the* best views of any restaurant in Greater Vancouver (see the Places to Eat chapter for details).

Keep in mind that if you are going up just for the views and there is the slightest hint of cloud around the mountain, wait until it clears because once you're at the top you won't see a thing. Also consider going up in the late afternoon so you can see the city's lights come on.

Skiers and hikers have been making the trek here since the early 1900s, which at that time was a roundtrip journey of about three days. With the completion of a toll road to the base of the mountain, the first chalet opened in 1926 and was eventually followed by North America's first double chairlift in 1949. The original chalet burned down in 1962 and was replaced with the current facility.

Grouse Mountain is famous for its Swiss-built, 125-passenger **Skyride**, the largest aerial tramway in North America that, in about eight minutes, takes you from the base to the chalet, 1100m above sea level. It operates daily, departing every 15 minutes from 9 am to 10 pm, and costs $17/15/11/6 adults/seniors/youths (13 to 18)/children. These prices are slightly higher if you are going up to ski, and there is no charge if you have made reservations in the restaurant.

After exiting the tramway you enter the top floor of the stone-and-wood chalet (check out the carved wood-to-ceiling posts in the foyer) where you'll find the restaurant and Bar 98. On the ground floor there are shops, a cafeteria and the 110-seat **Theatre in the Sky**, admission to which is included with your Skyride ticket. The theater's 25-minute film, a history of Grouse Mountain and an overview of southwestern BC from an eagle's point of view, is shown every half-hour in summer and every hour in winter. The ski runs and lifts to the summit (1230m) are in front of the chalet.

For more information on Grouse Mountain, see the Activities section later in this chapter. To get to the mountain, take bus No 236 from Lonsdale Quay.

Lynn Canyon Park

Set in thick woods, this 250-hectare park provides a good example of the temperate rain-forest vegetation found throughout the coastal Pacific Northwest. There are many hiking trails throughout the park where you can find your own picnic spots and swimming spots in deep-water pools. Originally built in 1912, a **suspension bridge** crosses over the canyon with the river some 50m below and, although not as big as the Capilano Suspension Bridge, it's much the same and it's free. Near the bridge, the **Ecology Centre** (☎ 604-981-3103), 3663 Park Rd, has interactive displays, films and slide shows about the biology of the area and is open daily from 10 am to 5 pm.

To get to the park, take bus Nos 228 or 229 from Lonsdale Quay. If driving, take the Trans Canada Hwy (Hwy 1) to Lynn Valley Rd and follow it north to Peters Rd, turn east (right) and the parking lot is at the end.

Mt Seymour Provincial Park

This park (☎ 604-986-2261), at an altitude of about 1000m, is a quick escape from the city. The road travels up to a parking lot and from there a chairlift goes to the peak. The park, which is only 16km from Vancouver, has 10 hiking trails varying in difficulty and length (the easiest being Goldie Lake Trail) which make their way past 250-to-800-year-old Douglas firs. Some areas are very rugged, so visitors going on overnight trips should register at the park office, where trail maps are available. There's also skiing in winter, including night skiing (see the Activities section later for details).

There are parking lots for RVs but no real tent campgrounds, although you can pitch a tent along the many alpine trails. There really isn't any public transportation into the park although, from Phibbs

Exchange, bus No 215 will get you to the bottom of Mt Seymour Rd, where you might be able to hitch a ride to the top. If driving, take the Trans Canada Hwy (Hwy 1) to the Mt Seymour Pkwy (near the Second Narrows Bridge) and follow it east to Mt Seymour Rd, which then heads north to the parking lot.

If you do drive, stop at the two **lookouts** along the way for spectacular views of Indian Arm, Vancouver, Washington State's Mt Baker and Olympics to the south, and all the way to Vancouver Island to the west.

Seymour Demonstration Forest

Seemingly part of Mt Seymour Provincial Park but actually administered by the GVRD, this 5600 hectares of wilderness area in the lower Seymour Valley has 40km of trails (many are paved) which can be used by walkers, hikers, cyclists and in-line skaters. On the weekend, the forestry education center conducts tours explaining water and forestry management (hence the park's name) and identifying the vegetation and some of the 100 species of animals, birds and fish that live in the park. Call ☎ 604-987-1273 for information.

To get to the forest, take the Trans Canada Hwy (Hwy 1) to the Lillooet Rd exit and follow it north into the park. Be warned that near the park entrance the road is in very bad condition with potholes resembling small lakes, so the going is slow. There is no public transportation to the park.

Cates Park

While you are in the area you might want to go to Deep Cove to visit Cates Park on the Dollarton Hwy overlooking Indian Arm, especially if you are a Malcolm Lowry fan. What is now a relatively small park is where the writer, best known for his novel *Under the Volcano*, lived with his wife from 1940 to 1954. There is a walk dedicated to him that goes to the area where his squatter's shack was once located (ironically, when Lowry was squatting here the authorities did everything in their power to have him removed). In the park you will also find the remains of the Dollar Lumber Mill (in operation from 1916 to 1942), a 15m Native Indian war canoe, forest walks and a sandy beach.

Farther along is the small village of Deep Cove, which is worth visiting for its gift shops, restaurants and cafes, and for renting kayaks and canoes to explore Indian Arm (see the Activities section later in this chapter for details). If you want a drink or a meal, The Raven Pub is highly recommended (see Bars & Pubs in the Entertainment chapter for details).

To get to the park, or Deep Cove, take bus No 212 from Phibbs Exchange. If driving, take the Trans Canada Hwy (Hwy 1) to the Dollarton Hwy (near the Second Narrows Bridge) and follow it east.

WEST VANCOUVER (Map 8)

West of the Capilano River and extending east as far as Horseshoe Bay, West Vancouver (population 42,500) is where you'll find some of the Lower Mainland's wealthiest neighborhoods, particularly the British Properties, above the Upper Levels Hwy (Hwy 1), and Caulfeild off Marine Drive.

Close to the Lions Gate Bridge and straddling Marine Drive, the **Park Royal Shopping Centre** is Canada's first mall, although today with its 200 shops it's very different than it was in 1945 when it was located on the north side of the road only. Behind it, extending west from the mouth of the Capilano River to 13th St, is **Ambleside Park** with its sandy beach, playing fields, pitch-and-putt golf course, duck pond, dog park and historic ferry building. Continue west along Argyle Ave to **John Lawson Park** at 17th St and you'll hook up with the popular Centennial Seawalk that goes to the Dundarave Pier at 25th St.

Marine Drive continues west through **Ambleside and Dundarave**, collectively known as 'The Village.' This is the commercial center of West Vancouver (which is simply called West Van) and here you'll find designer shops, cafes and restaurants. This is a pleasant area to spend an afternoon browsing in the shops or having a meal. In fact, a couple of the Lower Mainland's better restaurants are located in West Van-

couver (see the Places to Eat chapter for details).

Marine Drive winds its way past expensive waterfront homes, rocky beaches and small coves hidden away from the road, with good views (especially from Lighthouse Park) looking back at Vancouver and across to Point Grey. Eventually Marine Drive reaches Horseshoe Bay where you can either spend some time wandering around the marina, catch the ferry to Bowen Island or, if you are driving, swing up onto the Upper Levels Hwy (Hwy 1) and return to Vancouver.

On your way back, stop off at **Cypress Provincial Park** (☎ 604-924-2200) where you can go downhill or cross-country skiing in the winter or hiking in the summer. It has eight hiking trails, including the Baden-Powell, Yew Lake and Howe Sound Crest Trails. The trails cut through forests of huge Douglas fir, yellow cypress and cedar, and there is a lake. On the way up the Cypress Access Rd you'll get great views all the way to Vancouver Island. There is no public transport to the park.

To get to West Van, take one of the West Vancouver Blue Buses (part of the BC Transit system) west on West Georgia St; bus No 250 travels between Vancouver and Horseshoe Bay, making frequent stops along the way. Also, BC Transit bus No 239 travels between Phibbs Exchange, Lonsdale Quay and Park Royal.

Lighthouse Park

This 75-hectare park is probably the easiest access to virgin forest you'll find in the Lower Mainland. Some of the 500-year-old Douglas firs stand as tall as 60m – these were big trees even in 1792 when Captain Vancouver mapped this coast and named Point Atkinson. You'll also see the unusual arbutus, a wide-leaf evergreen with orange peeling bark.

There are about 13km of hiking trails, with the most popular one leading to the Point Atkinson Lighthouse, which guards the entrance to Burrard Inlet from its rocky perch. The lighthouse, with its two-tone foghorn, was built in 1912 to replace the

Lighthouse, Cameras, Action!

Don't be surprised if you stumble over a film crew while walking around Lighthouse Park, or trip over electrical cables stretched across the forest trails, or see helicopters hovering overhead while you try to enjoy the views across to Point Grey. The park has become a very popular location for some of the many TV series and films shot in the Vancouver area.

Some neighbors have complained that film crews destroy vegetation by either trampling it or by removing bushes that aren't considered appropriate for the film. The crews also drill holes in the rocks, damage park equipment and fly helicopters only 7m above some of the surrounding homes.

One local resident, who became fed up with the Hollywoodization of the only old-growth Douglas fir forest in Greater Vancouver, told the West Vancouver council that 'Lighthouse Park has become a convenient escort-for-hire to producers of questionable cultural pulp – in the last eight years it has been the scene of death by decapitation, stabbing, gunshots and immolation.' Be that as it may, West Vancouver earns $1000 a day to let all this bloodshed and mayhem take place and it is unlikely to tell the film industry to take a hike. Pass the popcorn.

1875 original. This is one of the few staffed lighthouses left on the coast and it is not open to visitors. Park maps are available in the parking lot. The park entrance is at Beacon Lane off Marine Drive about 10km west of the Lions Gate Bridge. To get to the park, take bus No 250 west on West Georgia St.

Horseshoe Bay

The small coastal community of Horseshoe Bay marks the end of West Vancouver. It's a pretty spot, with great views across the bay and up Howe Sound to distant glacial peaks. There are several places to eat and shop,

most of which are situated along the waterfront on Bay St, near the marina.

But what Horseshoe Bay is really all about is the BC Ferries Terminal, where ferries travel between Nanaimo on Vancouver Island, Langdale on the Sunshine Coast (Sechelt Peninsula) and Bowen Island. If you aren't catching a ferry and it's a nice day, consider going on a skippered four-hour group **charter** to see some of the coastline, or rent a motorboat by the hour, half day or day from Sewell's Landing Marina (☎ 604-921-3474), 6695 Nelson Ave. Here you can also get maps, fishing gear and licenses.

Just beyond Horseshoe Bay, at the very end of Marine Drive, is **Whytecliff Park,** a great little park right on the water. Trails lead to vistas and a gazebo, from where you can watch the boat traffic and the ferries wend their way in and out of Burrard Inlet. The rocky beach is a great place to play, go for a swim or scamper over the large rock protruding from the beach. And as the park contains an underwater reserve, it's a favorite place with divers.

To get to Horseshoe Bay, take bus Nos 250 or 257 (express) west on West Georgia St.

Richmond

Bordered by the North and South arms of the Fraser River, the island city of Richmond, with a population of 157,000, is where many visitors to the Lower Mainland first arrive when they land at Vancouver international airport. But chances are, all you'll see is what passes by the window as you whisk through on your way to another part of the Lower Mainland, not to return until it's time to catch a flight home. However, Richmond actually has a few worthwhile attractions.

Even though Richmond has become closely identified with the recent influx of Hong Kong Chinese, to such an extent that it is often referred to as 'Asia West,' it began as an agricultural and fishing community. Even today, with its many shopping centers and housing developments, it still has some of the Lower Mainland's best farmland, much of it made useable by the many dikes that have been built to hold back the river, and it is home to BC's largest fishing fleet at Steveston, where there is also a historic fishing village.

Richmond is actually made up of a group of islands at the mouth of the Fraser River, the two largest being Lulu Island (named after Lulu Sweet, a popular San Francisco entertainer of the mid-1800s) and Sea Island, home to the international airport. Essentially, No 3 Rd is the main north-south thoroughfare while the Westminster Hwy (which indeed does go all the way to New Westminster) is the main east-west road. Hwy 91 also goes east to New Westminster before veering south to Delta by way of the Alex Fraser Bridge, eventually hooking up with Hwy 99 near Surrey.

Going directly south through Richmond, Hwy 99 crosses the North Arm of the Fraser River by way of the Oak St Bridge, and travels under the South Arm of the Fraser River by way of the George Massey Tunnel, which connects it to Delta. Hwy 99 continues south through Surrey, eventually ending at the Canadian-US border, bypassing Tsawwassen and White Rock on the way.

The city's hub is the **Richmond Town Centre** which runs along No 3 Rd south from about Bridgeport Rd to Granville Ave. Here you'll find two large malls – Lansdowne Shopping Centre and Richmond Square Shopping Centre – plus the smaller Asian-influenced shopping malls including the Yaohan Centre, President Plaza, Aberdeen Centre and Parker Place. A slice of Hong Kong, these Asian centers are filled almost exclusively with Chinese stores, Chinese products and Chinese shoppers, and most of the signs are in Chinese. You'll also find excellent Chinese food here at very reasonable prices. As you drive through the neighborhoods, take note of the enormous new homes favored by the Hong Kong immigrants.

While in Richmond it's worth visiting the **Buddhist Temple**, (☎ 604-274-2822), 9160 Steveston Hwy, near the south end of No 3 Rd, which is open to the public for viewing, meditation classes and tea ceremonies. This two-tiered building – with flaring eaves, flying dragons and a gold roof – is a beautiful example of traditional Chinese architecture surrounded by landscaped gardens, complete with bonsai plants. Open daily from 10 am to 5 pm. To get to the temple take bus No 403 from Howe St in downtown Vancouver.

To get to No 3 Rd, take bus Nos 401, 403, 406 or 407 from Howe St.

RICHMOND NATURE PARK (Map 1)

This 80-hectare park (☎ 604-273-7015), 11851 Westminster Hwy, is dedicated to environmental education and the preservation of what remains of a 3000-year-old peat bog. The park features boardwalks through various ecosystems (a marsh, a forest and a pond), with interpretive displays and signage. The Nature House Centre continues the theme with interactive exhibits designed with children in mind. Open dawn to dusk and admission is free.

To get to the park, take bus Nos 401, 403, 406 or 407 from Howe St, and transfer to No 405 at the Richmond Exchange. If driving, follow Hwy 99 south.

STEVESTON

In the southwest corner of Richmond is the old fishing village of Steveston, Canada's largest commercial fishing port. This has long been the center of the region's fishing operations, although today it's rather tame compared to the late 1800s when a fishing season population of 10,000 people lived here, many of whom worked in the dozen or so canneries that lined the river. Today, only BC Packers' Imperial Cannery, started in 1893, remains in operation.

Japanese immigrants were one of the main groups to settle Steveston in the early 20th century. However, like other minorities at that time, they were often treated as second-class citizens and it wasn't until 1949 that Japanese Canadians were granted the right to vote. During WWII, nearly all the Japanese Canadians in the province, and specifically Steveston, were sent to the interior of BC to live in internment camps, and their boats and homes were sold at auction without a penny from the sales going to the owners. Financial compensation was finally made by the government in 1988, money from which went toward building the Japanese Canadian Cultural Centre in Steveston.

If you're interested in the history of Steveston, stop by the **Steveston Museum** (☎ 604-271-6868), 3811 Moncton St, which tells the story of the town's fishing past and the internment of the Japanese; admission is free. Moncton St runs through the center of the old village that fronts on to the South Arm of the Fraser River, and is bordered by Chatham St to the north, No 1 Rd to the east and 4th Ave to the west. The village is quite charming, and has a selection of shops, good restaurants and pubs.

There's more history at the **Gulf of Georgia Cannery National Historic Site** (☎ 604-664-9009), at the foot of 4th Ave and Bayview St, which operated from 1894 to 1979 and was the largest cannery on the Fraser River. Inside there are exhibits and a theater showing the West Coast's fishing

White Rock & Crescent Beach

These scenic beachside communities, just a 45-minute drive south of Vancouver near the Canadian-US border, are great places to visit – particularly to stroll the promenade and pier at White Rock or to go for a swim at Crescent Beach on a warm summer day. Or, head to White Rock to try one of the many restaurants along Marine Drive, which runs parallel with the beachside promenade between Oxford St and Johnston Rd. In fact, there are so many restaurants along this strip, it's referred to as 'Restaurant Row.'

In White Rock, on the 2km promenade near the 537m pier, the tourist information booth is open July to October, daily from 9 am to 5 pm. Beside it, the small White Rock Museum & Archives (☎ 604-541-2222) is located in what was the station of the former Burlington Northern Railway. Just to the south of the pier on the beach is the large white rock from which the town gets its name.

Centennial Park, 14600 North Bluff Rd, offers a series of steep trails surrounding two ravines – the ocean views are worth the visit alone – and children will love Semiahmoo Park, 158th St and Marine Drive, where there is a playground equipped with swings and a slide in the shape of a whale.

The shallow and reasonably warm Semiahmoo Bay is a great place to kayak or canoe. Campbell River, on the east side of Semiahmoo Park, is a good place to launch a boat. Kayaks and canoes can be rented from either Natural West Coast Adventures (☎ 604-535-7985), 1308 Everall St, or Boundary Bay Water Sports (☎ 604-541-9191), 1-15531 24th Ave. Both charge about $15 an hour or $75 a day for rental. White Rock Cycle (☎ 604-531-8111), 1465 Johnston Rd, rents bicycles for $6/18 per hour/day, plus $2 an hour for a helmet. For golf enthusiasts, the two closest 18-hole courses, both in Surrey, are the Meridian (☎ 604-541-1213), 1054 168th St, and the Peace Portal (☎ 604-538-4818), 16900 4th Ave. The Peace Portal also has a nine-hole par-three course.

Crescent Beach, just a couple of kilometers north of White Rock at the tip of the South Surrey Peninsula on Boundary Bay, provides good, relatively warm swimming, vast stretches of sand to walk or run along during low tide, and the breakwaters and tidal pools are good places to see herons and other wildlife or to dig for clams. Restaurants and shops stretch for about two blocks along Beecher St to a beachfront cul-de-sac. This is a great place to watch a sunset.

To get to either White Rock or Crescent Beach by car, take Hwy 99 south from Vancouver, or take bus No 351 from Burrard Station, which runs every half-hour during the week, and hourly on weekends; the bus ride takes about an hour.

history, plus a 1930 to 1950 canning line. Open July to September daily from 10 am to 5 pm; and in May, June, September and October, Thursday to Monday from 10 am to 5 pm. Admission is $4/3/2 for adults/ seniors & students/children (six to 16), and $10 for a family.

Down on Government Wharf behind the cannery, PaJo's at the Wharf is a great little place if you're feeling hungry; all the seats are outside on the small dock and you order your fish and chips (starting at $3.50), burgers ($3.50) or clam chowder ($2.50) from the window. There's lots of activity along the waterfront where you can buy fresh fish off the boats docked at **Steveston Landing**, or wander around the complex with its restaurants (serving mostly fish and chips) and shops.

If you don't want to eat fish then try Persimmon's Cafe (☎ 604-275-3753), 210 - 3791 Bayview St, across the street behind the landing, which has toasted bagel sandwiches ($4), vegburgers ($5) or lasagna ($6). It also has a fireplace and live music on Friday night.

To get to Steveston, take bus Nos 401, 406 or 407 from Howe St.

Activities

The question is, what can't be done in Vancouver? With its access to forested parks, ski hills, the ocean and various sports centers, you don't have to look too hard to find some activity of interest. The activities listed here are certainly not inclusive but suggestions to get you headed in the right direction. For other suggestions, see the Books section in the Facts for the Visitor chapter.

BIKING, IN-LINE SKATING & RUNNING

A good way to get around the city and the numerous parks and beach areas is by bicycle – and often where you can cycle you can also in-line skate and run. There are a number of designated routes: the 10.5km seawall around Stanley Park; the 10km route around False Creek; the BC Parkway, which more or less follows the SkyTrain

from the Science World-Main St Station to the New Westminster Station; and the numerous trails for mountain bikers and runners in Pacific Spirit Regional Park and for in-line skaters in North Vancouver's Seymour Demonstration Forest. Plus, there are any number of routes you can create on your own just by following a city map.

A good ride, or run, is to follow the route from Granville Island through Vanier Park to Kitsilano Beach Park, then along Point Grey Rd to Jericho Beach Park and follow the shoreline to Spanish Banks Beach (it's about 15km roundtrip). However, from Spanish Banks you can follow North-West Marine Drive around Point Grey to the other side of the peninsula, then take Dunbar St north back to Point Grey Rd and Kitsilano. From Granville Island this is about 25km roundtrip.

If you are feeling really energetic, you can cycle through Stanley Park, over the Lions Gate Bridge to West Vancouver, and then along Marine Drive to Horseshoe Bay. If that's not enough for one day then take the ferry over to Bowen Island and cycle around it before making the trip back. From Vancouver to Horseshoe Bay is about 40km roundtrip. Of course you could always spend the night on Bowen Island in a B&B and return the following day. That is unless you decide to swing up on to Hwy 99 and cycle to Squamish (64km north of Vancouver), or Whistler (120km north of Vancouver).

See the Getting Around chapter for more information on cycling in the city, plus details on bicycle and in-line skate rental.

BOATING

From kayaking to sailing to windsurfing, if you are interested in exploring Vancouver's waterways then there are various options available. A good place to start for any of these activities is Granville Island. For information on renting motorboats and fishing gear, see the Horseshoe Bay section earlier in the chapter, or try Granville Island Boat Rentals (☎ 604-682-6287).

There are some things you should know before you hit the water. If you are paddling, you should not attempt to go under the

Lions Gate Bridge as the currents there are extremely strong; sailboards are not allowed at the mouth of False Creek between the Burrard and Granville Bridges; and in False Creek the maximum speed for boats is five knots and sails are prohibited. Before you head out on the water for the day, call ☎ 604-664-9010 for a marine forecast.

Kayaking

For either the beginner or the experienced, kayaking is a great way to see False Creek, English Bay, Burrard Inlet or one of the surrounding rivers such as the Fraser. Ecomarine Ocean Kayak Centre (☎ 604-689-7575), 1668 Duranleau St, Granville Island, hires out kayaks for two hours at $22 for a one-person kayak, $32 for a two-person kayak, or $42/62 for a full day. There are weekly rates as well. It has another outlet at the Jericho Sailing Centre at Jericho Beach near the hostel. Ecomarine also offers courses and educational tours of the islands in Georgia Strait and in Clayoquot Sound on the west coast of Vancouver Island.

Sailing

If you are an experienced sailor, you can rent sailboats for anything from an evening sail to a weeklong trip through the Gulf Islands from, among others, Blue Pacific Yacht Charters (☎ 604-682-2161), 1519 Foreshore Walk, or Cooper Boating Centre (☎ 604-687-4110), 1620 Duranleau St, both on Granville Island. A skipper can be pro-

vided if you're not confident about your skills. Three- to four-hour sailing cruises on English Bay are also offered but require a minimum of four people.

Windsurfing

For sailing of a different kind, windsurfing is another option. Try Windmaster (☎ 604-685-7245), at Denman St and Beach Ave at English Bay, or Windsure Windsurfing School (☎ 604-224-0615), 1300 Discovery St at the Jericho Sailing Centre; both offer lessons and rent boards.

CLIMBING

There's rock climbing close to Vancouver at places such as Juniper Point in West Vancouver's Lighthouse Park, the bluffs overlooking Indian Arm in Deep Cove or some of the peaks of the North Shore mountains. Aside from that, climbing is pretty much restricted to indoor centers, which generally charge about $12 for a day pass, plus $8 for the equipment.

Some indoor rock climbing centers to try are Cliffhanger Indoor Rock Climbing (☎ 604-874-2400), 106 West 1st Ave; Edge Climbing Centre (☎ 604-984-9080), 2 - 1485 Welch St, North Vancouver, just off Capilano Rd below Marine Drive, which is Western Canada's largest indoor center offering a variety of climbs and programs, including ones geared for children; and Rock House Indoor Climbing Centre (☎ 604-276-0012), 520 - 3771 Jacombs Rd, Richmond, near Bridgeport Rd and Knight St.

Serious climbers, however, head up to Squamish to scale the Stawamus Chief or the Smoke Bluffs (see the Excursions chapter for details), or farther north to Murrin Park and Cheakamus Canyon. For more information, or to find out about courses, contact the Federation of Mountain Clubs of BC at ☎ 604-737-3053.

GOLF

From Whistler to Hope there are more than 70 golf courses. Several large tournaments are held in Vancouver annually, including the prestigious Greater Vancouver Open, part of the US PGA Tour, which is played at the Northview Golf & Country Club in Surrey over Labour Day weekend.

If you want to play a round or two you can try these public courses close to the city.

University Golf Club
(☎ 604-224-1818) 5185 University Blvd; par 72, 6157 yards

Langara Golf Course
(☎ 604-280-7888) 6706 Alberta St, near West 49th Ave; par 71, 6100 yards

Fraserview Golf Course
(☎ 604-280-8633) 7800 Vivian Drive, near East 54th St; par 71, 6346 yards

Gleneagles Golf Course
(☎ 604-921-7353) 6190 Marine Drive, West Vancouver, near Horseshoe Bay; nine holes, par 35, 2800 yards

Mayfair Lakes Golf Course
(☎ 604-276-0505) 5460 No 7 Rd, Richmond, off Hwy 91; par 72, 6225 yard

If you want the quick version, then try one of the pitch-and-putt courses at Stanley Park, Queen Elizabeth Park, Central Park or Ambleside Park.

HIKING

Hiking opportunities abound in the many regional and provincial parks in the Lower Mainland (see the individual parks in this chapter for details).

For a serious hike on the North Shore, the Baden-Powell Trail extends 41km from Horseshoe Bay on Howe Sound to Deep Cove out Indian Arm, joining together most of the area's major mountainous trails.

In any of the North Shore parks be prepared for continually changing mountain weather conditions – the weather can change quickly and a warm sunny day in the city might not mean it's going to be the same, or stay the same, in the mountains. Take along a warm waterproof jacket, wear sturdy shoes and a hat, and carry a water bottle. For mountain weather forecasts call ☎ 604-664-9021 before heading out for the day.

A little farther out, but well worth the trip, is Golden Ears Provincial Park (☎ 604-463-3513), 50km east of Vancouver, with 11 hiking trails plus a campsite and picnic areas. To get there, take Hwy 7 east (which is Broadway in Vancouver and becomes the Lougheed Hwy in Burnaby) to Haney and follow the signs to Alouette Lake.

If you are interested in going on a guided hike (offered May to October) in the North Shore mountains, or a nature walk (available throughout the year) in some of the other parks such as Lighthouse Park or Lynn Canyon Park, contact Active Lifestyles Fitness Services (☎/fax 604-984-6032), 1222 Doran Rd, North Vancouver.

Hike BC (☎ 604-684-9722) also offers guided day-hike tours in the wilderness parks around Vancouver. Both companies charge around $60, which includes hotel pickup and drop off and a picnic lunch.

For general information about the parks administered by the GVRD, call ☎ 604-432-6350; to receive information about nature programs, call ☎ 604-432-6359; or write to GVRD, Parks Department, 4330 Kingsway, Burnaby, BC V5H 4G8.

For information about BC provincial parks in the South Coast Region, call ☎ 604-929-1291. Also worth investigating is the Provincial Ministry of Environment, Lands and Parks' program designed to promote wildlife viewing in BC; call ☎ 604-582-5200 for information.

For general information about hiking clubs and courses, contact the Federation of Mountain Clubs of BC at ☎ 604-737-3053.

RAFTING

With all those rivers roaring down from all those mountains, you would be right in believing there are some good whitewater rafting opportunities to be had outside the city. The serious rivers, such as the Upper Fraser, the Thompson and the Chilliwack, offer some pretty exciting trips through canyons, the very names of which are enough to scare the life out of you, such as Hell's Gate, Jaws of Death, Devil's Cauldron and the Washing Machine.

Rafting trips are also possible in the Squamish and Whistler areas, although without offering quite the adrenaline rush you'll experience on one of the interior rivers. Leisurely float trips are also offered on many of the rivers.

There are a number of companies offering a variety of trips, including Down to Earth Adventures (☎ 604-323-6350), 403 - 2020 West 2nd Ave; Great Expeditions (☎ 604-257-2040), 5915 West Blvd; or Hyak Wilderness Adventures (☎ 604-734-8622), 1975 Maple St.

SCUBA DIVING

There are some wonderful underwater sights around Vancouver for those who enjoy diving. Diving is restricted in the harbor, and if you plan to dive in Indian Arm, please notify the Harbour Master at ☎ 604-666-2405, or 666-6011. In BC waters divers will need a 6mm neoprene wetsuit as temperatures below the thermocline stay at about 10°C (50°F).

Areas popular for diving include Cates Park in North Vancouver (see that section earlier in the chapter for details); Lighthouse and Whytecliff Parks off Marine Drive in West Vancouver (see those sections earlier for details); and Porteau Cove on Hwy 99, 24km north of Horseshoe Bay, which is a provincial marine park and has an artificial reef made from pieces of old ships, plus there is a campsite with showers.

A number of outfitters offer equipment, training and trips, including International Diving Centre (☎ 604-736-2541), 2034 West 11th Ave, and Diving Locker (☎ 604-736-2681), 2745 West 4th Ave, both in Kitsilano.

SKATING

If you want to practice your ice-dancing routine, or just have fun, some skating rinks to try include the outdoor rink at Robson Square, open from November to early March; the West End Community Centre (☎ 604-257-8333), 870 Denman St, open from October to March; and the Britannia Community Centre (☎ 604-253-4391), 1661 Napier St, off Commercial Drive, which stays open throughout the year. Call the two indoor rinks for public skating times, and costs for both admission and rental.

SKIING & SNOWBOARDING

Around Vancouver there are some excellent downhill skiing and snowboarding areas as well as cross-country skiing trails, some of them just minutes from the city center. To get to the areas listed here, see their relevant sections earlier in the chapter.

Cypress Bowl (☎ 604-926-5612, 419-7669 for snow information), at Cypress Provincial Park in West Vancouver, has 23 runs with the longest being 3.2km, plus rental, instruction and night skiing until 10 pm. There are also cross-country ski trails and a toboganing slope. There is a shuttle service (☎ 604-878-9229) from Lonsdale Quay, Park Royal Shopping Centre and Horseshoe Bay. A downhill day pass is $33/15/28/17 adults/seniors/youths (13 to 18)/children, and $2 for kids six.

Grouse Mountain (☎ 604-984-0661, 986-6262 for snow information), North Vancouver, has 13 runs with the longest being 2.4km, snowmaking facilities, rental, instruction and night skiing until 10 pm. There is also the Munday Alpine Snow Shoe Park for those who would rather walk, plus cross-country ski trails and an outdoor skating rink. A downhill day pass is weekdays $19/15/9 adults/seniors/children (seven to 12) and weekends $25/15/15/. Family passes (two adults and two children) cost $55 on weekdays and $75 on weekends.

Mt Seymour Provincial Park (☎ 604-986-2261, 879-3999 for snow information), North Vancouver, has 25 runs with the longest being 2.4km, rental, instruction and night skiing until 10 pm. There is also snowshoe and cross-country trails and a tobogganing slope. There is a shuttle service operating on the weekends from the Mohawk service station at the foot of Mt Seymour Rd. A downhill pass is weekdays $18/14 for adults/seniors & children; on weekends $26/15, and $20 for youths (13 to 18).

Farther away from Vancouver (not including Whistler which is covered in the Excursions chapter) the ski areas include: Hemlock Valley (☎ 604-797-4411), 125km east of the city, which has 19 runs with the longest being 1.6km; Mt Baker in Washington State (☎ 360-734-6771), 120km south of the city, which has 48 runs with the longest being 3.2km; and Manning Park (☎ 604-840-8822), 240km east of Vancouver on

Hwy 3 between Hope and Princeton, which has *the* best cross-country skiing in, or close to, the Lower Mainland with 190km of trails.

SWIMMING
Beaches
There are 11 beaches around the city that are fine for swimming, and from the end of May to the beginning of September seven of them are patrolled by lifeguards, including Third Beach and Second Beach (Stanley Park), English Bay Beach (West End), Kitsilano Beach, Jericho Beach, Locarno Beach and Spanish Banks Beach (all on the West Side). The water is never exactly warm; it reaches a high in summer of around 21°C (70°F).

In West Vancouver there is a sandy beach at Ambleside Park, and some good swimming off the rocks at Lighthouse Park and at the beach in Whytecliff Park. Crescent Beach beside White Rock, near the Canadian-US border, is a popular beach during summer (see the White Rock & Crescent Beach boxed text earlier in this chapter).

Pools
The main aquatic centers in Greater Vancouver are open throughout the year, while two of the more central outdoor pools are open in summer only. Admission to any of these facilities is about $4/2.50/2 for adults/youths/seniors & children. Because times for public swimming in the indoor facilities vary widely throughout the year, it's best to call first for times.

Indoor Canada Games Pool (☎ 604-526-4281), 65 East 6th Ave, New Westminster, has a 50m pool, waterslide, toddler pool, water toys and a fitness center. Minoru Aquatic Centre (☎ 604-278-3178), 7560 Minoru Gate, off Granville Ave, Richmond, has a pool, sauna, universal gym and exercise facilities. UBC Aquatic Centre (☎ 604-822-4521), off University Blvd beside the bus loop, has a 50m pool, saunas and exercise areas open to the public.

Vancouver Aquatic Centre (☎ 604-665-3424), 1050 Beach Ave, at Sunset Beach beside the Burrard Bridge, has a 50m pool, whirlpool, diving tank, gym and sauna. West Vancouver Aquatic Centre (☎ 604-925-7210), 776 22nd St, just off Marine Drive, has a 37m pool, fitness room, sauna, whirlpool and teach pool.

The YMCA (☎ 604-681-0221), 955 Burrard St, is open to both sexes at coed swim times. The day pass for nonmembers allows access to all the facilities, including a gym, courts and sauna.

Outdoor The heated 137m Kitsilano Outdoor Pool (Map 6; ☎ 604-731-0011), Cornwall Ave and Yew St at Kitsilano Beach Park, is the only one in the city to use saltwater. The Second Beach Pool in Stanley Park is right beside the beach and has lanes for laps as well as a children's area with waterslides. Both pools are open May 17 to September 7, daily from about 7 am to 8.45 pm.

TENNIS
There is no shortage of courts in Vancouver, which is why you might wonder why it takes so long to get on one. This is a popular activity and because of the Lower Mainland's relatively mild winters, it can be played year-round. The public courts are free to use and, with a couple of exceptions, are outdoors.

Some of the more central courts include Stanley Park with 17 courts by the Beach Ave entrance and four courts by Lost Lagoon at the foot of Robson St; Kitsilano Beach Park with 10 courts; False Creek Community Centre, Granville Island, with three courts; Jericho Beach Park with five courts; UBC (East Mall and Thunderbird Blvd) with 10 outdoor and four indoor courts; and Queen Elizabeth Park with 20 courts.

Places to Stay

Vancouver is unusual in that a great many inexpensive and moderately priced hotels and motels remain in the otherwise very high-rent downtown area; these in addition to the landmark luxury and business hotels commonly associated with city centers. Unless you prefer staying on a motel strip some distance from downtown, there's no reason not to stay right in the center of things.

Summer is very busy in Vancouver; you should make reservations weeks, or even months, in advance, especially if you have your heart set on a specific hotel. The Travel InfoCentre (☎ 604-683-2772 for bookings, 800-663-6000) offers a free accommodations reservation service, which can be indispensable if you are trying to find a room at the last minute.

The prices quoted in this book are generally for the peak summer season, and for what you'll pay if you walk in off the street. If you book well in advance or if you're able to take advantage of corporate rates or the many packages offered, you should be able to get the room at a lower rate. You'll also find that many of the hotels have greatly reduced rates in the off season.

Over the past few years B&Bs have become numerous and popular in Vancouver but usually are not cheap, averaging $75 to $105 for a double with shared bathroom. Because B&Bs come and go rather quickly, it's a good idea to use a reservation service to book a room. The following services have rooms in all price ranges: Old English B&B Registry (☎ 604-986-5069), 1226 Silverwood Crescent, North Vancouver, BC V7L 1L3; and Town & Country B&B (☎ 604-731-5942), PO Box 74542, Vancouver, BC V6K 1K2.

Although not a booking agency, contact the Western Canada B&B Innkeepers Association (☎ 604-255-9199), PO Box 74534, Vancouver, BC V6K 4P4, for a brochure with listings in Vancouver and throughout the province.

Accommodations are listed according to price range, type of accommodations and neighborhood location.

BUDGET
Camping
There are no public campgrounds in the Vancouver area and, except for one, the RV parks right in Vancouver do not allow tenting.

East Vancouver East of the city, *Burnaby Cariboo RV Park* (Map 1; ☎ 604-472-1722), 8765 Cariboo Place, Burnaby, is also open year-round and has tent sites, an indoor pool, lounge, laundromat and a convenience store. Sites start at $21. To get there from Hwy 1, take the Cariboo exit, turn right at the first traffic light, immediately turn left and the next right is Cariboo Place.

North Shore (Map 8) In North Vancouver, but a short walk to the Park Royal Shopping Centre in West Vancouver, the *Capilano RV Park* (☎ 604-987-4722), 295 Tomahawk Ave, has everything including a Jacuzzi; tent sites start at $22. Exit onto Capilano Rd south off the Upper Levels Hwy (Hwy 1), or from the Lions Gate Bridge, stay in the right lane and turn right at Capilano Rd, then follow the signs.

South Vancouver There are other campgrounds south of the city, on or near Hwy 99. South of the Middle Arm of the Fraser River, *Richmond RV Park* (Map 1; ☎ 604-270-7878), 6200 River Rd, Richmond, near Hollybridge Way is one of the closest to town. It's open from April to October and has sites starting at $16.50 for two people. *ParkCanada RV Inns* (☎ 604-943-5811), 4799 Hwy 17, Delta, is northeast of the Tsawwassen ferry terminal and is open year-round. It has free showers and sites start at $14.

Hostels

Travelers have an ever-increasing array of hostel choices, including some really dodgy old hotels trying to cash in on the increase in traffic; these didn't make it into this guide. Most of the good hostels are pretty much full through the summer and quite busy the rest of the year. It's a good idea to make reservations.

Downtown (Map 2) The *HI Vancouver Downtown* hostel (☎ 604-684-4565), 1114 Burnaby St at the corner of Thurlow St, is in a former nunnery and health-care center. There are 212 beds with no more than four in any one room. Family rooms are also available. Prices are $19 members, $23 nonmembers. Facilities include a patio, library and games room. This very convenient hostel is walkable from anywhere in the downtown area and is open 24 hours. A free shuttle service is provided between this hostel, the HI Vancouver Jericho Beach hostel and Pacific Central Station.

Formerly called Vincent's Backpackers Hostel, the *C&N Backpackers Hostel* (☎ 604-682-2441, 888-434-6060, backpackers@ sprint.ca), 927 Main St, has undergone major renovations, including new owners and a new name. It is not in the best of areas, but is within walking distance of downtown and not too far from the SkyTrain Science World-Main St Station and Pacific Central Station. Take bus Nos 3, 8 or 19 from downtown along Main St. The office is open 8 am to 11 pm, there's no curfew and the rates are low at $10/20/25 for a dormitory/single/ double. It can sleep 85 people and offers weekly rates.

The *New Backpackers Hostel* (☎ 604-688-0112), centrally located in the big hotel building at 347 West Pender St, is still operated by Vincent. This is generally a more spacious place than the Main St hostel, and the little outdoor courtyard, good for reading and relaxing, is pleasant. However, the $10 dorm beds go quickly and you may have to wait for a shower. Singles/doubles are $25/35.

The centrally located *Cambie International Hostel* (☎ 604-684-6466), 300 Cambie St at Cordova St, has dorm beds in two- or four-bunk rooms costing $20 for students or AYH/IYH members, and $27 for anyone else. Bedding is provided and bathrooms are down the hall. There are laundry facilities and bicycle storage. A bakery, cafe and bar on the ground floor make it a convenient and potentially noisy place to spend the night.

The *YMCA* (☎ 604-681-0221) is right downtown at 955 Burrard St. Depending on whether you want a TV, singles are $36 or $39, doubles are $44 or $46. Women and couples are allowed and quite a few travelers stay here. The only drawback is the constant sound of the unlocking of doors. There are gym and pool facilities and a small, inexpensive restaurant serving good-value breakfasts and sandwiches.

The *YWCA* (☎ 604-895-5830, 800-663-1424), 733 Beatty St, between West Georgia and Robson Sts near BC Place Stadium, is more like a hotel, and accommodates men, women, couples or families. There are 155 rooms in various configurations ranging from singles with bathrooms down the hall ($51) to family rooms and others with five single beds. Doubles start at $70; $79 with a private bathroom. Each room has a refrigerator but there are also communal kitchens, plus TV lounges and a laundry. Fitness facilities are available but are off the premises. The SkyTrain Stadium Station is a five-minute walk.

West Side (Map 6) Although away from the center of town, the original Vancouver HI hostel, *HI Vancouver Jericho Beach* (☎ 604-224-3208, fax 224-4852), 1515 Discovery St, Kitsilano, is in a great location. It's close to the beach at Jericho Beach Park on Burrard Inlet, about 20 minutes from downtown by bus, and not that far away from the restaurants and bars on West 4th Ave. The hostel is open 24 hours, although there is a 'quiet time' between 11 pm and 7 am. With 287 beds, it's the largest in Canada and has complete facilities. It runs a number of activities throughout the year that are available to members and nonmembers alike. The rates are $17.50 for members, $21.50 for nonmembers. From downtown take bus No 4 south on Granville St.

North Shore (Map 8) The *Globe Trotter's Inn* (☎ 604-988-2082), 170 West Esplanade, North Vancouver, is small and quiet, only a five-minute walk to the SeaBus at Lonsdale Quay, and close to all amenities (including the excellent Sailor Hagar's Brew Pub). It has a kitchen, laundry and a range of rooms. Rates are $17.50/30/40 for dorm/singles/doubles.

Student Accommodations

You don't have to be a student to stay at the facilities on the two university campuses. Travelers will find reasonably priced accommodations from May to the end of August, when most of the students are on their summer break.

West Side (Map 7) The *University of British Columbia* has singles/doubles with shared bathroom for $22/44 or you can get self-contained apartments from $69 to $99. Contact the Conference Centre (☎ 604-822-1010), Gage Towers, 5961 Student Union Blvd, UBC Campus, Vancouver. The pleasant campus has a cafeteria, some cafes, laundromat, pub and sports facilities.

East Vancouver (Map 1) *Simon Fraser University* rents out rooms; bathrooms are shared. Singles without bedding (bring your own sleeping bag) cost $19, with bedding $31, doubles with bedding $51. The university also has four-bedroom townhouse units for $115. For more information, contact the Housing & Conference Services (☎ 604-291-4503), Room 212, McTaggart-Cowan Hall, Burnaby.

Hotels

Downtown (Map 2) Vancouver has many inexpensive hotels right downtown, especially along Granville, Pender and Hastings Sts. While some are well kept and offer good value, many are long-term accommodations serving the downtrodden and those on very low incomes or government assistance, and aren't places most travelers would want to

stay (see the Right Price, Wrong Place boxed text).

The best low-cost hotel in town is the *Kingston Hotel* (☎ 604-684-9024), 757 Richards St. It was the city's first B&B hotel and still offers a morning meal (although it's just enough to get the eyes open). Singles are from $45 to $70, doubles from $50 to $80. Extras include a sauna, guest laundry and an overnight parking subsidy.

In Gastown, the old but renovated *Dominion Hotel* (☎ 604-681-6666), 210 Abbott St at the corner of Water St, dates from 1899. The rooms go for $82 with shared bathroom or $117 with private bathroom.

Hastings St, on either side of Main St, is a less-than-wholesome part of town (especially at night), but the *Hotel Patricia* (Map 4; ☎ 604-255-4301), 403 East Hastings St, breaks rank. It's large, clean, well kept and a very good value with rooms from $39/59/69/79 singles/doubles/triples/quads. All the rooms are self-contained and some rooms have fine views of the harbor.

One of the more central motels is *City Centre Motel* (☎ 604-876-7166, 800-707-2489), 2111 Main St, a 10 minute walk south of the SkyTrain Science World-Main St Station, with rooms for $70.

In the West End, the well-loved, if slightly faded, *Sylvia Hotel* (☎ 604-681-9321), 1154 Gilford St, has a marvelous location on English Bay and is close to both Davie and Denman Sts. The ivy-covered hotel was built in 1912 (the new low-rise wing was added in 1986) and has been declared a heritage building. There are 119 rooms, all with bathrooms, and 23 have kitchens. In the summer the Sylvia Restaurant has outdoor dining and the bar is a good place to watch the sunset, even if you aren't staying here. Rooms start at $65 for singles or doubles, and the kitchen suites start at $120.

Also next door to Stanley Park is *The Buchan Hotel* (☎ 604-685-5354, 800-668-6654), 1906 Haro St, a nicely appointed older hotel with singles/doubles for $70/80 with shared bath, or $98/108 with private bath. The *Shato Inn Hotel* (☎ 604-681-8920), at 1825 Comox St off Denman St, a couple

Right Price, Wrong Place for Budget Travelers

For many years the string of old hotels on Hastings St, three or four blocks on either side of Main St, has been home to people in need of low-cost housing – welfare recipients, drug addicts, persons with disabilities or HIV/AIDS sufferers. You need only to walk through this area during the day to feel the sense of desperation and hopelessness that exists here.

This part of the city is as close to grotty as you are likely to find in Vancouver, and the 6000 grungy hotel rooms are the main reason, although the beer parlors and cheap restaurants in the area are certainly other reasons why those who are down on their luck call this part of the city home.

This is not a good place for budget travelers to look for cheap accommodations, even if they could rent a room for the night. Most of the rooms are what are called 'single-room occupancy hotel units' (SROs) rented by the week or the month. This section of Hastings St has the largest concentration of the city's 7500 SROs (the others are in the central business district, mostly along Granville St), and about half of the SROs in the entire province are in Vancouver.

With this high concentration of SROs comes a serious crime problem that has spilled over to areas such as Chinatown and Gastown, much to the dismay of the local business people who say it's not uncommon to find drug addicts shooting up in the alleys or to have supplies stolen from the back of their premises. In recent years, groups such as the Chinatown Merchants Association and the Gastown Homeowners Association have pressed the city for solutions to these issues, one being that the city find ways to spread low-cost housing around Vancouver so that it's not concentrated in this one area.

In a move to help combat some of these problems, and to create affordable public housing, the provincial government purchased the Sunrise and the Washington Hotels along the 100 block of East Hastings St, and turned them into low-cost accommodations, complete with on-site health services. The government estimates that to build social housing will cost as much as $100,000 per unit, while the cost of renovating existing structures into habitable accommodations is only $30,000 a unit. Not only does this represent a huge savings for taxpayers, but it's a big step forward in helping to alleviate a problem that has existed for far too long.

of blocks from Stanley Park and English Bay Beach, has rooms, some with cooking facilities, for $85 for singles or doubles, and $95 for a queen-size bed.

The *Barclay Hotel* (☎ 604-688-8850), 1348 Robson St, has air-con, TV and a licensed lounge; rooms start at $75/95. A moderately priced motel, the *Burrard Motor Inn* (☎ 604-681-2331, 800-663-0366), 1100 Burrard St, is convenient and a favorite of families and budget travelers with rooms at $85/95.

West Side (Map 5) *Shaughnessy Village* (☎ 604-736-5511), 1125 West 12th Ave, is a high-rise complex with a B&B, hotel, resort, apartment building and amusement center

all rolled into one. The least-expensive rooms, tiny ship-like studio cabins, cost $78/87 with breakfast and come packed with every amenity; in the dead of winter the price plummets to $40/50. Ask for one of the limited parking spots when you reserve a room.

East Vancouver (Map 4) Just a few blocks west of Commercial Drive and close enough to the city center by bus (which run frequently along Hastings St), the *Waldorf Hotel* (☎ 604-253-7141), 1489 East Hastings St, is another good option with rooms at $60/70 with bathrooms. The Grove Pub on the ground floor has 18 different beers on tap and has a good selection of bar food.

There are a number of motels along Kingsway, a major road that branches off Main St southeast of East 7th Ave, and continues through Burnaby all the way to New Westminster. This is a good part of the city to stay in if you don't mind being out of the center; all of the hotels and motels along here have plenty of free parking, the Sky-Train runs parallel to Kingsway (although it's about three blocks away at most points), and there is a regular bus service along Kingsway that will take you straight into the city center. The cheapest option along here is the *2400 Motel* (Map 1; ☎ 604-434-2464, 888-833-2400), 2400 Kingsway, with rooms starting at $67 for singles or doubles. Another reasonably priced choice just down the road is *Eldorado Motor Hotel* (Map 1; ☎ 604-434-1341), 2330 Kingsway, with rooms starting at $85/95.

North Shore (Map 8) There really isn't any reason to stay in Horseshoe Bay, but if the need or urge arises, the *Horseshoe Bay Motel* (☎ 604-921-7454), 6588 Royal Ave, about a five-minute walk from the ferry terminal, has basic rooms starting at $75 for up to four people.

B&Bs

West Side (Map 5) *Windsor Guest House* (☎ 604-872-3060, 888-872-3060), 325 West 11th Ave, beside City Hall just off Cambie St, is an 1895 home with six rooms, one with private bathroom, ranging between $50 and $95. Just a couple of blocks away the same owners also operate *Douglas Guest House* (same phone numbers), 456 West 13th Ave, a six-room Edwardian house built in the 1920s; rooms range from $50 to $115.

In the same area, an inexpensive and popular place is *Paul's Guest House* (☎ 604-872-4753), 345 West 14th Ave, between Alberta and Yukon Sts, in a quiet residential area. Paul speaks 11 languages, which should cover most guests! Breakfast includes all the eggs you can eat. It's very clean and friendly, and there's a laundry service, TV room and free coffee or tea during the day. Singles/doubles are $65/75 from May to September dropping to $40/50 the rest of the year. If this place is full, Paul has another guest house nearby.

North Shore (Map 8) In North Vancouver try *Capilano B&B* (☎ 604-990-8889), 1374 Plateau Drive, which isn't far from Capilano Rd and the Upper Levels Hwy (Hwy 1). There are only two rooms, starting at $70/85, but if they're full the owners can suggest other B&Bs. *European B&B* (☎ 604-988-1792), 648 East Keith Rd, isn't far from the Second Narrows Bridge, and has rooms, some with shared bathroom, starting at $65. The owners speak German.

MID-RANGE
Hotels

Downtown (Map 2) A good deal is the all-suite *Century Plaza Hotel* (☎ 604-687-0575, 800-663-1818), 1015 Burrard St, starting at $119/144. For more good-value suites in a former apartment building, try the *Oceanside Apartment Hotel* (☎ 604-682-5641), 1847 Pendrell St, with suites starting at $150.

Robson St, west of the busy shopping district, has some good hotel deals in a prime area. *Riviera Motor Inn* (☎ 604-685-1301), 1431 Robson St, has apartments with fully equipped kitchens, beginning at $128. Some of the apartments have a good view of the North Shore. At the *Robsonstrasse City Motor Inn* (☎ 604-687-1674, 888-667-8877), 1394 Robson St, you get kitchenettes, free parking and a guest laundry for $120/130.

For a little more money you can get more amenities along Robson St. Heading east from Denman St, the appropriately named *Landmark Hotel* (☎ 604-687-0511, 800-830-6144), 1400 Robson St, affectionately known by locals as 'the eyesore,' is Vancouver's tallest hotel and has the views to prove it. On the top there's a revolving restaurant, Cloud Nine, and Sportscasters bar at the bottom. Rooms start at $179 for singles or doubles.

The *Greenbriar Hotel* (☎ 604-683-4558), 1393 Robson St, is a former apartment building that has also been transformed into a suite hotel. It's nicer than it looks from the outside, as each room has a full kitchen and sitting area. Rooms range between $149 and $169 for a single or double.

Continuing up Robson St, the ***Tropicana Motor Inn*** (☎ 604-687-6631), 1361 Robson St, another high-rise option with similar amenities, plus a pool and sauna, has rooms starting at $139 for a single or double. The ***Pacific Palisades Hotel*** (☎ 604-688-0461, 800-663-1815), 1277 Robson St, is an all-suite hotel that has rooms equipped with kitchenettes for $195 for a single or double. The ***Blue Horizon Hotel*** (☎ 604-688-1411, 800-663-1333), 1225 Robson St, with rooms at $175 for singles or doubles, has great views, balconies (one of which is featured in a rather disturbing scene in the film *Star 80*), an indoor pool, restaurants and a bar.

From False Creek heading north along Howe St there are quite a few lodging options. ***The Executive Inn*** (☎ 604-688-7678), 1379 Howe St, has 98 rooms and 32 suites starting at $139/149. The ***Quality Inn at False Creek*** (☎ 604-682-0229, 800-663-8474), 1335 Howe St, has spacious rooms at $160/180. The ***Travelodge Vancouver Centre*** (☎ 604-682-2767, 800-665-2080), 1304 Howe St, has basic but fine rooms for $99/109, and there's a heated outdoor pool.

The ***Holiday Inn Vancouver Downtown*** (☎ 604-684-2151, 800-663-9151), 1110 Howe St near Davie St, is a class act for a chain hotel, with large rooms, pool, health club and some rooms with kitchens; rooms start at $179/199. One of the best deals in the city is ***Bosman's Motor Hotel*** (☎ 604-682-3171, 800-663-7840), 1060 Howe St. It's extremely central, has free parking and is everything most people will ever need in a moderately priced lodging; rooms range between $129 and $139.

The ***Dufferin Hotel*** (☎ 604-683-4251), 900 Seymour St, has prices beginning at $95/100 for singles/doubles. It's a good choice and gets the overflow from the Kingston Hotel (see the Budget category). There's a dining room and free parking.

The ***Best Western Downtown*** (☎ 604-669-9888), 718 Drake St, near the Granville Bridge, offers all the usual amenities, including a continental breakfast; rooms start at $180 for singles or doubles.

In the heart of the theater and club scene, the ***Hotel Dakota*** (☎ 604-605-4333, 888-605-5333), 654 Nelson St at Granville St, has recently been renovated, plus it's close to Yaletown and the sports facilities. Rooms start at $104 for singles or doubles. Farther along Granville St, the ***Best Western Chateau Granville*** (☎ 604-664-7070), 1110 Granville St, runs the gamut of price categories, with the 36 rooms in the 'motel section' starting at $89 for singles or doubles, while the 112 suites in the tower start at $195.

Along Davie St there are a couple of moderately priced hotels. Just north of Thurlow St, the ***Parkhill Hotel*** (☎ 604-685-1311, 800-663-1525), 1160 Davie St, offers business services and has convention facilities for up to 300 people. Plus, there are two restaurants: Taiko for Japanese food and Byron's Lounge & Grill for continental cuisine. Rates start at $160 for singles or doubles. Also close to Thurlow St and just one block south of Davie St, the ***Sunset Inn*** (☎ 604-688-2474), 1111 Burnaby St, is a converted apartment building and the rooms, which all have kitchens and balconies, start at $158 for singles or doubles.

At the far end of Davie St near Denman St, the ***Best Western Sands Hotel*** (☎ 604-682-1831), 1755 Davie St, has rooms starting at $179 for singles or doubles. The hotel's lounge, the Bayside Room, is a good place to catch an English Bay sunset.

The ***Day's Inn Vancouver Downtown*** (☎ 604-681-4335, 800-329-7466), 921 West Pender St, is at a great location, and the small but nicely furnished rooms start at $145 for singles or doubles. The ***St Regis Hotel*** (☎ 604-681-1135, 800-790-7929), 602 Dunsmuir St at the corner of Seymour St, is right in the heart of the city. This older hotel has been recently renovated and the plain but functional rooms, starting at $120 for singles or doubles, are a good deal considering the location.

If you want to be ideally situated for sporting events at GM Place or BC Place Stadium, or for theatrical presentations at the Queen Elizabeth, Playhouse and Ford theaters, there are a couple of options. The

Sandman Hotel Downtown (☎ 604-681-2211, 800-726-3626), 180 West Georgia St, with the popular Shark Club Bar & Grill on the ground floor (it gets packed before and after a game), has rooms starting at $180 for singles or doubles.

The *Georgian Court* (☎ 604-682-5555), 773 Beatty St, is a very nicely decorated European-style hotel with fabulous service. Rooms start at $180/200 for singles/doubles.

West Side (Map 5) There aren't many mid-range choices on the West Side. The *Holiday Inn Vancouver Centre* (☎ 604-879-0511), 711 West Broadway, with rooms at $189/209 for singles/doubles, is a large complex with a pool and two restaurants. The *Ramada Vancouver Centre* (☎ 604-872-8661, 800-663-5403), 898 West Broadway, has rooms with balconies for $170/185. *The Plaza 500 Hotel* (☎ 604-873-1811, 800-473-1811), 500 West 12th Ave at Cambie St, has some spectacular views of the city from some of the rooms, most of which come with a private balcony. Rooms start at $180 for singles or doubles.

East Vancouver (Map 4) The closest motel strip to downtown is along East Hastings St around Hastings Park and east into Burnaby. This is a convenient area, close to the Second Narrows Bridge leading over Burrard Inlet to North Vancouver. The *Best Western Exhibition Park* (☎ 604-294-4751), 3475 East Hastings St on the corner of Cassiar St, has rooms from $150 for singles or doubles. Another good deal is the *Atrium Inn* (☎ 604-254-1000, 800-663-8158), 2889 East Hastings St, with rooms for $135/165, which includes a continental breakfast and a free shuttle service to the airport and the city center.

Closer to the city is the *Biltmore Motor Hotel* (☎ 604-872-5252), 395 Kingsway at East 12th Ave, with rooms starting at $124. Continuing down Kingsway, there are other moderately priced hotels. The *Kingsway Lodge Motel* (☎ 604-876-5531), at 2075 Kingsway, has rooms for $139/149, although these prices plummet to $49/59 in winter. A continental breakfast is included.

Quality Inn Metrotown (Map 1; ☎ 604-433-8255), 3484 Kingsway, is a typical chain hotel with the usual facilities, lots of free parking, plus it's close to Central Park. Rates start at $119/139. Not far from the large Deer Lake Park, *Best Western Kings Inn* (Map 1; ☎ 604-438-1383), 5441 Kingsway, is another chain hotel with rates starting at $125 for singles or doubles.

Even though New Westminster is a pleasant enough area to visit for the day, it's not a place you are likely to want to call home while visiting Vancouver. However, it is only about a 25-minute ride on the SkyTrain from the city center and is ideally situated for trips around the southeast section of the Lower Mainland. There are a couple of places to try here.

The Met Hotel (☎ 604-520-3815, 888-512-5511), 411 Columbia St, right next to the SkyTrain Columbia Station, is a European boutique-style hotel geared to business travelers. The 30 rooms have computer plug-ins, services such as faxing and photocopying are free, secretarial services ($22 for the first hour and $12 for each additional hour) can be arranged, and there is an attractive bar and restaurant on the ground floor. The rooms are a great value at $125 for singles or doubles, which includes a large continental breakfast. In the low season this rate drops to $85, making this an outstanding deal.

The *Inn at Westminster Quay* (Map 1; ☎ 604-520-1776, 800-663-2001), 900 Quayside Drive, is built over the water beside the Public Market – every room boasts a view of the Fraser River – and it is close to the SkyTrain New Westminster Station. Rooms start at $150 for singles or doubles.

North Shore (Map 8) Another motel area is in North Vancouver, close to the Lions Gate Bridge and not far from Grouse Mountain. Look along Marine Drive and north up Capilano Rd. The motels along here are pretty much the same both in terms of facilities and rates. The *Lionsgate Travelodge* (☎ 604-985-5311), at 2060 Marine Drive, has rooms starting at $120 for singles or doubles.

Going up Capilano Rd, *The Grouse Inn* (☎ 604-683-4558), 1633 Capilano Rd, has rooms with kitchenettes at $129 for singles or doubles. Across the road, the *Capilano Inn* (☎ 604-987-8185), 1634 Capilano Rd, has rooms starting at $105, and suites with kitchens start at $150. Next door the *Canyon Court* (☎ 604-988-3181), 1748 Capilano Rd, charges $120/125 for singles/doubles, while beside it the *Holiday Inn Express* (☎ 604-987-4461), 1800 Capilano Rd, has rooms starting at $135 for singles or doubles.

Traveling east along Marine Drive, the *Avalon Motor Hotel* (☎ 604-985-4181), 1025 Marine Drive, is about a five-minute drive from the Lions Gate Bridge and has rooms at $95 for singles or doubles.

In West Vancouver, beside the north section of Park Royal Shopping Centre just off Taylor Way, the *Park Royal Hotel* (☎ 604-926-5511), 44 Clyde Ave, is a small 30-room hotel that has the feel of an English country inn, complete with a pub. Rooms start at $144/155.

Richmond/Airport (Map 1) If you want to stay close to the airport, or simply like the idea of staying in Richmond, there are numerous hotels that fall into this price bracket.

Howard Johnson (☎ 604-270-6030), 9020 Bridgeport Rd, between No 3 and No 4 Rds, has standard accommodations starting at $100 for singles or doubles. *Stay 'n Save Inn* (☎ 604-273-3311), 10551 St Edwards Drive, part of which runs beside and parallel to Hwy 99 between Cambie and Bridgeport Rds, has rooms starting at $109/119 for singles/doubles.

Executive Inn (☎ 604-278-5555), 7211 Westminster Hwy, close to Gilbert Rd, has rooms starting at $119/139. Holiday Inn has two hotels here, which both use ☎ 604-821-1818; the *Holiday Inn Express*, 9351 Bridgeport Rd, beside Hwy 99, has rooms starting at $119 for singles or doubles, while rooms at the *Holiday Inn Airport*, 10720 Cambie Rd at the corner of Shell Rd, start at $129 for a single or double.

The Tudor-style *Abercorn Inn* (☎ 604-270-7576), at 9260 Bridgeport Rd, beside Hwy 99 and the Oak St Bridge, is a bit different from the standard hotels; rooms start at $149/159. The *Best Western Richmond Inn* (☎ 604-273-7878), 7551 Westminster Hwy, next to Minoru Blvd, has rooms starting at $159 for singles or doubles. One of two Delta hotels in Richmond, *Delta Pacific Resort* (☎ 604-278-9611), 10251 St Edwards Drive, next to Hwy 99, has rooms starting at $169 for a single or double.

B&Bs

Downtown (Map 2) The *West End Guest House* (☎ 604-681-2889), 1362 Haro St, is just a block away from the shopping and restaurants on Robson St. The 1906 Victorian guesthouse with period furnishings is like stepping into another world. There are eight rooms, each with its own bathroom, a small living room and a sundeck; the large room has a fireplace. Rooms range from $110 to $210 for a single or double.

West Side (Map 5) There are a few choices in the area close to Kitsilano Beach and Vanier Park, where you are only minutes by mini-ferry to the city center or Granville Island, or a 10-minute drive to the city center or UBC. *Ogden Point B&B* (☎ 604-736-4336), 1982 Ogden Ave, is a lovely oceanfront heritage home that has three rooms ranging from $100 to $160 for a single, $110 to $180 double. In the same area, *Walnut House B&B* (☎ 604-739-6941), 1350 Walnut St, is another heritage home that has three rooms with private bathrooms for $105/115. *Maple House B&B* (☎ 604-739-5833), 1533 Maple St, just off Cornwall Ave, is a 1900 heritage home with five rooms starting at $95 for singles or doubles.

The *Kenya Court Guest House* (☎ 604-738-7085), 2230 Cornwall Ave, is a refurbished apartment building right across from Kitsilano Beach. The large one- and two-bedroom apartments sleep up to six and breakfast is served on the rooftop solarium. Rates start at $135 based on double occupancy. Just two blocks from Kitsilano Beach, *Mickey's Kits Beach Chalet* (☎ 604-739-3342), 2142 & 2146 West 1st Ave, has four rooms, all with bathrooms, ranging from $95 to $120 for a single, $105 to $130 double.

Not far from City Hall, ***Pillow 'n Porridge Guest Suites*** (Map 5; ☎ 604-879-8977), 2859 Manitoba St, between West 12th and 13th Aves, isn't technically a B&B: it has dropped the 'porridge' component from its service. However, this is a lovely place to stay. The executive travel suites are in a 1910 heritage corner-store building and in two converted coach houses. Rates start at $115 for a one-bedroom suite and go to $160 for a two-bedroom suite; all rooms include private bathrooms. Monthly rates are also available.

William House B&B (☎ 604-731-2760), 2050 West 18th Ave, is a bit farther away from the city center, but the lovely farmhouse setting close to Arbutus St might just make it worthwhile. There are five rooms starting at $95, and the top-floor suite is $195. For a more modern alternative, try ***Treehouse B&B*** (Map 1; ☎ 604-266-2962), 2490 West 49th Ave, with contemporary decor, Jacuzzi tubs and private bathroom; the three rooms start at $110.

North Shore (Map 8) In North Vancouver there are numerous mid-range B&Bs. One worth mentioning is ***Thistle Down House B&B*** (☎ 604-986-7173), 3910 Capilano Rd, north of the Upper Levels Hwy (Hwy 1). Close to the Capilano Suspension Bridge and the Capilano Salmon Hatchery, and on the road to Grouse Mountain, this 1920s house on a half-acre lot has a country inn feel to it. The gourmet breakfast is scrumptious and, if you're around in the afternoon, there are homemade cakes, pastries and other delicious items for tea. All five rooms are en suite and range from $110 to $189. Buses run along Capilano Rd.

In West Vancouver it's worth trying ***Beachside B&B*** (☎ 604-922-7773), 4208 Evergreen Ave, off Marine Drive and right on the beach with views of Point Grey and the Lions Gate Bridge. This B&B offers a seaside whirlpool, good breakfasts and the feeling that the city is far away when, in fact, a bus on Marine Drive gets you to the city in about 20 minutes. Rooms start at $120 and go up to $195 for an oceanfront view.

TOP END
Hotels
Downtown (Map 2) In the city center you'll find a number of brand new hotel towers with luxury-class accommodations as well as elegant older hotels. Despite the rising skyline, the ***Hotel Vancouver*** (☎ 604-684-3131, 800-441-1414), 900 West Georgia St, remains a city landmark recognizable by its green copper roof. This Canadian Pacific hotel is one of the largest and most famous in Vancouver, if not Canada, offering all the comforts known to the modern hospitality industry. A complete remodel recently brought this vintage doyenne even more up-to-date. Rooms begin at $360 for a single or double. Even if you're not staying here you can enjoy the traditional afternoon tea served daily at 2.30 pm, or dine at Griffins, the upscale buffet restaurant (see the Places to Eat chapter).

Built in the 1930s, and complete with wooden paneling, chandeliers and ornate brass elevators, the ***Hotel Georgia*** (☎ 604-682-5566, 800-663-1111), 801 West Georgia St, is a real charmer. For this class of hotel the rooms are a good value at $230/250 for singles/doubles, $450 for a suite. Vancouver's highest-rated hotel, the ***Four Seasons Hotel*** (☎ 604-689-9333, 800-268-6282), 791 West Georgia St, is above the Pacific Centre shopping complex. To get to the reception desk, you take the escalator to the left of the Buddha. Room prices vary widely, and start from $370/400. The hotel's restaurant, Chartwell, is considered to be one of the city's best (see the Places to Eat chapter).

If you want a more personalized experience, try the ***Wedgewood Hotel*** (☎ 604-689-7777, 800-663-0666), 845 Hornby St, another fantastic vintage boutique hotel with luxurious rooms starting at $200/220. Farther along Hornby St is ***The Residence Inn by Marriott*** (☎ 604-688-1234, 800-663-1234), 1234 Hornby St, offering only suites, complete with kitchens, starting at $200. It also has an indoor pool, fitness room and restaurant.

A stylish alternative is the *Sheraton Wall Centre Hotel* (☎ 604-331-1000, 800-663-9255), 1088 Burrard St, a modern high-rise in the center of the city with a distinctly arty and modernistic atmosphere. Rooms begin at $209 for singles or doubles. For those people who want to shop until they drop, *Sutton Place Hotel* (☎ 604-682-5511), 845 Burrard St, is close to Robson St and offers all the usual facilities with rooms starting from $345/365.

The *Hyatt Regency* (☎ 604-683-1234, 800-233-1234), 655 Burrard St, is right in the center of the city close to shopping, restaurants, entertainment and businesses. It has all the facilities you'd expect from a top-end hotel, and rooms start at $235/270 for singles/doubles. Two blocks over, the *Metropolitan Hotel* (☎ 604-687-1122), 645 Howe St, is a very swish establishment with a pool, fitness room and rooms starting at $329/349. Plus it has one of the top restaurants in the city, Diva at the Met (see the Places to Eat chapter).

On the shores of Burrard Inlet, by the harbor, are four notable hotels. *The Pan Pacific Hotel* (☎ 604-662-8111, 800-663-1515 in Canada, 800-937-1515 in US), 999 Canada Place, is a deluxe convention hotel with every facility imaginable, including three restaurants, a state-of-the-art health club and an outdoor heated pool open year-round. Even if you're not staying here it's worth going in just to see the eight-story atrium, complete with totem poles, the lobby and the lounge with 12m-high glass walls through which the views of the harbor are spectacular. You pay a lot for the location, with rooms at $400/430, but the views from the rooms are superb and the service extraordinary (or so they say). The hotel's top restaurant, Five Sails, has excellent views (see the Places to Eat chapter).

Across the road, *The CP Waterfront Hotel* (☎ 604-691-1991), 900 Canada Place, isn't as impressive as its rival but at $195/220 it's a lot more affordable and it's still a very nice hotel with an ideal location. Farther along toward Coal Harbour, the *Vancouver Renaissance Hotel - Harbourside* (☎ 604-689-9211), 1133 West Hastings St, is close to the waterfront with rooms starting at $194 for singles or doubles. If you want a room with a view the price goes up considerably. Inquire about the rooms on the 18th floor that include continental breakfast and free local phone calls.

At Coal Harbour, *The Westin Bayshore* (☎ 604-682-3377, 800-228-3000), 1601 West Georgia St, offers the same high-quality amenities from a location right on the waterfront and close to Stanley Park and Denman St. Aside from having doormen dressed in Beefeater outfits, the hotel is famous for having the billionaire recluse Howard Hughes as a guest for three months in 1972. Hughes rented the top two floors of the tower and, even though he had not been photographed for many years prior to his Vancouver visit, meandered through the hotel lobby in his bathrobe. He then stood on one of his balconies to watch a seaplane land before having all the windows in the rooms blacked out for the duration of his stay. Rooms start at $299/329 (ask about a reduced rate if you want to book a floor or two).

Just off Denman St, *The Coast Plaza at Stanley Park* (☎ 604-688-7711, 800-663-1144), 1733 Comox St, has spectacular views, indoor pool, exercise room and squash courts. Three floors are devoted to meeting, conference and banquet facilities, plus services for business travelers. Rooms start at $305/335.

Almost in Stanley Park, *Rosellen Suites* (☎ 604-689-4807), 2030 Barclay St, requires a minimum booking of three nights to stay in the one- or two-bedroom suites, which come with fully equipped kitchens, washing machines and dryers, private phone lines and twice-weekly maid service. The suites start at $175 and, quite literally, go up to $375 for the penthouse.

There are a couple of opulent choices along Robson St, the best of which is *Listel O'Doul's Hotel Best Western* (☎ 604-684-8461, 800-663-5491), 1300 Robson St. The modern, large, well-appointed rooms are $220/240, and the restaurant is very good. Another option is the *Rosedale on Robson* (☎ 604-689-8033, 800-661-8870), 838 Hamilton St at the corner of Robson St, not far from the Ford Centre and BC Place Stadium. This all-suite hotel offers full business facilities, plus all the usual comforts of a standard hotel. Suites start at $205 for singles or doubles.

West Side (Map 5) In one of the city's top locations, the *Granville Island Hotel* (☎ 604-683-7373), 1253 Johnston St, is a modernistic structure right on False Creek with great downtown views, especially from the sauna and Jacuzzi on the top floor. The 54-room hotel is near the island's famed market, art and craft galleries and theaters, and you are just seconds away from the mini-ferries to downtown or Kitsilano. Suite-style rooms are $209/219.

North Shore (Map 8) In North Vancouver, the *Lonsdale Quay Hotel* (☎ 604-986-6111), 123 Carrie Cates Court, has a pretty

unbeatable combination: great views of the city, the SeaBus close at hand and the Lonsdale Quay Market to explore. Rooms start at $200/250.

Richmond/Airport (Map 1) The *Delta Vancouver Airport Hotel & Marina* (☎ 604-278-1241), 3500 Cessna Drive, on Sea Island by the Moray Bridge, has business-class rooms starting at $239.

B&Bs

Downtown (Map 2) The *English Bay Inn* (☎ 604-683-8002), 1968 Comox St, is a genuine treat. Each of the five rooms in this gem has a private bath and nice touches like a four-poster bed. There is an elegant parlor, a formal dining room and a small garden where you can relax on a sunny day. Be sure to book well in advance. Rooms range from $170 to $285.

Places to Eat

Vancouver is one of the most cosmopolitan restaurant cities in North America, which is good news for food lovers. You can journey gastronomically from country to country by wandering streets that are groaning with choices. You aren't confined by budget either, because all types of food are available in all price categories. Add the Northwest's natural bounty of farm, garden and sea, and you've got the makings of a cuisine capital.

As in any city, restaurants are scattered everywhere, but for the visitor there are some definite areas and streets where many of the restaurants are concentrated. For the purposes of this guide we have divided the city into price categories and then areas and/or streets to make it easier for you to find your way around.

Most restaurants are licensed to serve alcohol, even if it is just wine and beer, and in many cases they probably make a larger profit from liquor sales than they do from the food. If you are on a budget be careful how much you drink because it is seldom inexpensive – you can find that after a good evening of drinking, the liquor portion of your bill may actually cost more than the food.

Note that smoking in restaurants is not allowed in Vancouver, a bylaw that is strictly enforced. Some restaurants, if they have two completely separate sections, will offer the choice of smoking or nonsmoking seating, or a separate bar area where smoking is allowed. This hasn't stopped the martini and cigar craze from taking a firm hold, especially in the trendier establishments, but a separate smoking room must be provided. Even in winter, when it can be wet and cold, some restaurants provide covered outdoor seating so that serious smokers can enjoy a hit of nicotine with their meals.

Non-North Americans should also note that in this part of the world, main lunch or dinner dishes are usually referred to as entrées, which can be somewhat confusing for people who come from parts of the world where an entrée is the dish you have to start a meal (called appetizers or starters in North America).

The two best sources of restaurant information for Greater Vancouver are the *Zagat Survey* and *Anne Garber's Cheap Eats Vancouver,* by Anne Garber and John TD Keyes, available at bookstores throughout the city. There's also *CityFood*, a free quarterly publication, available at bookstores and cafes, which contains restaurant listings and food news and gossip for Vancouver, Whistler and Victoria. Restaurant reviews also appear weekly in the Thursday *Vancouver Sun* and in the *Georgia Straight*, which also has dozens of discount coupons for two-for-one dinners and lunches.

BUDGET
City Center (Map 2)

This section wouldn't be complete without mentioning the *White Spot.* A Vancouver institution famous for its 'Triple-O' hamburger (you either love it or hate it), this chain of family restaurants was started by Nat Bailey in 1928. With over 30 locations in greater Vancouver, they serve standard food at reasonable prices every day. There's one on West Georgia St between Seymour and Granville Sts in the city center.

Granville St There are plenty of cheap greasy-spoon cafes and restaurants along Granville St, with a few that stand out. *Kitto Japanese House* (☎ 604-687-6622), 833 Granville St, is sometimes described as the McDonald's of Japanese food. Be that as it may, the food is good, fast and inexpensive; there's a second restaurant at 833 Bute St. The six combination dinners cost $8, while other items start at around $6.

A European-style cake shop and tearoom, *Notte's Bon Ton* (☎ 604-681-3058), 874 Granville St, can't be beat for delicious pastries and cakes. At the back of the shop, past glass counters bulging with extremely fattening items, there's a small cafe decorated like a Bavarian town square. Here you'll get ham and cheese in a crusty roll for $3.25. The scrumptious French pastries are $1.50, while the cheesecake with whipped cream and cherries is $3.55.

Step back into a '50s diner at *The Templeton* (☎ 604-685-4612), 1087 Granville St, a great retro-style cafe with jukeboxes in the booths. The diner menu has a distinctly New Orleans' feel with veggie chili ($6), Cajun creole ($8) and seafood jambalaya ($10). Open daily from 9 am to late, brunch is served on the weekend and holidays until 3.30 pm.

Robson St Heading north toward Denman St, *Pezzo* (☎ 604-669-9300), 1100 Robson St, is a lively place for gourmet pizza by the slice ($3.50), or spaghetti ($5) and lasagna ($6), both of which come with a salad. Head up the stairs to the *Thai House Restaurant* (☎ 604-683-3383), 1116 Robson St, where most dishes are around $10 and the lunch special is $7.

The Bread Garden Bakery & Cafe (☎ 604-688-3213), 812 Bute St, just around the corner off Robson St, serves things like quiche or wraps ($4.50) and chicken pot pie ($5). The restaurant, which is open 24 hours, even has a take-out window designed for skateboarders. Don't forget to take a number inside if you want to be served.

Just like a restaurant you'd find in Tokyo, *Harbour Moon* (☎ 604-688-8777), 1230 Robson St, has plastic models of food in the window. The reasonable prices, however, are something you won't find in Japan; ramen noodle soup costs $5.50, prawn and vegetable tempura costs $4.50 and the chicken teriyaki on rice is $6.

Although the *Fogg n' Suds* (☎ 604-683-2337), 202 - 1323 Robson St, one of three you'll find in Vancouver, specializes in beer (there are 24 on tap and 200 bottled varieties), it also offers a wide selection of food, none of it done particularly well, like beef wraps, vegetable stir-fry and burgers, all for around $8.

A great find is the tiny *Ezogiku Noodle Cafe*, 1329 Robson St, which specializes in big bowls of steaming noodles; a shuya ramen is $6, the seafood ramen is $9 and there's beef curry on rice for $6. You might have to wait to get a seat, but be patient, it's worth it. The large and noisy *Hon's Wun Tun House* (☎ 604-685-0871), 1339 Robson St, is a slice of Hong Kong with the usual selection of Chinese dishes for around $8.

Farther down you'll find the *Robson Public Market*, 1610 Robson St, with fresh fruit and vegetables, cheese, bread and other ingredients for a picnic. Upstairs is a small food court with a selection of take-out food. Across the street, *Capers*, 1675 Robson St, is a combination whole-foods market, deli, bakery, and fruit and vegetable market with an emphasis on 'organic' and fresh. After shopping, have a coffee and snack in the corner cafe. Open daily from 8 am to 10 pm.

De Dutch Pannekoek House (☎ 604-687-7065), 1725 Robson St, specializes in Dutch pancakes and is a good place for a filling breakfast or lunch. The servings are huge and two people could make a meal of one of the 'platters' ($7), or try the omelettes ($6 to $12) or the sandwiches ($7). Open daily from 8 am to 3.30 pm (3 pm on the weekend). There are several around the city.

Denman St Close to Stanley Park, this is another lively, pleasant street to stroll along, offering lots of eating options. At the *Great Wall Mongolian BBQ* (☎ 604-688-2121), 717 Denman St, you create your own stir-fry with ingredients from a buffet then watch as the chef cooks it up in front of you. The all-you-can-eat lunch ($6) and dinner ($10) deals are hard to beat. *Musashi Japanese Restaurant* (☎ 604-687-0634), 780 Denman St between Robson and Alberni Sts, is cozy, casual and cheap with dishes for $6 or combination dinners for $15. Closed Monday. For Montreal-style chicken and ribs – which means they're barbecued – try the *Rooster's Quarters* (☎ 604-689-8023), 836 Denman St, where the chicken dinners start at $8, and ribs at $9. There's a children's menu and live folk music on the weekend.

There's nothing fancy about this small restaurant in the West End Community Centre, but the **Denman Garden Inn** (☎ 604-669-3623), 870 Denman St, offers bargain meals, including Chinese dishes or Canadian food like pork chops for around $7. The breakfast special is a real steal at $3. Open from 8 am to 8 pm. **Bud's Halibut & Chips** (☎ 604-683-0661), 1007 Denman St, is a good place for fish and chips starting at around $8.

Forget the diet and let your willpower go for a walk while you indulge yourself at the desserts-only **Death by Chocolate** (☎ 604-899-2462), 1001 Denman St. All the items are around $7. However, if you are feeling particularly decadent, 'A Multitude of Sins' is a selection of six items for $15.

Davie St While the **Bombay Curry House** (☎ 604-688-9930), 1726 Davie St, might look like a plain cafe inside, the prices are excellent, such as the lamb biryani dinner for $10, and the tandoori chicken leg or the 'seesh kababs' for $5. For good hamburgers, great milkshakes and interesting clientele, **Hamburger Mary's** (☎ 604-687-1293), 1202 Davie St, is worth a visit, especially on a warm night when you can sit outside and watch life go by. Most hamburgers are around $7 and pasta is $8. Open daily from 7 am to 3 am.

Another good place for hamburgers, plus a variety of other great-value meals, is **Fresgo Inn** (☎ 604-689-1332), 1138 Davie St. Items include beef stew ($7), submarine sandwiches big enough for two to share ($7), and of course the burgers ($3 to $6). Open Monday to Saturday from 8 am to 3 am, and Sunday from 9 am to midnight.

For spicy Portuguese-style chicken try **Tigãlos** (☎ 604-331-0051), 1157 Davie St, where the chicken breast fillet with two side dishes is $7 and chicken burgers are $5. **Stepho's Souvlaki Greek Taverna** (☎ 604-683-2555), 1124 Davie St, is the local favorite for Greek cooking. A large helping of moussaka or souvlaki is $9, but come early, especially on the weekend, because there's often a line to get in.

Yaletown (Map 2)

Tradewinds Cafe (☎ 604-687-1010), B11 - 1020 Mainland St, is a small place with burgers and sandwiches for $6 and stir-fries for $8. It's tricky to find; go straight through the doors off 1020 Mainland St, through the doors at the far end and turn right down the stairs. Open Monday to Friday from 8.30 am to 6 pm.

Like something you'd expect to find in a converted New York City loft, hence its name, **Soho** (☎ 604-688-1180), 1144 Homer St, is a great place to relax over a Manhattan sandwich ($5.50) or play a game of pool on one of the six tables at the back. The art displayed on the brick walls is for sale, too. Open daily from 9 am to 1 am.

Gastown (Map 3)

A great place for breakfast ($3, served all day) or lunch is the **Bavaria Restaurant & Deli**, 203 Carrall St, which serves up such items as corned beef sandwiches ($4), pierogies with salad ($4.50) and goulash ($4). Almost next door, **Blake's on Carrall** (☎ 604-899-3354), 221 Carrall St, has nightly entertainment with 'magic nights,' 'comedy nights' and jazz. They also offer tapas and main courses like lasagna, quiche and fajitas, all for around $7.

Buzz into Gastown for a caffeine fix

Coffee Shops and Caffeine Fixes

No matter whether you call it espresso, cappuccino or latte, Vancouver is awash in good coffee. If you want to relax over a cup of java and a muffin, you don't have to look far – coffee shops are everywhere. The big-name chains found throughout the city include local roasters-made-good Blenz, Canadian giants Grabbajabba and Second Cup, and Seattle coffee-magnates Starbucks (in fact, Starbucks even has two outlets kitty-corner from each other on Robson and Thurlow Sts).

However, there are many small independent coffee shops offering equally good hot beverages, and in some cases delicious treats as well. For a real taste of Vancouver, try Delany's on Denman Coffee House, on Denman St in the West End; Benny's Bagels on West Broadway at Larch St on the West Side; Continental Coffee and Torrefazione Coloiera, both on Commercial Drive in East Vancouver; and the Savary Island Pie Company on Marine Drive in West Vancouver.

For soup-and-sandwich lunches, try either the ***Cottage Deli***, 131 Water St, which has views of Burrard Inlet, or ***La Luna Cafe***, 117 Water St, where daily specials are around $6, and there are lots of baked goodies. The ***Thai Palace*** (☎ 604-331-1660), 100 Water St, specializes in seafood dishes for around $12, while other Thai favorites start at $10.

The Old Spaghetti Factory (☎ 604-684-1288), 53 Water St, is part of a large chain offering good-value pasta-based dinners; kids are welcome. The eye-catching decor includes old machinery, stained-glass Tiffany lamps and even a 1910 Vancouver streetcar. Entrées range from $8 to $13.

For fabulous Indian cuisine, the ***Jewel of India*** (☎ 604-687-5665), 52 Alexander St, has entrées for around $9. Tandoori dishes, the house speciality, are around $11, while the lunch specials are around $7. There is live sitar music on Friday and Saturday evenings. Check into the breeding ground of new and inventive pizza (from $8 to $20) at ***Incendio*** (☎ 604-688-8694), 103 Columbia St, or try the excellent pasta ($10).

Another restaurant worth mentioning, which is just on the outskirts of Gastown, is ***The Only Seafood Restaurant*** (☎ 604-681-6546), 20 East Hastings St, near Carrall St. A Vancouver tradition since 1912, this restaurant still serves up great fresh seafood at reasonable prices. Don't be put off by the shabby interior (there are just 17 stools around the counters and two booths), or the rough neighborhood. The clam chowder with bread is $3.25; items such as salmon, cod and halibut are between $8 and $10; or try one of the daily specials such as three fried oysters, a cup of chowder and a coffee for $8. Open daily from 11 am to 8 pm.

If you got a hankering for good inexpensive Japanese food, head east out of Gastown to the 300 block of Powell St, where there are a few restaurants offering great deals. At one time this was known as 'Little Japan' before Japanese restaurants blossomed throughout the rest of the city. A personal favorite here is ***Hoko Japanese House*** (☎ 604-685-4656), 362 Powell St, where the $11 dinner special combination includes soup, salad, rice and three items off the menu, or pay $16 for all you can eat. Individual pieces of sushi are $1 to $3, or go for the Hoko Sushi Special for only $6 and get miso soup and 18 pieces of sushi. Open

Monday to Friday from 11.30 am to 10 pm, Saturday to 11 pm and closed Sunday.

Chinatown (Map 3)

One of the largest restaurants in the area, although on the outskirts of Chinatown, is the *Pink Pearl* (Map 4; ☎ 604-253-4316), 1132 East Hastings St, a good place for dim sum. The seemingly out-of-place *Bodai Vegetarian Restaurant* (☎ 604-682-2666), 337 East Hastings St, serves several appetizing dishes, some of which include simulated meat. At lunch, dim sum specials go for around $2.50, while other dishes are around $8. Closed Tuesday.

Next door is the *Pho Day Vietnamese Restaurant* (☎ 604-488-0508), 333 East Hastings St, with $4 specials. Just down the street, the 24-hour *Pho Pasteur* (☎ 604-689-8258), 290 East Hastings St, is another Vietnamese restaurant serving soups for $5.50, rice dishes for $8, or chicken curry with French bread for $5.

Kam's Garden Restaurant (☎ 604-669-5488), 509 Main St, specializes in wonton and barbecue dishes, with a bowl of wonton soup going for $4, or the dinner-for-one combination for $8. Across the street, the *Gold Pavilion Bakery & Restaurant* (☎ 604-688-6708), at 518 Main St, has daily specials like spareribs with black bean sauce on rice or black pepper chicken on rice for $4, or one of the filled buns for 80¢.

On East Pender St, down from Main St, try the *Buddhist Vegetarian Restaurant* (☎ 604-683-8816), 137 East Pender St, where you get chow mein dishes for $8, one-person set dinners for $8.50 or deluxe vegetarian dishes for $12. Right across the street, the *New Town Bakery & Restaurant* (☎ 604-681-1828), 158 East Pender St, has specials ($5) and a buffet lunch ($7) or dinner ($8). For children you pay 55¢ per year of the child's age.

Along Keefer St, the heart of Chinatown, you'll find lots of restaurants, including *The Gain Wah* (☎ 604-684-1740), 218 Keefer St, with 16 different varieties of congee (a rice or noodle soup loaded with goodies) starting at $4; *Kent's Kitchen* (☎ 604-669-2237), 232 Keefer St, with daily specials for $4; and

Hon's Wun-tun House (☎ 604-688-0871), 108 – 268 Keefer St, with a huge selection of noodle dishes for around $5.

Around the corner between Keefer and East Georgia Sts, *Kim Heng Noodles* (☎ 604-681-3188), 617 Gore Ave, isn't much to look at and there are only six tables, but you get large meals for about $4 and the selection of egg and rice noodles is truly astounding.

West Side

Granville Island/False Creek (Map 5)

For gourmet dining on a budget, try the *Pacific Institute of Culinary Arts* (☎ 604-734-4488), at 1505 West 2nd Ave, right by the entrance to Granville Island, where cooking students prepare the food and serve the public. You can get some delicious surprises in the small and tastefully decorated dining room, where a three-course lunch is around $16, an entrée costs around $10; on Monday there are two-for-one lunch and dinner specials. Open weekdays for lunch from 11.30 am to 2 pm, and for dinner from 6 to 9 pm.

West 4th Ave (Map 6)

The *India Grill* (☎ 604-734-5777), 1835 West 4th Ave, has good curries and vegetarian dishes for $9, while up the street the *Surat Sweet Restaurant* (☎ 604-733-7363), 1938 West 4th Ave, serves vegetarian-only Gujarati Indian cooking with most dishes costing about $6. For spicy Chinese, the *Won More Szechuan Cuisine* (☎ 604-737-2889), 1944 West 4th Ave, charges around $8 for most items, with a $6 lunch special.

Joe's Grill (☎ 604-736-6588), 2061 West 4th Ave, is the kind of cafe they just don't make anymore, with items like a two-egg breakfast for $3, burgers for $5 or splurge for the vegetable à la Creole for $9. Almost next door, *Sophie's Cosmic Cafe* (☎ 604-732-6810), 2095 West 4th Ave, is a more up-to-date cafe with lots of stuff on the walls and an impressive range of omelettes ($7), burgers ($8) and enchiladas ($10). The homemade desserts are a real delight.

The *Veggi Kitchen* (☎ 604-733-9668), 2135 West 4th Ave, is a fairly small Chinese

Buddhist vegetarian restaurant making some delicious food, most of which is around $6 for a small portion or $10 for a large. There are also lunch specials and dim sum on the weekend.

A relic of Kitsilano's hippie past, the 24-hour *Naam* (☎ 604-738-7151), 2724 West 4th Ave, is a vegetarian health-food restaurant serving stir-fries ($9), burger platters ($9) and pizza ($10). There is live guitar music nightly from 7 to 10 pm, including folk, jazz, classical and flamenco.

West Broadway (Map 5) Broadway, roughly between Cambie and Granville Sts, is a small Chinatown where you'll have no trouble finding an inexpensive place to eat. *Mongolie Grill* (☎ 604-874-6121), 467 West Broadway, specializes in choose-your-raw-ingredients brazier cooking, which can cost as little or as much as you want – you pay according to the weight of your uncooked food (about $2.20 per 100g). *Golden Great Wall Szechuan Restaurant* (☎ 604-872-0328), 525 West Broadway, has a good local reputation, specializing in spicy Shanghai cooking; most dishes are around $10.

Just off Broadway, the *Normandy* (☎ 604-738-3115), 2675 Granville St, between 10th and 11th Aves, is an old-style diner with breakfast specials from $2 and weekday dinner specials like curry seafood for $6. Open weekdays from 7 am to 9 pm, it opens at 8 am on the weekend. Back on the strip close to Pine St, *Szechwan Chongqing Seafood Restaurant* (☎ 604-734-2668), 1668 West Broadway, was recently voted by readers of the *Vancouver Sun* as the favorite Chinese restaurant in Vancouver. Not only does the staff serve up searing-hot delicacies, they also deliver. Most dishes are around $10.

At the very end of Broadway, *True Confections* (Map 6; ☎ 604-222-8489), 3701 West Broadway, on the corner of Alma St, is a dessert lover's paradise with up to 40 different selections. Cheesecakes, layer cakes and pies are the specialty. Most items are around $6 for a piece which, even if you're not on a diet, can feed two people. It supplies desserts

to many of the restaurants in town, and, if you want to take a whole cake back to your room, ask to see the 'whole item' price list. There is also a branch (☎ 604-682-1292), 866 Denman St at Haro St, in the West End.

East Vancouver (Map 4)
Commercial Drive The *Café Deux Soleil* (☎ 604-254-1195), 2096 Commercial Drive, is a very funky and child-friendly restaurant, offering 'kid food' selections for $2.25, and a play area on the small stage where bands perform on the weekend. For adults the food includes veggie chili ($5), a soup & sandwich special ($7), and stir-fries and pasta ($8).

The *Old Europe Restaurant* (☎ 604-255-9424), 1608 Commercial Drive, is like a cafe you might find down a side street in Budapest. The goulash and borscht is $4.50, veal stew with dumplings is $7.50, and Wiener schnitzel is $9. *Juicy Lucy's Good Eats* (☎ 604-254-6101), 1420 Commercial Drive, has lots of healthy dishes like dhal, chili ($4) and a nine-grain waffle topped with whipped cream, fresh fruit and maple syrup ($5).

The *Mekong Vietnamese Restaurant* (☎ 604-253-7088), 1414 Commercial Drive, has some great deals, such as the two-item lunch combo for $5, or the main dishes like sizzling lamb with curry on rice for $8. *Havana* (☎ 604-253-9119), 1212 Commercial Drive, is a Spanish-Caribbean tapas bar offering tapas for $7 and main dishes like the Shanghai-Havana Connection (red snapper with black beans and soy sauce) for around $10. Check out the small art gallery and performance space in the back.

El Cocal (☎ 604-255-4580), 1037 Commercial Drive, specializes in Salvadoran and Brazilian food, with more familiar Mexican dishes thrown in for good measure, with items like *feijoada* (pork stew) and *mukeka de peixe* (fish stew) for around $10. A good, cheap place to have lunch, *Andy's Bakery* (☎ 604-251-5667), 935 Commercial Drive, has soups for $1.25, sandwiches for around $4 and an array of delicious baked goods. Open weekdays from 9.30 am to 5 pm, Saturday from 9 am to 4 pm, and closed Sunday.

Punjabi Market (Map 1) The section of the city running south along Main St from East 48th to East 51st Aves is the Indian section, complete with street signs in Punjabi. There are three restaurants along here that are great value for excellent food.

Zeenaz Restaurant (☎ 604-324-9344), 6460 Main St, offers an all-you-can-eat buffet with a selection of about eight items which change daily; for lunch (noon to 3 pm) it's $9, and for dinner (3 to 9 pm) it's $11. You can also select items off the regular menu for around $12, but with a smorgasbord as good as this one, why bother? Closed Tuesday.

Not to be outdone, the *All India Sweets & Restaurant* (☎ 604-327-0891), 6505 Main St, has a 40-item all-you-can-eat vegetarian buffet for just $6. And, as the name implies, the specialty is the Indian sweets (of which the selection here seems endless). Down the street, *Pabla's Himalaya Restaurant* (☎ 604-324-6514), 6587 Main St, also has a fabulous selection of sweets, and the samosas are highly recommended. Vegetable dishes are $4, meat dishes are $5 and specialty dishes like goat curry are $6.

New Westminster (Map 1) *Judy's Restaurant* (☎ 604-522-0015), suite 101, 56 6th St, is a real find and almost worth a separate trip out here. The small restaurant is very tastefully decorated, including a baby grand piano in the center of the room which gets a workout on the weekend. There is a varied menu offering seafood dishes ($12), roast beef ($10) and pierogies ($9).

One block up from Columbia St, *The Old Spaghetti Factory* (☎ 604-524-9788), 50 8th St, on the corner of Carnarvon St, offers its usual assortment of inexpensive pasta dishes and 1920s decor.

The *Royal Tandoori Restaurant* (☎ 604-521-2247), 700 Columbia St, has some great deals, especially the daily specials posted on the outside board, and the all-you-can-eat dinner buffet on Wednesday for $9. Other items such as the vegetarian dishes are $7, while meat dishes are $8. Open daily except Sunday.

North Shore (Map 8)

North Vancouver Lonsdale Quay Market has lots of places to munch at or to buy food to take out. The British-style *Cheshire Cheese Inn* (☎ 604-987-3322), on level 2, sells traditional British food like steak and kidney pie and shepherd's pie, as well as chicken, ribs and steak for around $10. The *Thai House Restaurant* (☎ 604-987-9911), 180 West Esplanade, just above the quay, has to be one of the lovelier premises you'll find, with hand-cut wood posts and beams, tile floors, and floor-to-ceiling windows. It's almost like being in Thailand. Most of the dishes are around $10, however, the all-you-can-eat lunch buffet on the weekend is a great deal at $7.50. There are four other Thai House Restaurants in the Lower Mainland.

Sailor Hagar's Brew Pub (☎ 604-984-7669), 235 West 1st St, a couple of blocks up and over from the quay, not only produces some excellent beer (about eight on tap at any one time, including a couple of seasonal specialties), but also makes pretty good food. Items such as sandwiches, burgers, pizza, and fish and chips go for about $8. Weekend brunch, including holidays, is served from 11 am to 2 pm.

Over in the other direction just east off Lonsdale Ave, the *Flavour of India* (☎ 604-985-5477), 175 East 3rd St, offers good food at good prices. Items off the menu are around $10, but the real deal is the all-you-can-eat buffet dinner on Sunday and Monday for $10. Open for lunch weekdays from noon to 2 pm, and for dinner daily from 5 pm.

Farther up at 1301 Lonsdale Ave at the corner of 13th St, *Nando's* (☎ 604-990-1531), prepares delicious spicy Portuguese-style grilled chicken that you can eat there or takeout. A quarter-chicken meal is $7 while the half-chicken meal is $9, and the family meal (serves three to four hungry people) is a good deal at $22.

West Vancouver The *Dundarave Cafe* (☎ 604-926-8838), 2427 Marine Drive, is a real find and the large patio area at the front is ideal on a sunny day. Most items on the menu, such as the beef and mushroom pie,

Fruit of the Vine – BC Wine

British Columbia may not be up there with the great wine producing regions of the world, but in recent years the province's wineries have been unveiling some outstanding wines – and have the international awards to prove it.

The province's 40 wineries are found in four regions: Okanagan and Similkameen, both in the southern interior and probably the premier wine-growing regions in the province; Fraser Valley just east of Vancouver; and southern Vancouver Island. Some of the better wines being produced include Chardonnay, Riesling, Gewürztraminer, Pinot Blanc, Pinot Noir, Cabernet Sauvignon, Merlot, Cabernet Franc, Meritage and the expensive ice-wine.

A system has been developed in recent years to help consumers understand exactly what is meant by BC wine, especially since many people aren't even aware such a thing exists until they come here for a visit. Wineries are classified into three groups: large wineries that produce unlimited quantities for a mass market with both imported and BC grapes supplied by contract growers; estate wineries that use only grapes grown in BC, with at least half of those grown in their own vineyards; and farm wineries that use only grapes grown in their vineyards.

To complement this there is the Vintners Quality Alliance (VQA) that, much like Italy's DOC or France's appellation system, is a guarantee of authenticity. Even though this is a voluntary system, most vineyards choose to participate in it. The wine carrying this distinction must be made from 100% BC-grown grapes and must conform to an accepted varietal style. Keep in mind that unless a wine carries the VQA tag, it may not be made with 100% BC grapes and, in fact, may not even contain any BC grapes. By the same token, there are a small number of estate wineries producing good single-varietal wines that have chosen not to participate in the VQA program.

Some labels to look out for include Blue Mountain, Domain Combret, Gray Monk, Hawthorne Mountain, Inniskillin Okanagan, Mission Hill Grand Reserve, Quail's Gate, Sumac Ridge and Summerhill. BC wines are sold in liquor stores and privately operated wine stores, often found in shopping centers. For a great selection of VQA wines, visit the Broadway International Wine Shop (☎ 604-734-8543), 2752 West Broadway.

the braised lamb shanks or the legendary Sunday roast beef dinner are around $10. They also put on great weekend brunches from 10 am to 3 pm.

MID-RANGE
City Center (Map 2)

Granville St The *Goulash House Restaurant & Pastry Shop* (☎ 604-688-0206), 1065 Granville St, is in an unfortunate part of the city but worth the walk past the adult video stores and seedy hotels just for the delicious food at great prices. Try the stuffed cabbage rolls ($8.50), beef goulash ($11) or vegetable ragout with chicken schnitzel ($12.50).

Robson St Even though the address is 780 Thurlow St, *Café il Nido* (☎ 604-685-

6436) can be accessed by way of a ramp beside Manhattan Books & Magazines. The food here is highly recommended and most dishes are in the $15 range. Above the *Cactus Club Cafe* (☎ 604-687-3278), 1136 Robson St, a chain restaurant serving Tex-Mex dishes, burgers ($8) and ribs ($14), is the very popular *Zefferelli's* (☎ 604-687-0655) in a large open room serving pastas for $13, while other main dishes are around $18.

Across the street, *Milestone's* (☎ 604-734-8616), 1145 Robson St, is a modern, high-tech, trend-conscious bar and restaurant with burgers ($7), pasta ($11) and fish dishes ($14). There are a few of them around the Lower Mainland. Next door above London Drugs is a Vancouver chain restaurant, *Earls* (☎ 604-669-0020), 1185 Robson St. It serves the usual assortment of selections including burgers ($8), gumbo ($9) and chicken dishes ($14).

Da Pasta Bar (☎ 604-688-1288), 1232 Robson St, has a great early-bird dinner special daily from 4 to 6.30 pm, where you get one entrée at the regular price and the second for just $2. The regular menu offers a selection of pastas and sauces which you put together for around $14 (the ostrich sauce looks like an interesting choice).

For Vietnamese food at good prices, *Greenhut Vietnamese Cuisine* (☎ 604-688-3688), 1429 Robson St, has curries for $11, brochettes for $12, dinner-for-two plates for $27 and lunch specials starting at $6. If you'd prefer Greek cuisine, then a block or so down is *Yiamis Restaurant* (☎ 604-681-8141), 1642 Robson St, a Robson St original that still serves up delicious food inside the authentic looking Greek taverna. Lamb ($15) is the house specialty, but try the souvlakis ($14) or the vegetarian moussaka ($11).

Denman St The *Kafe Europa* (☎ 604-683-4982), 735 Denman St, serves reasonably priced Eastern European food such as goulash for $9, schnitzels for $10 and roasted duckling for $14. Only open for dinner Thursday to Sunday. For authentic Mexican, try *Poncho's* (☎ 604-683-7236), 835 Denman St, with standard dishes for around $10, while dishes like *carne a la Tampiqueña* (marinated beef) are $14.

With lots of hanging lamps, knickknacks on the walls and a large fireplace at one end, the *Brass Monkey* (☎ 604-685-7626), 1072 Denman St, is like being in someone's living room. The small menu offers pasta ($12), seafood ($16) and roast beef ($18).

Stanley Park Of the three restaurants in the park (see the Top End section for the other two), *Prospect Point Cafe* (Stanley Park Map; ☎ 604-669-2737), behind the gift shop, offers the best prices along with great views of the Lions Gate Bridge and Burrard Inlet. Salmon is the specialty, with the salmon platter going for $13 while the salmon steak is $17. There are also other items such as steamed mussels for $13 or steak for $18. Sunday brunch is served from 11 am to 4 pm.

Davie St Set in a beautiful Queen Anne stone mansion built in the early 1900s, *Romano's Macaroni Grill* (☎ 604-689-4334), 1523 Davie St, has a bag of tricks to bring in the business – including opera singers, cooking exhibitions and pay-what-you-drink jugs of wine. Oh yes, there's food here too, including pizza ($10), chicken ($12), pasta ($12) and meat dishes ($15).

The Japanese restaurant *Kisha Poppo* (☎ 604-681-0488), 1143 Davie St, specializes in all-you-can-eat dining. For lunch (daily from 11.30 am to 3 pm) there are 30 items ($11 weekdays, $12 weekends), and for dinner (daily from 5 to 10 pm) there are 40 items ($17 weekdays, $18 weekends).

Elsewhere Downtown *A Kettle of Fish* (☎ 604-682-6661), 900 Pacific St at the corner of Hornby St, is a well-established restaurant specializing in fresh fish and seafood for under $20. Not far away, *La Bodega* (☎ 604-684-8814), 1277 Howe St, is probably the most authentic Spanish restaurant in Vancouver, which is probably why you'll find a lot of Spanish ex-pats here. The sangria is good as are the tapas, the specialty, which ranges in price from about $3 to $7. A small menu offers items such as the outstanding paella for $16.

Yaletown (Map 2)

This warehouse-and-loft district is also home to some of Vancouver's trendiest restaurants. A real find here is *Deniro's Bistro* (☎ 604-684-2777), 1039 Mainland St, where you'll be served cosmopolitan cuisine in retro-diner ambience; pastas go for $10 while other main dishes cost around $15. There's a dinner special Sunday to Tuesday, in which all pastas go for $7.

Although a brewpub, the *Yaletown Brewing Company* (☎ 604-681-2739), 1111 Mainland St, also offers restaurant dining next to the pub. The pizza is around $11, pastas are $13, or try the oriental spicy lamb stir-fry for $14. They do make excellent beer (about seven to choose from).

The **Hamilton Street Grill** (☎ 604-331-1511), 1009 Hamilton St, with booths in the front and old posters on the walls, specializes in steaks, which go for around $20, while other entrées such as sea bass or grilled chicken are around $14. A block south, **Capones** (☎ 604-684-7900), 1141 Hamilton St, is a long, narrow restaurant that seems to go on forever (until you see the stage at the back where jazz bands play Wednesday through Saturday). Expect to pay around $14 for pizza and pasta dishes.

The sister to WaaZuBee on Commercial Drive in East Vancouver, **Subeez Cafe** (☎ 604-687-6107), 891 Homer St, has a steel, concrete and glass decor with lots of techno blasting out (there are DJs on the weekend). It specializes in fusion cuisine, and dishes are around $12.

Gastown (Map 3)

Both a brewpub and a restaurant, **Steamworks Brewing Co** (☎ 604-689-2739), 375 Water St at The Landing beside Waterfront Station, offers an array of overpriced mediocre food with good brewed-on-the-premises beer. If you do want to eat here expect to pay $11 for pizza or around $15 for other entrées. A better bet for a good meal is the **Water Street Cafe** (☎ 604-689 2832), 300 Water St, housed in one of the few buildings to escape the Great Fire of 1886, where you'll get pasta for $13 and other entrées for around $18.

For a touch of the neo-Gothic, **Mick's Restaurant & Rhythm Bar** (☎ 604-684-2883), 332 Water St, has sandwiches ($8), pasta ($8 to $12) and other entrées like beef stroganoff ($10) and New York steak ($18). Downstairs in the music lounge you can hear Latin, techno and jazz on Friday, Saturday and Monday nights. Meant to be a low-ticket version of the cucina at other Umberto's restaurants, **Umberto Al Porto** (☎ 604-683-8376), 321 Water St, is where to go for a small-scale Italian splurge, without threatening the limit on your credit card, with pasta for around $15 and meat and fish dishes for around $20.

La Ventana Restaurant (☎ 604-682-8667), 162 Water St, specializes in Spanish cuisine in surroundings that make you feel like you're dining in Barcelona. Tapas range from $6 to $13, paellas from $13 to $18 and other main dishes are around $18. At **Brother's Restaurant** (☎ 604-683-9124), 1 Water St, the decor has a monastic theme complete with Gregorian chants emanating from the front door and wait staff dressed in monks' habits. The 'Brothers' serve items like the Monastery burger ($8), pasta ($10), seafood and poultry ($12).

For Italian and Greek food, **Characters Restaurant** (☎ 604-681-6581), 1 Alexander St, offers calamari or moussaka ($14), roast lamb ($15) and a seafood plate ($17) in surroundings that are a cross between the Parthenon and a Greek taverna. Behind it in a converted railway dining car, **The Chew Chew Club** (☎ 604-688-2439), 106 Carrall St, has items like potato-crust pizza ($11) and crab cakes or gnocchi ($12), plus a good selection of wines, martinis and cigars.

Just a block south **The Irish Heather** (☎ 604-688-9779), 217 Carrall St, not only pours the best Guinness in town but serves up some good food such as sandwiches (around $6), beef in Guinness or vegetable stew ($13) and, of course, Irish stew ($14).

Chinatown (Map 3)

A local favorite, the **Park Lock** (☎ 604-688-1581), 544 Main St, specializes in great seafood dishes ($15), but there are also noodle and rice dishes ($10) and especially good dim sum; don't let the modest street-level entry put you off. Open daily for lunch from 10 am to 3 pm, and for dinner from 5 pm.

For Cambodian cuisine, go to **Phnom Penh** (☎ 604-682-5777), 244 East Georgia St, just off Main St, where you can expect to pay around $12 for most dishes.

West Side
Granville Island/False Creek (Map 5)

With the public market so close at hand, you would rightly expect Granville Island to feature fresh and tempting food. Both a jazz club and a Creole restaurant, **Mulvaney's**

Brunch – a Vancouver Tradition

If Vancouverites aren't zipping off to the ski hills first thing Sunday morning, or setting the sails up on their boats for a day on the water, they are probably heading to their favorite restaurant to relax over brunch. This Vancouver tradition is so popular that any restaurant worth its weight in eggs Benedict and blueberry waffles is almost obliged to serve brunch on the weekend, especially Sunday.

Most restaurants serve brunch from about 11 am to 2.30 pm and offer everything from the traditional bacon and eggs, omelettes and pancakes, to more exotic fare such as eggs served on smoked salmon, or dim sum.

The following is just a very small selection of places to try for brunch and, besides the good food, offer either great views of the city or have items that are a bit out of the ordinary. The establishments listed here are also described in more detail in this chapter. You can expect to pay from $10 to $15 for brunch at most of these restaurants.

For the best brunch-time view of the city, you won't do much better than the **Salmon House on the Hill** (Map 8; ☎ 604-926-3212), 2229 Folkestone Way, in West Vancouver. Another great location in West Vancouver with good views, even if they are more down-to-earth, is the **Beach House at Dundarave Pier** (Map 8; ☎ 604-922-1414), 150 25th St. For brunch with a difference take the ferry from Horseshoe Bay to Bowen Island, or sail there if you have a boat, and relax at Snug Cove in either **The Breakfast Cafe** (☎ 604-947-0550) or **Doc Morgan's Inn** (☎ 604-947-0707), both of which are just up the road from the marina.

In North Vancouver not far from Lonsdale Quay, **Sailor Hagar's Brew Pub** (Map 8; ☎ 604-984-7669), 235 West 1st St, has good views of the city skyline, some of the best beer in the Lower Mainland and good food as well. If you are planning to spend Sunday afternoon exploring Stanley Park, two good places to build up your energy levels are **Prospect Point Cafe** (Stanley Park Map; ☎ 604-669-2737), with views of Lions Gate Bridge and Burrard Inlet, and **The Teahouse Restaurant** (Stanley Park Map; ☎ 604-669-3281), at Ferguson Point, with views of English Bay.

A longtime Vancouver favorite for brunch, and serving some of the best eggs Benedict in the city, is **O'Doul's Restaurant & Bar** (Map 2; ☎ 604-684-8461), 1300 Robson St. For more great views of the city, but from a southern perspective with the North Shore mountains as a backdrop, try **Seasons in the Park** (Map 1; ☎ 604-874-8008) in Queen Elizabeth Park.

For a Thai brunch with views of False Creek looking across to Granville Island, the **Chili Club Restaurant** (Map 2; ☎ 604-681-2890), 1018 Beach Ave, offers a 20-dish buffet that will really set your taste buds up for the rest of the day. For dim sum, two of the better places to try are the **Grand King Seafood Restaurant** (Map 5; ☎ 604-876-7855), 705 West Broadway, and the huge and busy **Pink Pearl** (Map 4; ☎ 604-253-4316), 1132 East Hastings St.

(☎ 604-685-6571), 9 Creekhouse - 1535 Johnston St, brings New Orleans to BC, with fresh fish a specialty and main dishes at around $20. If you like your fish on the rare side, Kamei Royale Ocean (☎ 604-602-0005), 1333 Johnston St, is one of the city's best sushi bars and Japanese restaurants with entrées at around $18.

On a warm summer evening, there's no place like **Bridges** (☎ 604-687-4400), 1696 Duranleau St, with its large outdoor deck and great views. The food isn't bad either, mostly pub fare on the patio or more serious Northwest cuisine in the upstairs dining room, where you'll pay around $14 for most entrées.

Farther east around False Creek, close to West 6th Ave and the Cambie Bridge, **Monk McQueen's** (☎ 604-877-1351), 601 Stamp's Landing, has good views of the city and charges around $18 for most main dishes, although the rack of lamb is $32. There is also live jazz Wednesday to Sunday from 7 to 11 pm.

On the north side of False Creek, across from Granville Island, there are a couple of choices. The **Chili Club Restaurant** (Map 2; ☎ 604-681-2890), 1018 Beach Ave, tucked beneath the Burrard Bridge on the Granville Seawalk, is an upscale Thai restaurant with most items on the menu going for about $10. The Sunday buffet brunch, served from 11.30 am to 2 pm, has 20 varieties of Thai food for $13, or $7 for children under 12. For the best views, ask to be seated upstairs.

Follow the Granville Seawalk east toward the Granville Bridge and you'll come to *The Riley Waterfront Cafe* (Map 2; ☎ 604-684-3666), 1661 Granville St, where the views of Granville Island get even better. Most entrées go for about $12, although burgers and sandwiches are available for around $9. Of course, you can always forget about the food and just have a drink on the patio.

Yew St (Map 6) Running south between Cornwall and West 1st Aves across from Kitsilano Beach Park, Yew St offers a handful of interesting choices. If music is what you're after, *Rossini's* (☎ 604-737-8080), 1525 Yew St, is a very happening place with live jazz nightly and weekend afternoons, serving pasta ($10), cannelloni ($11) or other dishes like chicken cacciatore ($15). Across the street, the *Urban Well* (☎ 604-737-7770), 1516 Yew St, which has a large screen TV, couches in front of a fireplace and a long bar to sit at, serves burgers ($8), wraps ($9), pasta and stir-fries ($10).

Very close to Yew St, the *Sunset Grill* (☎ 604-732-3733), 2204 York Ave, is a bar and restaurant serving burgers ($8), pasta ($12) and other entrées ($13). It has a large-screen TV, a good selection of beer on tap and live music on the weekends. A block south, *Da Pasta Bar* (☎ 604-738-6515), 2201 West 1st Ave, offers the same pasta and sauce menu as the Robson St branch (see Robson St under the Mid-Range/City Center section).

West 4th Ave (Map 6) A combination Greek and Italian restaurant, *Simpatico* (☎ 604-733-6824), 2222 West 4th Ave, has long been a Vancouver favorite, and some say it makes the best pizza ($12) in town. Other selections include pasta ($8), calamari and moussaka ($11).

The *Topanga Cafe* (☎ 604-733-3713), 2904 West 4th Ave, serves up Californian-Mexican dishes that are a good value such as the enchilada and burrito combo for $15, as well as their standard dinners for $10. Crayons are provided, too, so that you and your kids can color in the menu over dinner.

For a great cultural experience, the *Nyala Restaurant* (☎ 604-731-7899), 2930 West 4th Ave, serves Ethiopian food to be eaten without the use of cutlery – you use bread instead. Prices range from $9 for vegetarian dishes to $13 for most meat dishes. An all-you-can-eat dinner buffet is offered on Wednesday and Sunday for $11 ($6 for children). Every Saturday night, there's African or Caribbean music and dancing.

West Broadway (Map 5) The *Afghan Horseman* (☎ 604-873-5923), 445 West Broadway, has been serving up delicious Middle Eastern dishes since 1974. Ask to be seated in the Afghan Room, where low tables and cushions are the feature. Most meat dishes are around $14 while vegetarian dishes are closer to $11.

Just next door, *Rasputin* (☎ 604-879-6675), 457 West Broadway, brings fine Russian dining to Vancouver with dishes like cabbage rolls ($14), chicken Kiev ($19) and Rasputin's Feast ($25). For real family-style Greek cooking, cross the street to *Kalamata Greek Taverna* (☎ 604-872-7050), 478 West Broadway, where most items on the small menu are between $10 for the calamari to $15 for the prawn and scallop souvlaki.

Worth making a detour for, *Grand King Seafood Restaurant* (☎ 604-876-7855), 705 West Broadway, has perhaps the city's best dim sum ($4 a dish), and dinner entrées are uniformly excellent and innovative ($15). *Tojo's* (☎ 604-872-8050), 202 - 777 West Broadway, has top-notch sushi and inventive, unusual Japanese main dishes for around $18. To get to this restaurant, which has fabulous views from the dining room, go through the front entrance of the building and take the elevator to the 2nd floor.

Carnegie's (☎ 604-733-4141), 1619 West Broadway, calls itself an 'American bar & grill' and is very much like a place you might find in uptown Manhattan. It's a very happening place on the weekends, and if you want to meet people grab a seat at the bar. The entrées off the menu are around $15, although for $9 the thin-crust pizza is very good.

The *Picasso Cafe* (☎ 604-732-3290), 1626 West Broadway, manages to pull off good health-conscious French cuisine. The food is uniformly good and prepared with a light hand on the sauces and butter. Pastas go for about $12 and main dishes like braised lamb cost $15. The staff is part of a restaurant training program for homeless kids trying to make a change.

While not exactly a bargain, the Italian-by-Northwest cuisine at *Ecco il Pane* (☎ 604-739-1314), 2563 West Broadway, is a good value when compared to its peers. The bakery here is one of the best in town and dinner entrées go for less than $20. You'll often have to wait in line to get in, even at lunch.

The 3000 block of West Broadway is sometimes known as 'Little Greece.' Among several popular places in this area is the *Acropol* (☎ 604-733-2412), 2946 West Broadway, which has vegetarian dishes for $10, traditional dishes for $12 or a combination platter for two for $35. *Orestes* (☎ 604-738-1941), 3116 West Broadway, best described as being kind of funky Mediterranean, serves pasta ($12), souvlaki ($13) and lamb ($14 to $20). The very good *Ouzeri* (☎ 604-739-9378), 3189 West Broadway, is open till the early hours serving casual tapas-style snacks.

The ethnic mix also includes *Andale's* (☎ 604-738-9782), 3211 West Broadway, which serves a variety of tasty Mexican and Spanish dishes from tacos for around $6 to sautéed prawns for $14; check out the $1 'happy hour tacos' Monday to Friday from 3 to 4.30 pm.

Queen Elizabeth Park (Map 1) *Seasons in the Park* (☎ 604-874-8008), at Cambie St and West 33rd Ave, offers great views of the city with the North Shore mountains as a backdrop. Prices here are reasonable, all things considered, with most of the Northwest-inspired entrées under $20, about $5 less for lunch items. Open weekdays for lunch from 11.30 am to 2.30, daily for dinner from 5.30 pm; brunch is served from 11 am to 2.30 pm.

East Vancouver (Map 4)

Commercial Drive *Spumante's* (☎ 604-253-8899), 1736 Commercial Drive, serves excellent hearty fare in a tasteful setting. The menu selection is astonishingly broad with pasta for around $11 and meat dishes for around $16. The *WaaZuBee Cafe* (☎ 604-253-5299), 1622 Commercial Drive, has huge painted murals of Italian mountain-and-lake scenes on the walls and great metal sculptures hanging from the ceiling. A chicken WaazuBwich is $9, pasta is $11 and the Thai curried seafood stew is $12. There's also a good selection of local beer on tap and a good wine list. Subeez Cafe on Homer St in Yaletown is its sister restaurant.

The *Arriva Ristorante* (☎ 604-251-1177), 1537 Commercial Drive, has lovely decor which comes complete with linen tablecloths, arched doorways and the feeling that you have just stepped into a restaurant in Tuscany. Pasta dishes are around $12, while the seafood and meat dishes are closer to $17. The *Latin Quarter* (☎ 604-251-1144), 1305 Commercial Drive, is a Mediterranean-influenced restaurant that also doubles as a venue for music such as blues, jazz and flamenco in the evening. Main courses such as fajitas, paella (the house specialty) and grilled salmon are around $14. There is also a selection of cold and hot tapas.

Nick's Spaghetti House (☎ 604-254-5633), 631 Commercial Drive, has been here forever serving up large portions of the old favorites such as spaghetti and meat balls ($12), lasagna ($13) or the rack of ribs with spaghetti ($20).

North Shore (Map 8)
North Vancouver Located on the 3rd floor of the Lonsdale Quay Market, *The Q Cafe* (☎ 604-986-6111) has great views of the city, and on a nice day you can sit out on the patio. Breakfast selections are around $9, lunch starts at around $6 for sandwiches and burgers, while the dinner menu offers entrées for around $17. Open from 7 am to 2.30 pm, and again from 5.30 to 9.30 pm.

Several restaurants are concentrated near the corner of Lonsdale Ave and Esplanade, but one that stands out is *Corsi Trattoria* (☎ 604-987-9910), 1 Lonsdale Ave, a very homey Italian trattoria where everything is made on the premises, including the pasta and bread. Entrées cost between $10 and $20.

In another part of North Vancouver, *The Tomahawk* (☎ 604-988-2612), 1550 Philip Ave, just south of Marine Drive about six blocks east of Capilano Rd, is worth the trip. For more than 70 years this Native Indian art-filled restaurant has been serving large logger-style breakfasts, good burgers, steaks and homemade desserts – the fruit pies are a highlight – with most entrées costing around $12.

West Vancouver Some say *Chez Michel* (☎ 604-926-4913), 1373 Marine Drive, is one of the best French restaurants on either side of the Lions Gate Bridge. Most entrées are around $19 and include sautéed sweetbreads in a port wine sauce, and the fabulous bouillabaisse loaded with West Coast seafood and fish.

TOP END
City Center (Map 2)
Robson St The *Hermitage* (☎ 604-689-3237), 115 - 1025 Robson St, tucked away in a small alcove off the street, serves classic French cuisine at around $25 for most entrées. Right beside it in the same alcove, *Café De Medici* (☎ 604-669-9322), 109 - 1025 Robson St, is a classy and elegant Florentine restaurant that some say is the best of its type in the city; expect to pay around $17 for a pasta or $25 for other entrées.

For steaks, oysters, grilled fish and other stalwarts of the traditional Northwest cooking, go to *Joe Fortes* (☎ 604-669-1940), 777 Thurlow St, just off Robson St, where most main dishes, such as the swordfish or the crusted tuna, are between $20 and $25. There is an early-bird two-for-one dinner special between 5 and 6 pm.

Only moderately extravagant in price, *Cin Cin* (☎ 604-688-7338), 1154 Robson St, is a top downtown Italian restaurant with a sophisticated ambiance offering dishes from $18 to $28.

O'Doul's Restaurant & Bar (☎ 604-684-8461), 1300 Robson St, is a large open room with lots of windows, antique maps, and a huge globe that hangs from the ceiling. The Northwest-Cajun-Creole menu has items such as a West Coast seafood hot pot or Pacific Northwest jambalaya. Most dishes run about $20. The small bar has a good selection of beer on tap and single-malt whiskies. It's also very popular for its Sunday brunch.

Denman St *Café de Paris* (☎ 604-687-1418), 751 Denman St, is a very upscale French restaurant considered by some to be the best in the city. Expect to pay between $16 and $23 for most items on the menu. Farther down the street, the elegant *Raincity Grill* (☎ 604-685-7337) at 1193 Denman St, has a menu that changes with the seasons and offers vegetarian choices for about $15, while the other selections range from $18 to $25.

Stanley Park These two restaurants both serve very good food, plus they have the advantage of being in the park, which somehow makes them feel that much more special. *The Teahouse Restaurant* (Stanley Park Map; ☎ 604-669-3281), at Ferguson Point, was built as a WWII garrison and officer's mess when Ferguson Point was a military installation. There are wonderful views out to the ships moored in English Bay and over to West Vancouver. Most items, such as seafood, lamb or duck, are around $22, and about $5 less for lunch. Open for lunch Monday to Saturday from

Lunch al fresco at
Stanley Park's Teahouse Restaurant

11.30 am to 2.30 pm, for dinner daily from 5.30 pm, and for Sunday brunch from 10.30 am to 2.30 pm.

The Fish House (Stanley Park Map; ☎ 604-681-7275), 8901 Stanley Park Drive, is a very elegant restaurant with decor that has old-world charm in contemporary colors. If you are here for lunch, ask to be seated near the windows looking out at the tennis court. For dinner ask for the room with the large fireplace. Entrées like the salmon cakes start at about $16 and go up to $25 for the mixed-fish plate. The early-bird special from 5 to 6 pm is a three-course salmon dinner for $20.

Davie St Pacific Northwest dining doesn't get much better, or more authentic, than the *Liliget Feast House* (☎ 604-681-7044), 1724 Davie St. The Native Indian cuisine and unique setting make this a real cultural experience, with dishes like venison steak ($22), Arctic caribou tenderloin ($30) or one of the 'feast' dishes for two ($40).

Mescalero (☎ 604-669-2399), at 1215 Bidwell St, just off Davie St, is a trendy combination Spanish and Tex-Mex restaurant serving the usual assortment of items, plus paella ($22), ostrich ($23) and tapas ($5 to $10).

Elsewhere Downtown At the Georgian Court hotel is *William Tell* (☎ 604-688-3504), 773 Beatty St, just off Robson St, a long-established top-end restaurant serving continental cuisine. Entrées include certified Angus beef – from an 8oz New York cut ($22.85) to a

serving of chateaubriand ($29.50) – as well as dishes for fish and fowl lovers, and vegetarians. Open for dinner at 5.30 pm, last seating at 9 pm. Closed on Monday.

Griffins (☎ 604-662-1900), 900 West Georgia St, an upscale restaurant in the Hotel Vancouver, serves hot and cold buffet lunches ($12.95 to $15.95) weekdays from 11.30 am to 2.30 pm, as well as a Sunday brunch. Dinner entrées range from sandwiches ($12.75) and burgers ($13.50) to ribeye 'steak frite' ($18.25) and dungeness crab cakes ($18.50). Open daily from 6.30 am to 10 pm.

Famous for its fantastic wine list and considered to be one of the city's best restaurants, *Chartwell* (☎ 604-689-9333), 791 West Georgia St, in the Four Seasons Hotel, is an expensive treat. With plates that start at $20 for butternut squash risotto up to $35 for Novia Scotia lobster, plus $8 to $12 appetizers and an obligatory glass of wine, you'll be richer in calories than dollars. Breakfast is served daily from 6.30 to 11 am, lunch from 12 to 2.30 pm and dinner from 5 to 10 pm.

The Metropolitan Hotel has one of the top restaurants in the city, *Diva at the Met* (☎ 604-602-7788), 645 Howe St. For a taste of heaven try 'a taste of Diva,' a prix-fixe meal which includes grilled black tiger prawns, a squash, Mascarpone and sun-dried tomato tortelloni, roasted lamb chops and vanilla cake with pistachio ice cream ($48.50). Open weekdays 6.30 to 11am, 11.30 am to 2.30 pm for breakfast and lunch, with an à la carte brunch on Sunday. Dinner is served from 5 to 10 pm Sunday to Wednesday, till 11 pm Thursday to Saturday.

The Pan Pacific Hotel's top restaurant, *Five Sails* (☎ 604-662-8111), 999 Canada Place, has views to match the bill you'll get at the end of the evening. The menu has an extensive list of surf-and-turf options, including ahi tuna topped with foie gras ($28), venison loin in gingerbread sauce ($32) and prix-fixe dinners from $47 to $62. To put a sweet end to the meal, all entrées include ice chocolate bonbons. Open for dinner daily from 6 to 10.30 pm.

The Umberto's chain of Italian restaurants has done a lot to put Vancouver on the cuisine map. The original restaurant, *Il Giardino di Umberto* (☎ 604-669-2422), 1382 Hornby St, is still one of the city's best for Tuscan cooking. In a lovely old house in the downtown core, some say this is the finest Italian restaurant in the city. Most items on the menu are around $30, although the pastas are around $15 and the certified Angus beef Florentine is $70 for two. Just up the street, *Etoile* (☎ 604-681-4444), 1355 Hornby St, updates French classics and introduces sauces to Northwest meat and seafood. There are two prix-fixe menus at $28 and $38.

A block over, *Bandi's* (☎ 604-685-3391), 1427 Howe St, is a Hungarian restaurant in a lovely old house. Items run from $17 for the pan-fried trout to $25 for the filet of deer; the items on the lunch menu are about $5 less. Open for lunch weekdays from 11.30 am to 2 pm, and for dinner daily from 6 pm.

A real favorite, *Le Crocodile* (☎ 604-669-4298), 101 – 909 Burrard St, specializes in satisfying dishes from Alsace, set in a sumptuous dining room, with most entrées costing about $30.

Le Gavroche (☎ 604-685-3924), 1616 Alberni St, bridges the Northwest larder with French haute cuisine; an excellent choice for a romantic dinner.

Yaletown (Map 2)

Mangiamo (☎ 604-687-1116), 1116 Mainland St, is a stylish Italian restaurant, with a great open kitchen and patio, specializing in fresh fish. Expect to pay $16 for a basic pasta up to $34 for the rack of lamb, or try the swordfish for $29.

For some, the center of fine dining in this trendy area is *Century Grill* (☎ 604-688-8088), 1095 Hamilton St, while for others it's the place to be seen and to hang out with the celebrities and sports stars who frequent it. There is a long bar where you can enjoy a drink or get fresh oysters. Main courses are generally in the $22 range, although a basic pasta dish is only $13, while the roast duck is $26.

Farrago (☎ 604-684-4044), 1138 Homer St, serves Mediterranean-style cuisine in an elegant dining room. All the art is for sale so take a good look around while you eat. Entrées are around $22, although pasta and pizza cost $11 and tapas are $5.

West Side

False Creek (Map 2) On the north side of False Creek looking across to Granville Island, *Anderson's* (☎ 604-684-3777), 1661 Granville St, below the bridge, specializes in beef which comes with your choice of sauce for $25. Open daily for lunch from 11 am to 2.30 pm, and for dinner from 5.30 pm.

West 4th Ave (Map 6) *Bishops* (☎ 604-738-2025), 2183 West 4th Ave, is the other top-flight restaurant in Kitsilano. Chef John Bishop has cooked for a private get-together with presidents Clinton and Yeltsin, as well as a host of celebrities. The main courses are too eclectic to categorize easily – mingling Thai, Chinese, French and Italian – but absolutely fresh ingredients, strong but complementary flavors and ingenious presentation are the hallmarks that make this a very memorable restaurant. Expect to pay over $30 for most dishes.

West Broadway (Map 6) The *Lumiere* (☎ 604-739-8185), 2551 West Broadway, prepares a kind of French-fusion cooking that brings in the best of world cuisine and then drapes it in wonderful sauces. There are two prix-fixe menus, both with four courses, one for $70 and a vegetarian option for $50.

East Vancouver (Map 4)

In the industrial warehouse and dock area is the *Cannery Seafood Restaurant* (☎ 604-254-9606), 2205 Commissioner St, near Victoria Drive, which has some great views looking back at the city. Inside, the decor has a sort of rustic charm with lots of wood, two fireplaces, suspended lifeboats and hanging rope ladders. The daily fresh-fish menu, with about 14 items on it, runs about $20 while lamb or beef is $28. There is an extensive wine list that might take you most of the evening to read through. Open for lunch weekdays, and daily for dinner.

North Shore (Map 8)

North Vancouver The next best thing to a dinner cruise is having dinner on the *Seven Seas Seafood Restaurant* (☎ 604-987-3344), at the foot of Lonsdale Ave to the east of the quay, where dinner comes with great views of the city. This floating restaurant, built in 1941, was originally a ferry that traveled between North Vancouver and Vancouver before the Second Narrows Bridge was completed in 1957. The restaurant serves up, among other things, a remarkable seafood smorgasbord with a selection of 27 cold and 22 hot dishes to feast on, including a selection of cheeses and desserts, for $35. There is also a full selection of items on the regular menu for around $20. Open for dinner only from 5 to 10.30 pm.

When it comes to restaurants, the views in Vancouver don't get any better than those from the *Grouse Nest Restaurant* (☎ 604-984-0661), at the top of Grouse Mountain. As you might expect, dinner isn't cheap, ranging from $17 for the wild mushroom and leek raviolis to $26 for the ostrich medallions. Aside from the view, which is probably enough in itself, there isn't anything special about this small restaurant. Open daily for dinner from 5 pm; the cost of the Skyride is included if you have reservations.

West Vancouver With Vancouver at your feet, the *Salmon House on the Hill* (☎ 604-926-3212), 2229 Folkestone Way, is tough to beat when it comes to views. Indeed, this is the sort of place Vancouverites bring out-of-towners for dinner. The decor is lots of wood and Native Indian art that sets off the Northwest cuisine. As you'd expect, fish dominates the menu, with most items costing around $20. Open for lunch Monday to Saturday from 11.30 am to 2.30 pm, and for dinner daily from 5 pm. It's also open for Sunday brunch from 11 am to 2.30 pm.

The *Beach House at Dundarave Pier* (☎ 604-922-1414), 150 25th St, with spectacular views of the city lights across the water, has entrées ranging in price from $16 for the spaghetti with rock prawns to $31 for the rack of lamb. If you really feel like splurging, start with the beluga caviar with boiled quail eggs and iced Stolichnaya for $85.

Entertainment

As the third-largest city in Canada, and the only major city west of Calgary and north of Seattle, Vancouver is an entertainment mecca offering anything and everything you could possibly hope to find. The *Georgia Straight* does a great job of listing everything that's going on in the city on a weekly basis, as do the two daily newspapers, the *Vancouver Sun* and the *Province*, especially their Thursday and Friday editions. Vancouver's free monthly, *Playboard*, is a good source for reviews and dates of events in the visual and performing arts, as are the many free weeklies distributed around the city (see the Newspapers & Magazines section in the Facts for the Visitor chapter for details).

Tickets for most events are available from Ticketmaster (☎ 604-280-3311 for the performing arts, 280-4444 for concerts, 280-4400 for sports). For details on professional theater, dance, music, opera, museums and visual art exhibitions, call the Arts Hotline ☎ 604-684-2787.

The **casinos** you see throughout Greater Vancouver are fairly new to the entertainment scene. Open daily, they are partly operated as a fund-raising facility – organizations rent the casinos for the day and/or night, and half of the earnings is theirs to keep (so at least you know your money is going to a good cause). However, we aren't talking Las Vegas or Monte Carlo here: these casinos are small and rather drab, alcohol is prohibited and many of the people at the tables don't exactly look like they are having the time of their lives.

BARS & PUBS

It has only been since Expo 86 that Vancouver, and all of BC for that matter, has had reasonably liberal drinking laws. It wasn't even until the mid-1970s that entertainment was allowed in bars, which were large taverns attached to hotels. In those days it was technically illegal to walk around a bar with a beer in your hand (if you wanted to change tables you had to ask the waiter to move your beer) and on Sunday the only way you could get a drink was by ordering a meal in a restaurant.

All of that has changed. Small neighborhood pubs and bars are common, open daily and often have a good selection of both local and international beer available on tap and in bottles. Some pubs also serve good food and have entertainment, even if only on the weekend. In recent years the 'sports bar' concept has become popular, where one or several large TV screens are tuned into a cable-TV sports channel.

One of the best things to come out of the relaxed liquor laws is the advent of brewpubs, where a selection of beer is brewed on the premises for sale in the pub. Along with this has come the growth of small breweries producing draught and bottled beer that you'll find for sale in many pubs and restaurants (see the For the Love of Beer boxed text).

The following are recommendations of some interesting pubs and bars around Vancouver that are worth checking out, but keep in mind this list is by no means complete.

Downtown (Map 2)
Dover Arms Pub (☎ 604-683-1929), 961 Denman St, was one of the first 'neighborhood pubs' in the city, but today is more of a sports bar with lots of TVs, a fireplace and a reasonable selection of beer. ***DV8*** (☎ 604-682-4388), 515 Davie St, is a hip lounge that is open late. ***Fred's Tavern*** (☎ 604-605-4350), 1006 Granville St, in the Hotel Dakota, is a comfortable, pub-like place.

The Irish Heather (Map 3; ☎ 604-688-9779), 217 Carrall St, not only pours the best Guinness in town – order your second one about halfway through your first – but supposedly sells the second-most pints of the dark stuff in Canada. There are other Irish beers on tap and a good selection of whiskies, as well as live Irish music. See the

For the Love of Beer – Brewpubs & Microbreweries

If you enjoy beer then you've come to the right place. Brewpubs and microbreweries have been a feature of BC's beer-drinking landscape since the beginning of the 1980s when the provincial government began to relax the liquor laws, and there is no better place in the province to sample this selection of brews than in Greater Vancouver and Victoria.

The first brewpub in Canada, at least in recent times, was The Troller Pub in Horseshoe Bay where the legendary John Mitchell started brewing his own draught beer in 1982. Mitchell went on to establish Spinnakers Brew Pub & Restaurant in Victoria, which is now the oldest licensed brewpub in Canada, and helped set up the Howe Sound Inn & Brewing Company in Squamish. Sadly, The Troller Pub no longer produces beer. Also in Victoria is Swans Brewpub, and in Whistler the Brewhouse is the resort's first brewpub (see the individual sections in the Excursions chapter for details of these pubs).

Brewpubs in Vancouver include: **Steamworks Brewing Company** (☎ 604-689-2739), 375 Water St, in Gastown; **Yaletown Brewing Co** (☎ 604-681-2719), 1111 Mainland St; and **The Creek Restaurant Brewery & Lounge** (☎ 604-685-7070), 1253 Johnson St, in the Granville Island Hotel.

On the North Shore, **Sailor Hagar's Brew Pub** (☎ 604-984-7669), 235 West 1st St, North Vancouver, produces some excellent beer that it also bottles, and in West Vancouver the **Square Rigger Pub** (☎ 604-926-3811), 150 - 1425 Marine Drive, is a small neighborhood pub tucked away in the Village Square. Farther out of the city in Mission, off the Lougheed Hwy (Hwy 7), there is the **Mission Springs Brewing Co** (☎ 604-504-4200), 7160 Oliver St, overlooking the Fraser River.

Although they don't produce their own beer, many pubs and restaurants do offer draught beer produced by some of BC's microbreweries. Granville Island Brewing, opened in 1984, has the distinction of being Canada's first microbrewery and there are now 18 small independent breweries in the province, not to mention scores of others across the country. Some of the beers are excellent while others are simply mediocre, but all are worth trying and of course the final judgment is a matter of personal taste and preference. When ordering a beer in a restaurant or pub, be sure to ask if there are any local beers on tap.

A great way to sample a variety of BC beer is to pick up a selection from a liquor or cold-beer store, although the first time you walk into a liquor store to make a beer purchase the choice can be a bit daunting. Various breweries produce a variety of beer including ales, bitters, lagers, pilsners, bocks, porters, stouts and fruit beer (Bowen Island Brewing has even developed a hemp-based beer, Hemp Cream Ale). If you are around the city in June you

Places to Eat chapter for more details on the restaurant.

Mahoneys Sports Grill (☎ 604-662-3672), 222 - 1025 Robson St, as the name implies, is a sports bar serving the usual assortment of bar-type food. For a sports bar that has live music a couple of days a week and a good selection of food, try ***Malone's Bar & Grill*** (☎ 604-684-9977), 608 West Pender St.

Rose & Thorne (☎ 604-683-2921), 755 Richards St, in the Kingston Hotel, has lots of partitioned areas with comfy couches and chairs and a great selection of beer.

Shark Club Bar & Grill (☎ 604-687-4275), 180 West Georgia St, in the Sandman Hotel Downtown, is a popular bar especially before or after a game (it's close to GM Place and BC Place Stadium) and has a good selection of beer.

The ***Steamworks Brewing Company*** (☎ 604-689-2739), 375 Water St, features an ocean view, cushy chairs, fireplaces and homebrews.

might want to attend the Vancouver Brewmasters Festival (☎ 604-331-0907) which is a good way to sample a variety of beer. For more information about brewpubs and breweries in BC check out the website www.realbeer.com.

Three 'independent' BC breweries that do not fall into the microbrewery category include Capilano Brewing in North Vancouver, a subsidiary of the giant Canadian brewer Molson; Columbia Brewing Co in Creston, a subsidiary of the other national giant Labatt; and Pacific Western Brewing in Prince George.

The following is an alphabetical list of the BC microbrewery beers you can expect to find on the shelves (although not all stores stock every one):

Bowen Island Brewing Co (West Vancouver)
Bear Brewing Co (Kamloops)
Coquihalla Brewery (Delta)
Granville Island Brewing (Vancouver)
Horseshoe Bay Brewing Co (North Vancouver)
Mt Begbie Brewing Co (Revelstoke)
Nelson Brewing Co (Nelson)
Okanagan Spring Brewery (Vernon)
R&B Brewing Co (Vancouver)
Russell Brewing (Surrey)
Shaftebury Brewing Co (Delta)
Storm Brewing Ltd (Vancouver)
Tall Ship Ale Co (Squamish)
Tin Whistle Brewing Co (Penticton)
Tree Brewing Co (Kelowna)
Vancouver Island Brewing Co (Victoria)
Whistler Brewing Co (Whistler)
Wild Horse Brewing Co (Penticton)

West Side

Arts Club Theatre Backstage Lounge (Map 5; ☎ 604-687-1354), 1585 Johnston St, on Granville Island, is a pleasant place to sample one or two of the 50 Scotches and to listen to some live music. *Darby's Pub* (Map 6; ☎ 604-731-0617), 2001 Macdonald St at West 4th Ave, is a pleasant neighborhood bar in which to have a drink and a game of darts, and there's music from Friday to Sunday. *The Side Door* (Map 6; ☎ 604-733-2821), 2291 West Broadway, is tucked away down an awning-covered walkway with a dance floor that jumps to the newest sounds.

North Shore (Map 8)

The Raven Pub (☎ 604-929-3834), 1060 Deep Cove Rd, North Vancouver, is a great place to come if you've been for a stroll along Malcolm Lowry's Walk in Cates Park and want to pay your respects to the great man, who was known to enjoy a drink or two himself. There are 26 beers on tap plus a good selection of Scotch in this friendly pub with a circular fireplace in one corner. The food here is very good, too. No doubt Lowry would have been a regular if this pub had been around in his day.

Rusty Gull (☎ 604-988-5585), 175 East 1st St, North Vancouver, just a short walk up from the quay, is very comfortable with a good selection of beer and pub food.

The Troller Pub (☎ 604-921-7616), 6422 Bay St, Horseshoe Bay, West Vancouver, was the first brewpub in the province, but unfortunately the brewmaster moved on and the pub stopped making its own beer. Still, it's not a bad place to have a drink before getting on the ferry, and there's a standard bar menu.

CINEMAS

There is a great selection of cinemas throughout the city from first-run multiplexes to independent repertory theaters. Generally, admission to first-run films for evening showings is $8.75/5.25 for adults/seniors & children, while weekday matinees (prior to 6 pm) cost $5 for anyone, and weekend matinees cost $6.50/5.25. On Tuesday tickets are $5 for all shows. Admission prices to repertory cinemas vary from $3 to $7. All cinemas listed below show first-run films, unless specified.

Downtown (Map 2)

Vancouver Centre (☎ 604-669-4442)
650 West Georgia St

Capitol 6 (☎ 604-669-6000) 820 Granville St

Granville 7 Cinemas (☎ 604-684-4000)
855 Granville St

Caprice (☎ 604-683-6099) 965 Granville St

Denman Place Discount Cinema
(☎ 604-683-2201) 1737 Comox St

Paradise Theatre (☎ 604-681-1732)
919 Granville St (repertory)

Pacific Cinematheque (☎ 604-688-3456)
1131 Howe St (repertory – shows films you aren't likely to see anywhere else in the city)

West Side

Fifth Avenue Cinemas (Map 6; ☎ 604-734-7469)
2110 Burrard St at West 5th Ave

Ridge Theatre (Map 6; ☎ 604-738-6311) 3131
Arbutus St and West 16th Ave (also repertory)

Hollywood (☎ 604-738-3211)
3123 West Broadway (repertory)

Varsity (Map 4; ☎ 604-222-2235)
4375 West 10th Ave

Dunbar (☎ 604-228-9912)
4555 Dunbar St and West 30th Ave

Park (Map 5; ☎ 604-876-2747) 3440 Cambie St
and West 19th Ave

Oakridge Centre (☎ 604-263-1944)
Cambie St and West 41st Ave

East Vancouver

Van East Cinema (Map 4; ☎ 604-299-9000 ext
3278) 2290 Commercial Drive (specializing in foreign films)

Raja Cinema (Map 4) 639 Commercial Drive
(specializing in Indian films)

Dolphin Discount Cinemas (☎ 604-299-9000 ext
3457) 4555 East Hastings St, Burnaby

Station Square 5 Cinemas (☎ 604-435-3575) 6200
McKay Ave, Burnaby

Station Square 7 Cinemas (☎ 604-434-7711)
Metrotown, Burnaby

New West Cinema (☎ 604-420-0321) Unit 299 555
6th St, New Westminster

North Shore (Map 8)

Esplanade 6 (☎ 604-983-2762) Esplanade and
Chesterfield Ave, next to Lonsdale Quay,
North Vancouver

Park & Tilford Cinemas (☎ 604-985-3911)
Cotton Rd and Brooksbank Ave, near the
Second Narrows Bridge, North Vancouver

Caprice Park Royal (☎ 604-926-6699)
Marine Drive on the south side of Park Royal,
West Vancouver

Island Cinema (☎ 604-947-9438)
Bowen Island, West Vancouver

Richmond

Richport Cinemas (☎ 604-270-7788)
No 3 Rd and Ackroyd Rd, near Westminster
Hwy

Richmond Centre 6 Cinemas (☎ 604-273-7173)
Minoru Blvd, near No 3 Rd and Westminster
Hwy

Silver City (☎ 604-681-4255) No 6 Rd and
Steveston Hwy (very state-of-the-art)

COFFEEHOUSES

If you are looking for poetry, literary readings, music or performance art with your coffee, or in some cases with your alcoholic beverage, check out the following Vancouver venues.

Both *Forbidden Cafe*, (Map 5), 2404 Main St, and *Generations Espresso Bar* (☎ 604-421-4931), 4563 North Rd, Burnaby, have readings by local writers; the former focuses mostly on gay themes. *Myles of Beans* (☎ 604-524-3700), 7010 Kingsway, has various types of live music throughout the week. *Olde Times Cafe* (☎ 604-876-0845), Pender and Homer Sts, presents poetry readings. *South Hill Candy Shop* (☎ 604-876-7463), 4198 Main St, has a mixture of live music from Tuesday to Saturday starting at 8.30 pm, while *Stone Table Coffee House* (☎ 604-255-3338), 1135 Thurlow St, has live music on Friday and Saturday only starting at 8 pm.

The *Vancouver Press Club* (☎ 604-872-2902), 2215 Granville St, presents readings by local authors and has local bands on the weekend. The *Vancouver Public Library* (Map 2; ☎ 604-331-3602), 350 West Georgia St, presents a series of readings by authors.

COMEDY CLUBS

Vancouver has two full-time venues for mirth and frivolity where you can see stand-up comics from around the city or from across North America, including *Yuk Yuk's* (Map 2; ☎ 604-687-5233), 750 Pacific Blvd, and *Lafflines Comedy Club* (☎ 604-525-2262), 26 4th St, New Westminster. The Arts Club Revue Theatre on Granville Island is home to the 'improv' group, TheatreSports League (see the Theater section later in this chapter for more information). Many other clubs, restaurants and theaters have comedy nights as part of their weekly line-up.

MUSIC

From classical to techno, there isn't a style of music you won't hear in Vancouver. For a description of what's happening musically in Vancouver, see the Music section in the Facts about Vancouver chapter. Generally, unless it's a big-name act, you shouldn't have problems getting tickets for most performances by phoning ahead or even just showing up at the door on that night (that is, if you don't mind where you sit).

Many big-name acts on tour perform at BC Place Stadium, GM Place, the Queen Elizabeth Theatre or the Orpheum Theatre.

For more information or to make bookings call the venues direct, or call Ticketmaster. For information on what's going on in the jazz clubs, or on international artists performing in the city, call the Jazz Hotline ☎ 604-682-0706. Some restaurants provide music in the evening or on the weekends; many of these are described in the Places to Eat chapter.

Keep in mind that some of the more popular clubs have lines outside by mid-evening, especially on the weekend, so get there early if you want to be guaranteed entry without spending half the night standing in a line. Many of the music clubs are found along Granville St, while many of the dance clubs are along Richards St. There are also a variety of clubs in Gastown and the West Side, with a few in East Vancouver.

Classical

Chan Centre for the Performing Arts (Map 7; ☎ 604-822-5574), 6265 Crescent Rd, at UBC, often presents classical music performances. The *Orpheum Theatre* (Map 2; ☎ 604-876-3434), 884 Granville St, is the home of the Vancouver Symphony Orchestra, which performs here regularly as well as at other venues in the city. This is also the home of the 130-voice Vancouver Bach Choir (☎ 604-921-8012) that performs about six times a year. The Vancouver Recital Society (☎ 604-602-0363) and the Vancouver Chamber Choir (☎ 604-738-6822) also perform here. The *Vancouver Academy of Music* (Map 6; ☎ 604-430-8029), 1270 Chestnut St, presents work by contemporary and classical composers.

Rock, Blues & Jazz

These days it's difficult to categorize the types of music any given venue might present. Some clubs offer just straight rock, jazz or hip-hop, while others present a real mixed bag of styles over the course of a week. The descriptions accompanying the following selections are just a rough guide to what you can expect to find.

Downtown (Map 2) *The Brickyard* (Map 3; ☎ 604-685-3978), 315 Carrall St, presents local rock bands while the *Chameleon Urban Lounge* (☎ 604-669-0806), 801 West Georgia St, in the Hotel Georgia, has a mix of Latin jazz, deep house, hip-hop, jazz and jungle. Also located in the Hotel Georgia, the *Georgia St Bar & Grill* (☎ 604-602-0994) features local jazz bands. *Club Millennium* (☎ 604-684-2000), 595 Hornby St, is a posh club with Las Vegas-style acts.

The Gate (☎ 604-608-4283), at 1176 Granville St, presents a mixture of swing, salsa, rock and Celtic music. *Lamplighter's Pub* (Map 3; ☎ 604-681-6666), 210 Abbott St, in the Dominion Hotel, presents Top-40 bands and a Celtic night on Tuesday. The *Piccadilly Pub* (☎ 604-682-3221), 620 West Pender St, presents local rock and blues bands with a bit of house or acid jazz midweek.

The *Railway Club* (☎ 604-681-1625), 579 Dunsmuir St, is like a private club (except it isn't – just sign in at the door) with a variety of music seven nights a week and good-quality, original jazz on Saturday afternoons. The *Roxy* (☎ 604-684-7699), 932 Granville St, has local and sometimes big-name rock bands. The *Starfish Room* (☎ 604-682-4171), 1055 Homer St, is one of the city's top venues for local and international rock bands. *Uforia* (☎ 604-685-7770), 860 Burrard St, is a restaurant presenting live jazz Thursday to Saturday.

At 918 Granville St is the *Vogue Theatre*, a converted cinema which has found new life as a venue for touring international bands and local bands. Call Ticketmaster for information. The *Yale* (☎ 604-681-9253), 1300 Granville St, is one of the best blues bars in the city, if not the country.

West Side (Map 5) The *Anza Club* (☎ 604-876-7128), 3 West 8th Ave, presents local rock and blues bands. The *Blue Note Jazz Bistro* (Map 6; ☎ 604-733-0330), 2340 West 4th Ave, is a club and restaurant featuring jazz and blues bands. The *Cellar Jazz Cafe* (Map 6; ☎ 604-738-1959), 3611 West Broadway (downstairs), is also a restaurant presenting local jazz groups. The *Cotton Club* (☎ 604-738-7465), 1833 Anderson St, Granville Island, is a restaurant with live jazz on various nights. The *Fairview Pub* (☎ 604-872-1262), 898 West Broadway, in the Ramada Vancouver Centre, presents live blues and jazz bands. The *Hot Jazz Club* (☎ 604-873-4131), 2120 Main St, has jazz, swing, Dixieland and big-band music.

East Vancouver (Map 4) The *Garage Pub* (☎ 604-254-1000), 2889 East Hastings St, in the Atrium Inn, features local rock and blues bands. The *WISE Hall* (☎ 604-736-3022), 1882 Adanac St, one block north of Venables St and close to Victoria Drive, often presents folk artists. In Burnaby, on the 6200 block of Kingsway, *Studebakers* (☎ 604-434-3100) presents live Top-40 dance and progressive dance.

Dance Clubs

Big Bam Boo (Map 5; ☎ 604-733-2220), 1236 West Broadway, presents Top-40 dance music and ladies' night twice a week with male exotic dancers. *Club 212* (Map 3; ☎ 604-682-2126), 212 Carrall St, presents the latest in progressive dance music. *Luv-A-Fair* (Map 2; ☎ 604-685-3288), 1275 Seymour St, is an alternative dance club with various DJs. *Madison's* (Map 2; ☎ 604-687-5007), 398 Richards St, presents hip-hop, reggae and R&B.

MaRS (Map 2; ☎ 604-662-7707), 1320 Richards St, is the hottest place to dance downtown, with amazing light effects and a huge fiber-optic screen above the dance floor. The *Palladium Club* (Map 2; ☎ 604-688-2648), 1250 Richards St, presents the latest dance music with live presentations thrown in, too. The *Purple Onion* (Map 3; ☎ 604-602-9442), 15 Water St, presents both dance music and bands in the club and lounge.

Richard's on Richards (Map 2; ☎ 604-687-6794), 1036 Richards St, was once sneeringly referred to as 'Dick's on Dicks,' which the club now uses to its advantage by calling itself 'Dix on Dix.' It has long been one of the 'in' places to dance the night away, and presents dance music as well as live acts.

The Rage (Map 2; ☎ 604-685-5585), 750 Pacific Blvd, presents cutting-edge music

Hastings Park – From Exhibitions to Parkland

For many years the sports-and-exhibition center of Vancouver was situated in the large park at East Hastings and Renfrew Sts near the Second Narrows Bridge. This 70-hectare site is once again being called by its original name, Hastings Park, after being called Exhibition Park for many years, and is being converted to its original purpose – a green space complete with streams, trees and gardens.

Among other activities and events, this had been the site of the Pacific National Exhibition (PNE), a combination agricultural fair, midway, carnival, entertainment and trade-show venue that went from the middle of August to Labour Day. In 1996 the city decided to no longer hold the PNE here and to relocate it to one of the outer suburbs combining it with a state-of-the-art theme park (at the time of writing the details of this were still uncertain).

Besides the PNE, this site was the location of several of the city's major facilities including: Empire Stadium, built for the 1954 British Empire Games and the original home of the BC Lions football team before they moved to BC Place in 1983 (the stadium was demolished in 1993); the Pacific Coliseum, built in 1968 and home to the Vancouver Canucks before they moved to GM Place in 1995, as well as at one time being the city's largest venue for concerts and trade shows; the Forum, another arena that, when built in 1930, was the largest artificial ice surface in North America; Playland, an amusement park open daily in the summer and on weekends in the spring; and Hastings Park Racecourse, a thoroughbred race track (see the Horse Racing section later in this chapter for details).

The race track will remain but the future of the other buildings and attractions is still undecided. One thing is certain, and that's the enjoyment people will derive from spending time in what is to become East Vancouver's largest green space.

and a deafening sound system. *Sonar* (Map 3; ☎ 604-683-6695), 66 Water St, presents a mixture of progressive house, soul, hip-hop, R&B, reggae and other types of electronic music.

Downtown the *Stone Temple Cabaret* (Map 2; ☎ 604-488-1333), at 1082 Granville St, presents Top-40 and progressive dance, lounge and swing, R&B and hip-hop. The *Sugar Refinery* (Map 2; ☎ 604-683-2004), 1115 Granville St, presents a mixture of deep house and trip-hop fusion with DJs and live bands.

Latin

In the Hotel Dakota, *Babalu* (Map 2; ☎ 604-605-4343), 654 Nelson St at Granville St, is a lounge offering live and recorded Latin music. *Club Mora* (Map 3; ☎ 604-689-1634), 6 Powell St, presents live Latin sounds on the weekend and the recorded version during the week. The dance floor really hops in this place.

Gay & Lesbian Clubs

Vancouver's large gay population means there's a lot happening in the club scene, some of it drag-oriented. The place to dance and dish is the *Dufferin Hotel* (Map 2; ☎ 604-683-4251), 900 Seymour St, complete with drag karaoke. The *Royal Hotel* (Map 2; ☎ 604-685-5335), 1025 Granville St, is the city's only gay bar with live music.

The biggest gay bar in Vancouver is *Celebrities* (Map 2; ☎ 604-689-3180), 1022 Davie St, with DJ dancing and crowds every night of the week. Close by is *Numbers Cabaret* (Map 2; ☎ 604-685-4077), 1098 Davie St. *Denman Station Cabaret* (Map 2; ☎ 604-669-3448), 860 Denman St, is a lot of fun, with dancing, darts, drag acts and other entertainers, and theme parties; catch the Electrolush Lounge on Thursday. In the Heritage Hotel (Map 3; ☎ 604-685-7777), 455 Abbott St, you can choose between the *Lotus Club*, Vancouver's only dance club for women and their friends (on Friday it's strictly women only), *Charlie's Lounge* and *Chuck's Pub*.

Odyssey (Map 2; ☎ 604-689-5256), 1251 Howe St, is the wildest gay dance club with go-go boys, shower-room viewing and theme nights.

THEATER

Theater, from mainstream to fringe, is flourishing in Vancouver, and the quality of the productions is generally world class. Tickets to most productions can be purchased through Ticketmaster or the theater directly. For same day, half-price theater tickets check the small booth on the ground level in Robson Galleria, 1025 Robson St, open from noon to 1 pm and from 4:30 to 6 pm Monday to Saturday.

There are many theaters and theater companies operating in the Lower Mainland. Some of the main ones follow.

The *Arts Club Theatre* (Map 5; ☎ 604-687-1644) has three stages in the city, two on Granville Island – Mainstage and Revue, both at 1585 Johnston St – and one in the newly refurbished 1930s *Stanley Theatre*, on Granville St a few blocks south of Broadway. The TheatreSports League, the famed 'improv' troupe, performs about four nights a week at the Arts Club Revue Theatre.

The *Firehall Arts Centre* (Map 3; ☎ 604-689-0926), 280 East Cordova St, in a heritage fire station, presents plays by Canadian and foreign playwrights. The *Ford Centre for the Performing Arts* (Map 2; ☎ 604-280-2222), 777 Homer St, specializes in grand Broadway musicals and big splashy dance productions.

The *Frederic Wood Theatre at UBC* (Map 7; ☎ 604-822-2678), 6354 Crescent Rd, has a variety of productions presented by the drama department. *Gateway Theatre* (☎ 604-270-1812), 6500 Gilbert Rd, Richmond, is actually two theaters presenting small and large productions geared toward multicultural audiences.

Looking Glass Theatre (Map 2; ☎ 604-253-6333), 722 Richards St, is a small theater presenting fringe and experimental produc-

tions. *Malkin Bowl* (see the Stanley Park Map; ☎ 604-687-0174), or Theatre Under the Stars as it's also known, is an outdoor theater in Stanley Park where, weather permitting, musicals are presented nightly in July and August.

Metro Theatre (☎ 604-266-7191), 1370 South-West Marine Drive, is home to one of the city's most prominent community theater companies.

Pacific Theatre (Map 5; ☎ 604-731-5518), 1440 West 12th Ave, presents a variety of productions. *Performance Works* (Map 5; ☎ 604-253-5122), 1218 Cartwright St, on Granville Island, is a multipurpose venue in an old warehouse where theater, dance and music are presented.

The *Playhouse* (Map 2; ☎ 604-873-3311), Hamilton and Dunsmuir Sts, presents plays from Canadian playwrights to Shakespeare, as well as concerts. *Queen Elizabeth Theatre* (Map 2; ☎ 604-280-4444), Hamilton and Dunsmuir Sts, presents major international productions, including drama, music and dance. It's home to Ballet British Columbia (see the Dance section) and the Vancouver Opera (☎ 604-683-0222). There is also the Theatre Restaurant (☎ 604-665-2373) that serves a lovely gourmet buffet dinner for about $17.

Presentation House Theatre (Map 8; ☎ 604-990-3474), 333 Chesterfield Ave, North Vancouver, presents local productions. *Shadbolt Centre for the Arts* (☎ 604-203-2000), 6450 Deer Lake Ave, Burnaby, has three theaters presenting a variety of productions, the main one being the James Cowan Theatre. The *Vancouver East Cultural Centre* (Map 4; ☎ 604-254-9578), 1895 Venables St, presents theater, dance and a wide variety of music.

Vancouver Little Theatre (☎ 604-876-4165), 3102 Main St, presents new experimental productions. *Waterfront Theatre* (Map 5; ☎ 604-685-6217), 1410 Cartwright St, on Granville Island, is the venue for a number of local theater companies.

DANCE

The main dance companies in Vancouver include *Ballet British Columbia* (☎ 604-

732-5003), which performs at the Queen Elizabeth Theatre; *Experimental Dance and Music* (EDAM; ☎ 604-876-9559), which adopts a multimedia approach to its presentations; and the *Karen Jamieson Dance Company* (☎ 604-872-5658).

Some of the resident companies that perform regularly throughout the city are Battery Opera Dance Company, Dancecorps, the Goh Ballet, Judith Marcuse, Jumpstart, Kinesis Dance, Kokoro Dance, Mascall Dance and the Vancouver Moving Theatre. For information call the Vancouver Dance Centre at ☎ 604-606-6400.

SPECTATOR SPORTS

Depending on when you are in town, Vancouver has a variety of sports events to attend. Tickets for even the big-league teams are generally easy to get right up to game time, although the seat selection might not be the greatest. Visiting top teams, like the NBA's Chicago Bulls for example, will bring out the crowds, so tickets for these games might be more difficult to come by.

As in any city, scalpers circle the entrances to the stadiums like vultures waiting to pounce, and close to game time they may be able to offer you a better seat than you'll get at the box office, but you'll also pay a premium for this 'service.' However, if you wait until the game has just started, you might strike a good deal as the scalpers will be anxious to recoup their losses. Advance tickets for most sports events can be purchased by calling the numbers provided in the text or through Ticketmaster.

Baseball

The Vancouver Canadians (☎ 604-872-5232), of the Pacific Coast League (PCL), play their home games at 7500-seat Nat Bailey Stadium (Map 1), 4601 Ontario St and West 30th Ave next to Queen Elizabeth Park. The season runs from April to September, and there are both afternoon and evening games. The Canadians' major-league parent team is the Oakland A's (was the Anaheim Angels) so this is high-caliber

Nat Bailey Stadium – the best little ballpark in North America

playing at a great place to watch a ball game. Admission is $10.50/8.50/5.75 for box/reserved adult/reserved senior & youth, and $6 for general admission. To get to the stadium, take bus No 3 south on Main St to West 30th Ave and walk one block west.

Basketball & Hockey

Both the Vancouver Grizzlies (☎ 604-899-4667) of the National Basketball Association (NBA) and the Vancouver Canucks (☎ 604-899-4625) of the National Hockey League (NHL) play at the 20,000-seat GM Place (Map 2), 800 Griffiths Way, near Beatty St and Pacific Blvd. Both seasons go from October to mid-April – longer if the team is fortunate enough to make the playoffs. Tickets for the Grizzlies range from $25 to $258, while for the Canucks they are from $30 to $99. See the Organized Tours section in the Facts for the Visitor chapter for the special boat, dinner and game packages. To get to GM Place, take the SkyTrain to Stadium Station, or bus No 17 on Burrard St.

Football

The BC Lions (☎ 604-589-7627) of the Canadian Football League (CFL) play Canadian-style professional football from June to late October in the 60,000-seat BC Place Stadium (Map 2), 777 Pacific Blvd South, at the foot of Robson and Beatty Sts. Tickets for the games are from $13.50 to $43.

Football Canadian-Style

Those unfamiliar with the Canadian version of football may not be aware that it and its US cousin are variations of the same game. The first documented game in North America was played at the University of Toronto in 1861. Eight years later it was being played in the USA where, in 1869, Rutgers and Princeton universities played a soccer-football game using modified rugby rules – tries became touchdowns and goals from the field became field goals. From that time, rugby gained in popularity and modern Canadian/American football began to develop.

The first professional association, the National Football League (NFL), began in the USA in 1902 with just three teams. It wasn't until 1909 when Albert Henry George, the fourth Earl of Grey, donated a silver trophy called the Grey Cup that the 'modern' version of the Canadian Football League (CFL) began with four teams – University of Toronto, Parkdale Canoe Club, Hamilton Tigers and Ottawa Rough Riders.

The Grey Cup has been awarded to the CFL champions every year since then, except for interruptions during WWI and WWII. The modern Grey Cup celebration in Canada is said to have begun in 1948 when Calgary Stampeders' fans caused an uproar by invading a Toronto hotel on horseback. From it was born the tradition of using the championship game as an excuse to get drunk and brag about which side of the country, east or west, won the game.

While the game of football slowly evolved from rugby, it also developed on either side of the Canadian-US border with slight variations. For instance, the number of players on a team was reduced from rugby's 15 to 12 in Canadian football and 11 in American football. In Canadian football the offensive team is required to gain 10 yards on three downs to maintain possession of the ball, while in American football the team is allowed four downs. The field length and width is slightly larger in the Canadian game. And in Canadian football a rouge (pronounced 'rue-ja') was added for a single point off a missed field goal – this is the hardest aspect of the game for American football fans to appreciate as they believe a team should not be rewarded for doing something 'wrong.'

The game as a whole continued to evolve: in 1925, the huddle system was introduced, with players standing in a circle while the quarterback, or signal-caller, calls a pre-diagrammed 'play'; and the overhand forward pass to advance the ball was instituted in 1929 replacing the 'rugby-style' lateral pass.

Although a large number of US players make up the rosters on Canadian teams, and despite the introduction of teams in US cities in the early '90s which have since left the league, the CFL is the last remaining professional sports league made up entirely of Canadian teams. There are currently eight teams – Montreal Alouettes, Toronto Argonauts, Hamilton Tiger-Cats, Winnipeg Blue Bombers, Saskatchewan Roughriders, Calgary Stampeders and Edmonton Eskimos – with the BC Lions representing Vancouver. The Lions came into the league in 1954 and have won the Grey Cup in 1964, 1985 and 1994. The 1994 championship was the first time a game was played against a US team, the Baltimore Stallions (the underdog Lions won 26-23).

Supporters call the CFL the most exciting brand of football in North America mainly because it has more scoring than the NFL and the ball has to be passed more often in order to gain yardage. Unfortunately, the CFL is struggling financially because it can't compete with the marketing dollars that drive the NFL and because many Canadians do not want to pay high ticket prices to watch teams play in what they feel is a second-rate league. Falling attendance, the popularity of the NFL and all things American, the lack of a big TV contract, and the emergence of major-league baseball, basketball and hockey in the large markets of Montreal, Toronto and Vancouver all combine to make the CFL a tough sell.

Kent Spencer, a Vancouver journalist

To get to the stadium, take the SkyTrain to Stadium Station, or bus Nos 15 or 17 on Burrard St.

Horse Racing
Hastings Park Racecourse (Map 4; ☎ 604-254-1631), at McGill and Renfrew Sts, near the Second Narrows Bridge, is where the thoroughbreds race from mid-April to the beginning of November. Here you'll find a covered grandstand and the Table Terrace Restaurant, with great views of Burrard Inlet and the North Shore. Post times are weekdays 6.30 pm and weekends and holidays 1.15 pm. To get to the track take bus Nos 4, 10 or 16 north on Granville St.

Fraser Downs, also called Cloverdale Raceway (☎ 604-576-9141), 17755 60th Ave, Surrey, off 176th St (Pacific Hwy 15), is the home of harness racing from October to April. There is a 3300-seat glass enclosed grandstand, clubhouse and cafeteria. Race times are Monday, Wednesday and Friday at 6.50 pm, and weekends and holidays at 1 pm. To get to the track, take the SkyTrain to Surrey Central Station and then bus No 320.

Betting only takes place at the tracks as there is no off-track betting in BC.

Lacrosse
This fast and exciting indoor version of the game originally played by Native Indians is worth catching if you are around during the sport's short season. The six teams in the professional Western Lacrosse Association (WLA) league – Burnaby Lakers, Coquitlam Adanacs, Maple Ridge Burrards, New Westminster Salmonbellies, North Shore Indians and Victoria Shamrocks – play their games from the beginning of May to the end of July in their local arenas. Tickets are $6.

For information on lacrosse games call ☎ 604-421-9755.

Soccer
The Vancouver 86ers (☎ 604-589-7627) of the American Professional Soccer League (A League) play at Swangard Stadium, in Central Park at Kingsway and Boundary Rd, Burnaby (Map 1). The season goes from May to October, and they also play exhibition games against international teams. Tickets for the games are from $13 to $18. To get to the stadium, take the SkyTrain to Patterson Station, or take bus No 19 east on Pender St.

Shopping

WHAT TO BUY
Antiques

If you are in the market for collectibles, or just enjoy browsing around antique stores, you'll have a field day along Antique Row. There are about 20 antique stores, covering the entire range from top-of-the-line to kitsch, along the six blocks of Main St north of King Edward Ave (Map 1). A couple to check out are Sugar Barrel Antiques (☎ 604-876-5234), 4285 Main St, and Second Time Around Antiques (☎ 604-879-2313), 4428 Main St.

The area referred to as South Granville, Granville St south from about West 8th to 16th Aves (Map 5), is where you'll also find some antique dealers. Ambleside in West Vancouver is worth a look, too. If you are shopping for Asian antiques, try Marvelous Arts & Antiques of China (Map 5; ☎ 604-879-7500), 3011 Cambie St, which specializes in objects and furniture from China.

Books & Magazines

From all the bookstores that seem to thrive in Vancouver, you would have to draw the conclusion that this is a very literate city, which begs the question: How do Vancouverites find the time to pursue so many outdoor activities?

Duthie Books is a longtime Vancouver retailer with eight stores throughout the city and one at Vancouver international airport. The main stores include one (Map 2; ☎ 604-689-1802) at 650 West Georgia St at the corner of Granville St, another (Map 2; ☎ 604-684-4496) at 919 Robson St and a third (Map 2; ☎ 604-602-0610) at Library Square. Duthie's on West Georgia and Granville Sts is a large store with sections on any topic imaginable, including a store within a store specializing in technical, scientific and professional books, a great travel section downstairs and a cafe where you can have coffee and a snack while perusing your new books. All the stores are open Monday to Saturday from 9 am to 9 pm, and the downtown stores are open Sunday from noon to 5 pm. You can also visit Duthie's Virtual Bookstore at www.literascape.com.

Book Warehouse has several outlets around the city, including the downtown store (Map 2; ☎ 604-685-5711), at 1181 Davie St, and another (Map 5; ☎ 604-872-5711) at 632 West Broadway. It specializes in bargain books and discounted best-sellers. Blackberry Books (Map 5; ☎ 604-685-4113), 1663 Duranleau St, Granville Island, is a good bookstore with a great selection.

The Chapters bookstores are simply huge places with an unbelievable selection of books. There are several locations throughout Vancouver: (☎ 604-682-4066) 788 Robson St; (☎ 604-731-7822) 2505 Granville St; (☎ 604-431-0463) 4700 Kingsway at Metrotown; and (☎ 604-303-7392) 8171 Ackroyd in Richmond.

Another simply huge bookstore with an unbelievable selection is the University Bookstore (Map 7; ☎ 604-822-2665), 6200 University Blvd, UBC.

If you're interested in books about Vancouver, see the Books section in the Facts for the Visitor chapter.

Specialty Titles For books that have more to do with alternative lifestyles, meditation, organic gardening and herbal therapies try Banyen Books (Map 6; ☎ 604-732-7912), 2671 West Broadway. Women in Print (Map 6; ☎ 604-732-4128), 3566 West 4th Ave, specializes in books about women, for women and by women. Little Sister's Book and Art Emporium (Map 2; ☎ 604-669-1753), 1238 Davie St, specializes in gay literature specifically geared for women. For those who are into comic books, new and used, check out the impressive selection at The Comicshop (Map 6; ☎ 604-738-8122), 2089 West 4th Ave.

If your children don't lose themselves at Kidsbooks (Map 6; ☎ 604-738-5335), 3083

West Broadway, then you just might. It has a fabulous collection of every kind of book imaginable for children, plus assorted toys and games. There is a second location in North Vancouver (☎ 604-986-6190) at 3040 Edgemont Blvd.

If you are looking for cookbooks then head to Barbara-Jo's Books to Cooks (Map 2; ☎ 604-688-6755), 1128 Mainland St, in Yaletown. It features more than 2500 titles, a demonstration kitchen where dishes from the books are prepared, and a series of talks on Thursday from 6.30 to 8 pm (and if the urge to cook gets to be too much, go next door to find out about having a kitchen built).

Wilkinson's Automobilia (Map 5; ☎ 604-873-6242), 2531 Ontario St, deals in new and used out-of-print books, shop manuals, sales literature, vintage magazines and videos on all things to do with automobiles. You'll also find other collectibles like model cars and limited-edition prints. If the mystery genre is more your cup of tea, you'll enjoy browsing through the Mystery Merchant Bookstore (Map 6; ☎ 604-739-4311), 1952 West 4th Ave.

Travel One of the best stores in the city for travel guides and maps for just about anywhere in the world, not to mention the province, is World Wide Books and Maps (Map 2; ☎ 604-687-3320), 552 Seymour St, a block or so north of West Georgia St. Wanderlust (Map 6; ☎ 604-739-2182), 1929 West 4th Ave in Kitsilano, is another very good store with travel guides galore and a luggage department next door. If you want information from a guide you'll have to buy it at this store because the sign at the front door clearly states: 'Feel free to browse but please NO NOTE TAKING.' Also in Kitsilano is Travel Bug (Map 6; ☎ 604-737-1122), 2667 West Broadway, where you'll find a good selection of books, maps and travel accessories.

Used If you like poking around in secondhand bookstores, you'll have a good time in Vancouver. When you're in one of these used bookstores ask for the pamphlet

Browse more than 100,000 titles at Duthie's flagship store on Robson St

Guide to the Secondhand & Antiquarian Bookstores of Greater Vancouver. For a good selection of general literature and antiquarian books, try MacLeod's Books (Map 2; ☎ 604-681-7654), 455 West Pender St. Not far away, Antiquarius (Map 2; ☎ 604-669-7288), 341 West Pender St, has an interesting collection of books as well as photos, posters and magazines. Lawrence Books (☎ 604-261-3812), 3591 West 41st Ave, is a real find and has a fantastic selection of books.

Magazines Manhattan Books & Magazines (Map 2; ☎ 604-681-9074), 1089 Robson St, is owned by Duthie's. Here you'll find a great selection of newspapers and magazines from around the world, with special emphasis on French, German, Italian and Spanish language publications. Mayfair News (Map 5; ☎ 604-738-8951), 1535 West Broadway near Granville St, is also a great place for newspapers and magazines from around the world. Magpie Magazine Gallery (Map 4; ☎ 604-253-6666, fax 255-6913, magpie@lynx.bc.ca), 1319 Commercial Drive, has the largest selection of magazines in the city with 2000 separate titles.

Native Indian Art & Crafts

There are many shops and galleries in Greater Vancouver that sell a wide range of Native Indian art, from the tacky tourist stuff to the very best in contemporary designs and images. However, as with aboriginal art in other countries, Native art in Canada has become very popular and in recent years, and while the demand has increased significantly, the quality has decreased in some cases.

If you are in the market for a piece of Native art, take your time and shop around. This will give you a good idea of what's available in your particular price range, as well as an understanding of what the art is about. Not only will the acquired knowledge help you to make an informed purchase, but it will also give you a deeper appreciation of the art, and the artist who created it.

A few artists whose works are worth looking out for include: Luke Anowtalik, Kenojuak Ashevak, Kaka Ashoona, Joe David, Beau Dick, Joy Hallauk, Judas Ooloolah, Tim Paul, Kanaginak Pootoogook, Bill Reid, Kov Takpaungai, Lucy Tasseor, George Tataniq and Oviloo Tunnillie. For more information about Native artists, see the Painting & Sculpture section in the Facts about Vancouver chapter.

Arctic Canada (Map 2; ☎ 604-688-5330), 355 Burrard St, has clothes – such as traditional jackets, vests and moccasins – and blankets, carvings and paintings.

Canoe Pass Gallery (☎ 604-272-0095), 115 - 3866 Bayview St, Steveston, represents artists from BC's Northwest Coast to Eastern Canada with carvings, prints, jewelry, books and Haida art.

Coastal Peoples Fine Arts Gallery (Map 2; ☎ 604-685-9298), 1072 Mainland St, Yaletown, specializes in Northwest Coast art, including (small) totem poles, jewelry, masks, wood sculptures and original painting and prints.

Douglas Reynolds Gallery (Map 5; ☎ 604-731-9292), 2335 Granville St, exhibits Northwest Coast art including masks, paintings, prints and jewelry.

Leona Lattimer Northwest Coast Indian Art (Map 5; ☎ 604-732-4556), 1590 West 2nd Ave, specializes in jewelry, carvings, bent boxes, drums, masks and prints.

Hill's Indian Crafts (Map 3; ☎ 604-685-4249), 165 Water St, is a large three-story shop selling items more geared to the tourist market than some of the others listed here. As well as prints, masks and carvings, you'll find T-shirts, books and Native music.

Images for a Canadian Heritage (☎ 604-685-7046), 164 Water St, specializes in Inuit sculpture and Northwest Coast woodcarvings, jewelry and argillite, as well as work in marble, bronze, ceramic and glass.

Inuit Gallery of Vancouver (Map 3; ☎ 604-688-7323), 345 Water St, has some of the foremost collections of Inuit and Northwest Coast art, including masks, ceremonial bowls, bent boxes, tapestries, drawings, carvings in wood and argillite, and sculpture in stone and bone by some of the region's best artists.

Khot-La-Cha (Map 8; ☎ 604-987-3339), 1500 McGuire Ave, North Vancouver, a block east of Capilano Rd just south of Marine Drive, sells work by Coast Salish artists and craftspeople, including carvings, jewelry, masks, Cowichan sweaters, moccasins and prints.

Marion Scott Gallery (Map 2; ☎ 604-685-1934), 481 Howe St, has Inuit prints, drawings and wall hangings as well as sculpture.

Spirit Wrestler Gallery (☎ 604-669-8813), 8 Water St, specializes in Inuit and Northwest Coast art, especially sculpture and graphics that explore the themes of shamanism and transformation.

Clothing

Bargain For bargain-basement prices on clothes, including the best prices on Levi's in the city and other items generally found in a department store, you can't beat Army & Navy (Map 2; ☎ 604-682-6644), 27 West Hastings St, and in New Westminster (☎ 604-526-4661), 502 Columbia St. Another good place to shop for jeans and casual wear is Mark's Work Warehouse (Map 6; ☎ 604-736-2678), at 1885 West 4th Ave, which also has several other outlets around the city.

For more upscale clothes, Second Suit (Map 2; ☎ 604-732-0338), 2036 West 4th Ave, has discounted samples and quality used clothing for men and women. Turnabout (Map 5; ☎ 604-732-8115), 3121 Granville St, also sells quality used clothes.

Children's Hazel & Co Maternity & Kids (Map 6; ☎ 604-730-8689), 2209 West 4th Ave, has a good selection of clothes for children from newborns to eight-year-olds, as does Miki House (Map 1; ☎ 604-681-6454), in The Landing at 375 Water St.

Specialty If finding the right size is a problem, women can try: Fashion Addition (Map 2; ☎ 604-684-8344), in the Vancouver Centre at Granville and West Georgia Sts, which has sizes from 14 up; Petite Fashions (☎ 604-266-3577), 2153 West 41st Ave, which specializes in sizes 2 to 14 for women under 5'4"; Suzanne Bell's Fashions (☎ 604-324-7394), 5794 Victoria Drive, for sizes 16 and up, including 44 to 70; and Tall Girl (Map 2; ☎ 604-688-9238), 644-646 Hornby St, for tall sizes 8 to 20 and shoes in sizes 10 to 12. Men can try Repp Ltd Big & Tall (Map 2; ☎ 604-681-3548), 475 West Hastings St, which carries a complete range of sizes, styles and accessories.

For clothes with a difference, check out Dorothy Grant (☎ 604-681-0201), in the Sinclair Centre, where you'll find Haida designs incorporated into contemporary fashions for men and women, as well as jewelry and accessories. Vis-...-Vis Clothing (Map 5; ☎ 604-730-5603), 3109 Granville St, specializes in women's fashions by Canadian designers, from the well known to the more obscure.

A bit out of the ordinary is True Value Vintage Clothing (Map 2; ☎ 604-685-5403), 710 Robson St, which sells, rents, trades and buys 'vintage' clothes and accessories from the 1920s to the 1970s, including a huge selection of used Levi's. Tilley Endurables (Map 5; ☎ 604-732-4287), 2401 Granville St, which also has a store in North Vancouver, specializes in comfortable and durable travel and adventure clothing – complete with the 'give 'em hell' washing instructions and the famous Tilley Hat.

Galleries

A good way to see a cross section of contemporary Canadian art in various media, even if you're not in the market to buy, is to visit some of Vancouver's many private galleries. Owners are only too happy to talk about the artists they represent without making you feel like you have to make a purchase. Some of these galleries also exhibit works by international artists. For galleries specializing in Native Indian art, see the boxed text, and if you are looking for more craft-oriented items, check out Granville Island. Some galleries to visit include:

Art Works (Map 2; ☎ 604-688-3301), 225 Smithe St, has work by renowned Canadian and international artists covering the range of media plus poster reproductions.

Bau-Xi Gallery (Map 5; ☎ 604-733-7011), 3045 Granville St, exhibits gallery artists' work in various media.

Buschlen/Mowatt Fine Arts (Map 2; ☎ 604-682-1234), 1445 West Georgia St, features work by leading contemporary and international artists.

Charles H Scott Gallery (☎ 604-844-3809), 1399 Johnston St, Granville Island, exhibits thematic works by various artists and often shows the works of students from the Emily Carr Institute of Art and Design.

Diane Farris Gallery (Map 5; ☎ 604-737-2629), 1565 West 7th Ave, shows various media by gallery artists and guests.

Douglas Udell Gallery (Map 5; ☎ 604-736-8900), 1558 West 6th Ave, shows work by gallery artists.

Equinox Gallery (Map 5; ☎ 604-736-2405), 2321 Granville St, exhibits works by established Canadian artists.

Gallery Gachet (Map 2; ☎ 604-687-2468), 88 East Cordova St, shows the works of member artists.

Jack Gibson Gallery (☎ 604-276-9432), 8940A River Rd, Richmond, shows the works of gallery artists.

Keith Alexander Gallery (Map 2; ☎ 604-682-7777), 647 Howe St, shows the works of regional Canadian and international artists.

Uno Langmann Limited (Map 5; ☎ 604-736-8825), at 2117 Granville St, specializes in North American and European paintings from the 18th, 19th and early 20th centuries, plus objets d'art and antique furniture.

Petley-Jones Gallery (Map 5; ☎ 604-732-5353), 2231 Granville St, specializes in 19th- and 20th-century North American and European art.

Rendez-Vous Gallery (Map 2; ☎ 604-687-7466), 671 Howe St, shows paintings and sculptures by well-known BC and Canadian artists.

Third Avenue Gallery (Map 5; ☎ 604-738-3500), 1725 West 3rd Ave, exhibits works by local and Canadian artists.

Jewelry

Henry Birks & Sons (Map 2; ☎ 604-669-3333), 698 West Hastings St, plus other locations in shopping malls, has a long tradition in Vancouver for selling fine jewelry, and also designs its own watches and clocks. Potter's Jewellers – Potter's Gallery has two stores in The Westin Bayshore, 1601 West Georgia St, the lobby store (☎ 604-685-7412) and the tower store (☎ 604-685-3919). It has been producing one-of-kind jewelry since 1924, and sells fine porcelain flowers hand-crafted exclusively for Potter's by ceramist Kurf Sutton. It also sells Japanese and Chinese antiques.

Many of the private galleries, particularly those specializing in Native Indian art, sell original jewelry, as do some of the craft shops on Granville Island. Another place for jewelry and beads from around the world, circa 2500 BC to the present day, is Silver Moon (Map 5; ☎ 604-736-2323), at 3036 Granville St.

Also visit Jade World (Map 5; ☎ 604-733-7212), 1696 West 1st Ave, where not only can you watch huge pieces of jade being cut and carved (BC is the world's main supplier of jade), but you can also purchase jewelry and carvings. In the Punjabi Market, on Main St

between East 48th and 51st Sts, you'll find a lot of jewelers crammed into a small area, and in true Asian tradition bartering is acceptable.

Leatherware

The Leather Ranch (☎ 604-669-9188), 856 Granville St, has a large selection of Canadian designed and manufactured leather and suede garments for men and women. For shoes, Ingledews (☎ 604-687-8606), 535 Granville St, and several other locations in shopping centers, has a large selection of footwear for women in sizes 4 to 11, 4A to C, and for men in sizes 6 to 15, A to 3E. If you want western boots or trendy footwear then try David Gordon (☎ 604-685-3784), 1202 Robson St. Also along Robson St you'll find lots of expensive shoe stores for both men and women.

Markets

Aside from the large markets such as Granville Island, Lonsdale Quay and Westminster Quay, a fun place to check out is the Vancouver Flea Market (Map 4; ☎ 604-685-0666), 703 Terminal Ave, east of Pacific Central Station, where you are bound to find something you need at one of the 350 tables. Open weekends and holidays from 9 am to 5 pm. Admission is 60¢, and free for children under 12.

Music

The claim is made by some that Vancouver has the cheapest CD prices in North America, if not the world. This could well be true, but be that as it may, the number of stores in the city competing for the music buyers' dollar means the prices are low and the selection is second to none. In some of the larger stores you can expect to pay between $10 to $14 for recent releases and oldies-but-goodies can sell for as low as $5.

The larger stores and specialty outlets in the city include:

A&B Sound (Map 2; ☎ 604-687-5837), 556 Seymour St, with other outlets around the Lower Mainland, has a great selection. It can be difficult to find specific artists, however, because of how the shelves are organized. The weekend sales, which occur regularly, are a good way to stock up on old and new favorites. The jazz and classical section upstairs is very good. A full range of electronic equipment and videos are also available.

Black Swan (Map 6; ☎ 604-734-2828), 3209 West Broadway, is a small independent store specializing in blues, jazz, folk and hard-to-get rock.

Highlife Records and Music (Map 4; ☎ 604-251-6964), 1317 Commercial Drive, is a small shop specializing in reggae, Caribbean, African and jazz.

HMV (Map 2; ☎ 604-685-9203), 1160 Robson St, with other stores in shopping centers, has a general selection of music, although its probably best for Top-40 selections.

Magic Flute (Map 6; ☎ 604-736-2727), 2203 West 4th Ave, has a dedicated selection of classical, world music and jazz.

Odyssey Imports (Map 2; ☎ 604-669-6644), 534 Seymour St, specializes in imports from Europe and Japan.

Sam the Record Man (Map 2; ☎ 604-684-3722), 568 Seymour St, next door to A&B Sound, has a good selection of music covering the spectrum, and it's easy to go between the two stores to compare prices, which are very competitive; there are other outlets in some of the shopping centers.

Sikora's Classical Records (Map 2; ☎ 604-685-0625), 432 West Hastings St, specializes in new and used classical music, both vinyl and CD.

Virgin Megastore (Map 2; ☎ 604-669-2289), 788 Burrard St, on the corner of Robson St in the old library building, is the largest music and entertainment store in Canada and the selection is simply staggering.

Zulu Records (Map 6; ☎ 604-738-3232), 1869 West 4th Ave, is without a doubt the best independent music store in the city, specializing in rock with lots of hard-to-find imports, plus used CDs, vinyl and tapes.

Outdoor Equipment

There isn't a better city in Canada to shop for all things to do with the great outdoors, including hiking, camping and expedition equipment and supplies. You just about need overnight gear to get around Mountain Equipment Co-op (☎ 604-872-7858), 130 West Broadway. This is the largest outdoor-equipment store in Canada and, as it's a true

cooperative, you must pay the $5 lifetime membership to make a purchase.

Just a block west is Great Outdoors (☎ 604-872-8872), 222 West Broadway, and one block north on West 8th Ave between Main and Cambie Sts there are several other stores competing for the adventurer's dollar. Coast Mountain Sports (☎ 604-731-6181), 2201 West 4th Ave, and another outlet on the north side of the Park Royal Shopping Centre in West Vancouver, is another large store worth checking out.

Photo Supplies

Vancouver isn't known for bargains when it comes to camera equipment, but if you want to buy a new lens, get repairs done or buy specialty film, there are some good shops around. Dunne & Rundle Cameras has two locations in the city center, one (☎ 604-681-9254) at 891 Granville St, and another (☎ 604-689-8508) at 595 Burrard St in the lower level of the Bentall Centre. Kerrisdale Cameras (☎ 604-263-3221) is a local chain with the main store at 2170 West 41st St. Lens and Shutter (☎ 604-736-3461), 2912 West Broadway, is a large store with a huge selection. The camera department in London Drugs, located throughout the city but with an outlet at 1187 Robson St (☎ 604-669-8533), probably has the best prices and is a good place to get your film developed.

Ski & Snowboard Equipment

Vancouver is bursting at the seams with good stores selling ski and snowboarding gear, so if you are in the market, shop around and don't be afraid to bargain for the best price. Comor Wintersport (Map 2; ☎ 604-899-2111), on the northeast corner of Thurlow and West Georgia Sts, is a spacious place that not only sells equipment but also does repairs and tune-ups by certified ski technicians; open Monday to Saturday from 10 am to 9 pm and Sunday from 11 am to 6 pm. Just a block south at Thurlow and Alberni Sts, Sport Mart (Map 2; ☎ 604-683-2433) also offers everything from equipment to service and is open similar hours throughout the week.

On the West Side, Westside Sport & Ski has two locations, one (Map 6; ☎ 604-739-7547) at 2625 West 4th Ave and another (☎ 604-872-6860) 232 West Broadway. Also in this part of town is The Boardroom (Map 5; ☎ 604-734-7669), 1717 West 4th Ave, specializing in snowboard and wakeboard equipment sales, service and rental.

In the Park Royal Shopping Centre in West Vancouver there are two good shops, Cypress Mountain Sports (☎ 604-878-9229) and Sport Chek (☎ 604-922-3336), both on the south side of Marine Drive, offering sales and service.

WHERE TO SHOP
There are shopping centers underground, above ground, covering several city blocks, straddling roadways, along waterfront quays and inside converted heritage buildings. Vancouver is a shopaholic's dream come true, or worst nightmare, depending on how you see it. Some of these areas are mentioned elsewhere in the book, specifically in the Things to See & Do chapter, but are worth listing here again to make it easier for you to plan your shopping spree.

These are just a few of the major shopping areas and centers you'll find in Greater Vancouver.

Downtown
Chinatown (Map 3) is full of interesting shops selling traditional crafts and products as well as various markets (see the Things to See & Do chapter for details).

Gastown (Map 3) can seem like tourist central but there are some interesting galleries and shops to be found, including The Landing (see the Things to See & Do chapter for details).

Pacific Centre (Map 2; ☎ 604-688-7236), anchored by Eaton's department store, this is an underground mall extending north from Robson St almost three blocks to between Dunsmuir and Pender Sts, and is bordered on the east and west by Granville and Howe Sts. Here you'll find 200 stores, restaurants and services as well as a three-

story waterfall and glass skylights. Holt Renfrew is one of the other major stores in the center. Open Monday to Wednesday from 9.30 am to 6 pm, Thursday and Friday to 9 pm, Saturday to 5.30 pm, and Sunday from 11 am to 5.30 pm.

Robson St (Map 2), essentially the section extending west from Burrard to Jervis Sts, is a trendy shopping street crammed with shops, restaurants and services. The stores along here are open daily until about 9 pm. Farther west, closer to Denman St, you'll find another stretch of shops geared more toward 'everyday' needs.

Royal Centre (Map 2; ☎ 604-689-6711), 1055 West Georgia St at the corner of Burrard St, is an underground mall with about 60 stores, services and a food court.

Sinclair Centre (Map 2; ☎ 604-666-4483), 757 West Hastings St, features four heritage buildings under glass and consists of specialty shops, a restaurant and a food court. Open Monday to Saturday from 10 am to 5.30 pm.

Vancouver Centre (Map 2; ☎ 604-684-7537), at West Georgia and Granville Sts, is below The Bay department store and consists of 23 stores. Open the same hours as the Pacific Centre.

Waterfront Centre (Map 2; ☎ 604-893-3245), at Howe and Cordova Sts, is home to upscale shops and a food court that opens onto a sheltered plaza, and connects with Waterfront Station. Open daily 9 am to 5 pm.

Yaletown (Map 2) is the home of more designer furniture stores than you'd ever think could exist in one city, let alone in one small shopping precinct. There are lots of designer clothing stores as well (see the Things to See & Do chapter for details).

West Side
Broadway (Maps 5 & 6) is one very long avenue stretching west from Boundary Rd to Alma St where you'll find a lot of shops.

The most interesting stretch for visitors is more or less west from about Cambie St. One suggestion is to take the Broadway bus No 9 from about Cambie St and ride to the end, taking note of what looks interesting, then take the bus back and get on and off wherever your heart desires.

City Square (Map 5; ☎ 604-876-5102), 555 West 12th Ave, across from City Hall on Cambie St, is a lovely shopping center developed from two heritage buildings and is home to 90 shops and services. Open Monday to Wednesday and Saturday from 10 am to 6 pm, Thursday and Friday to 8 pm, and Sunday from noon to 5 pm. To get to the square, take bus No 15 south on Burrard St.

Granville Island (Map 5) has it all plus much more (see the Things to See & Do chapter for details).

Oakridge Centre (Map 1; ☎ 604-261-2511), West 41st Ave at Cambie St, is a large shopping mall with The Bay and 150 other stores and services, including cinemas. It's open Monday, Tuesday and Saturday from 9.30 am to 5.30 pm, Wednesday to Friday to 9 pm, and Sunday from noon to 5 pm. To get to Oakridge, take bus No 15 south on Burrard St.

South Granville (Map 5), as the stretch of Granville St south from about West 8th to 16th Aves is called, is where you'll find an abundance of galleries, antique dealers, jewelers, upscale clothing stores, restaurants and carpet and furniture stores. To get to South Granville, take bus Nos 8, 10 or 16 south on Granville St.

West 4th Ave (Map 6), west from about Burrard St, has a great selection of shops and restaurants and makes for a great afternoon walk (see the Things to See & Do chapter for details).

East Vancouver

Commercial Drive (Map 4) is an alternative down-market version of Robson St, and is a lot more interesting (see the Things to See & Do chapter for details).

Metrotown (Map 1), near Central Park on Kingsway between Willingdon and Nelson Aves, is the largest shopping complex in BC and includes just about every major department and specialty store imaginable. It actually comprises Eaton Centre Metrotown (☎ 604-438-4700) in the middle, Metrotown Centre (☎ 604-438-2444) on the east side and Station Square Metrotown (☎ 604-433-8438) on the west side. If you like to shop you'll think you've died and gone to heaven. Some of the 450 shops in themselves are mega-stores, and even with 4000 free parking spaces over 11 hectares it still can be difficult to find a place to park your car. Open Monday, Tuesday and Saturday from 10 am to 6 pm, Wednesday to Friday to 9 pm, and Sunday from 11 am to 5.30 pm. To get there, take the SkyTrain to Metrotown Station, or take bus No 19 east on Pender St.

Westminster Quay Public Market (Map 1) isn't a bad place to check out if you are out this way (see the Things to See & Do chapter for details).

North Shore

Lonsdale Quay Market (Map 8) is worth a ride on the SeaBus to check out (see the Things to See & Do chapter for details).

Park Royal Shopping Centre (Map 8; ☎ 604-925-9576), in West Vancouver close to the Lions Gate Bridge, is divided by Marine Drive – the south side is anchored by Eaton's and the north side by The Bay. There are more than 200 stores, with 100 of them unique to Park Royal. You'll also find a public market, cinemas, bowling lanes, restaurants and a golf driving range. Open Monday to Wednesday from 10 am to 6 pm, Thursday and Friday to 9 pm, Saturday from 9.30 am to 5.30 pm, and Sunday from noon to 6 pm (see the West Vancouver section in the Things to See & Do chapter for details).

Ambleside in West Vancouver, along Marine Drive west from 14th to about 21st Sts, and to a lesser degree **Dundarave,** farther west, is a lovely place to wander on a nice day with some exclusive clothing shops and interesting boutiques (see the Things to See & Do chapter for more details).

Richmond

Asia West is the name given to five malls found either on or just off No 3 Rd which consist of Asian-oriented retailers, including Aberdeen Centre (☎ 604-273-1234), 4151 Hazelbridge Way; Fairchild Square (☎ 604-273-1234), 4400 Hazelbridge Way; Parker Place (☎ 604-273-0276), 4380 No 3 Rd; President Plaza (☎ 604-270-8677), 8181 Cambie Rd; and Yaohan Centre (☎ 604-231-0601), 3700 No 3 Rd. Open daily; call for hours.

Lansdowne Park (☎ 604-270-1344), No 3 Rd at Alderbridge Way, has 120 shops and services, plus Bonkers Indoor Playground for children. Open Monday, Tuesday and Saturday from 9 am to 5.30 pm, Wednesday to Friday from 9.30 am to 9 pm and Sunday from noon to 5 pm. To get there, take bus Nos 403 or 406 on Howe St.

Richmond Centre (☎ 604-273-4828), No 3 Rd and Westminster Hwy, has 255 shops and services under a sky of glass. Open Monday and Tuesday from 10 am to 6 pm, Wednesday to Friday from 10 am to 9 pm, Saturday from 9.30 am to 5.30 pm, and Sunday from noon to 5 pm. To get there, take bus Nos 401, 403, 406 or 407 on Howe St.

Excursions

Victoria

Victoria, the provincial capital and, with a population of 300,000, the second-largest city in BC, lies at the southeast end of Vancouver Island, 90km southwest of Vancouver. Although bounded on three sides by water, it is sheltered from the Pacific Ocean by the Olympic Peninsula, across the Strait of Juan de Fuca in Washington State.

With the mildest climate in Canada, architecturally compelling buildings, an interesting history and the city's famed gardens and parks to attract people, it's not surprising that two million tourists visit Victoria annually. This quiet, traditional seat of civilization was once described by Rudyard Kipling as 'Brighton Pavilion with the

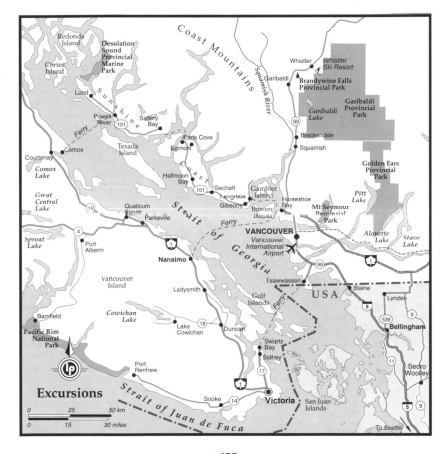

Himalayas for a backdrop.' Only three hours by car and ferry from Vancouver, Victoria can be visited in a day, although it is probably more enjoyable to stay for at least one or two nights (see the Organized Tours section in the Getting There & Away chapter for details about tours to Victoria from Vancouver).

ORIENTATION

The city lies at the southeast tip of Vancouver Island, actually closer to the USA than to the Canadian mainland. The small downtown area, bounded on two sides by water, has very few high-rise buildings and is an easy and pleasant area to explore on foot.

The focal point is the Inner Harbour, a section of Victoria Harbour surrounded by several of the city's most important structures, including the Empress Hotel and the enormous provincial Parliament Buildings. To the east of the Royal British Columbia Museum is Thunderbird Park, with its totem poles, and south of this is Beacon Hill Park, the city's largest. Surrounding the park and extending down to the ocean are well-kept residences, many with attractive lawns and gardens.

Along Wharf St, north of the Empress Hotel, is the central Travel InfoCentre, on the corner of the Inner Harbour. Following Wharf St along the water will take you through the Old Town, the restored original area of Victoria, to Bastion Square, the city's old central square and the site of old Fort Victoria.

Parallel to Wharf St and a couple of blocks east, Government St is a principal shopping area and tourist hub lined with historic buildings. One block east is Douglas St, downtown's main thoroughfare and busy commercial center.

The northern boundary of the downtown area is marked by Fisgard St, between Government and Wharf Sts, which has a small Chinatown with Asian-style street lamps and buildings, Chinese characters on the street signs and, of course, restaurants. Following Fort St east up the hill and then along Oak Bay Ave will lead you through the 'tweed curtain' to the wealthier, very British area of Oak Bay.

Both Douglas and Blanshard Sts lead north out of the city – the former to the Trans Canada Hwy (Hwy 1) and Nanaimo, the latter to the Patricia Bay Hwy (Hwy 17), Sidney and the BC Ferries Terminal at Swartz Bay. Also to the north, at the Douglas St and Hillside Ave intersection, Gorge Rd veers northwest, where it becomes part of the Island Hwy (Hwy 1A); it runs along the northern side of The Gorge and meets up farther west with Craigflower Rd and eventually the Trans Canada Hwy (Hwy 1). Gorge Rd is a good area to look for motels.

INFORMATION
Tourist Offices

The Travel InfoCentre (☎ 250-382-2127), 812 Wharf St, is by the water at the Inner Harbour, kitty-corner from the Empress Hotel. The InfoCentre has information on everything to do with the city and Vancouver Island, and operates a room-reservation service. It's open daily from 9 am to 9 pm and Sunday to 7 pm. There is also an office 1km south of Swartz Bay on Patricia Bay Hwy (Hwy 17), and another in Sidney.

To find out more about Victoria before you arrive, contact Tourism Victoria (☎ 250-382-2127), 710 - 1175 Douglas St, Victoria, BC V8W 2E1. Luggage can be left in lockers beside the bus station, 700 Douglas St. Tokens for the lockers, obtained inside the station, cost $2.50.

Money & Post

The major banks have branches along Douglas St and are open during business hours weekdays. The Toronto Dominion Bank, 1070-1080 Douglas St, is open on Saturday from 9.30 am to 4.30 pm. You can change money at Money Mart, 1720 Douglas St, opposite The Bay department store, and at Currency Exchange, 724 Douglas St, open daily from 7 am to 9.30 pm. You can also change money at American Express (☎ 250-385-8731), 1203 Douglas St. US currency is accepted by most businesses but at a much poorer exchange

Exterior of shop near Lonsdale Quay

North Vancouver's main drag, Lonsdale Ave

Everybody's happy at Lonsdale Quay Market

Grouse Mountain's 125-passenger Skyride

Chainsaw art sculpture, Grouse Mountain

Lighthouse Park, home to some of Vancouver's largest remaining stands of virgin Douglas firs

Enjoying the intricate network of cross-country trails at Cypress Provincial Park

Parliament Buildings, Victoria

Sunday rugby match, Victoria

Highland dancer, Victoria

Victoria's Market Square, where you can buy everything from beads to kayaks

Italian Garden at the Butchart Gardens

Skiers at Garibaldi Provincial Park

A perfect summer's day on Whistler's Alta Lake

rate. The main post office (☎ 250-381-6114) is in Broughton Square, 905 Gordon St; closed Sunday.

Media

The daily newspaper is the *Times Colonist*, and arts and entertainment news is featured in the weekly *Monday Magazine*.

Laundry

If your hotel doesn't have a laundry, then head to Maytag Homestyle Laundry (☎ 250-386-1799), 1309 Cook St, with self-service machines, drop-off service and a dry cleaners.

Medical Services

If your medical needs aren't serious, then avoid the emergency room and head to Mayfair Medical Treatment Centre (☎ 250-360-2282), 3147 Douglas St, in the Mayfair Shopping Mall. It's open daily and you don't need an appointment. The Royal Jubilee Hospital (☎ 250-595-9200, 595-9212 for emergencies) is located at 1900 Fort St.

THINGS TO SEE
Royal British Columbia Museum

This excellent museum (☎ 250-387-3701), 675 Belleville St, is a must-see, even for people who normally avoid such places. The wide variety of displays is artistically arranged, beautifully lit and accompanied by informative, succinct explanations. The museum provides free tours and is open daily in summer from 9.30 am to 7 pm, and in winter from 10 am to 5 pm. Admission is $7/3.25/2.15 for adults/seniors/students, or $14 for a family.

Helmcken House

This house (☎ 250-387-4697), in Eliot Square beside the Royal BC Museum, is the oldest in BC to have remained unchanged. The rooms are preserved much the way they would have appeared in the early 1850s. Open daily in summer from 11 am to 5 pm, and admission is $4.

St Anne's Pioneer Schoolhouse

Also in Eliot Square, this schoolhouse, operated as part of the Royal BC Museum, is one of the oldest buildings in Victoria still in use. Built sometime between 1840 and 1860, it was moved to its present site in 1974 from the grounds of St Anne's Academy.

Thunderbird Park

This small but interesting park beside the Royal BC Museum has a collection of both plain and painted wooden totem poles, some of which are labeled. In the Thunderbird Park Carving Studio you can watch Native Indian artists at work.

Parliament Buildings

The multi-turreted Parliament Buildings (☎ 250-387-6121), 501 Belleville St, or Legislative Buildings, as the complex is also called, was designed by Francis Rattenbury and completed in 1898. On top of the main dome is a figure of Captain George Vancouver, the first British navigator to circle Vancouver Island. Rattenbury also designed the Empress Hotel and the Parthenon-like Royal London Wax Museum, which was once a Canadian Pacific steamship terminal, and the building that now houses the Vancouver Art Gallery. The buildings are open daily from 8.30 am to 5 pm, and free 45-minute guided tours are offered daily in summer and weekdays in winter (call ☎ 250-387-3046 for times).

The paintings in the lower rotunda depict scenes from Canadian history. Around the upper rotunda are paintings of four of BC's main industries. The Legislative Chamber is where all the laws of BC are made (there is

JOHN ELK

Helmcken House Historic Site

Rattenbury & the Marble Palace

Only six months after arriving in BC in 1892 from Leeds, England, the 25-year-old British immigrant Francis Mawson Rattenbury was awarded the job of designing BC's new Parliament Buildings. It would take five years and nearly $1 million – a cost of twice the original budget – before this new home for the legislature would officially open on February 10, 1898.

One of the reasons the project was undertaken was to stimulate the economy. Therefore, much of the building was constructed from local materials. The foundation stone is granite from Nelson Island, north of the Sunshine Coast, while the building stones are from Haddington Island about 500km north of Victoria. The bricks were produced in Victoria and the roof slates are from Jervis Inlet.

Called the 'Marble Palace' by some, Rattenbury described the Parliament Buildings as being of a 'free classical style' and envisioned it surrounded by forest. When the government decided to cut down the trees that covered the site, Rattenbury became enraged and in a letter to the city's paper, *The Victoria Daily Colonist*, wrote: 'It makes me heartsick to see each tree as it falls to the ground. It is so rarely that an architect is fortunate enough to have the opportunity of erecting a large building amongst the delicate traces of woodland scenery.'

Rattenbury went on to become BC's most popular architect, designing the Empress Hotel, Crystal Garden, banks and mansions, and in Vancouver, the Courthouse (now the Vancouver Art Gallery). He was named the CPR's western architect in 1901, a position he held until 1908.

An affair with a woman 30 years his junior, Alma Victoria Clark Dolling Pakenham, outraged polite society so much that in 1929 he and his new young bride moved to Bournemouth, England. In 1935 Rattenbury was murdered by his chauffeur, George Stoner, who was having an affair with Alma. Stoner was sentenced to life in prison but was eventually released. Alma committed suicide.

no Senate in the provincial parliament). You can view the debates from the public gallery when the session is in. In the Legislative Library is the dagger used to kill Captain Cook in Hawaii, while on the lawn is a statue of Queen Victoria and a sequoia tree from California planted in the 1860s. The buildings are lit spectacularly at night by more than 3000 lightbulbs.

Pacific Undersea Gardens

A sort of natural aquarium, the gardens (☎ 250-382-5717), 490 Belleville St, on the Inner Harbour, descend beneath the water's surface and provide a glass-enclosed view of a range of corralled sea creatures such as octopuses, eels and crabs. Children especially find the gardens intriguing. Admission is $7/6.25 for adults/seniors, $5 for students (12 to 17), and $3.50 for children (five to 11).

Royal London Wax Museum

This wax museum (☎ 250-388-4461), 470 Belleville St, in front of the Parliament Buildings, contains more than 200 wax models of historical and contemporary figures. Open daily from 9 am to 9 pm, and admission is $7/6.50/3 for adults/seniors/students.

Miniature World

Probably of more interest to children, this attraction (☎ 250-385-9731), 649 Humboldt St, beside the Empress Hotel, has numerous layouts depicting various themes in exact detail, such as the world of Dickens. There's also a model train representing the development of the CPR from 1885 to 1915. Open daily from 9 am to 8 pm, and admission is $8/7/6 for adults/students/children.

Crystal Garden

This site (☎ 250-381-1277), 713 Douglas St, is one of the more popular commercial attractions. The principal draw is the colorful tropical-like garden complete with 65 varieties of endangered animals and birds, as well as free-flying butterflies. Designed by Francis Rattenbury, it was fashioned after London's Crystal Palace and built in 1925. Open daily in July and August from 10 am to 9 pm; it closes the rest of the year at 4.30 pm. Admission is $7/6/4 for adults/seniors/children.

Shopping Areas

Bastion Square, between Langley and Wharf Sts, is where Fort Victoria was situated, and held the courthouse, jail, gallows and brothel. The whole area has been restored and redeveloped and is a pleasant place to wander. The square's old buildings are now restaurants, boutiques, galleries and offices.

Farther north along Wharf St, on the corner of Johnson St, is **Market Square**, a former warehouse dating from the 1890s. Renovated in 1975, this compact, attractive area now has two floors of more than 40 shops and restaurants built around a courtyard shaded by trees. Busy **Government St** is especially attractive, with many fine shops and handsome Victorian buildings. It's especially lovely at night, when the structures are lit.

Maritime Museum

The museum (☎ 250-385-4222), 28 Bastion Square, near Government St, houses a collection of artifacts, models, photographs and naval memorabilia. Even if the museum is of limited interest, the elevator inside the front door is worth a look. Open daily from 9.30 am to 4.30 pm, and admission is $5/4/3/2 for adults/seniors/students/children.

Victoria Eaton Centre

Although this is a shopping center (☎ 250-382-7141), it's worth strolling around even if you aren't looking to spend money. The complex, which incorporates the facades of the original buildings, has five floors and houses 100 shops, restaurants and services.

Plus there are fountains, pools and a rooftop garden. It occupies two blocks between Government and Douglas Sts, and between Fort and View Sts.

Fisherman's Wharf

Just west of the Inner Harbour, around Laurel Point, is Fisherman's Wharf. It's a busy spot, with fishing boats and pleasure craft coming and going. You can sometimes buy fresh seafood from the boats or at the little shed, and nearby is Barb's Place selling fish and chips (see Places to Eat later in this chapter). Take a look at the mix of houseboats moored at one end of the dock.

Scenic Marine Drive

Starting either from Fisherman's Wharf or Beacon Hill Park, the Scenic Marine Drive, with great views out over the sea, skirts the coast along Dallas Rd and Beach Drive. The road heads north past some of Victoria's wealthiest neighborhoods and the retirement community of Oak Bay, where you can stop for afternoon tea at the Blethering Place Tearoom (see Places to Eat later in this chapter).

You'll see several parks and beaches along the way, though access to the shore is restricted because of private housing right on the coastline. The Gray Line double-decker bus includes Marine Drive in its tour (see the Organized Tours section later in this chapter).

Beacon Hill Park

Just southeast of the downtown area, along Douglas St, this 61-hectare park is Victoria's largest. The park is an oasis of trees, gardens, ponds, pathways and playing fields. You'll also find in the park the 'world's tallest totem,' a 100-year-old cricket pitch, a wildfowl sanctuary and a children's petting zoo. The southern edge overlooks the ocean and offers good views of the coastline. At the southwest corner of the park, the path along the water meets the **'Mile 0'** marker, the Pacific terminus of the Trans Canada Hwy. From downtown, take bus No 5 to reach the park, although it is very accessible by foot.

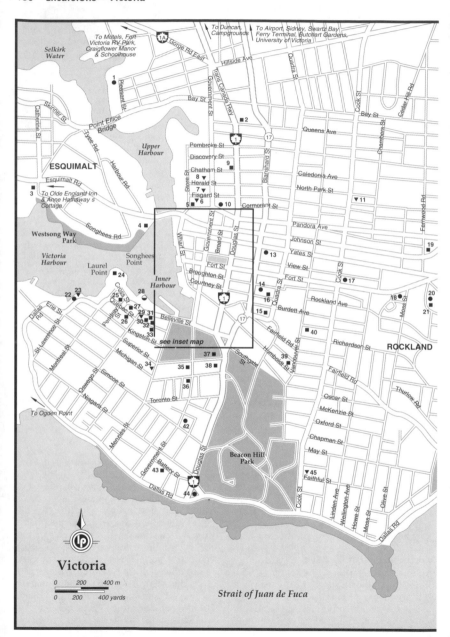

Victoria

0   200   400 m
0   200   400 yards

Strait of Juan de Fuca

PLACES TO STAY	PLACES TO EAT	OTHER
2 Traveller's Inn	6 Ocean Phoenix	1 Point Ellice House & Gardens
3 Spinnakers Guest House	7 Foo Hong Chop Suey	3 Spinnakers Brew Pub
4 Ocean Pointe Resort	8 Herald St Caffé	& Restaurant
5 Swans Hotel	11 Mount Royal Bagel Factory	10 McPherson Playhouse
9 Paul's Motor Inn	15 Bowman's Spare Rib House	13 Capital 6 (cinema)
12 Renouf House	23 Barb's Place	14 Royal Theatre
15 Cherry Bank Hotel	29 Harbour House Restaurant	17 BC Ferries Office
16 YM-YWCA	34 James Bay Tearoom	18 Art Gallery of Greater Victoria
19 Victoria Backpackers Lodge	47 Cook St Fish & Chips	20 Craigdarroch Castle
21 Craigmyle Guest House	47 Chandler's Seafood	22 Fisherman's Wharf
24 Laurel Point Inn	Restaurant	28 Ferry Terminal
25 Admiral Motel	48 Milky Way Cafe	41 Government House
26 Harbour Towers Hotel	52 John's Place	42 Carr House
27 Ramada Huntingdon Manor	55 Baan Thai	44 'Mile 0' Marker
30 Best Western Inner Harbour	56 Day & Night	46 E&N Railiner Station
31 Days Inn on the Harbour	57 Il Terrazzo	49 Market Square
32 Clarion Hotel Grand Pacific	59 The 1218 Restaurant	58 Odeon Theatre
33 Royal Scot Inn	60 Wharfside Eatery	63 Bastion Square
35 Birdcage Walk Guest House	61 Suze	65 Maritime Museum
36 James Bay Inn	62 Re-Bar	68 American Express
37 Helm's Inn	64 Camille's Fine	74 Post Office
38 Shamrock Motel	Westcoast Dining	78 Travel InfoCentre
39 Beaconsfield Inn	66 Le Petit Saigon	82 Royal London
40 Abigail's Hotel	67 Eugene's Restaurant &	Wax Museum
43 Battery St Guest House	Snack Bar	83 Pacific Undersea
50 Best Western Carlton Plaza	70 Koto Japanese Restaurant	Gardens
51 Hotel Douglas	71 Murchie's	84 Victoria Harbour Ferry
53 Victoria Regent Hotel	73 Pagliacci's	86 Miniature World
54 Victoria Hostel	76 Milestone's	89 Crystal Garden
69 Dominion Hotel	77 Sam's Deli	92 Parliament Buildings
72 Bedford Regency Hotel	79 Smitty's Family Restaurant	93 Royal British Columbia Museum
75 Strathcona Hotel	85 Empress Room,	94 Helmcken House &
80 Chateau Victoria	Bengal Lounge,	St Anne's Pioneer
81 Green Gables Hotel	Garden Café	Schoolhouse
85 Empress Hotel	87 Milos	95 Thunderbird Park
88 Executive House Hotel		96 Bus Station
90 Quality Inn Harbourview		
91 Embassy Inn		
97 Crystal Court Motel		

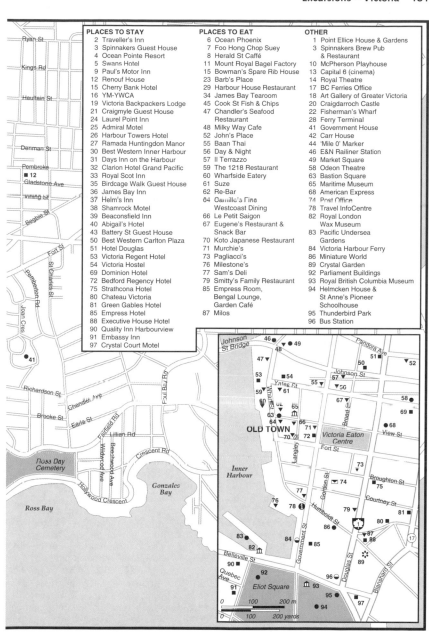

Carr House

South of the Inner Harbour, a short walk leads to the birthplace of Emily Carr, one of Canada's best-known painters (see The Life & Work of Emily Carr boxed text in the Things to See & Do chapter). Carr House (☎ 250-387-4697), 207 Government St, has displays on her life and work, including some of her paintings, many of which incorporated subject matter drawn from the culture of the Northwest Coast Native Indians, particularly the totem poles, and her writings. Open daily from 10 am to 5 pm, and admission is $4/3/2 for adults/seniors & students/children. Note that the Art Gallery of Greater Victoria has a permanent display of Carr's work.

Art Gallery of Greater Victoria

About 1km east of the downtown area, the art gallery (☎ 250-384-4101), 1040 Moss St, just off Fort St, is best known for its excellent Asian art, including the Japanese and Chinese collections. It also has artwork from other parts of the world and from widely varying periods of history, from pre-Columbian Latin American objects to contemporary Canadian paintings. Emily Carr's work is on permanent display and there are some good Inuit pieces. Open Monday to Saturday from 10 am to 5 pm, Thursday to 9 pm, and Sunday from 1 to 5 pm. Admission is $5/3 for adults/seniors & students, and free for children under 12. To get to the gallery, take bus Nos 10, 11 or 14 from downtown.

Government House

This house (☎ 250-387-2080), 1401 Rockland Ave, is the official residence of the province's lieutenant governor, and the six hectares of impressive gardens are open to the public daily from dawn to dusk (the house is closed to the public). To get there, take bus Nos 1, 11 or 14 from downtown.

Craigdarroch Castle

Near Government House, but off Fort St, this opulent house (☎ 250-592-5323), 1050 Joan Crescent, was built in the mid-1880s by Robert Dunsmuir, a coal millionaire. The castle-like house has been completely restored and is now a museum. Open daily in summer from 9 am to 7 pm, and the rest of the year from 10 am to 4.30 pm. Admission is $7.50/5/2 for adults/students/children (six to 12), and by donation for children under six. To get to the house, take bus Nos 11 or 14 from downtown.

Olde England Inn & Anne Hathaway's Cottage

This gimmicky but effective recreation of an English Tudor village (☎ 250-388-4353), at 429 Lampson St, is set among two hectares of gardens, in Esquimalt on the other side of the harbor. The highlights are the replicas of Shakespeare's birthplace and the thatched cottage of his wife, Anne Hathaway, complete with authentic 16th-century antiques. Open daily in summer from 9 am to 10 pm, and to 5 pm in winter. Admission is $7/4.75 for adults/children. To get to the village, take bus Nos 24 or 25 from downtown.

Point Ellice House & Gardens

This beautifully kept house (☎ 250-387-4697), 2616 Pleasant St, off Bay St at Point Ellice Bridge, was built in 1861 and has one of the most complete collections of Victorian furnishings and decorations in Western Canada. Afternoon tea is served in the garden. Open mid-May to mid-October, daily from 10 am to 5 pm. Admission is $4/3/2 for adults/seniors & students/children (six to 12 years), or $10 for a family. It's north of the downtown area, and to get there take bus No 14 from downtown.

Craigflower Manor & Schoolhouse

The restored Georgian-style farmhouse (☎ 250-387-4697), at Craigflower and Admirals Rds, northwest of the city, was built in 1856 and was the central home in the first farming community on Vancouver Island. Admission also includes a visit to the historic schoolhouse. The farmhouse is open daily from noon to 4 pm, and admission is $5/4/3 for adults/seniors & students/children, or $10 for a family. To get there, take bus Nos 10 or 14 from downtown.

Fort Rodd Hill National Historic Site

This scenic 17.6 hectare park (☎ 250-478-5849), 603 Fort Rodd Hill Rd, off Ocean Blvd, was originally a defense installation designed to protect Esquimalt Harbour and the Royal Navy yards. There are information signs around the park, as well as guides. The park is open daily from 10 am to 5.30 pm, Wednesday till 8.30 pm. Admission is $4, and ask about the candlelight tours. Also in the park is the **Fisgard Lighthouse**, Western Canada's first, which still works and has been in continuous use since 1860. The park is about 11km northwest of the city. To get to the site, take bus No 50 to within about 1km of the park.

Butchart Gardens

These gardens (☎ 250-652-5256, 652-4422), 800 Benvenuto Ave, about 21km north of Victoria at Brentwood Bay, are probably the most publicized of all Victoria's sights and one of the main reasons many people come here for a visit. Located on the site of a former limestone quarry, the 20 hectares of individual gardens were created by the family of a local cement manufacturer, beginning in 1904.

You can walk through the gardens in about 1½ hours, but plant lovers will want to linger much longer. In the evenings from June 15 to September 30, the gardens are illuminated, and there is a Christmas display from December 1 to the beginning of January. There are also concerts and puppet shows around dusk, and on Saturday nights in July and August there is a spectacular fireworks display set to music. The Blue Poppy and Dining Room restaurants are also in the gardens.

Open daily from 9 am to dusk, and admission is $14.50/7.50/2 for adults/students/children (five to 12). If you're driving, follow the Patricia Bay Hwy (Hwy 17) north, or take bus No 75 from downtown.

Dominion Astrophysical Observatory

On the way to the Butchart Gardens you could visit the observatory (☎ 250-363-0012), 5071 West Saanich Rd, on Little Saanich Mountain, where you can peer out to space through a 183cm telescope. There is a museum and equipment used to record earthquakes. Open Monday to Friday from 9 am to 4.30 pm, and Saturday from 7 to 11 pm; admission is free.

ACTIVITIES
Scuba Diving

Georgia Strait provides opportunities for world-class diving. The undersea life is tremendously varied and several excellent shore dive sites are found near Victoria, including Saanich Inlet, Saxe Point Park, the Ogden Point Breakwater, 10-Mile Point and Willis Point for deep diving. Race Rocks, 18km southwest of Victoria Harbour, offers superb scenery both above and below the water. Diving charters and dive shops in Victoria provide equipment sales, service, rentals and instruction.

Swimming

A good place to swim is the **Sooke Potholes**, about 37km west of Victoria on Sooke Rd (Hwy 14), by the town of Sooke on the southern shore. **Thetis Lake Municipal Park**, northwest of town (about a 20-minute drive), off the Trans Canada Hwy (Hwy 1) is popular. The Crystal Pool & Fitness Centre (☎ 250-380-4636), 2275 Quadra St, on the corner of Wark St, has a pool, sauna and whirlpool.

Whale Watching

A number of outfitters offer trips out into Georgia Strait to watch orcas (killer whales). Other wildlife you may see on these trips include bald eagles, dolphins, seals, sea lions and many kinds of sea birds.

A three-hour excursion generally costs from $75 to $85 for adults, and from $50 to $60 for children. For information and reservations try Ocean Explorations (☎ 250-383-6722, 888-422-6722), 146 Kingston St, at the Coast Victoria Harbourside Hotel near Fisherman's Wharf; Prince of Whales (☎ 250-383-4884), 812 Wharf St, just below the InfoCentre office; and Cuda Marine (☎ 250-812-6003), on the Wharf St pier.

Windsurfing & Kayaking

These are popular activities, especially in Cadboro Bay near the university, and at Willow's Beach in Oak Bay. Sailboards can be rented at both locations for around $17. Ocean River Sports (☎ 250-381-4233), 1437 Store St, rents canoes and kayaks, sells equipment and runs courses. Sports Rent (☎ 250-385-7368), 611 Discovery St, rents canoes and kayaks from $30 a day.

ORGANIZED TOURS

There are many types of tours available, from bus tours of downtown Victoria to quick trips around the island. Your best bet is to check with the Travel InfoCentre. Gray Line (☎ 250-388-5248), 700 Douglas St, offers a variety of bus tours, including a city bus tour costing $16 for 1½ hours that takes in some of the major historic and scenic sights. You can buy tickets and board the buses at the Empress Hotel.

Heritage Tours (☎ 250-474-4332), 713 Bexhill St, offers more personalized city tours in limousines seating six people for $75 for 1¼ hours, or $90 for two hours (the rate is for the car, not per person). Tallyho Sightseeing (☎ 250-479-1113) offers 45-minute city tours in a horse-drawn carriage for $30 for two people, and leaves from the corner of Belleville and Menzies Sts.

PLACES TO STAY

During the summer months, lodging in Victoria can be very expensive and hard to find. Make reservations as soon as you know your travel plans. In the downtown area there are several older hotels that have been renovated and are a good value. Otherwise, for inexpensive lodging try the hostels or one of the motel strips outside the city center. Prices for accommodations are very seasonal and if you travel outside of the main summer season, you'll save considerably on rooms, perhaps as much as $100 on some of the prices quoted here. If you're having trouble finding a room, the Travel InfoCentre's reservation service can help.

Camping

Closest to town is *Fort Victoria RV Park* (☎ 250-479-8112), 340 Island Hwy (Hwy 1A), 6.5km from the city center. The park caters mainly to RVs but it does have a few tent sites, although there are no trees and open fires are not allowed. It has full facilities including free showers and charges $26 per site. Take bus Nos 14 or 15 from downtown and get off at the bus stop at the gate.

A little farther out of town, *Thetis Lake Campground* (☎ 250-478-3845), 1938 Trans Canada Hwy, on Rural Route 6, is about a 20-minute drive northwest of the city center. All facilities are available, including laundry and a store, plus you can swim in the nearby lake. A site for two people is $15, plus $2 for electricity if you need it. The campground is open all year.

The best campground is *Goldstream Provincial Park* (☎ 250-391-2300), on the Trans Canada Hwy (Hwy 1), about 20km northwest of Victoria. A tent site costs $15.50 for one to four people, and you can go swimming, fishing and hiking. To get here, take bus No 50 from Douglas St.

South of Goldstream Provincial Park is *Paradise Campground* (☎ 250-478-6960), 2960 Irwin Rd, about 3km off the Trans Canada Hwy on Rural Route 6. It's part of a nature sanctuary and is open from early June to the end of September. It has full facilities, canoe and kayak rentals, and charges $18 for two people.

The Travel InfoCentre can give you information about other campgrounds not too far from town.

Hostels

The HI *Victoria Hostel* (☎ 250-385-4511), 516 Yates St, is in the old part of town just up from Wharf St. It has room for more than 100 people, with family rooms, a large common area, kitchen, laundry and a good notice board. A bed costs $15.50 for members and $19.50 for nonmembers. In peak season it's advisable to register before 4 pm. The hostel is open daily from 7 am to midnight.

Selkirk Guest House International (☎ 250-389-1213), 934 Selkirk Ave in Esquimalt over the Johnson St Bridge, is affiliated with Hostelling International. A dorm bed costs $18 and private rooms start at $50. Travelers with children can be accommodated economically and should feel right at home in this family-operated hostelry. Features include a garden with hot tub on the shore of The Gorge. The No 14 bus from Douglas St gets you within two blocks.

The *Victoria Backpackers Lodge* (☎ 250-386-4471), 1418 Fernwood Rd, has dormitory beds for $12 and private singles/doubles for $40/45. The hostel has no curfew and is close to the shops and restaurants of Fernwood Village. Buses east along Fort St will take you there and bus No 10 goes right past the door.

Also in the neighborhood is *Renouf House* (☎ 250 595 1771), 2010 Stanley Ave, which has beds in a coed dorm room for $20 (bunk and breakfast) in addition to several private B&B rooms (see B&Bs later in this section for information). The *YM-YWCA* (☎ 250-386-7511) are both in the same building at 880 Courtney St, but the residence is only for women. A dorm bunk with bedding costs $19. Private single rooms, when available, cost $37, though they're often fully booked with long-term boarders. There's also a cafeteria and a heated swimming pool.

The *University of Victoria* rents rooms from the start of May to the end of August. Singles/doubles are $38/50, including breakfast, and parking is $4 a day during the week but free on weekends. You can make use of the university's facilities and there are several licensed cafeterias on campus.

Contact Housing & Conference Services (☎ 250-721-8396), University of Victoria, PO Box 1700, Victoria, BC V8W 2Y2. To get to the campus, take bus No 14 on Douglas St, which takes about 20 minutes.

Hotels – Inner Harbour

Mid-Range While these prices certainly stretch the upper limits of the middle range, they're about the best you'll find in this much-sought-after area. The best deal here is the *Admiral Motel* (☎ 250-388-6267), 257 Belleville St, with rooms starting at $169, dipping as low as $79 in the winter. Hidden in a grove of trees, the *Best Western Inner Harbour* (☎ 250-384-5122, 888-383-2378), 412 Quebec St, has balconies and nicely decorated rooms starting at $149, although the price drops to $69 in winter.

Also in this price range is the *Ramada Huntingdon Manor* (☎ 250-381-3456, 800-663-7557), 330 Quebec St, where rooms start at $149. Across the street the *Harbour Towers Hotel* (☎ 250-385-2405, 800-663-5896), 345 Quebec St, has rooms starting at $169. You can't beat the location of the *Days Inn on the Harbour* (☎ 250-386-3451, 800-665-3024), 427 Belleville St, right across from the ferry terminal. Rooms start at $163, and there is an entrance at the back off Quebec St.

A block south of the harbor, *Embassy Inn* (☎ 250-382-8161, 800-268-8161), 520 Menzies St, has both an older and a newer wing with rooms starting at $119. Also just a block in from the harbor and from the Parliament Buildings, the *Royal Scot Inn* (☎ 250-388-5463, 800-663-7515), 425 Quebec St, offers studio, one- and two-bedroom suites starting at $139. There's more of a chain-hotel feeling to *Quality Inn Harbourview* (☎ 250-386-2421, 800-228-5151), 455 Belleville St, though some rooms have a good view; rooms range from $139 to $179. This hotel is attached to the more expensive Clarion Hotel, and the two hotels share the same check-in counter.

Top End The *Empress Hotel* (☎ 250-348-8111, 800-441-1414), at 721 Government St, is practically synonymous with Victoria.

Staying here on a honeymoon is a tradition throughout the Northwest and many well-heeled travelers wouldn't think of staying anywhere else. Rooms facing the city are $235 single or double, $60 more if you want a harbor view.

On the same scale of luxury, but much newer, *Laurel Point Inn* (☎ 250-386-8721, 800-663-7667), 680 Montreal St, with saunas, an indoor pool, balconies and incredible views, guards the entrance to the Inner Harbour; rooms start at $190.

At the *Clarion Hotel Grand Pacific* (☎ 250-386-0450, 800-458-6262), 450 Quebec St, rooms start at $199 single or double. In August the price goes up to $239, and between mid-October and the end of February it drops to $99 (add $20 to $40 for mountain or harbor views).

Hotels – Downtown & Old Town

Budget There are a few reasonable places right in the downtown area. The centrally located *Hotel Douglas* (☎ 250-383-4157, 800-332-9981), 1450 Douglas St at the corner of Pandora Ave, has rooms starting at $85/95, $40 for budget rooms without private bathroom. It shares its lobby with an art gallery. There is a 24-hour restaurant and bar downstairs – check the bar for daily food and drink specials.

At the *Strathcona Hotel* (☎ 250-383-7137, 800-663-7476), 919 Douglas St, a couple of blocks east of the Inner Harbour, rooms start at $89/99. There is free parking, several bars and a restaurant. *Crystal Court Motel* (☎ 250-384-0551), 701 Belleville St at the corner of Douglas St, across the road from the bus station and Crystal Garden, has rooms for $75/78, and a kitchen is an extra $2.

Mid-Range The totally renovated *Dominion Hotel* (☎ 250-384-4136, 800-663-6101), 759 Yates St, has rooms from $114/124 singles/doubles, plus $5 a day for parking, and there is a restaurant. Attractive *Green Gables Hotel* (☎ 250-385-6787, 800-661-4115), 850 Blanshard St, is close to the Inner Harbour and has an indoor pool, as well as a sauna and restaurant. Rooms start at

$110/125, kitchen studios are an extra $10 and weekly or monthly rates are available.

Executive House Hotel (☎ 250-388-5111, 800-663-7001), 777 Douglas St, is a high-rise tower a couple of blocks from the waterfront with good views and rooms starting at $175 for a single or double. The *Best Western Carlton Plaza* (☎ 250-388-5513, 800-663-7241), 642 Johnson St, is an older hotel that's been totally refurbished and offers a free continental breakfast and free valet parking, with rooms starting at $109. One of the nicest of the refurbished hotels is *Swans Hotel* (☎ 250-361-3310, 800-668-7926), 506 Pandora Ave, in a gem of a building in the Old Town area, right on the waterfront, with suites starting at $165, $185 for a two-bedroom suite.

Top End The *Bedford Regency Hotel* (☎ 250-384-6835, 800-665-6500), 1140 Government St, is a renovated vintage hotel right at the center of the city's prime shopping and dining area with rooms starting at $150. *Victoria Regent Hotel* (☎ 250-386-2211, 800-663-7472), 1234 Wharf St, near the corner of Yates St, is an all-suites hotel and has some of the best views in the city. Rooms start at $159 for singles or doubles, which includes a continental breakfast.

Chateau Victoria (☎ 250-382-4221, 800-663-5891), 740 Burdett Ave, is in a good location just behind the harbor area, with all the usual facilities, plus two restaurants. Rooms start at $147 for singles or doubles.

Hotels – Victoria Environs

Victoria is a very compact city and the following hotels and motels are just a few minutes from the downtown sights.

Budget East of the downtown area, *Cherry Bank Hotel* (☎ 250-385-5380, 800-998-6688), 825 Burdett Ave, opened in 1897, is a simple but reasonable value at $55/63 with shared bathroom, or $70/80 with private bathroom. Prices include breakfast but rooms have no TV or telephone. A popular restaurant and a bar are on the premises.

Just north of downtown along Douglas St is an area of inexpensive motels. *Paul's*

Motor Inn (☎ 250-382-9231), 1900 Douglas St, has a 24-hour restaurant and rooms are $75 for singles or doubles. *Traveller's Inn* has four motels in Victoria, but the two closest to the city are at 710 Queens Ave at Douglas St (☎ 250-370-1000, 888-753-3774) and two blocks down at 1850 Douglas St at Caledonia Ave (☎ 250-381-1000); the large rooms are $70/80. The *Doric Motel* (☎ 250-386-2481), 3025 Douglas St, is a five-minute drive, or 20-minute walk, north of the downtown area and has rooms for $74/79. Another good area for motels, not far from downtown, is northwest along Gorge Rd, which forms a section of Island Hwy (Hwy 1A). From Gorge Rd it's about a 10-minute drive to town.

Mid-Range *Helm's Inn* (☎ 250-385-5767, 800-665-4356), 600 Douglas St, has one-bedroom and studio suites with kitchen from $99/114. Opposite is the *Shamrock Motel* (☎ 250-385-8768), 675 Superior St, where rooms are $99/109. *James Bay Inn* (☎ 250-384-7151, 800-836-2649), 270 Government St, is a large old hotel with bay windows; rooms start at $100.

Top End One of the classiest places to stay in Victoria is *Abigail's Hotel* (☎ 250-388-5363, 800-561-6565), 906 McClure St, a small boutique hotel just east of downtown. This Tudor-style mansion has 16 exquisitely furnished rooms, with fresh flowers, goose-down duvets and other niceties; rooms start at $149.

Across the Inner Harbour from downtown and the Parliament Buildings, and with tremendous views of both, the *Ocean Pointe Resort* (☎ 250-360-2999, 800-667-4677), 45 Songees Rd, combines luxury-class rooms with spa facilities. On-site amenities include an indoor pool, hydrotherapy services, racquetball and squash courts, tennis courts and sauna. The rooms are top-notch and start at $129, or $199 for a full Inner Harbour view.

Beaconsfield Inn (☎ 250-384-4044), 998 Humboldt St, is an Edwardian mansion a few blocks east of the downtown area and a couple of blocks north of Beacon Hill Park. Rates start at $200, including breakfast.

There is also a beach cottage available for $395 but this does not include breakfast.

Oak Bay Beach Hotel (☎ 250-598-4556), 1175 Beach Drive, is a seaside hotel east of the downtown area overlooking Oak Bay, with rooms starting at $169. During the summer the hotel provides a shuttle service into the city center and offers lunchtime cruises.

B&Bs

There are several B&B associations with members offering rooms from $45 to $75 for singles, and from $55 to $120 for most doubles, though some go up to as much as $190. A couple of associations to try are All Seasons B&B Agency (☎ 250-655-7173), PO Box 5511, Station B, Victoria, BC V8R 6S4; and Victoria Vacationer B&B (☎ 250-382-9469), 1143 Leonard St, Victoria, BC V8V 2S3. Many B&Bs advertise independently and have pamphlets at the Travel InfoCentre. A few of them are listed here.

Northeast of the city center, *Renouf House* (☎ 250-595-4774) is a 1912 heritage home at 2010 Stanley Ave. Private rooms with a shared bathroom start at $35/55 for singles/doubles, rooms with a private bathroom start at $50/70. It can cater to people with special diets and has home-baked bread. Kayaking (one of the owners makes kayaks) or sailing tours are offered here through Intertidal Explorations. For information on its dorm rooms, see Hostels near the beginning of the Places to Stay section.

Marion's B&B (☎ 250-592-3070), 1730 Taylor St, about a 10-minute bus ride from downtown, has rooms for $35/55. The good breakfasts are enormous and the owners are friendly and helpful. *Battery St Guest House* (☎ 250-385-4632), 670 Battery St, is in an 1898 house south of downtown near Beacon Hill Park, with rooms for $50/85. *Craigmyle Guest House* (☎ 250-595-5411), 1037 Craigdarroch Rd, about 1km east of downtown, is next to Craigdarroch Castle, with rooms for $65/70.

Convenient to sights on the Inner Harbour, *Birdcage Walk Guest House* (☎ 250-389-0804), 505 Government St, offers five guest rooms with ensuite bathrooms in a historic home for $89/99. Perhaps the most upscale B&B in Victoria, and surely the one with the best view, is the *Gatsby Mansion* (☎ 250-388-9191, 800-563-9656), at 309 Belleville St, right on the Inner Harbour, with rooms for upwards of $200 a night; call to inquire about weekend packages.

A lovely place to stay, away from the city center, is *Spinnakers Guest House* (☎ 250-386-2739), 308 Catherine St, on the northwest side of the harbor, where rooms in the 1884 heritage building are $150 a night. Each room is well appointed with lovely furnishings and a Jacuzzi bath, and some even have a fireplace. You're also right next to the Spinnaker Brew Pub (see Brewpubs & Bars under Entertainment later in this chapter) to sample all that good beer.

PLACES TO EAT

Though a small city, Victoria has a varied array of restaurants due in part to its many visitors, and prices are generally good. As befits a tourist town, especially one with British roots, there are numerous cafes and tearooms. Some dining rooms offer good lunch specials but are fairly pricey in the evening. The pubs in town are also good for reasonably priced meals.

Budget

Restaurant food can be pricey in Victoria, particularly in summer. A place to shop around for a good, inexpensive meal is Chinatown (Fisgard St between Douglas St and the harbor), or in the Market Square shopping center at Johnson and Wharf Sts, where there are a number of casual eateries and food booths.

For a $3 breakfast served until 4 pm check out the *Milky Way Cafe* (☎ 250-360-1113), 126 - 160 Johnson St; $6 dinner specials are also available. *Foo Hong Chop Suey* (☎ 250-386-9553), 564 Fisgard St, is small and basic yet has good, simple Cantonese food with most dishes costing $6. The *Ocean Phoenix* (☎ 250-382-2828), at 509 Fisgard St, offers a small, neat dining room, an extensive menu and good food with most dishes costing $8 and Cantonese lunch specials for $7.

The modest and casual *Day & Night* (☎ 250-382-5553), 622 Yates St, is good for any meal, with good-value plain food, including one of the cheapest breakfasts in town, and sandwiches and pasta dishes from $4. *Smitty's Family Restaurant* (☎ 250-383-5612), 850 Douglas St, is an old standby and best for cheap pancake breakfasts for around $7, including coffee; it's open from 6 am to midnight.

Sam's Deli (☎ 250-382-8424), under the maroon awnings at 805 Government St at the corner of Wharf St and diagonally opposite the main Travel InfoCentre, is a perfect spot to have an espresso and write a postcard. Their $6 sandwiches are so big that two people can easily share one and call it lunch.

It's worth joining the crowds at colorful *John's Place* (☎ 250-389-0799), 723 Pandora Ave, for the large portions at breakfast or lunch. In Bastion Square, opposite The Planet dance club, is *C'est Bon* (☎ 250-381-1461), a small French-style bakery with croissants, coffee and lunchtime soups; open Tuesday to Saturday from 7 am to 4.30 pm.

Fish and chips are excellent in Victoria. *Barb's Place* (☎ 250-384-6515), at 310 St Lawrence St, at Fisherman's Wharf, is a wooden shack on the dock serving fish and chips wrapped in newspaper; fresh crabs can be bought from the boats nearby. *Cook St Fish & Chips* (☎ 250-384-1856), 252 Cook St, near Beacon Hill Park, and *Brady's* (☎ 250-382-3695), 20 West Burnside Rd, by the corner of Harriett Rd, are also good spots for fish and chips.

A cheap but good place is the busy *Eugene's Restaurant & Snack Bar* (☎ 250-381-5456), 1280 Broad St, offering simple, basic Greek food at about $4 to $8, served cafeteria style. The *Mount Royal Bagel Factory* (☎ 250-380-3588), 1115 North Park St (but with the door on Grant St) in the Fernwood Village area, has fresh Montreal-style bagels.

Mid-Range

A popular place for good light meals and drinks is *Suze* (☎ 250-383-2829), 515 Yates St, with a menu that includes pizza ($9), pasta ($11) and fresh seafood dishes ($16). The lounge, with exposed brick and a vintage 7.5m-long mahogany bar, is a comfortable place to have a drink.

Perhaps the most happening place in town is the **Re-Bar** (☎ 250-360-2401), 50 Bastion Square, with an eclectic, international menu and funky decor to match, plus an on-site bakery. Re-Bar is busy all day, serving breakfasts, coffees, desserts, salads and main dishes, which are mostly vegetarian and cost between $7 and $12.

Afternoon Tea – A Victoria Tradition

English-style afternoon tea in Victoria is one tradition that should not be missed during your visit. Aside from being a decadent way to load up on unwanted calories, afternoon tea, with the accompanying sandwiches, cakes and pastries, offers a touch of relaxed elegance admist the hustle and bustle of the city.

Tea at the **Empress Hotel** (☎ 250-348-8111, 800-441-1414), 721 Government St, is judged to be so mandatory an experience by many visitors that without it a trip to Victoria wouldn't be complete. While afternoon tea isn't usually considered a meal in itself, this extravagance of sandwiches, clotted cream, berries, scones, lemon tarts and cakes will surely ruin your appetite for an evening meal. The Empress has its own house blend made from Darjeeling, China and Ceylon teas. The tearooms at the Empress are lovely, and you should dress up a bit for the experience (in fact, there is a dress code). However, tea isn't cheap, costing $30 a person during the summer and $20 during winter. Reservations are mandatory in all but the dead of winter.

Another favorite place for afternoon tea is the **James Bay Tearoom** (☎ 250-382-8282), 332 Menzies St. Here you will get the usual assortment of sandwiches, scones and cakes as well as traditional English trifle. Tea costs $7. This very English restaurant is also a good place for lunch and dinner with standards like steak and kidney pie or roast beef and Yorkshire pudding. **Murchie's** (☎ 250-383-3112), 1110 Government St, between View and Fort Sts, is a quality West Coast tea and coffee merchant that also serves a decadent assortment of pastries and chocolates.

Popular with locals, the **Blethering Place Tearoom** (☎ 250-598-1413), 2250 Oak Bay Ave, is in a 1912 heritage building, away from the center of town in Oak Bay Village. It has 16 varieties of tea along with sausage rolls, sandwiches, scones and homemade jam, and delicious butter tarts. The price is from $9 to $12. **Bentley's on the Bay** in the Oak Bay Beach Hotel (☎ 250-598-4556), 1175 Beach Drive, offers tea with a delicious assortment of cakes and pastries along with great views of the Strait of Juan de Fuca. Tea costs $17, and reservations are required in winter.

Combine a trip to **Butchart Gardens** (☎ 250-652-8222), 800 Benvenuto Rd, with afternoon tea, served either in the main dining area, the conservatory or outside in the garden. Not only will you be surrounded by beautiful arrangements of flowers while you enjoy your tea, but you'll also be looking out onto the gardens and Tod Inlet. A selection of 15 teas is offered, plus sandwiches, scones and homemade jams, tarts, slices and cakes. Tea costs $18 in addition to the admission price to the gardens.

High tea at the Empress Hotel

If the weather's good and dining on an outdoor deck is appealing, then the *Wharfside Eatery* (☎ 250-360-1808), 1208 Wharf St, is your best bet. While fresh seafood is the specialty for around $20, the menu also offers wood-fired pizza for $14 and burgers for $10. Bustling and popular, *Il Terrazzo* (☎ 250-361-0028), 555 Johnson St, is the best place in Victoria for Italian pastas, grilled meats and tempting pizza, with most main dishes at around $14. Victoria has a number of good Greek restaurants, but *Milos* (☎ 250-382-5544), 716 Burdett St, with the windmill on the roof, has the reputation for the best roast lamb for around $15; stay late for the belly dancers.

Bowman's Spare Rib House (☎ 250-385-5380), in the Cherry Bank Hotel, 825 Burdett Ave, is a good place for rib dinners ($17 for a 1lb rack), steaks ($15) and seafood ($13). There's also a children's menu ($4 for most items) and live honky-tonk piano entertainment.

Pagliacci's (☎ 250-386-1662), 1011 Broad St, between Fort and Broughton Sts, is a moderately priced Italian restaurant, with pasta for $11 and other main dishes for $17. At night this is a busy place, for the food and for the live music. *Herald St Caffé* (☎ 250-381-1441), 546 Herald St, is a small Italian restaurant serving delicious pastas for $12 to $15. It also has vegetarian dishes, great desserts and a wine bar that gets busy after 10 pm.

Le Petit Saigon (☎ 250-386-1412), 1010 Langely St, is recommended for Vietnamese meals with selections of meat, fish and vegetarian dishes ranging in price from $9 to $15. *Milestone's* (☎ 250-381-2244), 812 Wharf St, right on the harbor below the Travel Info-Centre, has an incredible view of the Parliament Buildings and the Inner Harbour, with burgers for $7, pasta for $11 and most main dishes for around $12. While it doesn't have a regular liquor license (you'll need to order food to have a drink), many people come here for a cocktail and a snack. *Baan Thai* (☎ 250-383-0050), 1314 Government St, is the best place in town for authentic Thai cuisine with vegetarian dishes for $8, noodle dishes for $10 and seafood dishes for $14.

Top End

The Empress Hotel (☎ 250-384-8111), 721 Government St, has an array of dining options, including the formal *Empress Room,* offering top-quality food and service, and prices to match, with Northwest cuisine main dishes starting at around $30; the *Bengal Lounge*, complete with a tiger skin on the wall, is a real treat, serving seafood and poultry, a daily curry special for $16 and a lunch buffet for $12; and the *Garden Café* downstairs, where lunch is standard fare at regular prices.

Chandler's Seafood Restaurant (☎ 250-385-3474), near the Victoria Regent Hotel and the corner of Yates and Wharf Sts, is an established dining room specializing in ocean fare with prices ranging from $19 for the seafood pasta to $30 for the Victoria Seafood Platter. Overlooking the harbor, *Harbour House Restaurant* (☎ 250-386-1244), 607 Oswego St, is a formal, elegant seafood and steak house with prices ranging from $18 to $27.

Koto Japanese Restaurant (☎ 250-382-1514), 510 Fort St, just up from Wharf St, serves mainly seafood and has a sushi and salad bar, with main courses costing from $16 to $26. *The 1218 Restaurant* (☎ 250-386-1218), 1218 Wharf St, offers nouveau Northwest cuisine from $12 to $26 in a very attractive dining room with good views over the harbor.

Camille's Fine Westcoast Dining (☎ 250-381-3433), 45 Bastion Square, has the reputation of being Victoria's most inventive restaurant, combining Northwest ingredients with eclectic, international cuisine. Most main dishes are around $16, although the rack of lamb is $23.

ENTERTAINMENT
Brewpubs & Bars

Spinnakers Brew Pub & Restaurant (☎ 250-386-2739), 308 Catherine St, is a friendly place serving some of the best beer in BC (there are up to nine beers on tap – try the ESB), and when the weather is fine there is deck seating with views over the Inner Harbour. The spent grains from the brewery are used to feed cattle and turkeys.

Swans Brewpub (☎ 250-361-3310), 506 Pandora St, is half the main floor of Swans Hotel. Besides the good beers and ales, the other reason to come here is to admire the owner's extensive modern art collection which graces the pub. The food here is pretty good. Also in the hotel is *The Fowl & Fish Cafe, Ale & Oyster House* (☎ 250-361-3150), 1605 Store St, where you can sample the beer while dining on fresh oysters, tapas or Northwest cuisine.

Although they don't make their own beer, three other pubs worth trying are *The Flying Beagle Pub* (☎ 250-382-3301), 301 Cook St, with 16 beers on tap, good food and live jazz on Sunday night; *Garrick's Head*, 69 Bastion Square; and *The Sticky Wicket Pub* (☎ 250-383-7137), 919 Douglas St, in the Strathcona Hotel, with a great selection of international beer on tap as well as good food.

Coffeehouses

Besides a good cup of coffee, at *Bean Around the World* (☎ 250-386-7115), 533 Fisgard St, you can also get into one of the discussion groups. *Java Coffeehouse* (☎ 250-381-2326), 537 Johnson St, is a classic coffeehouse with more standard entertainment like live music and poetry readings, as is *Mocambo Coffee* (☎ 250-474-5489), 1028 Blanshard St.

Theater & Performing Arts

Victoria has a number of live theaters that provide venues for plays, concerts, comedies, ballets and operas. Victoria's Fringe Theatre Festival is held in late August and early September. The *McPherson Playhouse* (☎ 250-386-6121), 3 Centennial Square, on the corner of Pandora Ave and Government St, regularly puts on plays and comedies, and is also the home of Pacific Opera Victoria (☎ 250-385-0222). The box office is open Monday to Saturday from 9.30 am to 5.30 pm.

The elegant *Royal Theatre* (☎ 250-386-6121), 805 Broughton St, between Blanshard and Quadra Sts, hosts a range of performances, including the ballet, dance and concerts, and is the home of the Victoria Symphony Orchestra (☎ 250-846-9771).

Other theaters worth checking out in and around Victoria are the *Belfry* (☎ 250-385-6815), 1291 Gladstone Ave, northeast of the downtown area, and the *Phoenix Theatre* (☎ 250-721-8000), on the University of Victoria campus. The *International Recital & Chamber Music Society of Victoria* (☎ 250-477-7759) performs at the University Centre Auditorium. More experimental theater is staged by Dark Horse Theatre at the *Kaleidoscope Playhouse* (☎ 250-475-4444), 520 Herald St.

Live Music

In the same building as the Strathcona Hotel (☎ 250-383-7137), 919 Douglas St, you'll find two venues: *Legends*, a long-standing club presenting a variety of live music, including rock, country, blues and flamenco as well as DJs spinning the best in dance music; and *Big Bad John's*, which features country & western music. *Steamers Pub* (250-381-4340), 570 Yates St, just below Government St, is a good blues and jazz bar and has Sunday afternoon sessions.

Thursday's (☎ 250-360-2711), 1821 Cook St, features blues bands, as does *Victoria's Blues House* (☎ 250-386-1717), at 1417 Government St. Try the *Esquimalt Inn* (☎ 250-382-7161), 856 Esquimalt Rd, for country rock music. *Vertigo Night Club* (☎ 250-472-4311), in the Student Union Building at the University of Victoria, has a mixture of dance and live bands.

Victoria's best live jazz venue is *Millennium Jazz Club* (☎ 250-360-9098), 1601 Store St, beneath Swans Brewpub. *Pagliacci's* (☎ 250-386-1662), 1011 Broad St, is popular not only for its food but also for entertainment, including jazz and comedy sessions. *Hermann's Jazz Club* (☎ 250-388-9166), 753 View St, is another good place for live music. For information about jazz around town, call the Jazz Hotline at ☎ 250-658-5255.

The Limit (☎ 250-384-3557), 1318 Broad St, has live regional bands on weekends and DJs during the week.

Dance Clubs

One of the more popular dance clubs is *The Planet* (☎ 250-385-5333), 15 Bastion Square on the corner of Wharf St. Across the street and down the stairs beside the Wharfside Restaurant is *Uforia* (☎ 250-381-2331), 1208 Wharf St, the main straight dance club, with a young crowd and regular theme nights. The *Drawing Room* (☎ 250-920-7797), 751 View St, is a good place to dance to the latest in hip-hop and progressive dance.

The hottest dance club is *Rumours Cabaret* (☎ 250-385-0566), 1325 Government St, a friendly gay-oriented disco with a lively clientele. *BJ's Lounge* (☎ 250-388-0505), downstairs at 642 Johnson St, is another gay men's dance club.

Cinemas
Admission at commercial cinemas such as the *Capital 6* (☎ 250-384-6811), 805 Yates St, and the *Odeon Theatre* (☎ 250-383-0513), 780 Yates St, is reduced to $5 on Tuesday.

SHOPPING
There are a number of shops along Douglas and Government Sts selling Native Indian art and craftwork such as sweaters, moccasins, carvings, jewelry and prints. For Native Indian art that is truly unique, and where you can see some of the artists working in the upstairs studio, visit Ravensong (☎ 250-382-2787), 1221 Wharf St. Here you'll find traditional and contemporary Native carvings, Inuit sculpture, paintings, prints and jewelry, all original works. Many of the artists will create special orders; however, the selection in the gallery is usually enough to keep most customers satisfied.

GETTING THERE & AWAY
Air
Victoria international airport is in Sidney, about 26km north of the city off the Patricia Bay Hwy (Hwy 17). Two airlines with offices in Victoria are Air Canada (☎ 250-360-9074), 20 Centennial Square, and Canadian Airlines (☎ 250-382-6111), 901 Gordon St. See the Getting There & Away chapter for details of air services between Victoria and Vancouver. Keep in mind that if you're flying to Vancouver and beyond, the cost of a ticket from Victoria is just a few dollars more than one from Vancouver itself, so it's

not worth paying the cost of the ferry ride to catch a flight directly from Vancouver.

Horizon Air (☎ 800-547-9308, 206-762-3646 in Seattle), has service between Victoria and Seattle, Port Angeles and Bellingham. North Vancouver Air (☎ 800-228-6608) links Vancouver, Victoria and Tofino.

Bus
Although Greyhound has no service on the island or to the Mainland, it does have an office (☎ 250-385-5248) in the bus station at 700 Douglas St where you can get information and purchase tickets.

Pacific Coach Lines (PCL; ☎ 250-385-4411) operates buses to Vancouver every hour between 6 am and 9 pm; the one-way fare, which includes the cost of the ferry, is $25. It's the same price to Vancouver international airport; buses connect with the airport shuttle bus at Delta Pacific Resort in Richmond. The bus to Seattle, via Sidney and Anacortes, leaves at 10 am and arrives at 5.30 pm; the one-way fare is $39.

Island Coach Lines (☎ 250-385-4411), sometimes referred to as Laidlaw Lines, covers Vancouver Island. There are eight buses a day to Nanaimo and northern Vancouver Island.

Train
The Esquimalt & Nanaimo Railiner, or E&N Railiner, operated by VIA Rail (☎ 250-383-4324, 800-561-8630), connects Victoria with Nanaimo, Parksville and Courtenay. There is one train in each direction per day – northbound from Victoria at 8.15 am, southbound from Courtenay at 1.15 pm. The journey, through some beautiful scenery, takes about 3½ hours. The *Malahat*, as the train is known, is very popular so book ahead. Some one-way fares from Victoria are: $19 to Nanaimo, $24 to Parksville and $36 to Courtenay. Seven-day advance purchases are much cheaper.

For the full schedule, get a copy of the E&N Railiner pamphlet from the station, a travel agency or the Travel InfoCentre. The station, 405 Pandora Ave, is close to town, right at Johnson St Bridge, near the corner of Johnson and Wharf Sts. It's open from

7.30 am to noon, and from 1 to 3 pm. To get to the station, take bus Nos 23, 24 or 25.

Ferry

For information about getting from Swartz Bay to Tsawwassen on BC Ferries, see the Getting There & Away chapter. In Victoria you can contact BC Ferries (☎ 250-656-0757, 24 hours), 1112 Fort St at the corner of Cook St. BC Ferries also operates between Swartz Bay and five of the southern Gulf Islands: Galiano, Mayne, Saturna, Salt Spring and Pender. There are usually three or four ferry services a day.

Three passenger-only ferry services and one car-ferry service serve Washington State from the Inner Harbour ferry terminal at 430 Belleville St. The ferry MV *Coho*, operated by Black Ball Transport (☎ 250-386-2202), sails to Port Angeles, just across the Strait of Juan de Fuca, and costs $9.50 per person, or $39 with a car; during the summer months there are four 1½-hour trips a day leaving Victoria at 6.20 and 10.30 am, and 3 and 7.30 pm. The summer-only, passenger-only *Victoria Express* (☎ 250-361-9144) also goes to Port Angeles; the journey time is one hour and the roundtrip fare is $40. *Victoria Clipper* and *Victoria Clipper II*, run by Clipper Navigation (☎ 250-382-8100), sail to Seattle; the journey takes about three hours and in summer the one-way fare in these water-jet-propelled catamarans is $82. The passenger-only *Victoria Star*, operated by Victoria Cruises (☎ 800-443-4552), does a return trip once a day to Bellingham.

There are two other ferry options for those with cars. The *Princess Marguerite III* travels to Seattle and departs from Ogden Point off the northwest end of Dallas Rd; the journey takes 4½ hours and the cost is $41 per person, or $69 with a car. The Washington State Ferries (☎ 250-381-1551), 2499 Ocean Ave in Sidney, operates a ferry service from Swartz Bay through the San Juan Islands to Anacortes on the Washington mainland; the very scenic three-hour trip, which allows you to make stopovers on the islands, costs $10 per person or $41 with a car.

GETTING AROUND
To/From the Airport

PBM Transport (☎ 250-475-2010) operates the airport bus to Victoria international airport from any of 60 downtown hotels. It leaves every half-hour from downtown and the airport for the 26km trip and costs $15. A taxi to the airport from the downtown area costs about $40. City bus No 70 passes within 1km of the airport.

Bus

For local transit information call ☎ 250-382-6161 or get a copy of BC Transit's guide listing bus routes and fares from the Travel InfoCentre. The city buses cover a wide area and run quite frequently. The normal one-way fare is $1.50; $2.25 if you wish to travel into a second zone, such as the suburbs of Colwood or Sidney. Have the exact change ready. An all-day pass is $5 for as many rides as you want, starting as early as you like. These all-day passes are not sold on buses but are available from various places around town, such as convenience stores.

Bus No 70 goes to the BC Ferries Terminal in Swartz Bay; bus No 2 goes to Oak Bay. The Oak Bay Explorer double-decker bus costs just $1 and takes a 90-minute run between the Empress Hotel and Oak Bay; you can get off and on along the way.

Car

For rentals, shop around, as prices can vary. Two of the cheapest places are ADA Rent-A-Used Car (☎ 250-474-3455), 892 Goldstream Ave; and Rent-A-Wreck (☎ 250-384-5343), 2634 Douglas St.

All major rental companies are represented in and around the downtown area, including Avis (☎ 250-386-8468), 843 Douglas St; Budget (☎ 250-388-5525), 757 Douglas St; and Tilden (☎ 250-381-1115), 767 Douglas St.

Taxi

Two of several taxi companies are Victoria Taxi (☎ 250-383-7111) and Blue Bird Cabs (☎ 250-384-1155). You can get anywhere around the city center for about $6. You can also hire pedicabs, which are three-wheeled bicycle taxis, that cost about 75¢ a minute and operate from early April to late October.

Bicycle

Downtown you can rent bikes from Harbour Scooters (☎ 250-384-2133), 843 Douglas St, adjacent to the Avis office. Bikes are also available at Sports Rent (☎ 250-385-7368), 611 Discovery St, and at the HI hostel.

Mini-Ferry

Victoria Harbour Ferry runs an enjoyable, albeit short, ferry trip of about half an hour roundtrip from the Inner Harbour to Songhees Park (in front of the Ocean Pointe Resort), Fisherman's Wharf and Westbay Marina. The boat takes just a dozen people per trip and costs $3 one way.

Southern Gulf Islands

Lying north of Victoria, and off Tsawwassen on the Mainland, this string of nearly 200 islands in the Georgia Strait continues on to Washington State's San Juan Islands.

With a few important exceptions, most of the islands are small and nearly all of them virtually uninhabited, but this island-littered channel is a boater's dream. Vessels of all descriptions cruise in and out of bays, harbors and marinas much of the year. The fishing is varied and excellent: several species of prized salmon can be caught in season. BC Ferries connects with some of the larger islands, so you don't need your own boat to visit them. Lodging is tight, so reservations are mandatory, especially in high season. Pick up a copy of the free newspaper, *The Gulf Islander*, which details island happenings and lodging options.

Most of the restaurants on the Gulf Islands are associated with lodges, resorts and B&Bs. Campers should have cooking supplies, as casual restaurants can be hard to find on the island.

Due to the mild climate, abundant flora and fauna, relative isolation and natural beauty, the islands are one of Canada's escapist-dream destinations. Many of the inhabitants are retired people, artists or counterculture types of one sort or another. In fact, some of the 'farmers' take their harvest to Amsterdam where they compete in contests, much the way brewers compete for international medals.

Cycling the quiet island roads is a very popular pastime.

Getting There & Away

Ferry service to the islands is good, though potentially very confusing. Pick up one of the ferry schedules (available at most Info-Centres) and give yourself a few minutes to figure out the system. In general, there are more ferries in the morning than in the afternoon, so make sure you know when and how you're getting back if you're planning a day trip. Generally, here's what the service consists of.

Ferries connect to the Southern Gulf Islands from both Tsawwassen on the Mainland and Swartz Bay near Sidney on Vancouver Island. Tsawwassen-departing ferries go to Saturna, Mayne, Galiano, Pender and Salt Spring Islands. A one-way pedestrian passage is $8.50, or $34.50 for a car. Ferries from Swartz Bay go to all the above islands, except Mayne. One-way fare is $5 for a passenger, or $18 for a vehicle. For all these runs, reservations for cars are strongly advised in high season.

In addition to the ferries between the Mainland and Vancouver Island, there are also inter-island ferries; fares are $2.50 passenger, $6 for a car.

SALT SPRING ISLAND

Salt Spring Island is the largest island in both size and population; its population of more than 8500 swells to three times that size in summer. Artists, entertainers and craftspeople have chosen to live here. As a consequence, there are craft fairs and art galleries with national reputations. The island has a long, interesting Native Indian history, followed with settlement not by

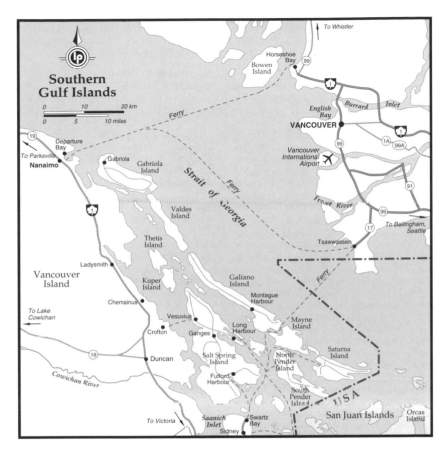

Southern Gulf Islands

white people but by pioneering US blacks. Seeking escape from prejudice and social tensions in the States, a small group of settlers formed a community at Vesuvius Bay. Unfortunately, the Native Indians didn't care for them any more than they cared for the British in the area. Still, the settlers stuck it out, began farms and set up schools. Later, immigrants came from Britain and Ireland.

Salt Spring Island has three terminals for ferries: Long Harbour serves Vancouver, Swartz Bay and the other southern Gulf Islands; Fulford Harbour serves Swartz Bay; and Vesuvius Bay is for ferries plying back and forth to Crofton.

Not far from the Long Harbour landing, **Ganges** is the principal village. It has the most accommodations and has a summer arts and crafts fair, a few tourist-oriented shops and a Saturday morning market. Artists welcome visitors to their studios – the Travel InfoCentre (☎ 250-537-5252), 121 Lower Ganges Rd, has a list. **Mouat Provincial Park** is nearby and has 15 campsites. Salt Spring Island Bus (☎ 250-537-2311) runs between Ganges and the ferry terminals.

South of Ganges, **Mt Maxwell Provincial Park** offers excellent views, fishing and picnic areas. In **Ruckle Provincial Park**, a former homestead 10km east of the Fulford

Harbour ferry terminal, you can enjoy hiking through forests and along the shoreline, plus fishing and wilderness camping.

Places to Stay

The campground at *Ruckle Provincial Park* (☎ 250-391-2300), on Beaver Point Rd, has 70 primitive campsites for $9.50. There are a few more campsites ($8) near Cusheon Lake at the *Saltspring Island Hostel* (☎ 250-537-4149), 640 Ocean Lake Rd, which also has dorm beds in either a cedar lodge or teepee for $14 (members) or $18 (nonmembers). The hostel is a short walk from the lake or ocean beach.

There are quite a few B&Bs on the island; the operators of most will pick you up at the ferry terminal. The breakfast is particularly good at the pastoral *Old Farmhouse B&B* (☎ 250-537-4113), 1077 North End Rd near St Mary Lake, a restored century-old farmhouse with four guest rooms ($125 to $150), all with private bathrooms and balconies.

Overlooking Ganges Harbour, the *Hastings House B&B* (☎ 250-537-2362), 160 Upper Ganges Rd, is the sort of ultimate B&B one would ordinarily reserve for a special occasion or big splurge. Lodgings are in one of four lavishly refurbished farm buildings; doubles start at $375. A five-course dinner is served in an elegant Tudor-style dining room. Children are not allowed.

Head to Ganges if you're looking for a motel. The *Seabreeze Inn* (☎ 250-537-4145), 101 Bittancourt Rd, has quiet rooms overlooking Ganges Harbour and a few kitchenettes; rooms cost $74/94 singles/doubles. A number of cottages along St Mary Lake go for roughly the same price as a motel room. The *Cottage Resort* (☎ 250-537-2214), 175 Suffolk Rd, features a sandy swimming beach, free canoes and rowboats, and small lakefront cottages with a few kitchenettes. Cottages rent for $75 to $105, depending on the size.

The health-oriented *Salty Springs Spa & Seaside Resort* (☎ 250-537-4111), 1460 North Beach Rd, in Vesuvius Bay, features upscale seaside chalets (some with kitchens) with fireplaces for $159/189 singles/doubles.

Rooms lack a TV or phone, as guests are expected to be busily rejuvenating themselves with massage and mud baths.

NORTH & SOUTH PENDER ISLANDS

These two islands, with a combined population of 1600, are joined by a small bridge. There are arts-and-crafts studios to visit and a golf course. For **beaches**, try Hamilton in Browning Harbour on North Pender and Mortimer Spit on South Pender (just after crossing the bridge). You might see some of the more-or-less tame deer around the islands. You can hike and camp at **Prior Centennial Provincial Park** on North Pender, close to **Medicine Beach** at Bedwell Harbour. On South Pender there are good views from the summit of the 255m-high **Mt Norman**.

Places to Stay

Accommodations are mainly in B&Bs and cottages. *Corbett House B&B* (☎ 250-629-6305), 4309 Corbett Rd, 1.5km from the ferry terminal, is a cozy heritage farmhouse with congenial hosts; rooms go for $70/85 singles/doubles. *Inn on Pender Island* (☎ 250-629-3353, 800-550-0172), 4709 Canal Rd, a small inn in the woods, is popular with cyclists. This is one of the least-expensive places to stay on the islands, with an on-site restaurant, and rooms with private entrances and coffeemakers for $60/70. *Cliffside Inn On-the-Sea* (☎ 250-629-6691), 4230 Armadale Rd, is an oceanfront B&B with great views (especially from the cliffside hot tub over the bay). All rooms have private bathrooms; this is a popular honeymoon destination.

SATURNA ISLAND

At Saturna Point by the ferry terminal in Lyall Harbour, there's a store and pub. **Winter Cove Marine Park** has a good sandy beach and swimming, fishing, boating and hiking. At the top of **Mt Warburton Pike** is a wildlife reserve with feral goats and fine views. You'll find good views of the Washington Cascades from the road on the island's leeward side. Just north of Saturna

Island is **Cabbage Island Marine Park**, with swimming, fishing and wilderness camping.

Accommodations on Saturna Island are limited to only a few B&Bs, so be sure to book in advance. *Breezy Bay B&B* (☎ 250-539-2937), 131 Payne Rd, on a farm about 1.5km from the ferry terminal, has singles/doubles for $55/65. All four rooms at the English-style *Stone House Farm B&B* (☎ 250-539-2683), 207 Narvaez Bay Rd, feature private bathrooms and balconies, and have views of the waterfront and Mt Baker; rooms cost $95/100.

MAYNE ISLAND

The ferry between Tsawwassen and Swartz Bay squeezes through Active Pass, which separates Mayne and Galiano Islands. Village Bay, on the southern side of Mayne Island, is the ferry terminal, although there are docking facilities for boaters at other points. There are some late-19th-century buildings at **Miners Bay**, including a museum which was formerly the jail.

Places to Stay

Mayne Inn Hotel (☎ 250-539-3122), 494 Arbutus Drive, is a small waterfront hotel; all the rooms have a view and start at $50/60 singles/doubles.

Fernhill Lodge (☎ 250-539-2544), 610 Fernhill Rd, is a secluded hilltop B&B about 5km from the ferry dock. The inn is loaded with character, with seven rooms in period theme, an herb garden and a sauna. Rooms start at $75/90. *Oceanwood Country Inn* (☎ 250-539-5074), 630 Dinner Bay Rd, is both pastoral and upscale. All rooms have private bathrooms and views of Navy Channel, some rooms have whirlpool tubs and private balconies. Rooms start at $120/130, tea service and breakfast included. The restaurant at the Oceanwood is one of the best restaurants in the Gulf Islands, with four-course Northwest cuisine dinners.

GALIANO ISLAND

Despite its relatively large size, Galiano Island has fewer than 1000 residents on its long, narrow landmass. About 75% of the island is forest and bush. There's a Travel InfoCentre (☎ 250-539-2233) at the ferry terminal in Sturdies Bay. Local artists and artisans invite visitors to their studios.

You can hike almost the length of the east coast and climb either **Mt Sutil** at 323m or **Mt Galiano** at 342m, and you can see the Olympic Mountains about 90km away from both mountains. If you're willing to tackle the hills, you can go cycling, while Porlia Pass and Active Pass are popular places for diving and fishing. The coast is lined with cliffs and small bays, and **canoeing** along the western shoreline is possible in the calmer waters. On the northeastern tip of the island is the rugged **Dionisio Point Provincial Park** with swimming, fishing, hiking and wilderness camping.

Places to Stay

You can camp at *Montague Harbour Marine Park* (☎ 250-391-2300), about 9.5km from Sturdies Bay ferry terminal for $12; sites are primitive and reservations are available. Around the island there are B&Bs and several places with cottage rentals. *Sutil Lodge* (☎ 250-539-2930) dates from the 1920s and is on the beach at Montague Harbour. It has singles/doubles from $60/75 and offers free use of canoes.

Bodega Resort (☎ 250-539-2677), 120 Monasty Rd, is a favorite family destination for its horseback-riding trails and trout-fishing pond. The two-story log cottages have three bedrooms and kitchens, and start at $40/60. *Woodstone Country Inn* (☎ 250-539-2022), on Georgeson Bay Rd, about 3km from the ferry, is more formal and upscale (children not allowed). There are 12 spacious rooms, all with private bathrooms, some with Jacuzzis and most with fireplaces. Tea and dinner are included in the room rate, which starts at $95/99 singles/doubles. The inn's restaurant is noted for its fine food, and is open to non-guests.

Bowen Island

At the entrance to Howe Sound and just a 20-minute ferry ride from Horseshoe Bay, this small island feels like it is about 1000km away from Vancouver instead of only 20km. West Vancouver's island suburb (although it's administered by the GVRD) has about 2700 permanent residents, half of whom commute to the Mainland each day. During the summer months, the island population swells to more than 4000, mostly due to the people who have cottages here.

The island was originally called Xwlil xhwm ('fast drumming ground') by the Squamish Indians who, along with the Salish Indians, used this as a meeting place. As was the case in so much of the Lower Mainland's history, logging was why the first white settlers came here. Within 30 years Bowen Island was supporting logging, fishing, whaling (Howe Sound was a home to humpback whales until about 1907, when all had been slaughtered), agriculture and dynamite production.

Tourism also played a big part in its history, going back as far as 1900 when Captain John Cates brought people here from Vancouver by boat (a road to Horseshoe Bay wasn't completed until 1928) to picnic, bathe in the sea and sit in the shade of the 300 fruit trees he had planted. Cates eventually built a hotel that became known for its clay tennis courts and lawn-bowling greens.

Under the management of the Union Steamship Company, which bought the hotel in 1920, Bowen Island (or the 'Happy Isle' as it was called) really hit its stride as a recreation mecca for Vancouverites. A dance hall that could hold up to 800 people was built in 1921, and by 1924 a ship was bringing in up to 1400 passengers at a time who wined, dined and danced all the way from Vancouver. The good times continued to 1946 when a record 101,000 people visited the island. However, in 1956, a planned resort that was to be North America's most luxurious dampened the enthusiasm of 'regular visitors.' The resort was eventually abandoned in the late '50s, and Bowen Island became a sleepy suburb. Recently, though, it has found new life as a weekend-escape destination.

With 260 hectares of parkland and 37km of coastline (good **swimming beaches** are found at Mannion Bay, next to Snug Cove, and Bowen Bay, on the west end of the island), this is a great spot to spend an afternoon, a day or a weekend. The small village of **Snug Cove**, where the ferry docks, has restaurants, bars, shops, B&B accommodations and a marina.

Most of the village straddles Government Rd, which runs straight up from the ferry terminal to a junction where it connects with two main roads – Miller Rd going north and Grafton Rd going southwest. **Visitors' information** is in the chamber of commerce office at the corner of Government and Grafton Rds. This is a pleasant area to wander around for an hour or so, then enjoy a meal or a drink. For more strenuous activity, you can rent a **kayak** from Bowen Island Sea Kayaking (☎ 604-947-9266), on the Bowen Island Marina adjacent to the ferry terminal, which also offers rentals, lessons and a variety of tours.

For walkers and hikers, **Crippen Regional Park** has several trails, from the easy 4km Killarney Lake Loop Trail to the more difficult 10km Mt Gardner Trail, which climbs 719m to the island's highest point. Or, take the 45-minute walk from Snug Cove to the picnic area at Killarney Lake, a habitat for birds which once served as the island's main source of water. Many of these hiking trails are also accessible to cyclists and horseback riders.

Places to Stay

If you want to stay here, there are quite a few B&Bs to choose from; the visitors' information office can provide you with a complete list. The accommodations listed here will give you somewhere to start. There are no camping or RV facilities on Bowen Island.

Right in Snug Cove, attached to Doc Morgan's Inn, is the *Union Steamship Marina & Historical Cottages* (☎ 604-947-0707), which has two cabins for $85 and a summer house for $125. Just north of the village off Miller Rd, *The Lodge at the Old Dorm* (☎ 604-947-0947), 460 Melmore Rd, was once the staff residence of the Union Steamship hotel and is a heritage building.

There are five rooms starting in price from $70 singles or doubles.

About a 15-minute walk directly south of Snug Cove and right on the water is *A Bit of Heaven B&B* (☎ 604-947-2242), 865 Hummingbird Lane, which has two rooms at $65 singles or doubles. Directly west of the village off Grafton Rd, about 2km from the ferry terminal, *The Vineyard* (☎ 604-947-0028), on Cates Lane, has a swimming pool, hot tub, gas fireplace in every room and a working vineyard. The food here is highly recommended. There are four rooms and two suites with prices starting at $140 singles or doubles.

Places to Eat

There are several places to choose from on this small island when it comes to food. *Doc Morgan's Inn* (☎ 604-947-0707), on the Boardwalk just up from the ferry terminal, is a pub-restaurant that is reminiscent of a seafarer's inn. There are lots of model ships and paraphernalia from the Union Steamship Company, plus there is an outdoor deck. Expect to pay around $17 for most items on the dinner menu, although you can have fish and chips or burgers for under $10. Brunch is also available on the weekends until 2 pm.

The Snug, up Government Rd from the ferry terminal, is a cozy little place serving breakfasts, sandwiches, chili and shepherd's pie all for around $5. Open weekdays from 5 am to 4 pm, and weekends from 7 am to 5 pm.

Also on Government Rd is an interesting place that is actually two restaurants in one, and comes very highly recommended. By day it's called *The Breakfast Cafe*, with most items costing about $6; closed Tuesday and Wednesday. At night it becomes *The Beggar's Purse* (☎ 604-947-0550), serving a set dinner for $30. Open Thursday to Sunday from 6 to 9.30 pm. There is a 'ferry-cam' pointed at the dock which you can watch in the restaurant to know exactly when you have to leave to catch the ferry.

The *Bowen Island Pub* (☎ 604-947-2782), at the top of Government Rd, is where you'll find a large TV screen, a pool table and an outdoor deck looking out to the cove. There

is a standard bar menu with sandwiches and burgers for $7, lasagna or fried chicken for $8 or pizza for $11.

Getting There & Away

BC Ferries operates between Horseshoe Bay and Snug Cove daily from 5.45 am to 9.45 pm. There is a sailing about every hour but call ☎ 604-669-1211 for exact times. The fare for a passenger is $5.75/3 adults/children, and $18.25/9.25/2.25/1.50 for car/motorcycle/kayak/bicycle. However, there is no need to take a car to the island if you are planning on staying around the Snug Cove-Crippen Park area.

A private 12-passenger water taxi operates an additional service daily to 11.30 pm, and on Saturday and Sunday to 12.30 am.

Sunshine Coast

A trip across Howe Sound from Horseshoe Bay in West Vancouver to Gibsons Landing on the Sunshine Coast makes for a great day trip. This trip can be extended into a longer excursion if you want to keep exploring the coastline, forests, inlets, harbors and lakes north along the Sechelt Peninsula and beyond to Powell River. Accommodations options range from good campgrounds to resort hotels complete with restaurants, recreational facilities and marinas.

The Sunshine Coast Hwy (Hwy 101) runs northwest from Langdale to Earls Cove. A ferry crosses Jervis Inlet to Saltery Bay where Hwy 101 continues to Powell River, with its large pulp and paper plant, and comes to an end 23km north at the tiny village of Lund. From Powell River you can take a ferry across Georgia Strait to Comox on Vancouver Island. In fact, BC Ferries offers a Sunshine Coast Circlepac which allows travel on four ferry routes linking the Mainland, the Sunshine Coast and Vancouver Island, taking up to 25% off the standard combined fares.

The region, with its excellent scenery, is relatively quiet compared to some other areas close to the Lower Mainland. Sechelt, 27km north of the BC Ferries Terminal at

Langdale, and Powell River, about 120km north of Langdale, are the commercial and activity centers of the coast. Aside from the good camping, hiking, kayaking, windsurfing, fishing and golf courses in the area, these towns are bases for some spectacular diving, especially between Halfmoon Bay and Egmont. The diving, however, is not for novices and local guides should be used – around Egmont, dive spots include wrecks and a beautiful bronze mermaid.

In **Sechelt,** the Travel InfoCentre (☎ 604-885-0662), in the Trail Bay Centre on Hwy 101, can provide information on accommodations, equipment rental and tours, as can the Travel InfoCentre in **Powell River** (☎ 604-485-4701), 4690 Marine Drive. Along the Sunshine Coast there are 11 regional parks and 13 provincial parks, seven of which are marine parks approachable only by water; these have campsites. From Powell River there is a 65km kayaking/canoeing circuit which takes five to seven days. North of Lund, **Desolation Sound Provincial Marine Park** has abundant wildlife, diving, kayaking and wilderness camping. For more information about the provincial parks in the region, call BC Parks at ☎ 604-898-3678.

GIBSONS LANDING

If you just want to sample the Sunshine Coast for the day, or even overnight, Gibsons Landing (often referred to simply as Gibsons) is a great spot to wander around in the shops, eat in some good restaurants and soak up the fishing-village atmosphere. Gibsons is just 5km from Langdale, which in turn is only a 40-minute ferry ride from Horseshoe Bay.

Gibsons is actually divided into two sections: the landing around Gibsons Harbour, which is the area of most interest to visitors; and the commercial strip farther up the hill along Hwy 101, where there are more motels, restaurants, fast-food outlets, shops and services. Around the harbor the main streets are Marine Drive (Hwy 101); Gower Point Rd, which runs west from Marine Drive; and School Rd, which runs northwest from the intersection of Marine Drive and Gower Point Rd.

The Gibsons Chamber of Commerce has a tourist information desk (☎ 604-886-2325) in the Sunnycrest Mall, just off Hwy 101 along the commercial strip. The post office is located at the corner of Gower Point and Winn Rds.

Things to See & Do

The real charm of this small village is the quaint shopping area along Gower Point Rd and the shoreline around the harbor with its public wharf and marina. You will probably notice the many references to *The Beachcombers*, a popular CBC TV series that was filmed here in the '70s – and you're forgiven for thinking that this was the only thing that has ever happened here. However, the two museums are worth a quick visit, especially if it looks like it's going to rain.

The **Elphinstone Pioneer Museum** (☎ 604-886-8232), 716 Winn Rd, across from the post office, has an eclectic collection, including bottles, period costumes, Native Indian baskets and seashells. On the 2nd floor you'll find old pieces of machinery, furniture and reconstructions of early-20th-century rooms. Perhaps the museum's oddest exhibit is the life-size model of an Inuit hunter spearing a narwhal – strange, considering neither Inuits nor narwhals ever lived anywhere near here. Open May to September daily from 9 am to 5 pm, with reduced hours the rest of the year. Admission is by donation.

The **Sunshine Coast Maritime Museum** (☎ 604-886-4114), Molly's Lane, behind Gower Point Rd (although by the time you read this it could have moved onto a tugboat docked at the marina), is a collection of model ships (of which there are plenty) and other bits and pieces to do with all things nautical. Open daily in the summer from 10 am to 4 pm, and in the winter from 11 am to 3 pm. Admission is free.

For good views of Howe Sound and Georgia Strait, follow the trail and staircase up to the top of **Soames Hill**, about a 20-minute walk. To get to the hill, follow North Rd off Marine Drive, not far from Langdale just southwest of the bypass.

For a swim or a picnic, **Armours Beach**, just northeast of the village below Marine

Drive, is a nice spot, or try **Chaster Park** around the point on Ocean Beach Esplanade (just follow Gower Point Rd).

Places to Stay

There are a few places to stay in Gibsons, including a motel and B&Bs, without your having to go to the commercial strip farther up Hwy 101. The *Days Inn Motor Hotel* (☎ 604-886-3343), 505 Gower Point Rd, is across from the marina at the corner of Dougall St and has rooms at $65/74 for singles/doubles; continental breakfast is included.

Lookout Adventures B&B (☎ 604-886-1655), 318 Shoal Lookout, on Gibsons Bluff at the far end of the village, looks onto the ocean where Howe Sound and Georgia Strait meet, with rooms starting at $75/85 singles/doubles. Also offered here are guided tours – such as hikes, boat rides and scenic drives – and holiday packages.

In the village just two blocks up from Gower Point Rd and off School Rd, *Maritimer B&B* (☎ 604-886-0664), 521 South Fletcher Rd, has a large deck looking down onto the marina and two very large rooms starting at $70/80. Just 1km north of the village toward Langdale and tucked below the road, *Marina House B&B* (☎ 604-886-7888), 546 Marine Drive, has wonderful views of Shoal Channel and has beach access; rooms start at $80/90.

Places to Eat

You'll find a good but small variety of restaurants here. *Molly's Reach* (☎ 604-886-9710), at the intersection of Marine Drive and Gower Point Rd (you can't miss it), has good harbor views and serves sandwiches and burgers ($6), seafood dishes and other main dishes ($14), and also has a children's menu ($6).

Harbour Cafe Oyster Bar & Grill (☎ 604-886-6882), 274 Gower Point Rd, doesn't offer any views, but the food is very good with a large variety of oyster dishes ($10), burgers and sandwiches ($9) and fresh seafood main dishes ($13).

For Tex-Mex selections, try *Howl at the Moon* (☎ 604-886-8881), 450 Marine Drive,

with most main dishes going for about $11, while salmon or steak is closer to $15. *Opa Japanese Restaurant* (☎ 604-886-4023), in Gibsons Quay on Gower Point Rd, has great window seats looking down onto the harbor. Dinner specials start at $11, while the boxed lunch is $8 and the boxed dinner is $14.

Jack's Lane Bistro & Bakery (☎ 604-886-4898), 546 Sunshine Coast Hwy, just up Hwy 101 as you climb out of Gibsons, is a small restaurant with spectacular views. The good food is mostly Mediterranean/Mid-Eastern-influenced, such as pita sandwiches ($6) or the kafta platter ($11). All baked items are made on the premises and the desserts are fabulous.

Getting There & Away

BC Ferries operates between Horseshoe Bay and Langdale daily in summer from 7.20 am to 10.10 pm, with a slightly reduced schedule the rest of the year. There is a sailing about every two hours but call ☎ 888-223-3779 for schedules and information, or ☎ 888-724-5223 for reservations. The peak-season roundtrip fare for a passenger is $8/4 adults/children, and $47.50/27.75/14/4/2.50 for RV/car/motorcycle/kayak/bicycle.

Maverick Coach Lines (☎ 604-662-8051, 255-1171) operates daily service from Pacific Central Station to Powell River. Another option is to take a BC Transit bus from Langdale to Gibsons, or as far as Sechelt. A transit bus leaves Langdale about every two hours in the morning (starting at 6.12 am) and hourly during the afternoon (starting at 12.12 pm) and early evening, with a final bus at 10.05 pm. The one-way fare is $1.50/1 for adults/seniors & students, and free for children under five. Call ☎ 604-885-3234 for information.

Sea to Sky Hwy

From Horseshoe Bay north to Whistler, the Sea to Sky Hwy (Hwy 99) offers a few sites of interest, including the BC Museum of Mining, Shannon Falls, Squamish and some excellent provincial parks.

BC MUSEUM OF MINING

This National Historic Site (☎ 604-896-2233, 688-8735), also a BC historic landmark, is at Britannia Beach about 12km south of Squamish. The once-active Britannia Mines began operation in 1888 and became the largest copper producer in the British Empire in the 1920s. By the time it ceased operation in 1974, it had produced more than 50 million tons of copper ore.

A small train takes visitors into one of the mine's 360m tunnels where demonstrations of the equipment and methods used to extract the ore are given. The huge Concentrator, itself a National Historic Site, is part of the tour, as are the various displays and photographs. A video presents the working and living conditions of the miners and their families. You can take a look at a 235-ton 'super' mine truck, pan for gold and visit the gift shop.

The museum is open to the public for tours mid-May to mid-October, weekdays from 10 am to 4 pm, and pre-booked tours are available the rest of the year. The interpretation center and the gift shop are open year-round. Admission is $9.50/7.50 for adults/seniors & students, and free for children under five.

If you're hungry, have one of the burgers from *Mountain Woman Take Out*, in a bus between the museum and the Britannia Creek General Store. It might just be the best burger you've ever eaten.

SQUAMISH

Located at the end of Howe Sound about halfway between Vancouver and Whistler, Squamish is primarily a forestry town, and the main service center for the area. There are a couple of attractions that make the town worth a stop, especially for outdoor enthusiasts. For information about the town and the region, visit the **Visitor & Business Information Centre** (☎ 604-892-9244), 37950 Cleveland Ave, which is also the station for the *Royal Hudson* steam train and the MV *Britannia* (see the Organized Tours section in the Getting Around chapter for details). Cleveland Ave is the town's main street and runs southwest off Hwy 99.

Just 3km south of Squamish, **Shannon Falls** is one of the highest waterfalls in Canada, with a vertical drop of 335m. There is a picnic area here as well as some hiking trails. In winter, when the falls freeze, climbers pick and pull their way to the top.

For rock climbers, this area is a mecca and the main attraction is the **Stawamus Chief**. Overlooking the town, this huge rock stands 652m high – the rest of it is spread out over some 195,000 hectares from Squamish to Pemberton, making it the second-largest granite monolith in the world (Gibraltar is the largest). The Chief takes its name from an image on the rock that looks like a sleeping Indian chief facing the sky. There are about 200 climbing routes, a trail that takes about three hours to hike and a walk-in campground. Other climbs include Malamute (across from the Chief), the Apron (about 400m north of the Chief) and Smoke Bluffs (overlooking the town). For information, guides or instruction, call Squamish Rock Guides at ☎ 604-892-2086.

One of the best places for windsurfing in Western Canada is the **Squamish Windsurfing Park** in Squamish Harbour at the head of Howe Sound. Winds from the mouth of the Squamish River can push sailboards to speeds of up to 60km/hr (in fact, Squamish is a Coast Salish word meaning 'Mother of the Winds'). For information on the weather and water conditions, call the Squamish Windsurfing Society at ☎ 604-892-2235.

Train buffs will want to visit the **West Coast Railway Heritage Park** (☎ 604-898-9336), Government Rd, west of Hwy 99 in the Squamish Industrial Park, for the 55 vintage railway cars and locomotives. The park is open May to October, daily from 10 am to 5 pm. Admission is $4.50/3.50 for adults/seniors & students, or $12 for a family.

To see the **bald eagles** at Brackendale, on the north side of Squamish, be in the area from late November to about mid-February. If you are around, don't miss it. Attracted by the dead salmon that float downstream after having spawned, as many as 3700 bald eagles live along a 15km stretch of the Squamish River, making this the largest gathering of these majestic birds in the world. There is a

Bring your binoculars for eagle-watching at the Brackendale Eagle Reserve

designated viewing area on the east side of the river, beside Government Rd, which is part of the 550-hectare Brackendale Eagle Reserve. Here you will not only be able to watch the eagles eating salmon on the riverbank or sitting in the trees, but you can read all about them from the information boards in the shelter.

Heading north on Hwy 99, not far from Squamish, outdoor recreation areas include **Garibaldi Provincial Park**, a great area for camping, serious hiking, mountain biking and cross-country skiing (a downhill-ski facility is being planned for this area); and **Alice Lake Provincial Park**, another area for camping, hiking and mountain biking, as well as boating and fishing. Closer to Whistler, you'll find camping and hiking at **Brandywine Falls Provincial Park**.

For information on getting to Squamish by either bus or train, see those sections in the Getting There & Away chapter.

Places to Stay & Eat

The **Squamish Hostel** (☎ 604-892-9240, 800-449-8614), 38490 Buckley Ave, with a fully equipped kitchen, has shared rooms for $15 ($40 for three nights) and private rooms for $25. The **Garibaldi Budget Motor Inn** (☎ 604-892-5204), 38012 3rd Ave, has basic rooms starting at $44. At the **Chieftain Hotel** (☎ 604-892-9119), 38005 Cleveland Ave, rooms start at $45/47 for singles/doubles, and **Baz's Grill** restaurant is here,

too. Or try **August Jack Motor Inn** (☎ 604-892-3504), 37947 Cleveland Ave, with rooms for $60/65.

A bit more upscale, the **Howe Sound Inn & Brewing Company** (☎ 604-892-2603), 37801 Cleveland Ave, has small rooms for $105 singles or doubles. The in-house restaurant, **The Red Heather Grill**, serves a good selection of food, including burgers ($7), pasta ($11), seafood hot pot ($17) and medallions of peppered venison ($19). The real highlight here is the comfortable brewpub, where you can enjoy one of the bar's nine varieties of beer while watching the climbers scale the Chief. There is also a good selection of Scotch.

Ocean's Cafe (☎ 604-892-5937), 37991 2nd Ave, has fish and chips ($8), steamed mussels ($7) and ribs ($12). The **Sunrise Japanese Restaurant** (☎ 604-898-2533), 40022 Government Rd, offers sashimi and noodle dishes for $7 and dinner combinations for $13. Also worth trying is the **Brackendale Art Gallery** (☎ 604-898-3333), on Government Rd, for the homemade soups, croissants and pastries. Owner Thor Froslev can give you information about the bald eagles.

Whistler

The world-class ski resort of Whistler, 120km north of Vancouver, is the destination for many people who travel the Sea to Sky Hwy, especially in winter. Since the late '70s, when it was a single ski hill with just a few facilities geared for local skiers, Whistler-Blackcomb has become a bustling village with two hills geared to an international market, and prices to match.

During the summer, this area, with its many lakes and rivers, also offers a large number of activities for outdoor enthusiasts such as camping, hiking, mountain biking, swimming, kayaking and fishing; Whistler's Gondola and Blackcomb's Express quad chairs stay open to make mountain-top walks and hikes more accessible. There are also seven golf courses in the area, some of which are of championship caliber.

In Whistler, hotels, restaurants, shops and services are open year-round. In the non-skiing season there are several festivals, including the Whistler Classical Music Festival in August (during which the Vancouver Symphony Orchestra gives a mountain-top performance), and the Whistler Fork Festival & Cheakamus Challenge in September, which includes a grueling bike race up and down the mountain.

Essentially, Whistler is divided into four main areas: Whistler Creekside, Whistler Village, Village North and Upper Village. Whistler Creekside, the original Whistler base, is the first area you will come to either by road on Hwy 99 as you approach from the south, or by train; this is where the BC Rail Station is located. Either way, this is a good place to stop to get maps and information from the chamber of commerce **visitor information** office (☎ 604-932-5528). You will also find some restaurants and services, a laundromat, and access to Alpha and Nita Lakes.

From Mountain High to Olympic Gold

Ross Rebagliati is the winner of Canada's first gold medal of the 1998 Winter Olympics, the winner of the first gold medal in the new Olympic sport of snowboarding and the first Canadian to nearly lose a medal for testing positive for marijuana.

Only 24 hours after speeding down the giant slalom course at Nagano and becoming a hero, the snowboarder from Whistler was living with the threat of having his medal taken away. A urine sample taken from the athlete the previous December showed marijuana concentrations of 90 to 120 nanograms per milliliter, which Rebagliati claimed was a product of secondhand smoke inhaled at a party. Be that as it may, marijuana is not a banned substance in snowboarding (banned substances vary from sport to sport).

The controversy lasted about three days before the 26-year-old was reinstated as the official gold-medal winner and became the single biggest thing ever to happen to Whistler. It wasn't long before he had signed a deal with IMG, the large international sports marketing firm that represents such high-profile athletes as Andre Agassi, Tiger Woods and Wayne Gretzky; Rebagliati stands to make millions of dollars through endorsements and corporate sponsorships.

And the marijuana controversy hasn't hurt Rebagliati in the least. It may have been a blessing in disguise, bringing him international attention that otherwise would have all but disappeared at the end of the Olympics. He appeared as a guest on *The Tonight Show* on US television where host Jay Leno jokingly referred to him as 'Nickelbag-liati,' and a Whistler park and a Blackcomb black-diamond run, 'Ross's Gold,' were named in his honor.

There are two things that in a sense complement the Rebagliati story – marijuana has long been a part of the snowboard culture's 'outlaw' image (there is even a snowboard magazine called *Blunt* which is slang for a rolled cigarette or joint), while BC has developed its own high-quality marijuana which has gained an international reputation for its potency and is estimated to be a billion-dollar industry.

The other three areas are about 4km up the highway past Alta Lake and sort of blur into one large village. If you are driving, turn east (right) onto Village Gate Blvd, which divides Whistler Village (the base of Whistler Mountain) and Village North, and follow it to the end. You'll find large parking areas on the other side of Blackcomb Way, which divides the other two areas from Upper Village (the base of Blackcomb Mountain).

This entire area is very spread out, with hotels, restaurants, pubs and shops everywhere, but a good place to start is Whistler Village, south of Village Gate Blvd and west of Blackcomb Way. This has the greatest concentration of facilities, plus the Whistler Activity & Information Centre (☎ 604-932-2394) and the central reservations desk in the Whistler Conference Centre, just west of the Village Square on Golfers Approach.

The post office is in Village North near the corner of Blackcomb Way and Lorimer Rd.

For information on transportation to and from Whistler by bus and train, or for organized tours to Whistler, see the Getting There & Away chapter. BC Transit operates bus service around the Whistler area for $1.50, as well as a free shuttle service between Whistler Village, Village North and Upper Village. The buses are equipped with outside ski racks and bicycle racks; call ☎ 604-932-4020 for information. Whistler Taxi is at ☎ 604-938-3333.

SKIING & SNOWBOARDING

Whistler and Blackcomb have the greatest vertical drop – 1530m and 1609m, respectively – and together are the largest ski and snowboarding area in North America. There are 200 marked trails over an area of 2800 hectares that take in three glaciers and 12 alpine bowls.

To get to all this territory, there are 12 high-speed lifts and 31 other lifts, making this the most extensive high-speed lift system in the world. The season runs from the end of November to the end of April, although on Blackcomb you can ski and snowboard Horstman Glacier through the beginning of August. There are rentals and instruction available for whatever it is you want to do. A downhill day pass is $55/47/27 for adults/seniors (over 65) & youth (13 to 18)/children (seven to 12).

For cross-country skiing, there are more than 28km of trails through Lost Lake Park and the valley. Other winter activities include heli-skiing, snowshoeing, skating, snowmobiling and sleigh rides.

PLACES TO STAY

There are a great number of places to stay in Whistler, but few of them are cheap, and in the winter you'll be lucky to get a room at all on the weekend if you haven't booked well in advance. You won't get a room much under $100 a night, and the average is closer to $150, especially if you want to be in the heart of things. Prices can go up to $350 a night at places like the luxurious *Pan Pacific Lodge* (☎ 604-905-2999, 888-905-9995) on Sundial Crescent in Whistler Village. To make general accommodations reservations, call ☎ 604-664-5625, or 800-944-7853 throughout North America.

For budget accommodations there are a few options. HI *Whistler Hostel* (☎ 604-932-5492), is in a beautiful setting on Alta Lake (West) Rd about 4km from Whistler Village. It costs $18 in summer and $20 in winter for members and a few dollars more for non-members. The office is open from 7 to 11 am and from 5 to 11 pm. The hostel has room for just 32 people, so it's a good idea to book ahead, especially during ski season. The BC Rail train will stop at the hostel upon request (the rail line follows the west side of Alta Lake).

Two places to try, but be sure to call first to make a reservation, are the *Fireside Lodge* (☎ 604-932-4545), 2117 Nordic Drive, with dormitory beds starting at $25, and the *UBC Lodge* (☎ 604-932-6604, 822-5851 in Vancouver), 2124 Nordic Drive, with dormitory accommodations from $13 to $23; both of these places are in Nordic Estates off Hwy 99 between Whistler Creekside and Whistler Village. The *Shoestring Lodge* (☎ 604-932-3338), at 7124 Nancy Greene Drive, in the Boot Pub, has basic doubles from $95.

PLACES TO EAT

The following is just a selection of some of the places you can try for a meal or to have a drink and maybe listen to some music. *La Brasserie des Artistes* (☎ 604-932-3569), near the Village Square in Whistler Village, is a small cafe/bar good for all-day breakfasts, lunch or dinner (burgers and pastas are $10), or just to have a beer.

Ingrid's Village Cafe (☎ 604-932-7000), just off the Village Square, is a great place for breakfast or lunch, and the prices are a steal: a large bowl of seafood chowder with bread is $4, sandwiches are $4.50 and the several varieties of vegetarian burgers are $5. Open daily from 7.30 am to 6 pm.

Moe's Deli & Bar (☎ 604-905-3167), on Main St in Village North, is in the large Delta Whistler Village Suites and has a bar on one side, a deli counter in the middle and a restaurant on the other side. The smoked meat is brought in from Montreal and a standard sandwich is $6, and there are other items such as fajitas ($12) and stir-fries ($13). The *Brewhouse* (☎ 604-905-2739), Blackcomb Way in Village North, is operated by Vancouver's Yaletown Brewing Company and produces some good beer of its own – try the Lifty Lager or the Big Wolf Bitter. The food is worthwhile, too, with pizza ($13), stir-fries ($16) and beef ribs ($23).

Black's (☎ 604-932-6945), on Mountain Square, close to the lifts in Whistler Village, has a great little bar upstairs with a good selection of local and imported beer and an even better selection of whiskies (if you've got $14 to spend on a drink, try the Glenlochy). The family restaurant downstairs is open all day.

Lonely Planet On-line
www.lonelyplanet.com *or* AOL keyword: lp

Whether you've just begun planning your next trip, or you're chasing down specific info on currency regulations or visa requirements, check out Lonely Planet On-line for up-to-the minute travel information.

As well as mini guides to more than 250 destinations, you'll find maps, photos, travel news, health and visa updates, travel advisories, and discussion of the ecological and political issues you need to be aware of as you travel. You'll also find timely upgrades to popular guidebooks which you can print out and stick in the back of your book.

There's also an on-line travellers' forum where you can share your experience of life on the road, meet travel companions and ask other travellers for their recommendations and advice.

And of course we have a complete and up-to-date list of all Lonely Planet travel products including travel guides, diving and snorkeling guides, phrasebooks, atlases, travel literature and videos, and a simple on-line ordering facility if you can't find the book you want elsewhere.

Lonely Planet Diving & Snorkeling Guides

Known for indispensible guidebooks to destinations all over the world, Lonely Planet's Pisces Books are the most popular series of diving and snorkeling titles available.

There are three series: **Diving & Snorkeling Guides**, **Shipwreck Diving** series and **Dive Into History**. Full colour throughout, the **Diving & Snorkeling Guides** combine quality photographs with detailed descriptions of the best dive sites for each location, giving divers a glimpse of what they can expect both on land and in water. The **Dive Into History** series is perfect for the adventure diver or armchair traveller. The **Shipwreck Diving** series provides all the details for exploring the most interesting wrecks in the Atlantic and Pacific oceans. The list also includes underwater nature and technical guides.

LONELY PLANET

Guides by Region

L onely Planet is known worldwide for publishing practical, reliable and no-nonsense travel information in our guides and on our Web site. The Lonely Planet list covers just about every accessible part of the world. Currently there are nine series: travel guides, shoestring guides, walking guides, city guides, phrasebooks, audio packs, travel atlases, diving and snorkeling guides and travel literature.

AFRICA Africa – the South ● Africa on a shoestring ● Arabic (Egyptian) phrasebook ● Arabic (Moroccan) phrasebook ● Cairo ● Cape Town ● Central Africa ● East Africa ● Egypt ● Egypt travel atlas ● Ethiopian (Amharic) phrasebook ● The Gambia & Senegal ● Kenya ● Kenya travel atlas ● Malawi, Mozambique & Zambia ● Morocco ● North Africa ● South Africa, Lesotho & Swaziland ● South Africa, Lesotho & Swaziland travel atlas ● Swahili phrasebook ● Trekking in East Africa ● Tunisia ● West Africa ● Zimbabwe, Botswana & Namibia ● Zimbabwe, Botswana & Namibia travel atlas
Travel Literature: The Rainbird: A Central African Journey ● Songs to an African Sunset: A Zimbabwean Story ● Mali Blues: Traveling to an African Beat

AUSTRALIA & THE PACIFIC Australia ● Australian phrasebook ● Bushwalking in Australia ● Bushwalking in Papua New Guinea ● Fiji ● Fijian phrasebook ● Islands of Australia's Great Barrier Reef ● Melbourne ● Micronesia ● New Caledonia ● New South Wales & the ACT ● New Zealand ● Northern Territory ● Outback Australia ● Papua New Guinea ● Papua New Guinea (Pidgin) phrasebook ● Queensland ● Rarotonga & the Cook Islands ● Samoa ● Solomon Islands ● South Australia ● Sydney ● Tahiti & French Polynesia ● Tasmania ● Tonga ● Tramping in New Zealand ● Vanuatu ● Victoria ● Western Australia
Travel Literature: Islands in the Clouds ● Sean & David's Long Drive

CENTRAL AMERICA & THE CARIBBEAN Bahamas and Turks & Caicos ● Bermuda ● Central America on a shoestring ● Costa Rica ● Cuba ● Eastern Caribbean ● Guatemala, Belize & Yucatán: La Ruta Maya ● Jamaica ● Mexico ● Mexico City ● Panama
Travel Literature: Green Dreams: Travels in Central America

EUROPE Amsterdam ● Andalucía ● Austria ● Baltic States phrasebook ● Berlin ● Britain ● Central Europe ● Central Europe phrasebook ● Czech & Slovak Republics ● Denmark ● Dublin ● Eastern Europe ● Eastern Europe phrasebook ● Edinburgh ● Estonia, Latvia & Lithuania ● Europe ● Finland ● France ● French phrasebook ● Germany ● German phrasebook ● Greece ● Greek phrasebook ● Hungary ● Iceland, Greenland & the Faroe Islands ● Ireland ● Italian phrasebook ● Italy ● Lisbon ● London ● Mediterranean Europe ● Mediterranean Europe phrasebook ● Paris ● Poland ● Portugal ● Portugal travel atlas ● Prague ● Romania & Moldova ● Russia, Ukraine & Belarus ● Russian phrasebook ● Scandinavian & Baltic Europe ● Scandinavian Europe phrasebook ● Scotland ● Slovenia ● Spain ● Spanish phrasebook ● St Petersburg ● Switzerland ● Trekking in Spain ● Ukrainian phrasebook ● Vienna ● Walking in Britain ● Walking in Italy ● Walking in Switzerland ● Western Europe ● Western Europe phrasebook
Travel Literature: The Olive Grove: Travels in Greece

INDIAN SUBCONTINENT Bangladesh ● Bengali phrasebook ● Bhutan ● Delhi ● Goa ● Hindi/Urdu phrasebook ● India ● India & Bangladesh travel atlas ● Indian Himalaya ● Karakoram Highway ● Nepal ● Nepali phrasebook ● Pakistan ● Rajasthan ● South India ● Sri Lanka ● Sri Lanka phrasebook ● Trekking in the Indian Himalaya ● Trekking in the Karakoram & Hindukush ● Trekking in the Nepal Himalaya
Travel Literature: In Rajasthan ● Shopping for Buddhas

LONELY PLANET

Mail Order

Lonely Planet products are distributed worldwide.They are also available by mail order from Lonely Planet, so if you have difficulty finding a title please write to us. North and South American residents should write to 150 Linden St, Oakland, CA 94607, USA; European and African residents should write to 10a Spring Place, London NW5 3BH, UK; and residents of other countries to PO Box 617, Hawthorn, Victoria 3122, Australia.

ISLANDS OF THE INDIAN OCEAN Madagascar & Comoros ● Maldives ● Mauritius, Réunion & Seychelles

MIDDLE EAST & CENTRAL ASIA Arab Gulf States ● Central Asia ● Central Asia phrasebook ● Iran ● Israel & the Palestinian Territories ● Israel & the Palestinian Territories travel atlas ● Istanbul ● Jerusalem ● Jordan & Syria ● Jordan, Syria & Lebanon travel atlas ● Lebanon ● Middle East on a shoestring ● Turkey ● Turkish phrasebook ● Turkey travel atlas ● Yemen
Travel Literature: The Gates of Damascus ● Kingdom of the Film Stars: Journey into Jordan

NORTH AMERICA Alaska ● Backpacking in Alaska ● Baja California ● California & Nevada ● Canada ● Florida ● Hawaii ● Honolulu ● Los Angeles ● Miami ● New England USA ● New Orleans ● New York City ● New York, New Jersey & Pennsylvania ● Pacific Northwest USA ● Rocky Mountain States ● San Francisco ● Seattle ● Southwest USA ● USA phrasebook ● Vancouver ● Washington, DC & the Capital Region
Travel Literature: Drive Thru America

NORTH-EAST ASIA Beijing ● Cantonese phrasebook ● China ● Hong Kong ● Hong Kong, Macau & Guangzhou ● Japan ● Japanese phrasebook ● Japanese audio pack ● Korea ● Korean phrasebook ● Kyoto ● Mandarin phrasebook ● Mongolia ● Mongolian phrasebook ● North-East Asia on a shoestring ● Seoul ● South-West China ● Taiwan ● Tibet ● Tibetan phrasebook ● Tokyo
Travel Literature: Lost Japan

SOUTH AMERICA Argentina, Uruguay & Paraguay ● Bolivia ● Brazil ● Brazilian phrasebook ● Buenos Aires ● Chile & Easter Island ● Chile & Easter Island travel atlas ● Colombia ● Ecuador & the Galapagos Islands ● Latin American Spanish phrasebook ● Peru ● Quechua phrasebook ● Rio de Janeiro ● South America on a shoestring ● Trekking in the Patagonian Andes ● Venezuela
Travel Literature: Full Circle: A South American Journey

SOUTH-EAST ASIA Bali & Lombok ● Bangkok ● Burmese phrasebook ● Cambodia ● Hill Tribes phrasebook ● Ho Chi Minh City ● Indonesia ● Indonesian phrasebook ● Indonesian audio pack ● Jakarta ● Java ● Laos ● Lao phrasebook ● Laos travel atlas ● Malay phrasebook ● Malaysia, Singapore & Brunei ● Myanmar (Burma) ● Philippines ● Pilipino (Tagalog) phrasebook ● Singapore ● South-East Asia on a shoestring ● South-East Asia phrasebook ● Thailand ● Thailand's Islands & Beaches ● Thailand travel atlas ● Thai phrasebook ● Thai audio pack ● Vietnam ● Vietnamese phrasebook ● Vietnam travel atlas

ALSO AVAILABLE: Antarctica ● Brief Encounters: Stories of Love, Sex & Travel ● Chasing Rickshaws ● Not the Only Planet: Travel Stories from Science Fiction ● Travel with Children ● Traveller's Tales

FREE Lonely Planet Newsletters

We love hearing from you and think you'd like to hear from us.

Planet Talk

Our FREE quarterly printed newsletter is full of tips from travellers and anecdotes from Lonely Planet guidebook authors. Every issue is packed with up-to-date travel news and advice, and includes:

- a postcard from Lonely Planet co-founder Tony Wheeler
- a swag of mail from travellers
- a look at life on the road through the eyes of a Lonely Planet author
- topical health advice
- prizes for the best travel yarn
- news about forthcoming Lonely Planet events
- a complete list of Lonely Planet books and other titles

To join our mailing list, residents of the UK, Europe and Africa can email us at go@lonelyplanet.co.uk; residents of North and South America can email us at info@lonelyplanet.com; the rest of the world can email us at talk2us@lonelyplanet.com.au, or contact any Lonely Planet office.

Comet

Our FREE monthly email newsletter brings you all the latest travel news, features, interviews, competitions, destination ideas, travellers' tips & tales, Q&As, raging debates and related links. Find out what's new on the Lonely Planet Web site and which books are about to hit the shelves.

Subscribe from your desktop: www.lonelyplanet.com/comet

Index

Text

A

accommodations 127-138
  B&Bs 127, 131, 134-135, 137
  camping 127
  Downtown 128, 129-130, 131-133, 134, 135-137
  East Vancouver 127, 129, 130-131, 133
  hostels 128-129
  North Shore 129, 131, 133-134, 135, 137
  North Vancouver 127
  Richmond/Airport 134, 137
  South Vancouver 127
  student accommodations 129
  West Side 128-129, 130, 131, 133, 134-135, 137
activities 122-126
Adams, Bryan 26
air tours 84
air travel 60-68, 76
  airlines 61
  airport 60, 76
  arriving in Canada 66
  baggage 65-66
  buying tickets 61-65
  Circle Pacific Tickets 64-65
  departure taxes 60-61
  leaving Canada 66
  round-the-world tickets 64
  to/from abroad 67-68
  to/from Victoria 66
  travelers with special needs 65
  within Canada 66
Ambleside 118
Ambleside Park 118
Angel of Victory 88

Aquabus 80
art galleries. See galleries
Art Gallery 112
Art Gallery of Greater Victoria 182
arts 23-29, 60
  public art 45

B

Baden-Powell Trail 124
bald eagles 202-203
Bannister, Roger 15
Barclay Heritage Square 98-99
Barnet Marine Park 111
bars & pubs 155-158. See also individual neighborhoods
baseball 163
basketball 163
BC Lions 161, 163-165
BC Museum of Mining 202
BC Place Stadium 89, 92
BC Sports Hall of Fame & Museum 89, 92
BC Transit 76-78
Beacon Hill Park 179
bicycling 80-81, 122
  rental 81
Birks clock 88
Bloedel Conservatory 108-109
boat tours 82-83
boating 122-123
books 42-44. See also literature
Bowen Island 197-199
brewpubs 156-157. See also bars & pubs
British Columbia Golf House Museum 105
British Empire Games 15
Buddhist Temple 120

Burnaby 110-112
Burnaby Art Gallery 111
Burnaby Heritage Village 111
Burnaby Lake Regional Park 111
Burnaby Mountain Park 111
bus tours 82
bus travel 69
  Canada Pass 69
business hours 54
business services 57-58
Butchart Gardens 183, 189
Byrnes Block 95

C

campuses 52
Canada Place 91-92
Canadian Craft Museum 86, 91
Canadian Football League 164
Canadian Pacific Railway 13, 88, 93, 96, 102
Capilano Indian Reserve 102
Capilano River Regional Park 116
Capilano Salmon Hatchery 116
Capilano Suspension Bridge 115-116
car travel 70-72, 78-79
  driveaways 72
  driving permit 35
  parking 78
  rental 79
Carr House 182. See also Carr, Emily
Carr, Emily 27, 89-91, 182
casinos 155
Cates Park 117-118
Cathedral Place 86
Central Park 111
Chief Khahtsahlanough 102
children's activities 51

Bold indicates maps.

Boxed Text

Vancouver Map Section

JOHN ELK

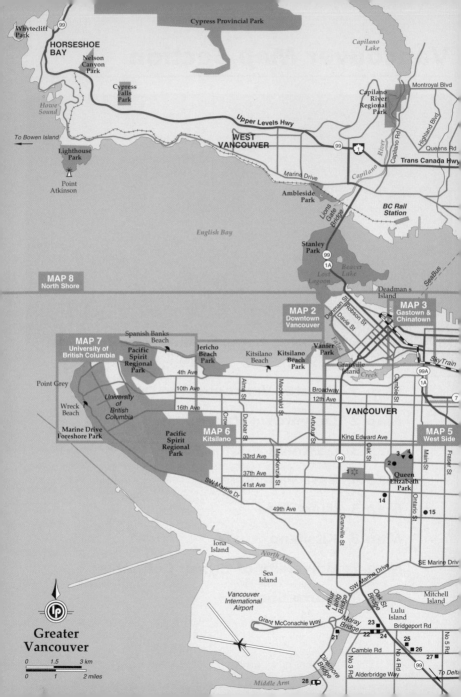

MAP 1

PLACES TO STAY

5 Kingsway Lodge Motel
6 Eldorado Motor Hotel
7 2400 Motel
8 Quality Inn Metrotown
10 Western Kings Inn
13 Burnaby Cariboo RV Park
16 Treehouse B&B
21 Delta Vancouver Airport
Hotel & Marina
22 Howard Johnson
23 Holiday Inn Express
24 Abercorn Inn
25 Delta Pacific Resort
26 Stay 'n Save Inn
27 Holiday Inn Airport
28 Richmond RV Park

PLACES TO EAT

3 Seasons in the Park

OTHER

1 VanDusen
Botanical Garden
2 Bloedel Conservatory
4 Nat Bailey Stadium
9 Swanguard Stadium
11 Burnaby Heritage Village
12 Burnaby Art Gallery
14 Oakridge Centre
15 Punjabi Market
17 Sikh Temple
18 Westminster Quay Public
Market & Esplanade
19 Travel InfoCentre
20 Irving House
Historic Centre

Lynn Headwaters
Regional Park

Dempsey Rd

Lynn Canyon
Park

29th St

Lonsdale Ave

Keith Rd

Grand Blvd

Lynn Valley Rd

Mountain Hwy

NORTH VANCOUVER

Mt Seymour Rd

Mt Seymour
Provincial
Park

Mt Seymour Pkwy

Deep Cove Rd

Deep Cove

Sasamat Lake

Dollarton Hwy

Second Narrows Bridge

Cates Park

Belcarra Regional Park

Burrard Inlet

Berry Point

Burrard Inlet

Barnet Marine Park

Barnet Rd

Hastings Park

Hastings St

Confederation Park

Inlet Drive

Burnaby Mountain Park

7A

Venables St

Clark Dr

Nanaimo St

Renfrew St

Boundary Rd

Parker St

Willingdon Ave

7A

Spering Ave

Curtis St

Simon Fraser University

Gaglardi Way

Clarke Rd

Blue Mountain St

BURNABY

MAP 4
East Vancouver

Rupert St

Canada Way

1

Lougheed Hwy

Burnaby Lake

7

Burnaby Lake Regional Park

13

Knight St

Kingsway

29th Ave

Joyce St

Moscrop St

Deer Lake Pkwy

Trans Canada Hwy

5

Victoria Drive

6

7

99A

1A

SkyTrain

Forest Glen Park

Royal Oak Ave

Deer Lake

11

12

Deer Lake Park

8

Central Park

Kerr St

Kingsway

Metrotown

Imperial St

10

Canada Way

10th Ave

6th St

8th St

McBride Blvd

Columbia St

16

Rumble St

99A

1A

19th St

Queen's Park

Royal Ave

Pattullo Bridge

99A

1A

17

Knight St Bridge

Marine Way

NEW WESTMINSTER

20

18

19

RICHMOND

North Arm

Fraser River

Queensborough Bridge

Fraser River

SURREY

Richmond Fwy

91

91A

Annacis Island

see Stanley Park map
between pages 96 and 97

Lost
Lagoon

Deadman's
Island

Coal Harbour

Stanley
Park

English Bay
Beach

English
Bay

Coal Harbour Rd

Pender St

WEST END

Barclay
Heritage
Square

Sunset Beach
Park

Vanier
Park

False Creek

Sunset Beach

Robson
Square

Burrard Bridge

Granville
Island

Granville
Bridge

to MAP 5
West Side

MAP 2

Burrard   Inlet

Downtown
Vancouver

0   150   300 m
0   150   300 yards

SkyBus to North Vancouver

Canada
Place
84
83

82

85

Hastings St
86
Sky Train

Waterfront Rd

87

(7A)

Sinclair
Centre

Waterfront

94

Waterfront
Station

93

Cordova St

95

Harbour
Centre

107

Water St

111

108

89

92

90

Granville St

91

100

103

105

104

106

116

118

117

115

114

119

109

110

120

121

122

GASTOWN

Powell St

Cordova St

Hastings St

97

98

99

101

102

Howe St

112

113

Pacific
Centre

Granville

CITY
CENTER

124

123

Seymour St

Dunsmuir St

Sky Train

125

see MAP 3
Gastown &
Chinatown

(7A)

127

CHINATOWN

Pender St

186

187

35

188

189

100

Georgia St

126

M Stadium

194

197

193

196

Robson St

Library
Square

192

Vancouver
Public Library

Smithe St

198

Hamilton St

199

202

201

200

99A
1A

GM
Place

Dunsmuir Viaduct

Quebec St

Main St

Station St

Pacific
Central
Station

203

05

204

Mainland St

Cambie St

Beatty St

Terry Fox
Plaza

Georgia Viaduct

206

208

209

ALETOWN

210

207

BC Place
Stadium

11

212

213

214

216

Pacific Blvd N

Pacific Blvd S

Sky Train

Science
World-
Main St

Thornton
Park

215

Cambie
Bridge

False Creek

99A
1A

DOWNTOWN VANCOUVER MAP KEY

PLACES TO STAY

PLACES TO EAT

Canada Place

DOWNTOWN VANCOUVER MAP KEY

206 Hamilton Street Grill
208 Century Grill
209 Deniro's Bistro
210 Tradewinds Cafe
211 Yaletown Brewing Company
213 Mangiamo

BARS, PUBS & CLUBS
21 Dover Arms Pub
23 Denman Station Cabaret
74 Mahoneys Sports Grill
76 Uforia
92 Club Millennium
99 Chameleon Urban Lounge,
   Georgia St Bar & Grill
104 Railway Club
105 Piccadilly Pub
106 Malone's Bar & Grill
141 Numbers Cabaret
142 Celebrities
148 Roxy
153 Royal Hotel
154 Fred's Tavern
167 The Gate
176 Yale
178 DV8
189 Rose & Thorne
193 Vogue Theatre
202 Shark Club Bar & Grill
205 Starfish Room

OTHER
1 Harbour Cruises
7 Spokes Bicycle Rental
   & Espresso Bar
11 Action Rentals
13 Alley Cat Bike Rentals
14 Stanley Park Cycle
29 Care Point Medical Centre
31 Denman Place Discount Cinema
38 Inukshuk (statue)
40 Roedde House

43 Buschlen/Mowatt Fine Arts
61 HMV
62 International Securities Exchange
68 Sport Mart
69 Comor Wintersport
70 Manhattan Books & Magazines
72 Thomas Cook
75 Virgin Megastore
77 Duthie Books
81 Court House
84 CN IMAX Theatre
85 Marine Building, Arctic Canada
86 Vancouver Travel InfoCentre,
   Waterfront Centre
88 Royal Centre
90 Christ Church Cathedral
91 American Express
93 Marion Scott Gallery
94 Pacific Theatre
95 Angel of Victory (statue)
97 Hongkong Bank,
   Pendulum (statue)
98 Cathedral Place,
   Canadian Craft Museum
100 Tall Girl
101 Rendez-Vous Gallery
102 Keith Alexander Gallery
107 Birks Clock
108 Harbour Centre Tower,
   The Lookout
109 Repp Ltd Big & Tall
110 Madison's
111 Payless Communications
112 Vancouver Art Gallery
115 Sam the Record Man
116 A&B Sound
117 World Wide Books and Maps
118 Odyssey Imports
119 MacLeod's Books
120 Sikora's Classical Records
121 Antiquarius
122 Woodward's Department Store

123 Vancouver Centre (cinema)
124 Duthie Books
126 Sun Tower
127 Carnegie Reading Room
128 Little Sister's Book
   & Art Emporium
131 Money Mart
132 Book Warehouse
137 BC Internet Coffee
139 Stone Table Coffee House
143 Davie Laundromat
144 St Paul's Hospital
146 Caprice (cinema)
147 Paradise Theatre
155 Babalu
157 Odyssey
158 Pacific Cinematheque
160 Sugar Refinery
162 Stone Temple Cabaret
163 Vancouver Aquatic Centre
177 Luv-A-Fair
180 MaRS
181 Palladium Club
185 Granville 7 Cinemas
187 True Value Vintage Clothing
188 Capitol 6 (cinema)
190 Looking Glass Theatre
191 Post Office (main)
192 Queen Elizabeth Theatre,
   Playhouse
194 Orpheum Theatre
196 Ford Centre for the
   Performing Arts
203 Richard's on Richards
204 ArtWorks
207 BC Sports Hall of Fame
   & Museum
212 Coastal Peoples Fine Arts Gallery
214 Barbara-Jo's Books to Cooks
215 Roundhouse Community Centre
216 The Rage, Yuk Yuk's

DOUG PLUMMER

The lobby of the Hotel Vancouver

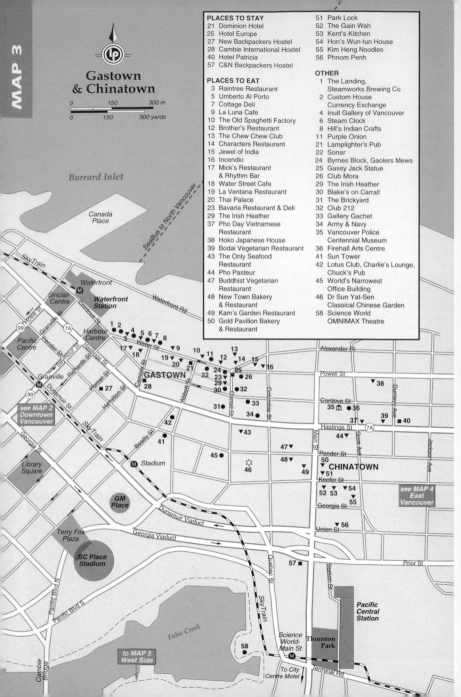

MAP 3

Gastown & Chinatown

0   150   300 m

0   150   300 yards

PLACES TO STAY
21 Dominion Hotel
25 Hotel Europe
27 New Backpackers Hostel
28 Cambie International Hostel
40 Hotel Patricia
57 C&N Backpackers Hostel

PLACES TO EAT
3 Raintree Restaurant
5 Umberto Al Porto
7 Cottage Deli
9 La Luna Cafe
10 The Old Spaghetti Factory
12 Brother's Restaurant
13 The Chew Chew Club
14 Characters Restaurant
15 Jewel of India
16 Incendio
17 Mick's Restaurant
   & Rhythm Bar
18 Water Street Cafe
19 La Ventana Restaurant
20 Thai Palace
23 Bavaria Restaurant & Deli
29 The Irish Heather
37 Pho Day Vietnamese
   Restaurant
38 Hoko Japanese House
39 Bodai Vegetarian Restaurant
43 The Only Seafood
   Restaurant
44 Pho Pasteur
47 Buddhist Vegetarian
   Restaurant
48 New Town Bakery
   & Restaurant
49 Kam's Garden Restaurant
50 Gold Pavilion Bakery
   & Restaurant

51 Park Lock
52 The Gain Wah
53 Kent's Kitchen
54 Hon's Wun-tun House
55 Kim Heng Noodles
56 Phnom Penh

OTHER
1 The Landing,
  Steamworks Brewing Co
2 Custom House
  Currency Exchange
4 Inuit Gallery of Vancouver
6 Steam Clock
8 Hill's Indian Crafts
11 Purple Onion
21 Lamplighter's Pub
22 Sonar
24 Byrnes Block, Gaolers Mews
25 Gassy Jack Statue
26 Club Mora
29 The Irish Heather
30 Blake's on Carrall
31 The Brickyard
32 Club 212
33 Gallery Gachet
34 Army & Navy
35 Vancouver Police
   Centennial Museum
36 Firehall Arts Centre
41 Sun Tower
42 Lotus Club, Charlie's Lounge,
   Chuck's Pub
45 World's Narrowest
   Office Building
46 Dr Sun Yat-Sen
   Classical Chinese Garden
58 Science World
   OMNIMAX Theatre

Gastown

Chinatown

Burrard Inlet

Powell St

Cordova St

Hastings St (7A)

see MAP 3
Gastown &
Chinatown

Dunlevy Ave

Gore Ave

Jackson Ave

Princess Ave

Heatley Ave

Campbell Ave

Pender St

Keefer St

Raymur Ave

MacLean Park

Union St

Prior St

Hawks Ave

Malkin Ave

Strathcona Park

Station St

Pacific Central Station

SkyTrain

see MAP 5
West Side

Terminal Ave

● 19

Glen Drive

Vernon Drive

Clark Drive

Vernon Drive

Odlum Drive

McLean Drive

Woodland Drive

Cotton Drive

Franklin St

3 ■

Hastings St

Pender St

Frances St

Georgia St

Woodland Park

Venables St

Parker St

Napier St

William St

Grandview Park

Charles St

Kitchener St

Grant St

Graveley St

Il Mercato Mall

1st Ave

2nd Ave

3rd Ave

4th Ave

5th Ave

6th Ave

7th Ave

Commercial Drive

McLean Drive

Woodland Drive

Salsbury Drive

2

6 ▼
7 ●

10 ▼

11 ▼

● 12

▼ 13

14 ▼
15 ●
16 ●
▼ 17
▼ 18

20 ▼

21 ✛

24 ▼

● 25

26 ●

▼ 27

● 28

▼ 22
▼ 23

East Vancouver

China Creek Park

0   200   400 m
0   200   400 yards

Grandview Hwy

SkyTrain

Broadway

MAP 4

McGill St
1 ▼
Wall St
McGill St
Nanaimo St
Eton St
Penticton St
Sloean St
Kaslo St
Renfrew St

Hastings Park
Racecourse

Cambridge St

Oxford St

Hastings
Park

Dundas St

Triumph St

Pandora St
Pandora
Park
Franklin St

5 ■

Hastings St
7A

To Best Western
Exhibition Park,
Burnaby,
Simon Fraser
University

Pender St
● 4

Ferndale St

Turner St

Templeton
Park
Georgia St

Adanac St

Venables St
8 ●
9 ●

Victoria Drive
Semlin Drive
Lakewood Drive
Templeton Drive
Parker St

Napier St

William St

Charles St

Kitchener St

Grant St

Graveley St

1st Ave

Nanaimo St
Renfrew St
2nd Ave

3rd Ave

4th Ave
McSpadden
Park

5th Ave

6th Ave

7th Ave

8th Ave

Broadway

PLACES TO STAY
3 Waldorf Hotel
5 Atrium Inn

PLACES TO EAT
1 Cannery Seafood Restaurant
8 Binh Dao]
6 Nick's Spaghetti House
10 Andy's Bakery
11 El Cocal
13 Havana
14 Latin Quarter
17 Mekong Vietnamese
Restaurant
18 Juicy Lucy's Good Eats
20 Arriva Ristorante
22 Old Europe Restaurant
23 WaaZuBee Cafe
24 Spumante's
27 Café Deux Soleil

OTHER
4 Tomson's Copy & Stationery
5 Garage Pub
7 Raja Cinema
8 WISE Hall
9 Vancouver East
Cultural Centre
12 Tony's Market
15 Highlife Records and Music
16 Magpie Magazine Gallery
19 Vancouver Flea Market
21 Care Point Medical Centre
25 Commercial Drug Mart
26 Vicious Cycle Laundro
& Leisurama
28 Van East Cinema

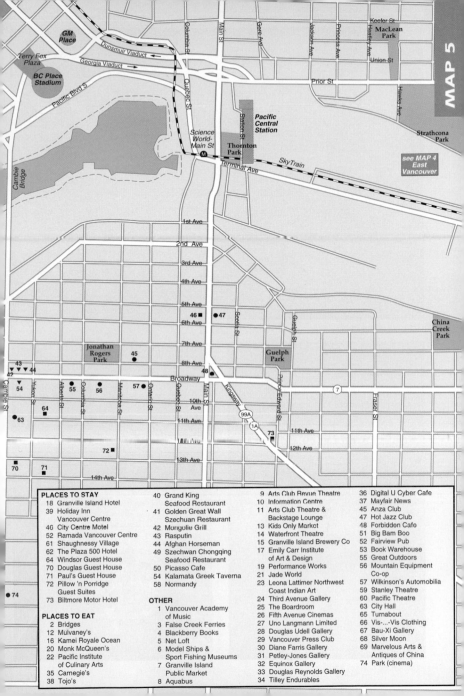

MAP 5

GM Place
Terry Fox Plaza
BC Place Stadium
Dunsmuir Viaduct
Georgia Viaduct
Pacific Blvd S
Cambie Bridge
Keefer St
MacLean Park
Union St
Columbia St
Main St
Gore Ave
Jackson Ave
Princess Ave
Heatley Ave
Hawks Ave
Prior St
Strathcona Park
Quebec St
Station St
Pacific Central Station
Thornton Park
Science World-Main St
Terminal Ave
SkyTrain
see MAP 4 East Vancouver
1st Ave
2nd Ave
3rd Ave
4th Ave
5th Ave
6th Ave
46 ■ ● 47
Scotia St
7th Ave
Jonathan Rogers Park
45 ●
8th Ave
48 ●
Guelph St
Guelph Park
China Creek Park
Broadway
43 ▼ ▼ 44
42 ▼
54 ●
Yukon St
Alberta St
Columbia St
55 ●
56 ●
Manitoba St
57 ●
Ontario St
Main St
Kingsway
Quebec St
10th Ave
Prince Edward St
7
Fraser St
Cambie St
64 ■
● 63
11th Ave
99A
1A
73 ■
11th Ave
12th Ave
72 ■
13th Ave
■ 70
71 ■
14th Ave
● 74

PLACES TO STAY
18 Granville Island Hotel
39 Holiday Inn Vancouver Centre
46 City Centre Motel
52 Ramada Vancouver Centre
61 Shaughnessy Village
62 The Plaza 500 Hotel
64 Windsor Guest House
70 Douglas Guest House
71 Paul's Guest House
72 Pillow 'n Porridge Guest Suites
73 Biltmore Motor Hotel

PLACES TO EAT
2 Bridges
5 Mulvaney's
16 Kamei Royale Ocean
20 Monk McQueen's
22 Pacific Institute of Culinary Arts
35 Carnegie's
38 Tojo's
40 Grand King Seafood Restaurant
41 Golden Great Wall Szechuan Restaurant
42 Mongolie Grill
43 Rasputin
44 Afghan Horseman
49 Szechwan Chongqing Seafood Restaurant
50 Picasso Cafe
54 Kalamata Greek Taverna
58 Normandy

OTHER
1 Vancouver Academy of Music
3 False Creek Ferries
4 Blackberry Books
6 Net Loft
7 Model Ships & Sport Fishing Museums
7 Granville Island Public Market
8 Aquabus
9 Arts Club Revue Theatre
10 Information Centre
11 Arts Club Theatre & Backstage Lounge
13 Kids Only Market
14 Waterfront Theatre
15 Granville Island Brewery Co
17 Emily Carr Institute of Art & Design
19 Performance Works
21 Jade World
23 Leona Lattimer Northwest Coast Indian Art
24 Third Avenue Gallery
25 The Boardroom
26 Fifth Avenue Cinemas
27 Uno Langmann Limited
28 Douglas Udell Gallery
29 Vancouver Press Club
30 Diane Farris Gallery
31 Petley-Jones Gallery
32 Equinox Gallery
33 Douglas Reynolds Gallery
34 Tilley Endurables
36 Digital U Cyber Cafe
37 Mayfair News
45 Anza Club
47 Hot Jazz Club
48 Forbidden Cafe
51 Big Bam Boo
52 Fairview Pub
53 Book Warehouse
55 Great Outdoors
56 Mountain Equipment Co-op
57 Wilkinson's Automobilia
59 Stanley Theatre
60 Pacific Theatre
63 City Hall
65 Turnabout
66 Vis-...-Vis Clothing
67 Bau-Xi Gallery
68 Silver Moon
69 Marvelous Arts & Antiques of China
74 Park (cinema)

Granville Island Public Market

False Creek & West End

Granville Island

Kitsilano Beach

Kitsilano storefront

Strait of Georgia

Jericho
Beach

Jericho
Beach
Park

Point Grey Rd

Hastings
Mill
Park

6

1st Ave

2nd Ave

3rd Ave

4th Ave

5th Ave

● 16

McBride
Park

Point
Grey
Park

Department of
National Defence

6th Ave

7th Ave

8th Ave

42 ▼

Broadway

43 ●

10th Ave

44 ●

46 48
▼ ●

to MAP 7
University of
British Columbia

41 ●

NW Marine Drive

Highbury St

Alma St

Dunbar St

Collingwood St

Waterloo St

Blenheim St

Trutch St

45 ▼

47 ▼

11th Ave

12th Ave

Almond
Park

13th Ave

14th Ave

15th Ave

16th Ave

King Edward Ave

PLACES TO STAY
1 HI Vancouver Jericho Beach
3 Ogden Point B&B
8 Kenya Court Guest House
13 Mickey's Kits Beach Chalet
14 Maple House B&B
15 Walnut House B&B
58 William House B&B

PLACES TO EAT
9 Sunset Grill
10 Da Pasta Bar
11 Rossini's
12 Urban Well
17 Nyala Restaurant
19 Topanga Cafe
21 Naam
24 Simpatico
28 Bishops
29 Veggi Kitchen
30 Sophie's Cosmic Cafe
32 Joe's Grill
36 Won More Szechuan Cuisine
37 Surat Sweet Restaurant
40 India Grill
42 True Confections
45 Andale's
46 Ouzeri
47 Orestes
50 Acropol
54 Ecco il Pane
55 Lumiere

OTHER
2 Jericho Sailing Centre
4 Vancouver Maritime
   Museum

5 Pacific Space Centre,
   Vancouver Museum,
   Gordon MacMillan
   Southam Observatory
6 Hastings Mill Store
   Museum
7 Kitsilano Outdoor Pool
16 Women in Print
18 Great West
   Coin Laundromat
20 Darby's Pub
22 Westside Sport & Ski
23 Blue Note Jazz Bistro
25 Hazel & Co Maternity
   & Kids
26 Magic Flute (records)
27 Coast Mountain Sports
31 The Comicshop
33 Second Suit
34 Mystery Merchant
   Bookstore
35 Wanderlust
38 Mark's Work Warehouse
39 Zulu Records
41 Varsity (cinema)
43 Cellar Jazz Cafe
44 Black Swan (records)
48 Hollywood (cinema)
49 Kidsbooks
51 KhatsahlanoMedical
   Clinic
52 Banyen Books
53 Travel Bug
56 The Side Door
57 Ridge Theatre

MAP 6

English Bay

Kitsilano Point

Vanier
Park

Kitsilano
Beach
Park

Ogden Ave
4
McNicoll Ave
3
5

Whyte Ave

Creelman Ave

Kitsilano
Beach
7

Cornwall Ave
8
11
12
York Ave
14
9
10
1st Ave
13
2nd Ave

Laburnum St
Walnut St
Cypress St
Chestnut St
15
Arbutus St
Maple St

3rd Ave
18
22
26 27
28
29
30 31
33
35
38 39
40
25
24
4th Ave
32
34
17
19
20
21
23
34
36 37
5th Ave
Bayswater St
Stephens St
Trafalgar St
Larch St
Balsam St
Vine St
Yew St
Burrard St

6th Ave

7th Ave
to MAP 5
West Side
8th Ave

49
51
52
54
56
10th Ave
50
55
Broadway
53
Cameron St
MacKenzie St
Macdonald St
11th Ave
Arbutus St
Maple St
Cypress St
Pine St

Connaught
Park
12th Ave

13th Ave

14th Ave

15th Ave
Granville
Park
57
16th Ave

Carnarvon
Park
18th Ave
58

19th Ave

20th Ave

21st Ave

22nd Ave

Kitsilano

Trafalgar
Park
23rd Ave
200   400 m
200   400 yards

West Blvd

1 Museum of Anthropology
2 Chan Centre for the
  Performing Arts
3 Frederic Wood Theatre
4 Gage Residence &
  Conference Center
5 Nitobe Memorial Garden
6 UBC Aquatic Centre
7 University Bookstore
8 The British Columbia
  Golf House Museum
9 UBC Botanical Garden

Acadia
Beach

NW Marine Dr.

Marine Drive
Foreshore
Park

Chancellor Blvd

Strait of Georgia

Westbrook Mall

Acadia Rd

Tower Beach

NW Marine Drive

1

2

East Mall

Crescent Rd

3

4

Student Union Blvd

Lower Mall

Memorial Rd

5

6
Bus Loop

Point Grey

University Blvd

7

University of
British Columbia

East Mall

Wreck Beach

Agronomy Rd

West Mall

Marine Drive
Foreshore Park

Thunderbird Blvd

Stadium Rd

9

Old Marine Drive

16th Ave

Fisheries Rd

SW Marine Drive

South Campus

Point No Point

University of
British Columbia

0   200   400 m
0   200   400 yards

MAP 7

Point Grey
Beach

Spanish Banks Beach

Locarno
Beach

Pacific Spirit
Regional Park

Belmont Ave

2nd Ave

3rd Ave

4th Ave

Chancellor Blvd

5th Ave

to MAP 6
Kitsilano

6th Ave

7th Ave

Point Grey
Park

8th Ave

University
Golf Course

Blanca St

9th Ave

Tolmie St

Sasamat St

Trimble St

8

10th Ave

University Blvd

11th Ave

12th Ave

13th Ave

14th Ave

15th Ave

16th Ave

Pacific Spirit
Regional Park

Rose Garden at UBC

Bill Reid's *The Raven and the First Men*, Museum of Anthropology, UBC

Sculpture at Waterfront Park, North Vancouver

Ferry leaving Horseshoe Bay

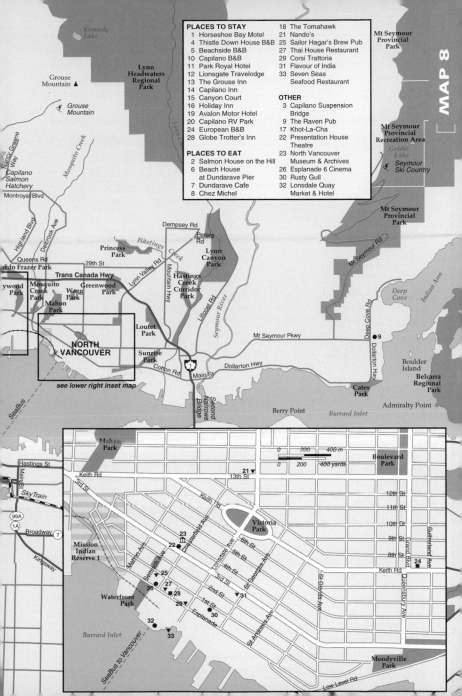

MAP 8

PLACES TO STAY
1 Horseshoe Bay Motel
4 Thistle Down House B&B
5 Beachside B&B
11 Capilano B&B
11 Park Royal Hotel
12 Lionsgate Travelodge
13 The Grouse Inn
14 Capilano Inn
15 Canyon Court
16 Holiday Inn
19 Avalon Motor Hotel
20 Capilano RV Park
24 European B&B
28 Globe Trotter's Inn

PLACES TO EAT
2 Salmon House on the Hill
6 Beach House
   at Dundarave Pier
7 Dundarave Cafe
8 Chez Michel

18 The Tomahawk
21 Nando's
25 Sailor Hagar's Brew Pub
27 Thai House Restaurant
29 Corsi Trattoria
31 Flavour of India
33 Seven Seas
   Seafood Restaurant

OTHER
3 Capilano Suspension
   Bridge
9 The Raven Pub
17 Khot-La-Cha
22 Presentation House
   Theatre
23 North Vancouver
   Museum & Archives
26 Esplanade 6 Cinema
30 Rusty Gull
32 Lonsdale Quay
   Market & Hotel

MAP LEGEND

BOUNDARIES

·–·–·–·–	International
–·–·–·–	State
– – – – –	County

HYDROGRAPHY

	Water
	Coastline
	Beach
)((	River, Waterfall
@	Swamp, Spring

ROUTES & TRANSPORT

	Freeway
	Primary Road
	Secondary Road
	Tertiary Road
= = = = =	Unpaved Road
	Pedestrian Mall
– – – – –	Trail
– – – – –	Ferry Route
+++++++	Railway, Train Station
–M–	Mass Transit Line & Station

ROUTE SHIELDS

①	Trans Canada Highway
⑤	US Interstate
⑩	Provincial, State Highway

AREA FEATURES

	Park, Garden
	Cemetery
	Building
	Plaza
⌐	Golf Course

MAP SYMBOLS

✪	**NATIONAL CAPITAL**	✛	Airfield	⚲	Mosque
◉	**Provincial, State Capital**	✈	Airport	▲	Mountain
		∴	Archaeological Site, Ruins	🏛	Museum
●	**LARGE CITY**	Ⓢ	Bank	⌂	Observatory
●	**Medium City**	🏖	Beach	←	One-Way Street
•	Small City	↔	Border Crossing	♣	Park
•	Town, Village	⊖	Bus Depot, Bus Stop	Ⓟ	Parking
○	Point of Interest	⊟	Cathedral	)(	Pass
		⌒	Cave	⋏	Picnic Area
		†	Church	★	Police Station
		◣	Dive Site	⌷	Pool
■	Place to Stay	℧	Embassy	⌑	Post Office
▲	Campground	⋈	Foot Bridge	❖	Shopping Mall
⊕	RV Park	⊖	Ferry Terminal	🎿	Skiing (Alpine)
		🛢	Gas Station	⚶	Skiing (Nordic)
▼	Place to Eat	⌐	Golf Course	🏛	Stately Home
☗	Bar (Place to Drink)	⊕	Hospital, Clinic	◼	Tomb, Mausoleum
⬗	Cafe	❶	Information	🚶	Trailhead
		⛩	Lighthouse	◢	Windsurfing
		☀	Lookout	🌿	Winery
		▲	Monument	🐘	Zoo

Note: Not all symbols displayed above appear in this book.

LONELY PLANET OFFICES

Australia
PO Box 617, Hawthorn 3122, Victoria
☎ (03) 9819 1877 fax (03) 9819 6459
email talk2us@lonelyplanet.com.au

USA
150 Linden Street, Oakland, California 94607
☎ (510) 893 8555, TOLL FREE (800) 275 8555
fax (510) 893 8572
email info@lonelyplanet.com

UK
10A Spring Place, London NW5 3BH
☎ (0171) 428 4800 fax (0171) 428 4828
email go@lonelyplanet.com.uk

France
1 rue du Dahomey, 75011 Paris
☎ 01 55 25 33 00 fax 01 55 25 33 01
email bip@lonelyplanet.fr
3615 lonelyplanet *(1,29 F TTC/min)*

World Wide Web: www.lonelyplanet.com *or* AOL keyword: lp
Lonely Planet Images: lpi@lonelyplanet.com.au